Culturally Affirmative
Psychotherapy With Deaf Persons

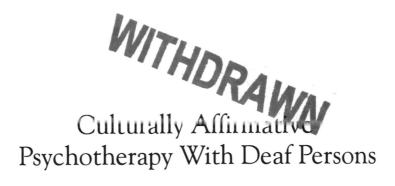

Culturally Affirmative
Psychotherapy With Deaf Persons

Edited by

Neil S. Glickman
Mental Health Unit for Deaf People
Westborough State Hospital
Westborough, MA

Michael A. Harvey
Boston University
Gallaudet University

LEA LAWRENCE ERLBAUM ASSOCIATES, PUBLISHERS
1996   Mahwah, New Jersey

Lawrence Erlbaum Associates, Inc., Publishers
10 Industrial Avenue
Mahwah, New Jersey 07430

Cover design by Gail Silverman

Library of Congress Cataloging-in-Publication Data

Glickman, Neil S.
Culturally affirmative psychotherapy with deaf persons / Neil
S. Glickman, Michael A. Harvey.
     p. cm.
  Includes bibliographical references and index.
  ISBN 0-8058-1488-4 (cloth : alk. paper). — ISBN
0-8058-1489-2 (paper : alk. paper)
    1. Deaf—Mental health. 2. Psychotherapy. 3. Deaf-
ness—Psychological aspects. I. Title.
  RC451.4.D4G56 1996
  616.89'14'0872—dc20

                    95-49691
                    CIP

Books published by Lawrence Erlbaum Associates are printed
on acid-free paper, and their bindings are chosen for strength
and durability.

Printed in the United States of America
10 9 8 7 6 5 4 3 2 1

Contents

Preface

The impetus for this volume is a growing awareness within the mental health and larger community of a culturally affirmative model for understanding and assisting Deaf people. In contrast to the medical–pathological model that treats deafness as a disability, the cultural model guides us to view Deaf persons in relation to the Deaf community: a group of people with a common language, culture, and collective identity. A primary tenet of culturally affirmative psychotherapy is to understand and respect such differences, not to eradicate them.

In this volume, we present a practical and realistic model of providing culturally affirmative counseling and psychotherapy for Deaf people. The three dimensions of this model have been delineated in the multicultural counseling literature, in particular, by Sue, Arredondo, and McDavis (1992) in their seminal article entitled "Multicultural Counseling Competencies and Standards: A Call to the Profession."

The organization of this volume reflects the recommendations of that research: namely, that culturally affirmative psychotherapy with Deaf persons requires therapist self-awareness, knowledge of the Deaf community and culture, and knowledge of culturally syntonic therapeutic interventions. These three dimensions are elucidated by Neil Glickman in the introductory chapter entitled "What Is Culturally Affirmative Psychotherapy?" This chapter also reviews the multicultural counseling and psychotherapy literature and presents important concepts that are further discussed in the remaining chapters.

The first dimension of culturally affirmative psychotherapy, therapist self-awareness, is the focus of the next two chapters. Primary attention is devoted to hearing therapist issues, as Deaf cultural issues are addressed throughout this volume. "Cultural Self-Awareness in Hearing People" by Harlan Lane presents a sociohistorical analysis of the relations between hearing and Deaf people. "Is There a Psychology of the Hearing?" by Robert Hoffmeister and Michael Harvey is an ironic play on the oft-cited notion of a psychology of the Deaf and presents a discussion of common psychological dynamics of hearing people who enter the field of deafness.

The second dimension is knowledge of the Deaf community and Deaf culture. Tom Humphries, in chapter 4, entitled "Of Deaf-mutes, the *Strange*, and the Modern Deaf Self," presents an analysis of Deaf empowerment and identity in relation to the Deaf and hearing communities. "The Development of Deaf Cultural Identities," by Neil Glickman, presents a developmental framework for understanding Deaf cultural identity.

The therapist must have a large repertoire of culturally syntonic interventions at his or her disposal. The remaining chapters are devoted to describing such interventions, the third dimension of providing culturally affirmative assistance. Michael Harvey, in "Utilization of Traumatic Transference by a Hearing Therapist," points out how childhood communicative isolation may be traumatic, how such trauma may affect the therapeutic relationship, and finally how such dynamics may be productively utilized by a hearing therapist.

Perhaps nowhere else is the intersection between the cultures of psychotherapy and the Deaf community greater than in their mutual concern with the telling of personal stories. Gail Isenberg, in "Storytelling and the Use of Culturally Appropriate Metaphors in Psychotherapy With Deaf People," discusses how stories can be used to make psychotherapy with Deaf People meaningful and powerful.

"Report From the Front Lines: Balancing Multiple Roles of a Deafness Therapist," by Sherry Zitter, discusses how clinicians manage the often conflicting role requirements of serving as a client's case worker, teacher, advocate, and psychotherapist. She presents a model to guide therapists in determining how many nontraditional activities one should assume and also presents innovative techniques for "managing" the managed health care context.

Tovah Wax, in "Mental Health Service and the Deaf Community: Deaf Leaders as Culture Brokers," presents a detailed example of collaboration between mental health professionals and Deaf paraprofessionals and discusses ways of engaging talented Deaf teachers as bridges between the Deaf and hearing communities. The final chapter is by Linda Lytle and Jeffery Lewis and is entitled "Deaf Therapists, Deaf Clients, and the Therapeutic Relationship." Their chapter presents intervention strategies and issues that Deaf clinicians (who themselves have Deaf cultural identities) commonly face when working with Deaf clients who have varying cultural identities.

We hope that this volume assists a broad array of professionals and paraprofessionals in the mental health field who work with Deaf and hard-of-hearing people.

Acknowledgments

Attempting cross-cultural psychotherapy, and then having the chutzpa to write about it, are humbling experiences. As members of the dominant group, in this case hearing people, we like to think we know what we are doing, what we are talking about. We would rather like to think of ourselves as experts. But at every step of the way of doing this kind of work we are faced not only with our limitations and our lack of competence but with our dependency on the very people we like to think we are helping. As hearing people we may, perhaps, credit ourselves with being receptive to a certain kind of knowledge. This knowledge is the perspective, the point of view, of the other, here Deaf people, who have taught us not only about their lives but, in so doing, about our own.

There are many Deaf people who contributed to our understanding of Deaf culture in general and to this work in particular. I began my education in Deaf culture through two superb Deaf teachers in Massachusetts, Nancy Becker and Marie Philip. The two people who contributed most to my understanding of Deaf culture, when we were at Gallaudet College, were Betty Colonomos and MJ Bienvenue, until recently codirectors of the Bicultural Center in Riverdale, Maryland. Betty and MJ set the highest national standards for the field of sign language teaching and interpreter education. Although I do not claim to come close to reaching these standards, my work, and my thinking about Deaf people, is enriched by having them before me.

Some of the other Deaf and hearing colleagues in this field with whom I have worked and become friends have informed and shaped my understanding of the Deaf world. These have included Michael Harvey, Sherry Zitter, Gail Isenberg, Carrie Upshaw, Susan Salinas, Patty Wilson, Steven Kimball, Mark Geiger, Ruth Moore, Greg Fisher, Jim Maher, Constance Gould, Jeannette Costa, Mark Dore, Lorna Leferriere, Robert Weinstock, Barb Walker, and Kathleen Fraini. Dr. Robert Pollard provided a focused, informed, and erudite critique of the Deaf identity development model outlined here.

The first draft of my introductory chapter was written as a comprehensive paper as part of my doctoral studies in Psychology at the University of Massachusetts in Amherst. My chapter on the development of Deaf cultural identities is derived from my dissertation research. Five faculty members at UMass guided and shaped my growing understanding of cultural issues in psychotherapy. Dr. Janine Roberts directed the family therapy training program and infused all her classes and work with constant reference to cultural implications of psychotherapy. On my dissertation committee, Dr. Brunilda de Leon and Dr. Ted Sloven provided consistent encouragement and a supportive and constructive review of my work. Dr. John Carey led me gently through the mine field of statistics, helping me conceptualize, organize, and present my statistical procedures and results. His personal attention to my intellectual project, and active encouragement of culturally informed research, made my doctoral training at UMass a rich and rewarding experience. My committee chair, Dr. Allen Ivey, kept my focus on the big picture and cautioned me helpfully about the ethical dilemmas of cross-cultural research. Dr. Ivey's skill in summarizing and synthesizing theoretical perspectives, his sensitivity to multicultural issues, his own model of developmental counseling, and his willingness to nurture creativity and professionalism in students made working under his guidance a life-shaping experience.

My research into the Deaf Identity Development Scale (DIDS) was facilitated by Drs. Kathleen Arnos and Pat Spencer of the Gallaudet Institutional Review Board. Dr. Neil Reynolds from the psychology department welcomed this research and gave me the use of the psychology department resources. Ms. Tammy Weiner served as Gallaudet faculty sponsor. Ms. Becky Piepho did a masterful and conscientious job of recruiting subjects and administering the DIDS. She also made many insightful comments on the research. Mr. Bob Weinstock also provided invaluable assistance in recruiting Deaf subjects.

I am indebted to the Board of Directors of the Association of Late Deafened Adults (ALDA)—Boston, especially Marilyn Howe, for supporting this research project. Their enthusiastic letter of support certainly contributed to the 75% return rate from ALDA—Boston members. Ms. Howe also contributed generously of her time in implementing a large mailing of the DIDS.

The English language version of the DIDS was translated into ASL twice: first by Steven Kimball, who also helped me think about the translatability of items; and again by Lorna Leferriere. Barb Walker produced a superb back-translation into English while working under considerable time pressure. Bill Russell filmed, edited, refilmed, and reedited several versions of the DIDS, and kept his sense of humor while putting up with my technical incompetence in video production.

My research into the DIDS was partially funded by a grant from the American Psychological Association, whose generosity is deeply appreciated.

My coeditor and colleague Michael Harvey has been a mentor for me for more than 10 years, supervising me in various jobs and capacities. He has provided a constant model of clinical excellence, which is also infused with an exquisite sensitivity to cross-cultural dynamics in psychotherapy. I am privileged to count him as a dear friend.

Michael Harvey and I extend much appreciation to Judith Amsel and Kathleen Dolan at Lawrence Erlbaum Associates for their encouragement, support and tolerance for extended deadlines and to Amy Olener and Anne Monaghan for their expertise and easy collegiality in shepherding the book through production.

On the home front, I want to thank my life partner Steven Riel for his meticulous proofreading of my chapters of this manuscript, for his painstaking work to create subject and author indexes, for his many invaluable suggestions, and for his constant love and support.

—*Neil S. Glickman*

The impetus for this book came from its first author, Neil Glickman, a colleague and friend. I appreciate his detailed and erudite feedback of my chapters; his gentle and consistent prodding for me to meet various deadlines; and, most of all, his obvious dedication.

It was fun to write a chapter with Robert Hoffmeister; we have complementary, but not competing, perspectives. Also, many thanks to Andrea Wohl, and the staff at the Learning Center for Deaf Children, for reviewing parts of manuscript.

Pamela Gunther was a key person in encouraging me to enter the field of deafness more than 15 years ago. She was the first person to tell me that ASL is different from English and that I should learn it from a Deaf teacher; and she spent more than 30 hours of her own time with me, elucidating many relevant sociocultural and psychological issues, complete with recommended readings.

We now find ourselves working together as coauthors, copresenters, and co-directors of a nonprofit corporation dedicated to reducing oppression. I thank her for her support, encouragement, erudite feedback and suggestions, and above all, for our continued dialogue.

Finally, much appreciation goes to all the chapter authors of this book. It has been an honor to have been part of this team effort.

—*Michael Harvey*

Reference

Sue, D. W., Arrendondo, P., & McDavis, R. J. (1992). Multicultural counseling competencies and standards: A call to the profession. *Journal of Counseling and Development, 70*(4), 477–486.

For Steven

and for Pamela, Allison, and Emily

Chapter 1

What Is Culturally Affirmative Psychotherapy?

Neil S. Glickman
Mental Health Unit for Deaf People
Westborough State Hospital
Westborough, MA

A NEW UNDERSTANDING OF DEAF PEOPLE

In the past 25 years, a radically new understanding of Deaf[1] people has appeared. This new understanding constitutes what Kuhn (1970) called a paradigm shift. The old and still dominant understanding of deaf people is that they have an unfortunate disability. For those unacquainted with the changes that have occurred in the consciousness of Deaf people (Padden & Humphries, 1988), this way of viewing deaf people makes sense. Most hearing people think of deafness as a terrible tragedy. It is common and usual to pity deaf people. Baker and Cokely (1980) called this viewpoint the *medical–pathological model*. In recent years, the Deaf community has put forward a fundamentally different model.

Baker and Cokely called the new model the *cultural model*. Its premise is that the Deaf community is "a group of persons who share a common language (ASL) and a common culture" (p. 54). According to this model, Deaf people are best thought of as culturally different. This paradigm shift in understanding of what it means to be deaf contains a world of implications for mental health practitioners who work with deaf persons.

---

[1]By now, it has become fairly conventional in this field to capitalize the word *Deaf* when referring to the Deaf community and culture or to culturally Deaf people. The uncapitalized word *deaf* is used to refer to the fact of hearing loss and to deaf people who do not identify with the Deaf community. I have also left deaf uncapitalized when referring generically to all deaf people.

Many paths led to the creation of the cultural model of Deaf people. The intellectual origin is found in the work of William Stokoe. In 1960, Stokoe, a linguist at Gallaudet College, published the first linguistic understanding of American Sign Language (ASL; Stokoe, 1978). Stokoe made the then-radical claim that the gestural system used by Deaf people was in fact a fully grammatical language capable of abstractions, subtleties, and linguistic development. He proved, in the words of Battison and Baker (1980, p. vii), "that American Sign Language is a language worthy of full recognition, study and use—on a par with all other languages of the world."

Before Stokoe's work, sign language was considered by deaf and hearing alike to be a kind of elaborate gesture, at best a truncated and primitive form of English and at worst a kind of "'back alley' talk, fit 'only for bathrooms'" (Garretson, 1980). Suddenly a professional linguist was taking sign language seriously. In 1965, Stokoe published his second work, A Dictionary of American Sign Language on Linguistic Principles (Stokoe, Casterline, & Croneberg, 1976), which included a study of "the linguistic community." Stokoe was already drawing the most obvious implication of his discovery. Not only do Deaf people have a full language, they also have a community and culture.

Throughout the next 25 years, Deaf people and professionals in the field learned of, assimilated, and drew further conclusions based on Stokoe's analysis. Professionals could no longer maintain that signing Deaf people were "nonverbal" or "low verbal" because they were less than fluent in the spoken language of the dominant society. Instead, they came to recognize that many of the deaf people they had so labeled were actually fluent and articulate sign language users. An educational movement called Total Communication relegitimized the use of sign language in schools for deaf children, although it has been the more English-like variants of sign that have dominated. Deaf consumers have come to increasingly expect professionals who work with them to master some variant of sign including ASL. In addition, deaf people have entered the helping professions in increasing numbers thereby providing models for hearing professionals of culturally appropriate treatment.

The study of the Deaf community and Deaf culture is complex. The past 25 years have seen Deaf histories (Gannon, 1981; Lane, 1984); sociological studies of the Deaf community (Benderly, 1980; Higgins, 1980; Nash & Nash, 1981); insider accounts of the norms, values, and perspectives of Deaf people (Jacobs, 1974; Padden & Humphries, 1988); as well as critical studies of Deaf culture (Bienvenue & Colonomos, 1985, 1986, 1988a, 1988b; Padden, 1980; Padden & Humphries, 1988; Wilcox, 1989).

In spite of these advances and the now-extensive recognition among deaf people and the professionals who work with them that ASL is a full language and that the Deaf community has a vibrant culture, very little has been written that draws out the implications of this perspective for clinical work with culturally Deaf people. A 1992 review of the literature on counseling or psychotherapy with Deaf people revealed only four articles that took an explicitly cross-cultural approach (these being: Anderson & Rosten, 1985; Glickman, 1983, 1986; Glickman & Zitter, 1989). Pollard (1993) edited a groundbreaking volume of articles for Rehabilitation Psychology, all of which, as he said in his introduction, assume a framework in which Deaf people are presented as "a frequently misunderstood and maligned minority which is better understood and embraced in the human spectrum of physical, linguistic and cultural diversity." Freedman (1994) developed the cultural model of counseling yet one step further.

Although the mental health literature has increasingly touted deafness as a cultural difference, it has more commonly stressed the negative psychological implications of deafness. These include deficits in English language development; limited communication in the family; parental grieving that interferes with the attachment, separation, and individuation process; impulsivity; and additional physical and neurological deficits that are associated with many of the aetiologies of deafness (Levine, 1960, 1981; Mindel & Vernon, 1971; Myklebust, 1964; Rainer & Althshuler, 1966; Schlesinger & Meadow, 1972). Although Deaf people are now recognized as having a culture, the medical–pathological model has remained dominant in educational and clinical work with deaf people.

If the Deaf community has a distinct culture, then Deaf and hearing people are, as groups, culturally different. When hearing clinicians attempt counseling or psychotherapy with members of the Deaf community, their work can be understood as a kind of cross-cultural treatment. If the Deaf community is a culturally distinct group, then the issues involved in making counseling and psychotherapy relevant and culturally affirmative in other cross-cultural situations would presumably apply here also.

CULTURALLY AFFIRMATIVE PSYCHOTHERAPY WITH OTHER MINORITY GROUPS

If we are going to draw out a model for a new understanding and approach to psychotherapy with culturally Deaf people, we need to review first what has been said about cross-cultural or culturally affirmative psychotherapy in other contexts. The Deaf community is one of many minority groups that has struggled against the mental health establishment's pathological construction of their psychology. The attempt to create a contrasting, progressive form of psychotherapy, one that respects and empowers the minority community with which it works, has a history dating back at least to the 1960s. Most of this introductory chapter is devoted to culling from the literature on cross-cultural psychotherapy a perspective and a procedure relevant to culturally affirmative therapy with Deaf people.

The civil rights struggles of the 1960s and 1970s created awareness in U.S. society of the oppression faced by minorities and women. Since then, increasing attention has been paid in all of the social science to the experience and points of view of disempowered people. One "front" of the minority critique of U.S. society was to document the abuses of the mental health establishment and to create an alternative, genuinely liberating kind of healing. This effort was sometimes called Radical Psychology (Brown, 1973), sometimes called Anti-Psychiatry/Psychology (Frank, 1979), and sometimes, for those with a socialist orientation, called Marxist Psychology (Brown, 1974).

Critics of the mental health establishment included Thomas Szasz (1963, 1970, 1974), R. D. Laing (1967), David Cooper (1970), and Michel Foucault (1965), as well as social groups who were finding their voices. Thomas and Sillen (1972) wrote a pioneering exploration of institutionalized racism within the mental health system. Chesler (1973) described the abuses of women by psychiatry and psychology. Bayer (1981) described the revolt of gay men and lesbian women against the American Psychiatric Association. This revolt resulted in the removal of homosexuality as a diagnostic category from the *Diagnostic and Statistical Manual*. Psychiatric patients organized against their treaters in groups like the Mental Patients Liberation Front. They published newspapers like *The Radical Therapist* and *State and Mind* both to expose the abuses of the mental health field and reinvent psychotherapy as an agent of positive social change. Harlan Lane's (1992) book, *The Mask of Benevolence: Disabling the Deaf Community*, parallels these earlier indictments of professional helpers and healers, this time uncovering the paternalism of the "audist" hearing establishment toward deaf people.

An important and influential text in the field of cross-cultural counseling is *Counseling the Culturally Different* by Derald W. Sue (1981; Sue & Sue, 1990). The chapter Sue devoted to "the politics of counseling" is clearly within this Radical Psychology tradition. Indeed, although the radical rhetoric and revolutionary agenda of the early critics of the mental health field are absent, the themes of those who wrote in the 1980s and 1990s about cross-cultural and multicultural psychotherapy are essentially the same as those who preceded them one generation back. Sue, like his predecessors during the civil rights era, challenged head-on the notion that the theory and practice of counseling are morally, ethically, and politically neutral. Such misconceptions, he said, have resulted in:

> a) a subjugation of the culturally different, b) perpetuation of the view that minorities are inherently pathological, c) perpetuation of racist practices in counseling, and d) provision of an excuse to the profession for not taking social action to rectify inequities in the system. (Sue, 1981, pp. 19–20)

In contrast, Sue outlined a vision of activist counseling that not only takes into account the conditions of oppression of the culturally different but seeks to turn the counseling profession into a proactive force for progressive social change.

The literature that has grown since the 1960s on counseling and psychotherapy with minorities is vast even with a narrow definition of the term minority. If one widens one's view to consider women, gay men and lesbians, and disabled people as minorities or oppressed people, then one finds an overwhelming amount of material to read and assimilate. Certainly we want this "wide lens" in this volume where we consider Deaf people as an oppressed cultural minority.

Working cross-culturally is nothing new. For as long as there has been a mental health field, Whites have "treated" Blacks, men have "treated" women, middle- and upper-class people have "treated" working class and poor people, heterosexuals have "treated" gay and lesbian people, hearing people have "treated" Deaf people. What is new is the attempt to do so self-consciously, with a culturally affirmative perspective and relevant skills. What is new is the attempt to base psychotherapy on a notion of individual and community self-empowerment, to link individual change with collective change. What is new is the project of understanding the sociocultural basis of psychotherapy and the need to adapt psychotherapy to make it a relevant form of healing for disempowered people. This new viewpoint began to be developed in the 1960s, and in the 1980s and early 1990s, a series of books appeared that attempted to present complete models for culturally affirmative mental health treatment. Some of the major texts include Levine and Padilla (1980); Sue (1981); Sue and Sue (1990); McGoldrick, Pearce, and Giordano (1982); Sue and Morishima (1982); Ho (1987); Pedersen (1988); Boyd-Franklin (1989), and Ivey (1991).

The term *culturally affirmative counseling and psychotherapy* is preceded in the literature by the terms *cross-cultural therapy* and *multicultural psychotherapy*, and for many purposes, their meaning can be considered synonymous. A useful definition of cross-cultural counseling and therapy was put forward in an important position paper (Sue et al., 1982) by some of the leading multicultural therapy researchers:

> Cross-cultural counseling/therapy may be defined as any counseling relationship in which two or more of the participants differ with respect to cultural background, values and lifestyle. In most cases, the mental health practitioner is generally a member of the majority group and the client is a minority group member or international (a citizen of another country). This definition of cross-cultural counseling also includes situations in which both the counselor/therapist and client are minority individuals, but represent different minority groups (Black–Hispanic, and so forth). It also includes situations in which the counselor/therapist is a minority person and the client a majority person (Black counselor–White client, Chicano counselor–White client, etc.). Additionally, it may include situations in which the counselor/therapist and client are racially and ethnically similar but may belong to different cultural groups because of other variables such as sex, sexual orientation, socioeconomic factors, religious orientation, and age. . . . In measurement terms, the degree of counselor/therapist–client similarity or dissimilarity in terms of cultural background, values and lifestyle would be the key determinants in discussing cross-cultural counseling/therapy. (p. 47)

This definition tends to focus on sociocultural differences between client and clinician. Because cultural differences are defined broadly, almost any dyadic encounter can be seen as cross-cultural. For what two people are not in some way culturally different?

In a major revision of their "multicultural counseling competencies and standards" position paper, Sue, Arredondo, and McDavis (1992) argued that it is useful to consider all forms of counseling as cross-cultural. At the same time, cross-cultural counseling requires some specialized training and skill.

> On the one hand, we believe strongly that all forms of counseling are cross-cultural, that cultural issues need to be seen as central to cross-cultural counseling (not ancillary), and that by focusing just on ethnic minority issues, we may be "ghettoizing" the problem. Yet, we believe that multicultural counseling is a specialty area as well. Although all of us are racial, ethnic and cultural beings, belonging to a particular group does not endow a person with the competencies and skills necessary to be a culturally skilled counselor. (p. 478)

A DEFINITION OF CULTURALLY AFFIRMATIVE COUNSELING

In this volume, we have chosen to use the term *culturally affirmative therapy* (CAT) as opposed to cross-cultural therapy because the former term puts the focus not on who the clinicians and clients are but on the nature of the work they do together.

Culturally affirmative therapy, as described here, refers to therapy that is socioculturally informed, that utilizes culturally relevant tools, and that seeks to empower clients and their communities. In this definition, culturally affirmative therapy is more nearly synonymous with multicultural therapy than with cross-cultural therapy, but we think the term we use is more straightforward and understandable.

The distinction between counseling and psychotherapy is made primarily by psychodynamically trained clinicians to mark a boundary between their presumably more complex and profound kind of interventions and those done by clinicians without their training. There are now, however, so many kinds of psychotherapy departing from the psychodynamic school that this distinction is increasingly difficult to make especially in the cross-cultural context where psychodynamic interventions are often considered culturally inappropriate. Therefore in this work, we use the terms counseling and psychotherapy interchangeably.

It is common to advocate for clinicians to be culturally sensitive. How often, for instance, have those of us in the deafness field seen the phrase "knowledge of Deaf culture" as a requirement for a job? But what exactly does that mean? What constitutes knowledge of a culture, and how does one know when one has enough of it? It has certainly been hard to operationalize what cultural sensitivity looks like as it pertains to counseling and psychotherapy. Yet if we are, as all of this literature advocates, to call on clinicians to do culturally affirmative treatment, we at least owe them a clear presentation of what such treatment looks like in practice. Many of the texts that appeared after 1980, cited previously, attempt to do that, and gradually an operational understanding of culturally affirmative therapy has emerged. Our task is to learn exactly how cultural issues bear on treatment. We want to know what culturally sensitive clinicians think and do differently that constitutes culturally affirmative treatment.

The main goal of this volume is, therefore, a practical one. We hope that after reading this volume, the reader will have some way to put into *practice* culturally affirmative therapy with Deaf people. Certainly we do not claim to offer the last word on the subject. The Deaf and hearing colleagues who have contributed to this volume offer, instead, a framework for culturally affirmative therapy and a beginning point.

Culturally affirmative therapy, although called a "therapy," is actually a set of principles and strategies that can work within the broad spectrum of existing psychotherapies. We assume that clinicians practicing culturally affirmative treatment work with a variety of theoretical perspectives such as psychodynamic, cognitive–behavioral, and family systems and in a variety of settings such as mental health clinics, vocational rehabilitation agencies, residential facilities, and independent living centers. What distinguishes them is not whether they are more or less psychodynamic or behavioral, but rather, as we show, the awareness, knowledge, and skills they bring to their work.

Culturally affirmative therapists strive to extend the relevancy and usefulness of psychotherapy to culturally different people. They think about social structure, culture, power, and oppression and seek to intervene in ways that (a) are relevant and sensible to the client, (b) empower the clients and the clients' community, (c) make connections between personal and collective experience, and (d) balance cultural and clinical considerations. To perform this, therapists must develop a flexible cognitive and therapeutic style. Just as good therapists base their therapeutic interventions on their assessment of their clients' diagnosis and strengths, so should they base their interventions on their clients' sociocultural context.

Culturally affirmative therapy is also an attitude set. Culturally affirmative therapists value cultural differences as healthy expressions of human diversity and see the connection between empowerment of a people, affirmation of their culture, and the individual mental health of the community's members. Culturally affirmative therapists are opposed, therefore, to any variant of racism or sexism that oppresses a group of people.

This principle is not as simple as it seems. One of the most difficult dilemmas of culturally affirmative therapy is what to do when the minority community espouses values that are, from the clinician's point of view, oppressive. If the client is from what appears to be a racist, sexist, or homophobic culture, does the clinician, in the interests of cultural affirmation, affirm those values? Suppose the client is a White supremacist or religious fundamentalist who believes that women's role is exclusively to serve men and raise children. Most mental health professionals work implicitly or explicitly with the values of human equality, individual freedom, and respect for human diversity. We hold these values not merely because we believe in them but because we believe they are psychologically healthy. If clinicians work from these principles, do they then risk being insensitive or irrelevant to clients from cultures where hierarchy and rigid social roles are valued? How do clinicians affirm a community that, in their eyes, oppresses their clients or other people? How does one balance respect for cultural difference with loyalty to one's own set of values and beliefs about what constitutes healthy and morally ethical living?

There are no easy answers to these questions. Our dilemma stems from our awareness that the practice of counseling and psychotherapy is based on assumptions about health, sickness and healing, and about good and bad ways of living that are relevant to particular social-historical contexts. As soon as one strives to extend the reach of psychotherapy to persons from other cultural contexts, cultural conflict happens.

It is difficult for hearing people to counsel Deaf people because of our cultural differences but also because, unlike when working with people of different nationalities, we often do not understand our differences as cultural. We become confused. To protect ourselves, we make all sorts of judgments about the supposed limitations of Deaf people. We forget that this cross-cultural encounter calls for adaptation on our part. How we must adapt as well as how we must remain the same is the juggling act culturally affirming therapists perform.

THE THREE DIMENSIONS OF CULTURALLY AFFIRMATIVE PSYCHOTHERAPY

Within the major professional organization for counselors, the American Counseling Association (ACA) and the major organization for psychologists, the American Psychological Association (APA), the last 25 years have seen a vigorous debate about the nature and role of culturally affirmative counseling/therapy competencies and standards. In 1982, a position paper on cross-cultural counseling competencies was published by a task force of the APA (Sue et al., 1982), and this paper, revised in 1992 (Sue, et al., 1992), has remained the guiding document in the field. A theoretical framework is put forward in these papers that one also finds in some of the leading texts on multicultural counseling and therapy (Pedersen, 1988; Sue & Sue, 1990).

In these papers, culturally affirmative counseling and psychotherapy are broken down into three dimensions: self-awareness, knowledge, and skills. Sue and Sue (1990) applied these three dimensions to describe the "culturally competent counselor." The following analysis is taken from the pivotal Sue et al. (1992) article:

> First, a culturally skilled counselor is one who is actively in the process of becoming aware of his or her own assumptions about human behavior, values, biases, preconceived notions, personal limitations, and so forth. They understand their own world views, how they are the product of their cultural conditioning, and how (they) may be reflected in their counseling and work with racial and ethnic minorities. The old adage "counselor, know thyself" is important in not allowing biases, values, or "hang-ups" to interfere with the counselor's ability to work with clients. Prevention of ethnocentrism is a key ingredient to effective cross-cultural counseling.

> Second, a culturally skilled counselor is one who actively attempts to understand the world view of his or her culturally different client without negative judgments. It is crucial that counselors understand and share the world views of their culturally different clients with respect and appreciation. This statement does not imply that counselors have to hold the world views as their own, but can accept them as another legitimate perspective.

> Third, a culturally skilled counselor is one who is in the process of actively developing and practicing appropriate, relevant, and sensitive intervention strategies and skills in working with his or her culturally different clients. Studies consistent reveal that counseling effectiveness is improved when counselors use modalities and define goals consistent with the life experiences and cultural values of clients. It is recognized that extrapsychic as well as intrapsychic approaches may be more appropriate and that differential helping strategies may be needed. (p. 481)

In this introductory chapter, we summarize a model based on the three dimensions of culturally affirmative therapy just mentioned. The next three sections of this introduction are organized following this framework and applied to the Deaf–hearing cross-cultural context. We discuss, in turn, the nature of the self-awareness necessary to work with deaf persons, the necessary knowledge of the Deaf community and culture, and the specialized skills this work requires.

THE SELF-AWARENESS DIMENSION

The first dimension of effective CAT is self-awareness. On the surface, this should come easily to therapists. Beginning with the psychoanalytic school and with Freud's own self-analysis, self-awareness has been championed as an essential characteristic of an effective therapist. Therapists are expected to be exceptionally self-aware, to have a clear understanding of how their past experiences have shaped who they are today, and to know their own values, attitudes, prejudices, and emotional blind spots. In culturally affirmative psychotherapy, we are not talking primarily about this kind of personal self-awareness. All of this remains crucial, but the emphasis here is on an additional kind of self-awareness: awareness of oneself as a social and historical being.

Culturally affirmative therapists seek to understand how their own constructions of reality are influenced by their own sociohistorical and cultural position. This means, for example, that if one is White in the United States, one needs to know the various ways that Whites as a group construct or attribute meaning. Particularly relevant is how Whites and African Americans understand skin color, themselves, and each other as racial groups. The color of one's skin, of course, has no inherent significance. What matters are the meanings that people have attached to skin color, the ways, for instance, that personality traits like intelligence, stupidity, industriousness, laziness, sexiness, virtue, and moral depravity have been ascribed to people of a particular color. Typically, White and African American people view Whiteness and Blackness differently. Their constructions also change as a result of sociohistorical forces. The Civil Rights movement, for instance, changed how both groups viewed themselves and each other.

"Disability," "handicap," and "deafness" are also social constructs or particular ways of understanding one dimension of human difference. Deaf people have helped hearing people become aware that each group constructs "deafness" differently; the former primarily as a cultural difference, the latter primarily as a disability. For Deaf people, deafness is a positive value in that it signifies a community, language, and culture with which one feels pride. For hearing people, deafness is a negative value, a tragic condition. Cultural self-awareness for hearing people means appreciating the full dimensions of the dominant hearing construction of deafness, then distancing oneself from this construction. In this volume, the chapters by Harlan Lane, Tom Humphries, Robert Hoffmeister, and Mike Harvey explore more fully what Hoffmeister and Harvey call the "psychology of hearing people."

The Obstacles of Humanism and Color-blindness

Probably many people reading this are, by now, ready to burst with objections. These objections might sound something like the following: "Wait a minute. I object to this way of thinking. It sounds like stereotyping to me. Yes, I am White, male, hearing, etc., but I don't believe that matters. I am a human being first and last. I try to treat all human beings equally and fairly. I try not to discriminate in any way but to judge people, as Martin Luther King Jr. said, by 'the content of their character.' I think you are engaging in labeling people. The full humanity of people is limited by labels such as these. What is important is to treat people simply as people without reference to whatever sociohistorical groups they belong to. Rather than focusing on what divides us—that I am hearing and you are Deaf—we should focus on our common humanity."

There are several names for the viewpoint that sociocultural differences should be irrelevant in consideration of how people are treated. Some call it humanism. In the political context, it has been referred to as color-blindness. It is a common perspective from which many counselors and therapists operate. This viewpoint, attractive as it seems, is probably the greatest obstacle to effective culturally affirmative therapy.

In the multicultural therapy literature, the notion of color-blindness is faulted as naive, hypocritical, and ultimately hostile to the interests of minorities. Sue et al. (1982) targeted this concept for special criticism:

> The culturally skilled counselor does not profess "color-blindness" or negate the existence of differences that exist in attitudes/beliefs. The basic concept underlying "color-blindness" was the humanity of all people. Regardless of color or other physical differences, each individual is equally human. While its intent was to eliminate bias from counseling, it has served to deny the existence of differences in client's perceptions of society arising out of membership in different racial groups. The message tends to be, "I will like you only if you are the same," instead of "I like you because of and in spite of your differences." (p. 50)

Many therapists have been influenced by this color-blind perspective. One frequently hears therapists assert that they treat all human beings as individuals, that they oppose prejudice of any kind, and that discussing one's Whiteness or maleness constitutes labeling and stereotyping that detracts from one's humanity. This perspective is appealing to therapists not only because it is consistent with dominant U.S. ideals about individualism but also because it is consistent with the humanistic treatment philosophy in which many therapists are trained.

Humanism is in many respects an appealing viewpoint. It calls for respect between people and opposition to persecution of any kind. The humanistic perspective highlights individual differences and downplays sociocultural differences. It tends to view considerations of culture or class as attempts at stereotyping or labeling. Humanists are concerned with the dignity and profundity of individual experience, certainly a worthwhile cause.

Compared with blatant racial prejudice, humanism is a significant advance. Moving from the view that one race is inferior to the view that race is irrelevant is a step in the direction of equality and freedom. Still, humanism is inadequate as a basis for culturally affirmative therapy precisely because it minimizes awareness of how sociohistorical categories *do* matter. It is not that one group has any inherent superiority over another, but that different groups have different experiences of the world, out of which grow different social constructions of realty. Some aspects of the world do indeed look different to Whites than to African Americans, hearing than to Deaf, and so on. Meaning has been attributed to race, gender, and disability; and people act toward each other on the basis on these attributions. In culturally affirmative therapy, one strives to work knowingly against the backdrop of these different social constructions of reality.

Boyd-Franklin (1989) noted, for example, that for White therapists to "join" with African American clients, the racial issue needs to be on the table. The client's life needs to be discussed from the client's viewpoint, and from this viewpoint, race is a salient issue. This requires the therapist to develop self-awareness as someone who is White, and in other contexts, it means self-awareness as a male, an Anglo, a heterosexual, a hearing person, and so on. Boyd-Franklin developed a systematic approach to psychotherapy with African American families. Her text is rich in information about African American culture, and she too placed great emphasis on the importance of racial self-awareness. African-American families, she noted, are very sensitive to the "vibes" put out by White therapists. They are acutely aware of the skin color of their therapist, consider it to be a matter of importance and relevance, and would be much more inclined to work with a therapist who can discuss race and skin color comfortably than one who claims that such issues do not matter.

A White clinician who has not thought through being White will have difficulty not emitting *vibes* that at least reveal discomfort, if not overt prejudice. Boyd-Franklin spoke about "racial countertransference." Clinicians may respond to individual African American clients on the basis of past experiences with and past perceptions of African American people. This racial countertransference includes conscious and unconscious racial stereotypes. Clinicians may, for instance, harbor a subtle fear of African American men. They may hold beliefs that African American people are to blame for their problems. Boyd-Franklin commented: "This may be articulated conceptually as, 'They are poor because they want to be' or 'They should pull themselves up by their bootstraps' or 'All other ethnic groups made it; why can't they?'—a process called 'blaming the victim'"(p. 98).

Views such as these are common enough in people who claim they are not prejudiced and that race does not matter. It is through a process of developing racial self-understanding that White therapists come to appreciate the subtle and varied forms that racism may take and through that process increase their ability to join therapeutically with African American clients.

Recently, some courses in culturally affirmative counseling and therapy have begun to include curricula to help White people with this collective soul searching process. Ponterotto (1988, cited in Ivey, 1991) had the most well-developed training model. Ivey (1991) saw White awareness training as "the frontier of multicultural training." It should be said that racist groups such as the Ku Klux Klan (KKK) also engage in a kind of White awareness training. The difference between what they do and what these models intend is that the KKK teaches White people to defend their power and privilege. Multicultural awareness training is designed to help Whites empower others.

The KKK probably has an easier time. The racist defenders of White culture are teaching self-empowerment, albeit at the cost of persecuting other groups. Their task is to reinforce natural tendencies for racial and cultural self-justification. It is unfortunately all too easy to encourage people to believe that their own group is naturally superior. On the other hand, when a White person confronts racism, a male confronts sexism, a heterosexual confronts homophobia, a hearing person confronts what Lane (1992) called *audism*, it is initially a disempowering experience because it involves learning that the advantages one enjoys are unfair and arbitrary. This goes against the fundamental human need to justify oneself and see oneself as good.

Effective cross-cultural and culturally affirmative work operates according to principles that are the opposite of fundamentalism, authoritarianism, racism, and cultural chauvinism. Rather than insisting on one truth, that of the therapist's own group, he or she sees and validates a diversity of truths. Rather than defensively denying the relative material advantages that some groups have over others, the therapist acknowledges the role that power differences play and seeks to further the self-empowerment of the disadvantaged. Rather than turning the "other" into a nonperson that can be exploited or a demon who must be destroyed, the therapist strives to appreciate and validate the full humanity of those different than he or she. I cannot help but believe that if human beings were as skilled in appreciating multiple constructions of reality as we are in individual and collective self-justification, that much of the evil in today's world would fade. In any case, it is probably this attitude set, more than any specific skill or knowledge base, that distinguishes the effective culturally affirmative therapist.

At some point, all White, or male, or heterosexual, or hearing therapists meet clients who are angry at them for being White, male, heterosexual, or hearing. Racially and culturally aware therapists are prepared for this and can respond nondefensively. Racially and culturally aware therapists do not respond by saying, "Well, it's a White (male, heterosexual, hearing) world, and you have to get along."

Instead, they respond, "Yes, it's a multicultural world, and we all have to change."

THE KNOWLEDGE DIMENSION

Understanding Oppression

The second dimension of culturally affirmative therapy is knowledge. Culturally affirmative therapists need to have broad knowledge of their society and knowledge of the specific groups and cultures with which they work. In this kind of therapy, the client's problems and the client–clinician relationship are understood in their sociohistorical context. This dimension is summarized by Sue et al. (1992, p. 482) as follows:

> 1. Culturally skilled counselors possess specific knowledge and information about the particular group they are working with. They are aware of the life experiences, cultural heritage, and historical background of their culturally different clients. This particular competency is strongly linked to the "minority identity development models" available in the literature.

2. Culturally skilled counselors understand how race, culture, ethnicity, and so forth may affect personality formation, vocational choices, manifestation of psychological disorders, help-seeking behavior, and the appropriateness or inappropriateness of counseling approaches.

3. Culturally skilled counselors understand and have knowledge about sociopolitical influences that impinge upon the life of racial and ethnic minorities. Immigration issues, poverty, racism, stereotyping, and powerlessness all leave major scars that may influence the counseling process.

Much of the knowledge dimension can be condensed into one concept: oppression. Culturally affirmative therapists need, probably above all else, to have a deep and intimate understanding of oppression. If one has not experienced significant oppression oneself, developing this understanding can be a formidable challenge. The world can look differently to oppressed people. Instead of seeing a world of opportunity, it can appear like a world of barriers, restrictions, and various forms of injustice.

Oppression grows out of the context of a society where wealth and power are distributed unequally and more powerful groups dominate less powerful groups. Typically, the members of the more powerful groups become professionals who "treat" what is viewed as pathology in less powerful groups. The oppressive domination of one group by another operates within every arena of life including the therapist–patient relationship. This oppressive domination means:

1. Each group has unequal access to material wealth, education, and high status employment.
2. Each group has unequal access to physical and mental health because they are influenced by material factors like money, housing, diet, and recreation.
3. Prejudice and discrimination work for some groups and against others.
4. Some groups use language forms that are considered correct and standard whereas others use language forms that are considered deficient. Dominant groups try to destroy or control the language used by subordinate groups (Glickman, 1984).
5. Members of some groups grow up with the expectation of failure or achievement limited to only specific arenas (e.g., sports, music). Members of other groups grow up with the expectation that they can achieve in any arena they choose.
6. Members of some groups grow up expecting to be treated respectfully, whereas members of other groups grow up expecting to be treated with fear, pity, or contempt.
7. The way of life of some groups is considered healthy, normal, or good, whereas the way of life of others is considered unhealthy, deficient, or bad.
8. Members of some groups grow up with a sense of self-worth and pride, whereas others grow up with a sense of self-hatred and shame.

Lane (1992) coined the term *audism* to refer to the oppression of Deaf people. His 1992 book, *The Mask of Benevolence: Disabling the Deaf Community*, is a powerful condemnation of the audist establishment of self-proclaimed benefactors of the Deaf community, including mental health professionals. In chapter 2 of this volume, Lane describes how a certain segment of the dominant hearing majority has come, for their own economic, professional, and psychological self-interest, to define themselves as helpers and healers of the "disabled" deaf community. Just as majority people come to define themselves as helpers and present their methods as neutral or objective science and medicine, so may their patients come to accept this dominant view of themselves, believing themselves disabled and needing the assistance of professional helpers. Without knowledge of the dynamics of deaf oppression, the practitioner inadvertently reinforces the notion of deaf people as disabled, impaired, dependent, and abnormal and prevents deaf clients from, as Tom Humphries describes, finding their own unique voice.

I noted that oppression may be difficult to understand if one has not experienced it directly oneself. I would like to share the story of how I discovered my oppression as a gay man because it illustrates, I believe, how these kinds of experiences can become a lens through which one interprets and makes sense of one's life.

It was 1976, the year of the bicentennial, and I was a college student in the small New York town of Ithaca. After years of denial, including one year of psychotherapy with a psychiatrist who told me that babies were naturally attracted to the opposite sex, I took the most difficult step of my life and publicly acknowledged my homosexuality. It took me months to build up the courage to attend a local gay persons group, and I remember being surprised at how boring the meeting was. Perhaps I expected an orgy, not the rather dry business meeting that actually occurred. After the meeting, I went with the others to a mixed gay and straight bar and there managed to summon the courage to dance with another man. The bar was filled with acquaintances, and I was embarrassed and afraid to be acknowledging my homosexuality in front of them. I also felt exhilarated and wildly happy. After we finished dancing, several men came over to us and started punching my partner. When I protested, one of these men picked me up, hurled me over a table, and pummeled me in the face. Eventually some people pulled him off of me. Nevertheless, I went home that night tremendously relieved. The pain of the physical beating was insignificant compared to the joy of hard-won self-acceptance.

This beating earned me overnight celebrity status in the small Ithaca gay and lesbian community. Word spread about the college student who was beaten up on his first night out. Within days, I had a whole new set of friends. I discovered something I had never experienced before, the power of a small, oppressed community to come together to support and affirm each other. Within a few weeks, I acquired a new identity, a community, perhaps even a sense of meaning and purpose. I was discovering in the gay community what many deaf people find in the Deaf community: a powerful sense of connection, a sense of "home."

Soon afterward, a businessman inquired at the local gay people's center about whether we would support a predominantly gay bar. We enthusiastically said we would, and a few months later this bar opened. The local gay and lesbian people flocked to it, but the owner changed his mind and started ejecting gay people. I was a middle-class, Jewish young man from Long Island. I was generally a well-behaved person, and it was quite a shock to me to find myself thrown out of a bar merely because I was dancing with another man. This simple gesture, dancing with a male partner, seemed to disturb many people. The gay and lesbian community organized a protest. One night all of us entered the bar in mixed male and female pairs but at exactly twelve o'clock we all changed partners, and suddenly the whole bar was filled with same sex couples. The owner stopped the music and turned up the lights. He yelled that we were not welcome there and should leave. A shouting match ensued. But that night we were in charge. We were gay and proud. No one would push us around.

Needless to say, the owner would not make the mistake of admitting us again. We began a nightly protest in front of the bar, circling it and chanting. It was during that summer of protest that I learned how oppression impacts every arena of one's life. We received almost no support from the local college or town community. Few straight people would walk with us, not even my best friends. Local teenage boys taunted us, threw cans and glass bottles at us, and beat up several of our members. One night I witnessed the bar owner push down and kick savagely one of our members. We all witnessed it. A policeman came over after the beating. The bar owner, in front of 20 witnesses, lied and said he had been attacked first. In spite of our protest, and the fact that our member was bruised and dazed and the bar owner was unhurt, the policeman believed the bar owner, not us, and walked away from the scene. Our efforts to get police protection so that we would not be beaten while protesting were unsuccessful. Most of us became fearful of walking through town alone. As a hitherto-privileged White boy, there had simply been nothing in my prior experience to shake my belief that the world was a safe, benevolent place. I now realized that my safety was dependent on my hiding or denying my homosexuality.

We tried to get favorable coverage in the local newspaper. The bar owner lied by asserting to the paper that we were having sex in the men's bathroom and on the dance floor. There was no truth to this, but due to ignorance and stereotypes, it was widely believed. To our surprise, we found the newspaper accounts fairly sympathetic to the bar owner and dismissive of the gay and lesbian victims. I began to realize that the public had a preconceived hostile attitude toward us that was easily confirmed by prejudicial reporting of our battle with the bar owner. More than fight for entry into a bar, we had to fight to be perceived as human beings worthy of respect. Even more basically, we had to fight to see ourselves as human beings worthy of respect.

We realized we had no civil rights protection in that town. We contacted each member of the local town council about establishing a gay rights ordinance and found, again to our surprise, most of them unsympathetic to us. We came to realize that these town council members were mostly local business people who tended to identify with the bar owner. They also felt threatened by us, and there was little support then for any kind of protective legislation for gay people. A decade later, such an ordinance would pass but only after an enormous society-wide effort to reconceptualize homosexuality as a human or cultural difference rather than a perversion. I first learned then how my oppression meant I had to fight to define myself on my own terms.

The nightly protests continued for 2 months. Night after night, we subjected ourselves to increasingly severe verbal and physical assaults. Throughout this experience, I found my gay identity solidifying. Although we did not win access to the bar, shortly afterward one member of our community opened our own bar. During this year, 1976, when Americans were celebrating 200 years of liberty, we received an education on one front of continuing injustice. Like every other oppressed group, we had to legitimize ourselves and claim our own place in society. No one would give us that place unfought for.

From this time of my socialization into the gay and lesbian subculture, I learned about my own oppression, and I would use that knowledge as a basis for understanding the struggles of other groups. Like many gay and lesbian people who find their way to work with the Deaf community, I empathized easily with the deaf experience of oppression, although it differs from my own. I have since come to appreciate my gay male perspective *to be a perspective* and therefore take some distance from it, but it would still be difficult for me to work, as a client, in psychotherapy with anyone who did not have some appreciation for the nature of homophobia. In this, I am very typical of gay and lesbian people who have found their way to self-acceptance. Likewise, to work in therapy with deaf people, with racial and ethnic minorities, requires knowledge of, and some feeling for, their particular experiences of oppression, especially as it shapes how they interpret their experience.

If one were to describe the elements of the oppression of Deaf people, the denial of language would certainly be central.

Deafness is often portrayed as a barrier to communication, and deaf children are thought to grow up with limited language skills *as if this were a natural, biological consequence of deafness.* The language difficulties of deaf people are not the result of deafness. They are the result of social policy toward deaf people. They are the result of the systematic attempts by hearing people to either destroy the language of the Deaf community (ASL), or distort it into a pale imitation of English. Hearing people generally think they act with the best of intentions. A hearing person might think, "After all, it's a hearing world and deaf children need to fit in." But the dynamics of oppression are the same as with any other minority group. Whenever Deaf people have organized, risen up and protested, affirmed themselves and their language and culture, their hearing benefactors, the doctors, teachers, audiologists, mental health professionals, and others have been there to oppose, to oppress, or, if these failed, to co-opt the struggle. As Lane pointed out, all these hearing benefactors have vested interests in maintaining Deaf people in their powerless positions. Their interests are financial (loss of income), institutional (loss of power), and psychological (loss of a sense of oneself as a benefactor).

The oppression of deaf people has meant in many instances the denial of Deaf culture and ASL; the profound and devastating impact of growing up with minimal access to language to explain one's experience; the poor quality of deaf education; the limited vocational and career opportunities for deaf people; the inaccessibility of almost all public, cultural, or educational events in society; the pathologization of deafness and stigmatization of deaf people; the inappropriate assessment and treatment by mental health professionals; the isolation of deaf children within mainstreamed educational facilities; and recently, the forced surgical implantation of cochlear devices in deaf children. All of this has been done with a maddening "mask of benevolence."

When minority people show some guardedness with the majority society, they are open to the charge of being considered paranoid. People who have written about the psychology of oppression have countered that minority people need to develop a healthy paranoia because the truth is that the world is not a safe place for them. As a consequence, deaf people commonly ask hearing people how and why they learned sign and became involved with the Deaf community. This is part curiosity, part suspiciousness, part sizing up the opposition. There are right and wrong answers to this question: Some answers facilitate joining with deaf people and some alienate them. The safest answer is probably that one was captivated by the beauty of sign language and Deaf culture. The worst answer is probably that one wants to help poor deaf children talk so they can fit into society.

For years I, like so many hearing peers, immersed myself in the Deaf experience, falling in love with everything Deaf, almost wanting to be Deaf and certainly wanting to be accepted by Deaf people. I realized that adopting a culturally affirmative view of deafness would facilitate the development of relationships with deaf people and would help mark me, at least to a small extent, as different from the majority of hearing oppressors. Why should acceptance by deaf people have so mattered to me? Was I, as some deaf people are inclined to suspect of hearing people who hang on the fringes of the Deaf world, a misfit in my own cultures? Did I seek a home in the Deaf community because I had no home outside of it? Hoffmeister and Harvey (chapter 3, in this volume), describe the psychology of hearing people like me who "get into deafness." I asked myself about my own motivation and eventually found an answer that felt true and satisfied me.

It is commonly noted that many of the hearing people who work with deaf people are gay or lesbian. Why should this be? In my own case, I eventually realized that concern with the struggles of deaf people provided me with a socially acceptable vehicle for expression of the rage I felt at my own mistreatment and marginalization as a gay man. I knew what oppression felt like. I was furious with the world. I found that by championing in a small way the struggles of deaf people I could express my anger but in a way that won me praise rather than further condemnation. Connecting with the deaf experience through my own experience of oppression has had mixed results. On the one hand, it has helped me understand and empathize with deaf people and thereby become a more effective counselor and advocate. I doubt I would have discovered cross-cultural counseling were I not gay. On the other hand, it may, at times, have lead to overidentification, and it has taken me away from the struggles of my own communities.

One way or another, hearing clinicians who work with deaf people need to develop an understanding of how hearing people as a group have oppressed deaf people. Culturally affirmative therapists work with knowledge of oppression, racism in all its forms, and prejudice. Culturally affirmative therapists try to distinguish themselves from this oppressive tradition. This is done first by acknowledging oppression, talking about it, and then by seeking ways to empower clients. Without this understanding and point of view, one easily and unwittingly becomes just another in the long line of "benefactors" who have exploited and abused the Deaf community.

Knowledge of Cultural and Racial Identity Models

Cultural and Racial Identity Development models (C/RID; Sue & Sue, 1990), or, as they used to be called, Minority Identity Development models (Ivey, 1991), are an important part of the knowledge dimension of culturally affirmative therapy. These models are all rooted in the changes in consciousness that have occurred among minorities in the United States beginning with the Civil Rights Era. They all describe a difference between what might be called the consciousness of the oppressed person and the consciousness of the liberated person. In the 1960s, this was often referred to as "false" and "true" consciousness. These models are important for many reasons. Most fundamentally, the attempt to connect individual therapy and community liberation is done by fostering, within therapy, the kind of change in consciousness that grows out of social struggle. Counseling and psychotherapy are used to help oppressed people become empowered. These models provide an understanding of how minority people commonly think, feel, and act before, during, and after the process of individual and collective liberation.

C/RID models usually have four or five stages. The stage names change depending on the theorist. In the most recent synthesis of these models (Sue & Sue, 1990), the stages are called conformity, dissonance, resistance and immersion, introspection, and integrative awareness. In the work of Helms (1990), the stages are called pre-encounter, encounter, immersion, and internalization. These stages chart the process from ignorance about, and denial of, racial/cultural differences (pre-encounter or conformity stage), to discovery or encounter with the reality of oppression, to immersion within the minority community and complete rejection of the larger society, to pulling back and searching for a more personal and integrated identity, to a final stage of biculturalism (the integrative awareness or internalization stage). In this final stage, which is presumed to be the most healthy, minority people have integrated their cultural difference in an affirmative way with their larger "personhood." They remain intolerant of oppression and comfortably proud of their heritage and community, but they are also able to recognize limitations of their community and positive aspects of the majority society.

There are many reasons why cultural and racial identity models are prominent in virtually all discussions of culturally affirmative therapy. A major theme in this literature is whether, or in which circumstances, a clinician from the majority culture can perform therapy with a client from a minority culture. Much of the literature of the 1970s on cross-cultural counseling between African Americans and Whites focused on the question of whether or when White clinicians could treat African American clients (Atkinson, 1985). The most common answer to this question is that it depends on the stage of identity development of the client. The more sophisticated answer to this question is that it also depends on the stage of identity development of the clinician. This question also needs to be posed in the hearing–Deaf context: How does the identity development of both Deaf and hearing people bear on their ability to work cross-culturally in psychotherapy?

These models also address the question of in which instances minority clinicians work effectively with minority clients. Anyone who has been in a position of looking to hire minority clinical staff for a mental health program that serves minorities faces this issue. It is necessary to hire minorities, but there is no guarantee that the person hired will be a good clinician or even be culturally aware. In some instances, minority clinicians can do far more damage to clients than majority clinicians precisely because they are assumed to be knowledgeable and credible when they are not. Sue (Sue & Sue, 1990) made this important point:

> A minority counselor at the conformity stage may cause great harm to clients at other stages. The counselor may intentionally and unintentionally (a) reinforce a conformity client's feelings of racial self-hatred, (b) prevent or block a dissonance client from looking at inconsistent feelings/attitudes/beliefs, (c) dismiss and negate the resistance and immersion client's anger about racism (he or she is a radical), and (d) perceive the integrative awareness individual as having a confused sense of self-identity. (p. 112)

Minority clinicians who work with majority clients also need cultural self-awareness, or they also risk what Boyd-Franklin (1989) and others called "racial transference" (e.g., the African American clinician who is motivated unconsciously by anger toward White people.) To be most helpful to minority clients, both minority and majority clinicians should have worked through their feelings about racial and cultural differences and be comfortably within the integrative-awareness stage.

A third reason C/RID models are important is because of the assumption that some stages of identity are more positively correlated with mental health than others. In particular, the conformity stage identities, connected as they are with contempt toward one's own group, are thought to be correlated with variables like low self-esteem. Conformity attitudes are demonstrated by attempts to hide one's stigma and pass as "normal." Goffman (1963) wrote about the psychological costs of such efforts. One way to research the "psychology of oppression" is to correlate various indices of mental health with the identity and consciousness characterized as pre-encounter.

Later in chapter 5 of this volume, I present a model of how cultural identity in deaf people may develop. This model has been used as a basis for creating an instrument, the Deaf Identity Development Scale (Glickman, 1993; Glickman & Carey, 1993), designed to measure cultural identity in deaf people. A major purpose of such an instrument would be to investigate whether there is, indeed, a relationship between cultural orientation toward deafness and various indices of mental health.

Because African American identity models have been in existence the longest, research into the psychological effects of oppression and liberation in African American people using this paradigm has begun to bear fruit. Helms (1990) summarized recent research studies that "have found deficiencies in personal identity (e.g., depression, low self-esteem, high anxiety, etc.) to be most characteristic of pre-encounter attitudes, and strengths (e.g., positive self-esteem, low anxiety) to be associated with encounter and/or internalization attitudes" (p. 102).

A correlation between psychological maladjustment and early stage identity development is probably most apparent in the case of gay and lesbian people. Pre-encounter homosexuals are people still "in the closet," denying and repressing their same-sex attractions. Garnets and Kimmel (1991) reviewed the literature on the process of lesbian and gay identity development. They found that:

> self-labeling as gay, accepting this label, self-disclosure, and feeling accepted by others have been found to be strongly related to psychological adjustment. Similarly, more positive gay male or lesbian identity has been found to be correlated with significantly fewer symptoms of neurotic or social anxiety, higher ego strength, less depression, and higher self-esteem. (p. 153)

A fourth reason C/RID models are important is that identity is the primary factor through which multicultural counseling and therapy approaches consider individual differences. Sue and Zane (1987) cautioned that a major risk of cross-cultural approaches to counseling is the tendency to overgeneralize and stereotype. Harvey (1989) gave the same warning when discussing cross-cultural counseling approaches to treatment of deaf clients. Whenever therapists highlight the clients' cultural context in counseling, making it figural, they invariably lessen the importance of individual differences, making them "ground." Probably the major criticism that can be directed at some culturally affirmative approaches to counseling is that they lose sight of the individual. The inclusion of theories of identity development is meant to account for individual differences among members of a culture. Similarly in the Deaf–hearing context, construction of models of deaf identity development, and ultimately of hearing identity development, helps avoid the danger of stereotyping deaf and hearing people.

A final reason C/RID models are important is that they provide a framework for majority clinicians to become culturally self-aware. In recent C/RID literature, increasing attention is devoted to the idea of White identity development (Helms, 1990; Ivey, 1991; Ponterotto, 1988). A logical extension of this is that one would want to understand the developmental process that Whites, males, heterosexuals, and hearing people go through as they discover the oppression that their minority counterparts have been subject to. Hearing identity development would refer to the presumably common experiences and developmental changes hearing people have as they learn about Deaf culture and the oppression of deaf people. Hoffmeister and Harvey, in chapter 3 of this volume, outline what they see as common elements of such identity changes in hearing neophytes in the field of deafness.

Knowledge of Minority People's Points of View

According to Rogers (1967), three characteristics of the therapist are essential if the client is to grow. The therapist must be congruent or genuine, show unconditional positive regard, and convey accurate empathic understanding.

What does it take to achieve congruence, unconditional positive regard, and accurate empathy across cultural barriers? What makes this difficult is not merely the task of appreciating another cultural viewpoint, but also the task of working within the context of oppression. One has to learn to appreciate the perspective of a group with a sociohistorical relationship to one's own group—a relationship characterized not by mutual acknowledgment of difference, but by entrenched patterns of domination and submission.

Each social group constructs reality somewhat differently. African Americans, for example, typically attribute great importance to race and racism, whereas Whites typically stress individual rather than racial differences. For gay and lesbian people, the concept of homophobia is very important. Heterosexual people rarely use a concept like homophobia unless they have a great deal of positive experiences with gay and lesbian people. Much intergroup conflict results from the different social vantage points of each group, their position in society relative to each other, and the consequently different lenses through which they understand the world. All these constructions of reality may be true in the sense that they provide a useable map of meaning for a particular group. There are endless number of "true" ways to interpret reality just as there are endless number of ways to map a particular terrain.

Culturally affirmative psychotherapy requires of a therapist the cognitive ability to move between different social constructions of reality. One has to be able to appreciate how the people with whom one works see the world: what they find important and irrelevant; which concepts they use to explain their own lives. The ability to appreciate diverse constructions of reality is an advanced cognitive skill. For people who are rooted in their own construction—who believe, for instance, that their own group is the sole possessor of some God-given truth—this skill may be impossible to acquire.

Aside from cognitive skills, there are emotional skills required before one can know a minority perspective. We have seen that minorities go through stages in the development of their cultural identity. At early stages, they may idealize the majority therapist, and at middle stages, they may become furious with the majority therapist. The emotional task is to maintain a clinical perspective both while one is idealized and while one is hated. In more clinical terms, we could say this means the therapist must be able to work with both a positive and negative racial transference.

It is problematic for a hearing person to present what he thinks is a Deaf worldview. Doing so may represent yet another assault on the struggles of Deaf people to define themselves. Nonetheless, I think it is relevant for me to attempt to describe here some of what I have learned from Deaf people about Deaf and hearing worldviews. I would like to suggest that a key element of a Deaf worldview is an affirmative view of deafness and a critical view of the hearing world. Deafness is seen as positive because of the enjoyment deaf people get from interaction in ASL with each other at their own social events. Culturally Deaf people know that precious communication happens with other culturally Deaf people. Communication with anyone else, including many hearing people who have learned sign, is usually strained, awkward, and frustrating. This positive attitude toward deafness is demonstrated by the desire of some deaf parents to have deaf children. From a hearing point of view, this desire is difficult to understand. One is even tempted to label it pathological. From a Deaf perspective, it is merely the desire many people have to raise children like themselves, to have one's children belong to one's own social group and culture.

The difference between a Deaf and hearing point of view was made clear to me at a funeral of a deaf man I once attended. During the eulogy, the preacher remarked that this man was now in heaven with his Lord and he was now "communicating with his hands in his pockets." He no longer needs sign, the preacher continued. He can now speak. He can now hear. He is now healed. The preacher's bias was caught by an astute Deaf woman who wondered why he assumed that deaf people go to Heaven and learn speech but not that hearing people go to Heaven and learn sign. "Does he think that when French people die, they go to heaven and learn English?" she asked, annoyed also by his assumption that deaf people are defective and that when they die they are "healed" and become hearing people. This Deaf woman, who had been a close friend of the deceased man, asked to say a few words at the grave site. Signing through an interpreter, she remarked that this man had signed all his life and that signing was his preferred mode of communication. She suspected he might be already at work with Laurent Clerc developing yet another kind of sign, Heaven Sign Language (HSL).

How does one understand this Deaf woman's response to the preacher? Was she unjustifiably defensive toward a well-meant, harmless remark? Was she showing some unreasonable militancy based in unresolved anger and resentment? Or was she countering the preacher's anti-deaf prejudice with a eulogy her Deaf friend would have wanted? Was the preacher celebrating the deceased man, as he intended, or insulting the deceased man and his community, as was perceived? This is a cultural conflict. The answer depends on whether one adopts a Deaf or hearing point of view.

In working with any minority group, one needs to understand how they typically interpret common experiences; that is, one needs to understand their worldview. Understanding how cultures make sense of experience is the basis for determining whether psychotherapy, with adaptations, can be culturally relevant. Although psychotherapists are not required to be anthropologists, the more they can switch into the culture's framework for understanding, the better their ability to establish rapport and intervene meaningfully. Some of the questions that therapists can keep in mind when working with different cultures are as follows:

1. What is seen as good (sacred) and what is seen as bad (profane)?
2. What is seen as right and what is seen as wrong? What is the basis for evaluations of right and wrong?
3. What is important (figural) and what is irrelevant (ground)?
4. How and why do things happen? Which common explanations are offered for success and failure?
5. How are health and illness, normality and abnormality understood?
6. What are the sanctioned forms of helping and healing?
7. What are the organizing constructs of the culture? What are the culture's most important ideas?

   8. What are the principal metaphors and symbols for community life?
   9. How does the language of the culture organize experience?

   How does one answer these questions with regard to the Deaf community and culture? How, in particular, do culturally Deaf people construe helping, healing, sickness, and health? Clearly, the notion of "helping" is colored for deaf people by their experience with paternalism and oppression. When hearing people say "help," it is possible that deaf people hear this more as "control." In the culturally affirmative therapy literature, true helping is often understood to mean empowerment and liberation. Is it possible for hearing people, who have long been the agent of oppression of deaf people, to serve instead as agents of empowerment?

   As part of the task of knowing Deaf culture, hearing clinicians need to dialogue with deaf people around these kinds of questions. *Indeed, the nature of such a dialogue is itself empowering as all these questions imply recognition of and respect for the Deaf community.*

   In the normative view of culture (McDonald, 1986), one tries to understand the world in the way members of the culture do. One tries to appreciate and work within the culture's "cognitive map." A large part of appreciating a culture's cognitive map involves focusing on the culture's language, both as a value in itself and as a means of organizing experience. Bernal, Bernal, Martinez, Olmedo, and Santisteban (1983), for instance, described the importance of Spanish for Latinos. "As part of the Hispanic heritage, the Spanish language serves a unifying function for all Hispanics by providing a link with their cultural roots and a means to perpetuate their values" (p. 71). Because Spanish is not the official language of the U.S., one can expect that not only does the use of Spanish unify Latinos, but it serves as a central organizing construct or symbol. Whether or not a particular Hispanic American speaks Spanish is a major index of acculturation. How close or far one is perceived to be in relation to Latino cultures may be determined largely by one's degree of fluency in Spanish. Many Latinos have championed the cause of bilingual education because they value Spanish and believe Spanish speaking builds the self-esteem of Latino children. Similarly, many Latinos see the political movement that aims to declare English the sole language of the U.S. and to insist that all official business be conducted solely in English as racist to the core. One simply can not affirm a culture and a people without affirming the language of the people.

   The parallel between Hispanic American and Deaf American cultures is obvious. ASL is not merely a means of communication for Deaf people, but support for ASL is a central value of the community. Degree of identification with the Deaf community is often determined largely on the basis of skill in ASL. Hearing people's skill in ASL and attitude toward ASL are primary determinants of how much they are viewed to be allies of the Deaf community. Bilingual education programs for deaf children are viewed as important not only because they foster a healthy communication environment but because they embody respect for a cultural view of deafness. In addition, because deaf people are subject so often to poor communication, strong and clear communication is valued in a way that people who generally experience clear communication cannot appreciate.

Working With Deaf People's Anger With Hearing People

If one works with minorities, one also has to be prepared to encounter their rage. Culturally aware minority people are usually very sensitive to behavior that appears to replicate oppression. Indeed, the particular form of oppression they face, be it racism for ethnic and racial minorities, anti-semitism for Jews, sexism for women, heterosexism for gay men and lesbians, or paternalism and language bigotry for Deaf people, can become a framework or lens through which they interpret much of their experience. Minority clients usually view majority therapists as having a class, race and/or cultural bias. Therapists who maintain, in a naive way, that they are not prejudiced, are likely to alienate many minority clients who know better. Therapists who can, on the other hand, acknowledge oppression, who can validate the healthy paranoia of minority clients and their reasons for being angry and on guard, have a much better chance of joining with these clients.

The enormity of this challenge becomes clear when majority people confront the anger of oppressed groups. It is never comfortable to be the target of anger. One can almost always argue that the clients' anger, especially if acted on, is "inappropriate." Angry people are often not reasonable, and when oppressed people discover their oppression, their response can be more extreme than the cool, detached, and balanced therapist would advise. Yet part of the liberation of minority people must involve discovery of their oppression and the expression of their anger. There is no way, in spite of the dangers, to avoid working with this anger.

Perhaps the acid test of effective culturally affirmative therapists is that they have enough knowledge of minority perspectives so that they can welcome the clients' anger when it comes, even and especially when therapists themselves are the target. This does not mean self-flagellation by the therapists, but rather the straightforward and nonself-deprecating acknowledgment of the reality of oppression. Recovering from racism, sexism, and so on is practiced within therapy.

Needless to say, there is some danger while clients are at the resistance and emersion stage of identity development where they discover their rage and reject the dominant society fully. Clients may take extreme actions, become violent, and get themselves into legal trouble. Clients may need help appreciating the difference between feeling angry and acting violently. "Owning" one's anger is important. Acting violently is rarely justified. There is some risk that clients will not move beyond this stage, that they will stay angry and hostile for long periods of time, especially if their anger is rooted also in characterological problems. Therapists need to know that an open and direct acknowledgment of oppression will facilitate client growth, whereas a defensive response may retard growth and ultimately lead to the therapists being written off as part of the problem. Therapists, however, need also to avoid overidentification with the clients' rage and simplistic rationalization of aggressive behavior.

How can therapists help their clients navigate this stage while avoiding excesses of violence? As mentioned, therapists should be on guard against a simplistic understanding of this dynamic that would lead them to encourage clients to take antisocial action. If anything, therapists should, in my opinion, model a "cooler head" and remain someone who understands oppression and opposes it in constructive, socially responsible ways. This can also be construed as ego-enhancing work, as facilitating the development of a sense of self and the ability to manage one's impulses and feelings. Secondly, therapists may, in some instance, be able to help clients "become meta to the process." That is to say, therapists might share information with clients about minority identity development, validate their anger as an important stage in their growth, validate the reality of oppression, but frame this whole experience as a step on the clients' journey towards recovery. In chapter 6 of this volume, Harvey gives a poignant case example and offers additional insights into this difficult issue.

Culturally affirmative therapists strive to help clients negotiate a delicate balancing act. On the one hand, minority clients have good reason to be angry and need to have this anger validated. On the other hand, simply blaming society for one's problems is unlikely to help after a certain point. Mental health seems connected to an internal locus of control and to the ability to assume responsibility for one's actions (Oler, 1989; Sue, 1981). Yet the experience of oppression may predispose minorities to an external locus of control. Even in the worst instances of oppression, the clinical question still boils down to this: "Given this context of oppression, how will you live your life?"

Knowledge of Barriers to Utilization of Mental Health Services

A point frequently made in the literature on counseling/therapy with disadvantaged ethnic and language minorities is that they underutilize mental health services. They are less likely to seek help from a mental health center and more likely than their White counterparts to drop out of treatment early. This point has been made with regard to Hispanic Americans (Abad, Ramos, & Boyce, 1974; Bernal et al., 1983; Dolgin, Salazar, & Cruz, 1987; Laval, Gomez, & Ruiz, 1983; Torres, 1983), Asian Americans (Sue & Morishima, 1982), and African Americans (Boyd-Franklin, 1989; June, 1986), especially with poor and working-class members of these communities. Clinicians need to understand these barriers well if they are to have any hope of overcoming them.

Minorities underutilize mental health services for many reasons, chiefly:

1. There are not enough bilingual and bicultural clinicians, especially clinicians who are themselves minorities;
2. Mental health agencies and providers may demonstrate attitudes ranging from cultural insensitivity to overt racism;
3. Mental health services are commonly not understood within the minority culture. Counseling and psychotherapy may not be validated forms of healing, and therapists may not be credible healers;
4. Minorities may perceive public mental health services to be arms of a government and system they distrust.

For instance, Boyd-Franklin (1989) believed that the low utilization of mental health services by African American families has to do with negative experiences many have had with welfare and other government agencies and with their need to protect family secrets from disclosure. She noted that many African American families have experienced welfare systems as intrusive, prying, and controlling, and they may be uncertain about the relationship between the mental health clinic and the welfare department. In addition, White social workers filing child abuse complaints against African American parents, whether or not they are justified, cannot help but exacerbate an African American client's difficulty in trusting professional helpers, especially if they are White.

I once attended a conference sponsored by the Massachusetts Department of Mental Health (DMH) on multicultural mental health services. At a workshop for managers of programs that serve cultural minorities, the agency directors identified three main barriers to the provision of culturally competent services. First was the difficulty of recruiting, hiring, and retaining bicultural staff. Most of the directors did not find this problem insurmountable, at least with regards to Spanish-speaking clinicians. A bigger problem was how to fund nonbillable hours of service. Community mental health clinics receive much of their funding from the provision of treatment to Medicaid clients. For this treatment to be billable, clients must have an appropriate *Diagnostic and Statistical Manual* (DSM) diagnosis, and the treatment must occur within the standard clinical hour. Yet much of what has to be done to make services culturally relevant involves making the appropriate linkages with the community, doing education and preventative work, as well as an enormous amount of case management, and Medicaid does not generally pay for such interventions. The problem has become more acute as Medicaid moves to managed care. All clinical services have to be justified as medically necessary. The push for financial accountability in mental health services may conflict with the need to establish culturally appropriate services, many of which fall outside the medical model and the billable clinical hour. In chapter 8 of this volume, Zitter discusses how she attempts to overcome such administrative barriers to providing non-billable services to deaf clients.

Another barrier is that the no-show rates among minorities are often greater. This high no-show rate shares all the causes cited previously for minority underutilization of mental health services. Higher no-show rates may result in lower performance statistics for therapists who serve these clients and less income brought into the clinic for these efforts. In addition, because minority clients often require more case management and advocacy, therapists who face ever increasing productivity demands have counterincentives to taking on a minority caseload.

Managers who care about providing appropriate services to cultural minorities also have to pay attention to the bottom line: clinic survival. Unless a mental health clinic is housed within a large minority community so that the bulk of its clientele are minorities, it may not be to the financial advantage of the clinic to be culturally accessible to everyone. Clinicians may hold an ethical commitment to providing culturally affirmative treatment, but they need the means to translate this commitment into practical and financially remunerative services. Historically, it has been government support that has made the provision of such services possible.

Another barrier faced by clinic managers in Massachusetts is the policy adopted by the Department of Mental Health to give priority treatment to clients with long-term or serious mental illnesses. This policy effectively prevents the provision of long-term services to the majority of minority clients who do not present with major mental illnesses. For instance, one manager of an Hispanic treatment program said that most of her Hispanic clients presented with problems related to physical or sexual abuse or substance abuse. Hispanic clients with a major psychotic or affective disorder were relatively infrequent. This new policy appears to be a way for the Department of Mental Health to manage at a time of dwindling resources. If the state can not increase its services, it can define more narrowly who is eligible for these services. Such narrow definitions impede multicultural work, the thrust of which is to broaden the scope of mental health services.

The vast majority of deaf people who use public mental health facilities are not psychotic and would not be eligible for public funding of treatment given this narrow definition of eligibility. Because there are relatively few deaf clients with severe mental illnesses such as schizophrenia, and deaf people who present at mental health clinics are not necessarily diagnosable as severely mentally ill, it will not be cost effective for any clinic to develop culturally affirmative treatment programs unless it casts its net quite broadly, serving a wide range of deaf clients and providing numerous services outside the billable hour. Yet the Massachusetts Department of Mental Health, at precisely the moment it recognizes the need to serve deaf clients, limits its scope of services so that few clinic directors see financial incentive to do more than hire one or two clinicians who sign. An isolated clinician who signs does not constitute a culturally affirmative treatment program.

National trends in the delivery of mental health services are also threatening the creation and maintenance of culturally affirmative mental health programs. Increasingly, treatment is narrowly defined as limited to that which occurs in this billable hour with the patient. Then the parameters of the treatment itself are further restricted. Treatment is expected to be brief, focused, goal directed, and so on. This model of treatment can be very appropriate for clients who come to their outpatient clinic "treatment ready." They understand at least the basics of the treatment contract; they recognize the process as potentially healing and the therapist as a credible healer; and they have enough motivation to participate in the process of therapy that they can get themselves to appointments. But very poor people, very overwhelmed people, and people with marked cultural differences often do not meet these criteria. They are not ready to contract for mental health services. All the appropriate and necessary pretreatment work that must be done to bring them into the treatment process requires funding sources that appear to be disappearing.

The task of establishing culturally affirmative mental health treatment for cultural minorities was daunting before the arrival of managed care. Current fiscal constraints may, in fact, make counseling for all but the most acculturated minority members improbable. We should not, however, lose sight of the vision just because political realities are, for the moment, unfavorable. As long as one can conceptualize what culturally affirmative services would look like, there is always room to nudge an organization in that direction.

THE SKILLS DIMENSION

Introduction

The third dimension of culturally affirmative therapy is the development of specialized skills. We have already seen that clinicians working cross-culturally need to have highly developed self-awareness and knowledge of the general society and the particular culture of the client. That is the beginning. Sue and Zane (1987) pointed out, "In actuality, therapists' knowledge of the culture of clients is quite distal to therapeutic outcomes, in the sense that the knowledge must be transformed into concrete operations and strategies" (p. 39). They then ask the pivotal question, "Given knowledge of clients' culture, what should therapists do?"

Even a cursory review of the literature reveals great vagueness in this area. Almost everyone says that clinicians need to be culturally aware and to make appropriate adaptations for the culture of the clients. Few try to operationalize these aspects of multicultural work, to break culturally affirmative therapy down into concrete, teachable skills. When specifics are listed, one runs into a basic confusion of this field.

On the one hand, some culturally affirmative therapists criticize the notion that minority clients are unsuitable for insight-oriented psychotherapy. It has been pointed out the minority clients are often given "quick and dirty" psychotherapeutic interventions such as medication; electroshock therapy (ECT); involuntary hospitalization; and directive, reality-based, short-term counseling. The "real stuff," that is, insight-oriented, psychodynamic psychotherapy, is reserved for the presumably more verbal and psychologically minded White middle- and upper-class client. Some therapists may argue that it is racist to believe that minority clients cannot be suitable for the most "prestigious" (i.e., expensive) forms of psychotherapy.

On the other hand, insight-oriented depth psychotherapy is criticized as culturally inappropriate for many minorities. Instead, therapists are told, for instance, to work with present-day, reality-based problems; to work in roles such as educator, case manager, and advocate; to adjust clinical boundaries in the direction of becoming a family friend or to be stern and formal when the culture demands it; to work along side of, or in an advisory capacity to, indigenous community helpers or paraprofessionals who may have no training in mental health; to be directive and give advice, and so on. All of these modifications can make psychotherapy more quick and dirty, and can appear to be depriving the minority client of access to insight-oriented treatment. Needless to say, to modify one's interventions in these manners, to avoid consciously a nondirective, insight-oriented approach, can also be construed as racist.

The same debate has occurred with regard to psychotherapy with deaf persons. Is long-term, psychodynamic psychotherapy appropriate for deaf people, and, if not, is that due to the limitations of the patient, the therapist, or the method? Of course, depending on the resources of the patient, the skills of the therapist, and the flexibility of the method, virtually any psychotherapeutic procedure will work with some deaf persons. It is risky to generalize. What one needs is a way to think about how and when to make accommodations in the treatment procedure. Zitter, in chapter 8 of this volume, presents one map for how therapists might make such accommodations.

In the following discussion, I have culled from the literature on culturally affirmative therapy four parameters that correspond to particular skills that can be learned and used to make therapy more culturally appropriate for minorities. This can be thought of as another map for thinking about how therapists may adjust treatment to make it relevant and useful for minorities. These parameters are: (a) skills in languages, nonverbal communication and collaboration with professional interpreters; (b) skills in expanding and flexing clinical roles; (c) skills in collaboration with indigenous healers, helpers, community leaders, and paraprofessionals; and (d) skills in selecting and designing cultural syntonic treatment interventions.

One theme does seem to pervade the literature on what one does in treatment of cultural minorities. The theme is empowerment. Following from the knowledge that most minority clients are oppressed and the awareness that one always works in the context of that oppression, the idea is that the dynamics of oppression must be part of the therapeutic conversation. A goal of therapy becomes the identification and understanding of oppression and the development of resources to combat it. Boyd-Franklin (1989), for instance, in her text on family therapy with African American families, cited empowerment as the overriding concept infusing all such work. Empowerment has often been cited as a central value of feminist therapy (Chaplin, 1988). Empowerment is the reverse of victimization. Although one can not change society in the course of therapy, one can demystify the processes of oppression and provide clients with tools for self-affirmation and self-empowerment within an oppressive society. Helping a homosexual client affirm a gay identity and affiliate with the gay community is another example of empowerment within the context of oppression. Helping a deaf client explore his or her Deaf identity and place in the Deaf community is another example.

Cross-Cultural Communication Skills

Verbal Communication.   Sue (1981) cited language differences as a major barrier to cross-cultural counseling. This is obviously true when client and counselor speak different languages but is also true when they speak different versions of the same language. Although there are expressive forms of psychotherapy such as art and movement therapy, and although there are body-centered therapies that utilize touch and movement to elicit feelings, counseling and psychotherapy of any sort are heavily dependent on the use of a shared language.

It is a simple truth that client and therapist need to share a language system. (The only alternative is to utilize an interpreter, which I discuss shortly.) Although this is a simple statement, probably no other multicultural skill is more difficult to acquire. For most adults, acquiring fluency in a second language requires immense effort. To succeed, one generally has to make this a major life goal. Many therapists who value the ability to speak other languages may be unable or unwilling to put in the years of time and effort required. Given the paramount importance of language skills, it is tempting to consider every other multicultural competency a luxury. As mentioned, in clinics that serve linguistic minorities, bilingual staff may be so needed that they are hired even if their other clinical and cultural competencies are limited.

Beyond basic communication of content, language patterns impact profoundly on psychotherapy in other ways. Marcos (1976a, 1976b, 1988; Marcos & Urguyo, 1979) has been in the forefront of those drawing out the clinical implications of patterns of language usage. His work is worth reviewing in light of the experience of deaf people.

Marcos (1976b, 1988) described some relevant linguistic dimensions of bilingualism. The concept of *language dominance* refers to the degree of command that bilinguals have in each language. True, proficient, or pure bilinguals display native abilities in both languages. *Subordinate* bilinguals have greater command of one language than another. *True* bilinguals conceptualize issues in the way natural to each language they use. Subordinate bilinguals, by contrast, are always engaged in the task of interpretation. They are always searching for the linguistic equivalents of the concepts as conceptualized in their native language. Most people who become deaf early in life are probably subordinate bilinguals. If they are fortunate enough to receive sustained exposure to ASL, they will probably become dominant ASL users and second language English users. If they enter adulthood without any clear and consistent exposure to any language, they will be profoundly handicapped in every aspect of their lives.

Subordinate bilinguals face a *language barrier* with important implications for psychotherapy. Because subordinate bilinguals do not process information easily in the second language, the language barrier influences what they say and how they say it. Surely anyone who has ever tried to learn a second language has experienced the frustration of having an inadequate vocabulary. Deaf people who are not fluent in English are like perpetual visitors to a foreign country, constantly trying to make themselves understood in just the way they intend. Hearing people not fluent in ASL are equally handicapped in making their exact intentions clear.

Language independence refers to "the bilingual's capacity to acquire, maintain and utilize two separate language codes, each with its own lexical, syntactic, phonetic, semantic and ideational components" (Marcos, 1988, p. 36). Language independence refers to the fact that bilinguals associate different memories, experiences, feelings, and points of view with each language. The choice of language used in therapy, therefore, has profound implications for which information is accessed. If one's early childhood experiences occurred in Spanish, the use of English in treatment, even for an adult proficient in English, is likely to keep these experiences from being remembered and refelt in a way that is therapeutic. Similarly, we should ask in which language, if any, a deaf child's early experiences are encoded and how trying to "recover" these experiences using some different language or communication modality affects what is remembered.

Marcos noted that this language independence can be both useful and destructive to therapy. Powerful emotional experiences that occurred in one language can be avoided by use of the other language. This may be helpful as a first step toward reapproaching experiences that would otherwise remain undescribed. Avoiding one language can also be a form of resistance. This suggests that deaf ASL users might modulate their experience of powerful emotion through their language usage. To "turn up the volume" of emotion, they might use ASL. To turn it down, they might use a variant of sign closer to English.

Marcos' discussion of the clinical implications of bilingualism is useful even when the clinician does not know both languages. Some time ago, I treated a second generation Portuguese American client who was a pure bilingual, fully fluent in both English and Portuguese. As I did not speak Portuguese, I asked him whether he preferred to see a Portuguese speaking therapist. He assured me that it did not matter, but I searched for one, unsuccessfully, anyway. As we began work, it became clear that he had a great deal of ferocious rage toward his mother. He told me what his mother said and did, but he would interpret her Portuguese into English for me. To facilitate his obtaining clarity about his emotions and to achieve some catharsis, we role played, and I usually took the role of his mother. The problem was that conversations with his mother occurred in Portuguese.

Remembering Marcos' work, I began to experiment with having him speak to me in Portuguese during role plays, even though I did not fully understand him. Fortunately, I have some knowledge of Spanish, and that knowledge combined with working with him for some time enabled me to get the gist of what he was saying. It did seem to me that his affect was more real, that he got much closer to his pain, when he spoke in Portuguese. Indeed, even though he was fluent in English, his childhood and family experience were embedded in Portuguese. I knew therefore, that if I wanted to move him closer to these experiences, I needed to direct him to use Portuguese. Similarly, when I wanted to help him structure and contain his rage, I suggested he use English.

Nonverbal Communication.   Cultural differences also pertain to nonverbal communication. Sue (1981) cited personal space, eye contact, and conversational conventions as examples of nonverbal behavior that differ culturally and that are easily misconstrued by the culturally naive clinician. Cultural differences in personal space include how different cultures define intimate, personal, and public space. Without cross-cultural training, people in cross-cultural interactions can easily misinterpret body space to conclude that someone is cold and distant or inappropriately intimate and pushy.

It might be useful to review some of the cultural differences in nonverbal communicative behavior that have been noted between deaf and hearing people. Baker (1977), for instance, did extensive research on conversational turn-taking behaviors in ASL. She noted that signers indicate their readiness to "yield the floor" by, among other things, establishing eye contact, decreasing their signing speed, and dropping their hands to a resting place. Desire to continue signing can be indicated by eye gaze away from the receiver, acceleration in signing rate, and refusal to come to a rest position. Hearing people also utilize rules for turn taking. We rely heavily on voice inflection to indicate our intentions. The rules for the two cultures differ, and a hearing person unaware of what to look for may find himself cutting a signer off, thus appearing rude; or responding late, thus appearing inattentive. Baker reported that "hearing counselors with deaf clients often report difficulty in knowing when their client has finished signing his thought and when it is appropriate to respond." The implications are obvious.

Related to turn-taking behavior are different rules about eye contact and eye gaze. In ASL, eye gaze may have a grammatical function in, for instance, the establishment of pronouns in space. Conversation between hearing speakers and deaf signers may differ in the length of eye contact considered necessary for the sender and receiver. Baker (1977) noted Kendon's report that "mutual gazes between previously unacquainted (hearing) interactants tend to last for little more than one second." Such eye contact rules vary with the context, the sex of the interactants and their roles. Her own research with deaf signers led Baker to conclude that "effective communication in sign requires a consistent mainte-nance of addressee eye gaze on the speaker, and periods of mutual eye gaze extending more than 5 seconds are not uncommon." This difference is not hard to understand as conversation in sign is largely dependent on vision.

Because of this necessity of eye contact, there is apparently a greater taboo in Deaf culture against refusing to meet someone else's gaze. Among hearing people in White, American, middle-class culture, failure to make eye contact may be interpreted as timidity, disinterest, or rudeness. Stokoe and Battison (1981) reported:

> In hearing people's conversations, eye contact, or a lack of it, is used to express respect, attentiveness, boredom, preoccupation, and various other states and affects. Since signers are visually dependent, lack of eye contact is naturally interpreted as something stronger than inattentiveness. If the receiver breaks eye contact, communication is broken. (p. 191)

Meadow (1972) reported that "when the conversational channel is sign lan-guage, avoidance of eye contact becomes a powerful form of conversational control" (p. 63).

Hearing people, possibly oblivious to the stricter rules Deaf culture imposes on eye contact, may make all sorts of social blunders. A culturally Deaf person, even one with a clear voice, does not seem to believe people are listening unless they are watching. Baker (1977) observed, "Deaf people frequently comment that hearing people seem to be inattentive to and uninterested in what is being said. Even more disturbing is the fact that hearing people are often perceived as being hostile because they avoid the intimacy of mutual eye gaze" (p. 231). Stokoe and Battison (1981) made a similar observation: "Hearing signers are notorious for their incorrect (i.e., unregulated and ungrammatical) use of eye contact, and often appear shifty-eyed and evasive to deaf people" (p. 191).

The physical distance maintained between conversational interactants is another behavior regulated by cultural norms. There seems to be little doubt that deaf people signing to each other prefer to sit or stand further apart than hearing people talking to each other, although race, ethnicity, and other factors influence spatial arrangements. Hearing counselors who insensitively arrange their offices with heavy chairs in spaces that hearing people find comfortable might find their deaf clients squirming in their chairs or struggling to push them backward.

In hearing society, it is generally considered rude to shout in a closed space. Yet at Gallaudet University, deaf people often shout to get someone's attention. Any hearing student living in Gallaudet's dorms can testify that norms regarding noise differ for deaf and hearing people; that, contrary to popular belief, deaf people are often louder than hearing people. Because of the visibility of sign language, it is possible to have a conversation while separated by a window or across the expanse of a room. In Gallaudet's auditorium, it is common to see a deaf person in the front row sign to someone in the balcony. Most hearing people would never dream of shouting over that distance. This visibility of sign, which is an advantage when one wants to communicate across a room, is a disadvantage when one wants to have an intimate conversation in public. The fact that anyone might be reading one's signs from afar can not help but influence the norms for signing in a public place.

These and other nonverbal rules for behavior operate in cross-cultural interactions, usually with the result of cultural misunderstanding. When one of the interactants is a clinician and the other is a client, the cultural misunderstanding inevitably takes the form of misdiagnosis. Because of the power differences, it is generally the clinician's culturally based constructions or misperceptions that constitute the "dominant narrative" that accounts for the interaction (White & Epston, 1990).

Working With Interpreters. It is obvious that competent students who already have foreign language skills, especially if they are cultural minorities themselves, need to be actively recruited if the field of counseling and psychotherapy is to become more multiculturally aware. Lytle and Lewis, in chapter 10 of this volume, argue there is no substitute for clear, direct communication between therapist and client in the language preferred by the client. For those with commitment to culturally affirmative treatment without the time, ability, or life circumstances to permit development of foreign language skills, there is no alternative, nonetheless, but to conduct such treatment in collaboration with interpreters. A common mistake of clinicians working cross-culturally is to use untrained people as interpreters. Sabin (1975) reviewed two cases where psychiatrists, working with Spanish-speaking case workers, failed to appreciate the depth of their patient's despair, resulting in failure to intervene to hospitalize when necessary. Sabin hypothesized that "while translation allows transmission of data that promote diagnosis of psychosis, it may not reduce interpersonal distance enough to facilitate vivid appreciation of the patient's affective state" (p. 198). Nothing in Sabin's article, however, would lead one to conclude that either he or the psychiatrists in his study have any sense of interpreting as a profession or have had any training in the appropriate ways to work alongside an interpreter in a clinical setting.

Marcos (1979) discussed three kinds of distortions likely to result from the use of lay interpreters. The first are distortions associated with the interpreters' language competence and translation skills. Interpreting is a highly sophisticated skill. Most schools of foreign-language interpreting such as those at Georgetown University and the Monterey (CA) Institute for International Studies require bilingual fluency as well as a bachelor's degree merely to begin interpreter training, which may last several years (Frishberg, 1986, p. 89). The common belief that any bilingual person can act effectively as an interpreter is naive. However, in practice, not only are untrained bilingual people often asked to interpret in linguistically and clinically complex situations but so may be mere beginners in the language.

I recall an instance on the deaf psychiatric inpatient unit on which I worked when staff had particular difficulty understanding one deaf client. The staff included several Deaf native ASL users as well as an exceptionally qualified interpreter—people sufficiently experienced and skilled in communication with deaf people to recognize when they were facing an unusual linguistic challenge. While this staff struggled, a hearing, rehabilitation counselor who was several weeks into his first sign language class announced confidently that *he* had no difficulty communicating with this client and asked the other staff members what their problem was. As the saying goes, "A little knowledge can be a dangerous thing."

The second distortion cited by Marcos is associated with the lay interpreter's lack of psychiatric knowledge. This may take the form of normalization of the patient's thought processes as in the following example cited by Marcos:

> Clinician to Spanish-speaking patient: "What about worries, do you have many worries?"
>
> Interpreter to patient: "Is it there anything that bothers you?"
>
> Patient's response: "I know, I know that God is with me, I'm not afraid, they cannot get me (pause) I'm wearing these new pants and I feel protected, I feel good, I don't get headaches anymore."
>
> Interpreter to clinician: "He says that he is not afraid, he feels good, he doesn't have headaches anymore." (p. 173)

Not only does psychotic thinking take training to recognize and identify, it takes exceptional skill to interpret it accurately into another language. It is a difficult enough interpreting task when each party to a transaction is speaking clearly, wishing to be understood. When one party is thought or language disordered, the meaning of a communication may not be at all clear, and the interpreter has the task of conveying into a second language *the same lack of clarity* in an equivalently disorganized form. The absurdity of asking an untrained person to do this should be apparent.

The third distortion identified by Marcos is associated with the lay interpreter's attitude. This is especially a problem when the interpreter is a friend or relation and has some interest in the outcome of the interview. I know of one instance where a deaf teenager stabbed, but did not kill, her mother. At the police station the wounded but functional mother, who was fluent in sign, was asked to interpret for the police and her daughter. Even if the mother were a professionally trained and certified interpreter, the nature of her relationship with the client, especially under these circumstances, would impose emotional barriers to her acting competently in that role.

Marcos advised that in the absence of a competent psychiatric interpreter, clinicians should be aware of these barriers to effective communication. He suggested that clinicians meet with lay interpreters to assess their language skills and clinical sophistication, as well as their attitude, and to educate them regarding confidentiality and various aspects of the diagnostic process. Marcos did not explain how a monolingual clinician can judge the bilingual skills of an interpreter. Nor did he explain how a 10-minute educational session is likely to overcome these barriers. The optimal solution is to bring in professional interpreters. Marcos did not discuss this as an option probably because in clinical practice with foreign language users it is rarely done.

Psychotherapy with deaf people is generally not defined in cross-cultural terms. Nevertheless, one area where the field of counseling with deaf people has taken the lead over other cross-cultural encounters is with regard to the sophisticated collaboration with professional interpreters that sometimes occurs. In Massachusetts, for instance, the state first established an interpreter referral service for Deaf and hearing people and then used that as a model for the utilization of foreign language interpreters in mental health settings.

I believe that because most therapists who do not already know a second language will not take the time and effort to learn one, training in utilization of professional interpreters should be part of a program in culturally affirmative counseling and therapy. This training should have three components: knowledge of the interpretation process, knowledge of the role of the interpreter, and knowledge of the clinical implications of inclusion of an interpreter within the therapy session.

First, students should learn something about language interpretation. Interpreting requires fluency in both languages as well as competence in reframing from one language to another. As mentioned, languages do not neatly map out, word for word, against each other. Much is not easily translatable. Cultural referents for similar concepts are different; for instance, the French word *pain* does not refer to the same concept as the English word *bread*. Information is organized differently in different languages. In English, we say, "What is your sex?" In American Sign Language, we sign, "Male. Female. Which?" with appropriate facial and body grammar (i.e., eyebrows raised, head tilted forward). Interpreters do not translate from one word to another but rather they reconstruct the concept in the framework of the second language (Seleskovitch, 1978). This process of interpretation requires that the meaning of the intended message be fully understood before the closest possible linguistic equivalents in the second language can be uncovered.

Secondly, students should learn about the role of the interpreter. The Codes of Ethics of the International Association of Conference Interpreters and of the Registry of Interpreters for the Deaf, Inc. (RID) can be studied and representatives from each organization brought in as presenters. Both codes emphasize confidentiality, professional boundaries and conduct, and accepting assignments according to one's skill level. The RID Code of Ethics also emphasizes that the interpreter convey faithfully the content and spirit of the message and not counsel, advise, or introject personal opinions. Any sign language interpreter credentialed by the RID must adhere to these guidelines.

Thirdly, students should be educated about the clinical implications of introducing an interpreter into the treatment setting. These implications have been explored with reference to sign language interpreters by Stansfield (1981); DeMatteo, Veitri, and Lee (1986); Frishberg (1986), and Harvey (1989). A few of the clinical issues are as follows:

1. With families with a deaf member, where communication style is likely to be a highly charged issue, introduction of a sign language interpreter is itself a powerful intervention. As Harvey (1989) demonstrated, the introduction of the interpreter constitutes a statement about the inability of the family to communicate on its own. Harvey treated this introduction as a strategic intervention that both comments on and changes intrafamily communication. It is rare, however, to find other linguistic minorities in which the parents and children literally do not share a common language. This clinical implication may, therefore, be unique to deaf member families.

2. An interpreter is a third party in the clinical setting who can be an object of both patient transference and therapist countertransference. Harvey (1989) utilized what the family says or fantasizes about the interpreter, as when a father concludes the interpreter disapproves of him because he never learned sign, as a means of eliciting the emotional dynamics of the family. DeMatteo et al. (1986) gave an example of a deaf client who became angry with the interpreter rather than the therapist and described the therapist's attempts to utilize this manifestation of transference. Harvey (1989, p. 177) discussed his own countertransference at having an interpreter, whom he felt the need to impress, as a third party in his clinical sessions.

3. The clinician and interpreter are colleagues in the same treatment and must develop a mutually respectful understanding of each other's roles. Harvey advocated for regular before- and after-session process meetings with the interpreter. This collaboration is not easy and automatic. Harvey noted that the interpreter's commitment to neutrality may conflict with the therapist's desire to use the interpreter "strategically" by, for instance, asking the interpreter not to interpret a particular communication.

4. Professional interpreters may differ on how they interpret their own Code of Ethics. In the field of deafness, some interpreters see themselves as "machines," moving objectively from one language to another. A newer model is interpreter as cross-cultural mediator. In this role, the interpreter might comment to one or both parties on the communication process itself, thus acting as a consultant on language and other cultural matters. In a mental health setting, interpreters with this view of their role might feel comfortable commenting on what they believe the client understands. The clinician, in turn, needs to be aware of how each interpreter understands what the profession's Code of Ethics permits.

5. The clinician who is linguistically naive may not appreciate how, in the process of interpreting, the question they ask may be reframed in the second language in a way that may invalidate its original intent. Stansfield (1981) noted that one cannot interpret into ASL the following English questions found on the Wechsler intelligence tests without giving away their answers: "How are a ball and a wheel alike?" and "In what direction would you travel if you went from Chicago

to Panama?" A therapist may ask a general question like, "How has your mood been lately?", but in ASL the notion of "mood" is indicated by listing specifics, for example, "Have you been feeling happy or sad or angry or what?" This linguistically correct interpretation might be construed as leading when the therapist specifically intended to be vague. These problems are familiar to professional interpreters. In a court setting, for instance, an attorney might ask a deaf witness to describe the "crime" without realizing that "crime" is a general category that is interpreted into ASL by listing specifics (e.g., steal, rape, kill, etc.). The clinician and interpreter, working together, need to discuss how specific ideas should be interpreted into ASL in ways that are linguistically accurate while still clinically relevant.

6. Highly charged emotional issues such as sex, death, intimacy, anger, abuse, and incest are commonly discussed in psychotherapy. The therapist, comfortable with such territory, needs to be sure the interpreter is not reacting emotionally to the material being discussed. Generally, interpreters who work in mental health settings are prepared for this. However, the client may feel inhibited from discussing such issues if he or she perceives the interpreter is the "wrong" gender or age. The therapist needs to be sensitive not only to how the client views the therapist but also how the client views the interpreter.

I recall working with a Vietnamese American hearing family and their deaf teenage daughter. As this family did not sign, an English/ASL interpreter was used in the family therapy. When I asked about the families immigration to U.S., a horrendous story about war trauma was told. It seemed the deaf teenage daughter, who was a baby at the time of the family's escape from Vietnam, had never been told the story of how and why they left because of the language barrier between her and her parents. As the family began to tell her and me the story, I observed with some discomfort that the interpreter was having a powerful emotional reaction to the families' story. It was crucial that I, as the therapist, be prepared not only to help the family but the interpreter as well deal with the powerful material discussed in therapy.

I cannot say that the literature on culturally affirmative therapy addresses interpreter issues well. Indeed, the absence of discussions of interpreters in the literature is more noteworthy than its presence, and what few articles exist are very inadequate. The field of mental health treatment of deaf clients has much to contribute here. In my experience, clinicians who work regularly with deaf people are often more prepared to collaborate with professional interpreters than clinicians who work with those who use other foreign languages. During the course of our own sign language training, clinicians who work with deaf people often become educated about how to work with interpreters. This may be one area of cross-cultural competency in which clinicians who work with deaf people commonly excel. Lytle and Lewis (chapter 10, in this volume) discuss in more depth the intersection of clinical and communication issues as pertains to psychotherapy with deaf clients.

Skills in Expanding and Flexing Clinical Roles.   An important skill cited by Sue et al. (1982) as necessary for culturally affirmative therapy is the ability to work as advocates, intervening for positive change in the clients' world outside of the therapy hour: "The culturally skilled counseling psychologist is able to exercise institutional intervention skills on behalf of his/her client when appropriate" (p. 51).

Certainly one of the major themes cited in the multicultural therapy literature is that therapists must address the clients' real-world problems—that is, housing, employment, poverty, violence, discrimination, and so forth. Therapists are expected to do this both as part of the therapeutic conversation and by intervening actively as a social-change agent. Therapists are expected to educate clients, when necessary, about their rights or about any issue that bears on client empowerment. Therapists should also not hesitate to act as case managers, coordinating services from many providers.

Clinicians who work with lower functioning deaf people in community mental health centers will be called on constantly to act in roles outside the boundaries of traditional psychotherapy. They may advocate for clients to get services such as residential placements or social security benefits. They may educate clients about issues such as the nature of counseling, their rights under various laws, and how to use the bus system. They may case manage services involving rehabilitation counselors, independent living skills centers, residential programs, substance abuse programs, and other service providers. They may need to be actively involved in crisis interventions, being unable to pass this work on to the local emergency service team that is untrained in deafness issues. In many instances, as Sherry Zitter illustrates so well in chapter 8, this volume, much of what the therapist does must occur outside the billable hour. Even inside that hour, the actual work performed may look very different from that with higher functioning, acculturated deaf or hearing clients.

Are there potential problems with expanding and flexing one's clinical boundaries and roles? The strengths and weaknesses of doing so are demonstrated by Ho (1987) in his text *Family Therapy With Ethnic Minorities*. Ho made a clear and, to my mind, extreme case for role flexibility on the therapist's part. It is worth examining his viewpoint because his clarity in encouraging departure from the traditional therapeutic stance of neutrality also illuminates the dangers of doing so.

Ho discussed family therapists' role when working with Native Americans. He said that in order to accommodate to ideas these communities have about healers, clinicians should:

1. Be willing to go to the client's home;
2. Adjust to their sense of time in scheduling and conducting appointments (i.e., not to expect rigid adherence to scheduled appointment times);
3. Allow for more reciprocity by accepting gifts;
4. Be willing to maintain a relationship with the client beyond the termination of treatment;
5. Accept the role of case-worker and be willing to help with practical problems; and
6. Be available at all times. (p. 1–83)

In addition, in those instances in which therapists are not accepted by the community, they should be willing to work in collaboration or consultation with an indigenous community helper.

The issue of "not terminating" is especially germane to how clinicians establish boundaries with Native American families. Ho elaborated:

> The termination process should take into consideration the American Indian client's concept of time and space in a relationship. Because the relationship has taken a long time to build, it will also take a long time to end. Some families may never want to end a good relationship. They learn to respect and love the therapist as a member of their family, and they may wish to maintain contact with the therapist even after the successful achievement of therapy goals. A therapist should learn to treasure such a natural relationship and not allow her "professionalism" to spoil a genuine human sharing. (p. 107)

One has to commend Ho for the lengths he is willing to go to help cultural minorities. One also wonders, however, what distinguishes this culturally rele-vant therapy from, say, good friendship. Is anything left, after all these adapta-tions, that resembles psychotherapy, as traditionally practiced? What if therapists prefer not to be available at all times but to work traditional business hours? How are therapists to arrange a schedule and see a variety of clients if adaptations regarding time make scheduling and planning irrelevant? How could clinicians maintain sufficient productivity to produce revenue to keep a clinic alive? Which clinical dangers are present when therapists are this "loose" about clinical boundaries?

Sherry Zitter (chapter 8, this volume) describes her work with a hearing family of a deaf Puerto Rican client. She was working especially closely with the client's mother: a poor, monolingual Spanish-speaking woman from rural Puerto Rico. Zitter would frequently do home visits and on one occasion found herself invited to stay for dinner. With an Anglo family, Sherry would have politely declined at least until she understood all the possible meanings the family might attribute to her joining them for dinner. With this Puerto Rican family, she accepted the invitation, and she did so even though the family was serving pork and she was a vegetarian. She knew she had to adopt looser clinical boundaries in order to foster her relationship with the family, and she was willing to yield her own values somewhat in the interests of this relationship. It seems to me that she acted in a culturally sensitive manner that would serve to advance her treatment of the family.

Might these role adaptations, however, pose some practical and ethical dilemma for therapists? What would happen if the invitations became more frequent, and Zitter was also invited to church and to community festivities? Ho would probably say Zitter should accept the invitations and rejoice at her growing acceptance by the community. But Zitter is not a traditional Puerto Rican woman. She is a Jewish Anglo woman and a professional therapist. She is willing to adapt her clinical boundaries but not to the point that she forgets her own values, interests, and communities. She is also concerned that in the process of her growing integration into the community, some of her ability to serve as a professional psychotherapist may become lost. How free will her client feel to express a negative transference toward a therapist she has served dinner to in her home? Will her client perceive her as someone without strict professional boundaries and therefore not trustworthy to maintain confidentiality? If the therapist believes that interpretation of the transference is the heart of psychotherapy, will her ability to make these interpretations be compromised by the "real" relationship she is developing with her clients?

Although the need to assume an advocate role seems a commonplace aspect of culturally affirmative thinking, it is still a controversial position in psychology at large. Keith-Spiegel and Koocher (1985), in their text on ethics in psychology, noted: "One of the most fundamental dilemmas related to therapy goals is whether to encourage a client to rebel against a repressive environment or to attempt to adjust to it" (p. 20). One reason this is controversial is because of recognition that therapists, especially those who do not consider notions of transference and countertransference relevant, may unconsciously push their own social agenda onto their clients. They may project onto clients their own feelings of rage, which their clients then act out for them. Similarly, acting on behalf of clients may unconsciously be a repetition of other paternalistic patterns in the clients' life, or it may be therapists acting out of the clients' rage. Dynamically oriented therapists have learned the importance of not taking matters purely at face value.

Adaptations in clinical boundaries may conflict with the American Psychological Association's ethical prohibition against "dual-role relationships"—that is, acting not merely as clinician and client but as partners in some other business or personal matter. Keith-Spiegel and Koocher noted:

> The Ethical Principles (EP: 6a) recognize the perils of relating to consumers on other than a professional level and counsel psychologists to remain continually aware of their own needs and their potentially influential position. The code admonishes psychologists to make every effort to avoid exploiting trust and dependency. Blending the professional role with another is to be shunned whenever professional judgment may be compromised or impaired. (p. 251)

Keith-Spiegel and Koocher discussed the prohibition against dual-role relationships as it extends to issues of social contact with clients. While noting a diversity of practice among psychologists, they nonetheless warned of the relevant dangers.

> Clients may be unsure of the boundaries of social relationships and experience anxiety or confusion. The therapists' capacity to function as an objective party may deteriorate. Dependencies may be reinforced. The roles are incongruent in the areas of power and trust. Finally, since people do not have to pay their friends for support and caring, the meaning of "friend" becomes perverted in this instance. (p. 271)

A core principle of the ethical guidelines for both psychologists and social workers is confidentiality. The adoption of more flexible clinical boundaries however may make the maintenance of confidentiality more problematic. Even where therapists tenaciously hold the line, their presence at many community functions and apparent friendship with community members may raise the concern of clients about the therapists' ability to maintain confidentiality. This is especially true if, as is often the case, there is a stigma associated with seeing a therapist. Therapists, then, may need to leave the sanctity of their offices and intervene in various roles in the community, but their boundaries cannot be so permeable that community members have reason to doubt their professionalism. Therapists who work with Deaf clients commonly face exactly this dilemma.

How does one resolve the conflict between on one hand, these kinds of ethical guidelines and on the other hand, the need to act in differing roles and capacities in culturally affirmative treatment? How does one promote individual growth in a cultural context where family and community are valued over the individual? When one acts as an advocate, how can one be sure one is not projecting one's own worldview onto clients or re-enacting patterns of paternalism or dependency the client may have previously experienced with significant others? I think the best answer currently available is that the culturally affirmative therapist learns to juggle all these conflicting notions simultaneously. The therapist develops skill in this balancing act. It is profoundly dangerous to disregard the insights of psychodynamic treatment, particularly with regard to transference and countertransference issues, based on the justification that it is irrelevant to culturally affirmative work. It is also dangerous simply to adopt cultural affirmation as one's primary value without considering the nature of the culture one is affirming. Culturally affirmative clinicians, in their effort to make therapy culturally relevant, do need to make some of these adaptations. The more traditional the community and culture with which one works and the more limited the internal and external resources of the client, the more therapists may need to stretch their roles and boundaries in order to be legitimized by the community. Zitter (chapter 8, this volume) presents a powerful model for how she makes decisions about her role and boundaries when working with deaf clients.

Skills in Collaboration With Indigenous Healers/Helpers, Leaders, and Paraprofessionals.   Because psychotherapy is a process alien to many minority communities, much of the literature stresses the importance of working collaboratively with indigenous community healers. Ho (1987) made this point often. With Hispanic Americans, Ho advocated for collaborative efforts with *espiritistas* or spiritual healers. With Asian Americans, Ho advocated for use of a family member as therapist-helper. Boyd-Franklin (1989) advocated in a similar vein for the utilization of ministers and other church leaders when working with African American families:

> The minister or pastor of a church has the potential of being a valuable resource, particularly in situations where he has already served as pastoral counselor for family members and knows them well. At the very least, with the family's permission, a minister who has served in this role should be contacted for information about his involvement. It has always been amazing to me that mental health practitioners will routinely contact other clinics, hospitals, or therapists who have worked with our clients but will not follow up on or often even inquire about help that the family may have sought from a minister, deacon, deaconess, or another church member. (p. 89)

Delgado (1979) gave more detailed consideration to the issue of collaboration with Hispanic folk healers. He found only three documented instances of such incorporation of folk healers. Two occurred in the heavily Puerto Rican South Bronx in New York City at the Lincoln Community Mental Health Center and the Treatment Crisis Center. The third involved the Navajo Indians of Arizona. In all three settings, the role of the folk healer was primarily that of consultant and trainer.

Delgado outlined five models of roles that folk healers could assume within mental health settings. These models are helpful because they present examples of exactly how community healers could become integrated within mental health programs. Type 1 represents a minimal degree of involvement and Type 5 represents the highest degree of involvement.

In Type 1, the folk healer acts purely in a training capacity to mental health staff. In Type 2, the folk healer assumes the role of both trainer and consultant to agency staff. In Type 3, the folk healer acts as a referral agent and sometimes accompanies the client into early stages of treatment to help bridge the cultural gap. In Type 4, reciprocal arrangements for referrals are made between the mental health agency and the folk healer. In Type 5, the folk healer becomes a cotherapist and has a relationship of equality with the therapist. Because of the difficulty of establishing such collaborative relationships, Delgado advocated beginning with modest goals and building on them as trust develops.

In addition to collaboration with indigenous healers and leaders, many mental health programs that attempt to be culturally affirmative utilize paraprofessionals from the community as staff. The ideal, of course, is to find community members who are themselves trained mental health workers, but for all the reasons that make mental health services inaccessible to minorities, these minority professionals are hard to find.

The alternative is to recruit the more bicultural and psychologically minded members of the community, or perhaps recognized community leaders, and provide enough training for them to serve in some direct service capacity. Wax (chapter 9, this volume) presents such a model for training Deaf paraprofessionals for work in mental health settings.

Use of paraprofessionals is especially necessary when professionals do not have the language skills needed. Paraprofessionals, although they usually do not have training as interpreters, often act in that capacity. The hiring of these community members as staff is needed to give a program credibility with the community, to help the community feel that the program is theirs.

Several culturally affirmative mental health programs have been established that have given prominent roles to paraprofessionals from the community. Dolgin et al. (1987) described an Hispanic inpatient treatment unit that was fortunate enough to hire a staff of 18 mental health professionals, all of whom were Hispanic and bilingual and all of whom lived in the same neighborhoods as the patients. Abad et al. (1974) described a model mental health program for Hispanic Americans where bicultural staff, many of whom were paraprofessionals, played a crucial role in creating a bridge between the program and the community. Sherry Zitter and I (Glickman & Zitter, 1989) developed an inpatient unit for deaf people that made the hiring of Deaf professional and paraprofessional staff a cornerstone of its treatment philosophy.

Hiring clinically unsophisticated members of the minority community is not without difficulties, however. Generally these paraprofessionals view their work from the perspective of the community. This is an advantage when creating culturally relevant treatment interventions but a disadvantage when confronted with other clinical, administrative, or practical problems. Abad et al. (1974) noted that conflicts between professional and paraprofessional staff nearly closed their Spanish clinic, and it was only the relationships established with key members of the Puerto Rican community that enabled the program to withstand this crisis.

Andrade (1978) described a program in rural Texas that was designed to provide mental health outreach services to Chicanos. This program was highly dependent on paraprofessionals, many of whom appeared to have had virtually no clinical training. In the beginning, recruiting these paraprofessionals and a director oriented to serving the community as the community defined the need helped the program establish credibility. The program's Chicano psychiatrist reflected on this: "One lesson I learned was the 'stop sign' lesson which says that when initiating mental health consultation you do first what your client wants you to do, even if it is to help him get a stop sign for a busy intersection" (p. 26).

The program director stressed the need to gain the confidence of the community rather than to begin with pre-established and inflexible ideas of what mental health services should look like:

> The impact of the . . . director's belief that the mental health problems of Mexican Americans were based in socioeconomic and sociopolitical institutional factors was of great significance. . . . He emphasized that the staff had to gain the confidence of the community and to assist the local residents in coming to a new awareness of what "mental health" actually meant. Thus, to promote public awareness and confidence in the program, services included such community functions as a Thanksgiving dinner for the elderly and a Christmas party for children, assistance with income tax returns and help in obtaining automobile license plates. (p. 29)

These initial gains in community acceptance became weaknesses as the program, now established, became concerned with returning to its clinical mission. An Anglo psychiatrist who worked with the program remarked that he saw such culturally relevant programs going through predictable developmental stages. In the first stage, credibility is key, so appropriate staff and community ties are paramount. As the program develops, more concern is placed on professional clinical services. Third party payments and credibility in the mental health community become important so program accreditation is sought. Accreditation, however, imposes a concern with proper staff training and credentials, and needless to say, many of the paraprofessionals hired lack the relevant degrees and clinical background. Gradually, administrative concern with professionalism takes precedence over concern with cultural appropriateness. The initial vision of the program may disappear as a new round of more "practical" and "realistic" administrators are hired.

In the Chicano example, the commendable goal of integrating the program into the community, of having the community own the program, became problematic when the community and the professional mental health establishment had different ideas about staff. The community leaders valued "loyalty to the Raza Unida Party and a militant Chicanismo often characterized by the overt hostility of the Party's leaders towards all gringos" (pp.78–79). The mental health professionals valued the appropriate clinical training and credentials. To make matters worse, there seemed to be a common perception among the Chicano community that any Chicano who came to value clinical training and credentials was becoming "vendido" or sold out.

The experiences of oppression faced by the Chicanos caused them to see racism as figural and to distrust Anglo institutions. The professionals, even if sensitive to oppression, probably saw it as a less central issue. The training and credentialing process they went through and the perspective on client problems that emerges from this training and socialization process were more salient concerns for them.

When Sherry Zitter and I opened the Mental Health Unit for Deaf People, we saw hiring culturally Deaf staff as crucial to our success. In our article describing our experiences creating this unit (Glickman & Zitter, 1989), we outlined why this was so:

1. They provide effective language and role models for patients, families, and hearing staff.
2. They insure effective communication will happen at least some of the time.
3. They decrease the likelihood that deafness per se is pathologized.
4. They lessen patients' ability to use their deafness as a defense ("If you were deaf, you'd understand.") and help patients feel safe enough to open themselves for treatment.
5. They enable a program to have credibility in the Deaf community, which increases referrals and promotes recruitment of new staff.
6. They have a dramatic ability to sensitize the hospital community to the needs and abilities of deaf persons.
7. They provide immediate, direct, and powerful training to new hearing staff.
8. They enable staff to feel their work environment is exciting and special, thus decreasing staff turnover.
9. They insure that a culturally Deaf viewpoint is at least factored into every decision.

We maintained these beliefs throughout our tenure at the Deaf unit, but we learned the hard way that staff without clinical training, whatever their cultural competence, can also seriously hurt a struggling mental health program. Many of our patients had severe neurological and behavioral problems. For our first 14 months, our staff were, on an almost daily basis, kicked, punched, scratched, bitten, spat at, and otherwise abused. I remember that on the morning of our open house for the community, I had one nurse apply a heavy dose of makeup to my face to camouflage the black eye a patient had given me 2 days before. Our deaf staff and we found that we had grossly overjudged the therapeutic power of a signing environment on these particular patients. We were astounded to discover that we needed expertise in behavior management at least as much as we needed expertise in deafness per se.

One incident symbolized this dilemma for us. A culturally Deaf staff person was eating her dinner in a common area when a patient knocked her tray of food off the table and lunged at her. After recovering, she commented, "The problem is communication." In saying this, she was voicing the viewpoint that culturally Deaf staff commonly held: the problem is communication. For deaf people, communication is always salient. But the more highly trained clinical staff increasingly took a different view: The problem is certainly exacerbated by poor communication, but goes "deeper" to an emotional and neurological disorder.

Thus, a tension developed between the viewpoints of some hearing mental health professionals, who held the administrative power, and some of the deaf staff, a large block of whom were paraprofessionals working as nursing assistants. The tension was about how much importance to attribute to communication barriers in understanding the problems of patients and how much emphasis to place on appropriate communication in designing therapeutic interventions. This tension came up every time we were faced with hiring new staff or implementing a new treatment. If there were no deaf candidates with mental health training, should we hire the hearing candidate with good clinical skills but without signing ability or the deaf native signer who had no clinical training? Was it easier to teach good clinicians about deafness and to sign or teach talented deaf paraprofessionals about mental health?

Initially we balanced this tension well. There was enough enthusiasm about our program in the Deaf community that qualified Deaf professionals and paraprofessionals flocked to us. We achieved a "critical mass" of deaf staff that gave us some leverage for hiring credentialed hearing nonsigners for certain positions. But once our program developed, we faced the need to become accredited, so we could charge for our services and remain viable. When concerns with accreditation replaced our initial emphasis on cultural appropriateness, we were forced to think more about the professional credentials of our staff. We needed people who were licensable in their respective disciplines. This pressure further marginalized the culturally Deaf paraprofessional staff who were without mental health credentials.

Here then is the dilemma faced by programs that seek to hire indigenous members of the minority community they serve. On the one hand, for minority mental health programs to achieve credibility they must be staffed at least partially by indigenous people and have appropriate relationships with community leaders. On the other hand, clinically untrained staff and indigenous healers with nonpsychological perspectives can impede the development of clinical services that, after all, are the raison d'etre of the program. As programs become more established, they become increasingly concerned with an accreditation process that stresses clinical expertise and documentation over cultural relevancy. This is especially true when programs look to third party insurance companies, rather than state grants, to pay for the mental health treatment of their clients.

Bridging the gap between community and mental health perspectives and collaborating effectively with community members who do not have a mental health perspective and who have reason to distrust institutions that fund and oversee such programs is a key multicultural competency, especially for anyone directing a program. Clinicians working cross-culturally must have this skill.

Essentially it is the ability to reframe from different cultural perspectives and to make connections. It is also the ability to negotiate, compromise, achieve balance, and bring people together.

Skills in Selecting and Designing Culturally Syntonic Treatment Interventions. Adapting treatment so that it becomes syntonic with a culture is a core skill in culturally affirmative therapy. However, this notion of adapting treatment to culture is fairly radical. It assumes that psychotherapy is a sociohistorical phenomenon itself that is embodied in, and reflective of, certain cultural experiences. It assumes that psychotherapy has real limits in its applicability cross-culturally. To strive to adapt treatment to a culture is to perceive how culturally loaded various treatment interventions are. This is a fundamentally different perception of therapy than seeing it as an extra-historical, neutral, or objective phenomena, applied like medicine to any hurt in any context. The idea is that only some kinds of interventions make sense culturally. Certainly, culturally affirmative therapy is the attempt to extend the applicability of psychotherapy, *yet there is always a tension in this effort between cultural relevancy on the one hand and clinical appropriateness on the other.*

Assessing the degree of match between a culture and a form of psychotherapeutic intervention is neither simple nor straightforward. Within the literature, four broad ways to match treatment to culture have been described. The first is to provide members of a community with psychoeducation about counseling and therapy. This approach assumes that any matching problems result from deficits in the client population's understanding and that psychotherapy per se need not be changed. The second approach is to frame interventions in culturally syntonic terms. This essentially cognitive approach pays particular attention to the metaphors common within a culture and tries to utilize them along with otherwise standard psychotherapeutic interventions. The third approach is to select or adapt treatment interventions or styles that seem to match the culture in question. This approach assumes that some kinds of psychotherapy, because of their different "cultural loadings," are more syntonic than others. The fourth is to begin with the culture itself and to try to develop a counseling or therapy style out of the culture's indigenous means of helping.

In the inpatient treatment program for Hispanic Americans described by Dolgin et al. (1987), the staff used approaches one and two in their effort to be culturally affirmative. The unit staff began with the common problem that many of their patients were not familiar with psychotherapy. To counter the patients' ignorance about psychotherapy, the staff provided an educational program called "pretherapy." In pretherapy, patients meet with a therapist who explains to them what psychotherapy is and what patients can expect from it.

Dolgin et al. reported that this kind of orientation to therapy decreased resistance to attending groups and helped patients feel more relaxed in discussing cultural issues, and personal and sexual problems: "It was our experience that pretherapy facilitated the psychotherapy process for both patient and therapist" (p. 292).

In the culturally affirmative therapy literature, pretherapy is a commonly cited strategy. In their text on psychotherapy with low-income and minority patients, Acosta, Yamamoto, and Evans (1982) argued that outpatient therapy clinics should develop patient orientation programs, and they provide an example of one. Sue and Morishima (1982) advocated for "pretherapy orientations" when working with Asian and Pacific Americans. Pretherapy orientation is easily done with psychologically unsophisticated deaf people as well. The University of California Center on Deafness has produced a videotape in ASL to introduce psychotherapy to these deaf clients. Pretherapy orientation is a very doable intervention, especially when one has some orientation materials. Showing deaf clients an ASL videotape is culturally syntonic in that it respects both the visual way deaf people take in information and the language of the Deaf community.

In the Hispanic Treatment program cited previously, Dolgin et al. also took the second approach of trying to frame interventions in the language and metaphors of the culture. For instance, they designed "macho groups" for male patients that "provided a safe atmosphere in which the individual could openly present his feelings and views without threat to his masculinity" (p. 292). Female groups were conducted, including one called, "Nuestras Cuerpas, Nuestras Vidas" (Our Bodies, Our Lives) to discuss basic human anatomy and functioning and the development of male–female relationships. Cultural identity groups used Hispanic cultural perspectives to "help patients look at themselves, their families, their environment and interpersonal relationships from a realistic perspective" (p. 293). Apparently, it was the utilization of an appropriate cultural frame on problems that allowed for nondefensiveness and engagement in the therapeutic process.

The skill of framing interventions in culturally syntonic terms is at the heart of community-education efforts regarding public health issues like drugs and AIDS. Many substance-abuse experts have argued, for instance, that telling inner-city minorities to "just say no" to illegal drugs is ludicrously out of touch with their frame of reference. One recalls the debates about federal funding for programs that provide sexually explicit information to gay men about safer sex. Arch-conservative Senator Jesse Helms obtained a copy of a brochure distributed in gay male bars in New York City by the Gay Men's Health Crisis that discussed sexual practices in a very straightforward manner. He argued that the government should not be promoting immoral sexual activity. If one's objective is to save lives, something that cannot be assumed in Senator Helms' case, and if one wants to reach sexually active gay men who frequent bars, then a culturally syntonic means would be to talk in their language that is explicit and graphic about sex. Sanitized versions of safer sex information may sell better in mainstream America but they are culturally inappropriate for sexually active gay men in New York City.

How does one know how to frame interventions in culturally syntonic terms? This is where knowledge of a culture, in particular the culture's worldview, comes in. It requires study, exposure, a respectful attitude, and a careful listening for the metaphors a community's members use to describe their daily lives. Gail Isenberg (chapter 7, this volume) discusses her experiences using stories and culturally appropriate metaphors in psychotherapy with Deaf clients.

The third approach is to select treatment interventions and approaches that are culturally relevant. Here the compatibility between Jewish culture and psychotherapy is noteworthy. Because so much of culturally affirmative psycho-therapy literature argues that insight-oriented therapy, in particular psychody-namic treatment, is culturally inappropriate, it is striking to find one culture that actually values analysis. Herz and Rosen (1982) argued that Jewish families are generally favorably inclined toward psychotherapy, especially insight-ori-ented models, because in Jewish culture self-expression is valued as are complex explanations of problems. The Jewish origins of psychoanalysis are well-known as is the fact that many analysts and dynamic therapists are Jews. One might even argue that psychodynamic psychotherapy emerged from a particularly Jewish sensibility. In my reading, I have not come across any other cultural group for whom psychodynamic approaches, so often disparaged in the cross-cultural therapy literature, would seem to be indicated for cultural reasons.

Much has been written on counseling and psychotherapy with African Americans (e.g., Atkinson 1985, 1987; Block, 1984; Gunnings & Lipscomb, 1986; Hillard, 1985; Jackson, 1983; Warfield & Marion, 1985). An argument frequently made in this literature is that White cultural therapies assume intrapsychic sources of client problems, whereas African American therapies place more stress on external, environmental sources of client problems. Thera-peutic strategies that empower African American clients to deal with their environment may be more culturally indicated. That is to say, African Ameri-cans may be more inclined to see environmental forces as "figural" and intrap-sychic forces as "ground," and culturally syntonic interventions would make use of these common ways of meaning making.

What therapeutic strategies are most syntonic to culturally Deaf people? I have discussed with many clinicians who work with deaf people how easy it is to use psychodrama and role play. When one conveys a conversation in ASL, one frequently uses body movements and facial expression to become each player in the conversation. This is the equivalent of "he said, she said" used in English. The dramatic quality of sign easily lends itself to role playing. On the Mental Health Unit for Deaf People (Glickman & Zitter, 1989), we also found that groups utilizing art and movement therapy, and a group we invented called "communication therapy," were easily accepted by many deaf patients.

Freedman (1994) described three kinds of interventions that he believed are "well suited to a visual/gestural mode of communication" (p. 16). The first is an intervention developed by White and Epston (1990) called "externalizing the problem." The spatial properties of ASL, in which abstract notions such as depression or anxiety can be located in space, are used to help patients achieve distance from and mastery over their problems. Freedman also drew on the spatial properties of ASL, in which time is located spatially alongside the signer's body, to develop "lifelines" in which clients visually represents their personal history. Finally, Freedman, like Isenberg (chapter 7, this volume) drew on "storytelling as a culturally sensitive counseling tool" (p. 22). Freedman's excellent article represents precisely the kind of creative, culturally affirmative treatment we need to see more of.

In the attempt to make psychotherapy culturally relevant, there is always a tension between psychotherapy as an established and culturally specific means of healing and the means of healing indigenous to another culture.

With pretherapy orientations, one attempts to bring the culturally different to the psychotherapists' worldview. At the other end of the continuum are attempts to create "culture-specific treatment," (Ivey, 1991) where the therapist moves completely to the worldview of the client's culture. This model seems to call for counselors to use the style of helping indigenous to the culture in question. Would that mean training counselors to become spiritual healers or medicine people? Can an outsider ever assume these roles? Ivey would at least have us ask ourselves how the community we seek to serve already performs helping and healing functions. A relevant line of investigation, one I have not yet seen undertaken, would be how helping and healing already occurs within the Deaf community.

Western counseling and psychotherapy are more appropriate for some cultural contexts than others, and their degree of relevancy can be enhanced. The methods described here are all designed to push the boundaries of psychotherapy so that it can be relevant and powerful for the widest possible group of people. The task for therapists is to recognize that implicit in models of psychotherapy and in cultures are worldviews and that the degree of match or fit between these worldviews can be fine tuned. Therapists who recognize that they are working with worldviews, with culturally based frames of reference, may have a freedom and therapeutic leverage that their culture-bound colleagues, unaware of the arbitrariness of their own perspectives, cannot imagine.

CONCLUSION

Whenever we try to adapt psychotherapy, essentially a form of helping most relevant to educated, Westernized, middle- and upper-class people, to people from non-Western societies or groups within Western society who are marginalized or disenfranchised, two questions arise. First, what in the nature of psychotherapy reflects universal elements of helping and healing? That is, what makes healing possible in any context, and how does psychotherapy utilize these core elements? Second, how do we make these universal elements relevant to this particular sociohistorical context? What in our psychotherapeutic approach needs to be adapted so that we can be effective with this community and culture? Taking into account these two questions—that of the universals and particulars of helping—what conclusions can we draw regarding the project of making psychotherapy relevant and affirmative for culturally Deaf people?

Torrey (1986) claimed that modern psychiatrists rely on essentially the same means of healing as do witchdoctors. He studied forms of healing found in diverse societies and concluded that all forms of healing have the same four elements in common. Given the harm that psychiatrists, in some situations, have done (Bayer, 1981; Chesler, 1973; Masson, 1988; Thomas & Sillen, 1972), I have sometimes felt this comparison does an injustice—to the witchdoctors. Nevertheless, it is instructive to note the four core components of healing Torrey identified. These are:

1) clients and healers have a shared world-view as to what constitutes the problem and the solution; 2) healers have personal qualities valued for healing by their culture and establish special, personal, helping relationships with clients; 3) clients "buy into" the process of treatment and expect to benefit; and 4) clients believe the treatment will provide them "with the knowledge, competence, insight and understanding necessary to master life's adversities" (Torrey, 1986, pp. 69–70).

If these are the universals of all psychological healing, consider the barriers imposed in cross-cultural treatment. First, clients and healers commonly lack a shared worldview. They differ on what constitutes the problem, the solution, and the process of cure. Second, healers are unlikely to be credible and to have personal qualities valued by the client. Indeed, therapists may even be perceived as agents of an oppressive establishment, people more likely to cause harm than good. Finally, clients are not likely to find the process of treatment to be meaningful. They may have no idea what therapists do, and when told, are likely to find the treatment bizarre and irrelevant.

These issues are commonly found in work with psychologically naive deaf clients who are often brought to therapy by someone else (such as a family member or caseworker), who usually lack an understanding of the therapeutic process, and who do not necessarily see the therapists, be they deaf or hearing, as credible helpers. These clients commonly have different perceptions of "the problem" and its solution. I recall many such deaf clients who expected me to tell them what to do, who saw no purpose in talking with me about such intangibles as feelings and early childhood experiences, and who expected me to give or get them something. For instance, I remember one client whose initial teletype (tty) conversation with me went as follows:

"Hello. Neil Glickman here. GA."

"I need a girlfriend. GA."

This client did not bother with the usual niceties like introducing himself, asking about services, and requesting an appointment. Instead, he went right to the point: "I need a girlfriend." In a cross-cultural encounter such as this, my first task is to try to bridge the huge chasm between our different understandings of the nature and purpose of our interaction.

To counter these formidable obstacles, therapists need to understand and work within the worldview of the clients. Therapists need to understand the clients' cultural and personal frame of reference and reframe interventions accordingly. The exciting challenge of culturally affirmative work is that it pushes clinicians to think differently, to enter a different cognitive reality, and then to help clients shift their own thinking about their problems.

Does this mean that my job *is* to find the deaf client mentioned previously a girlfriend? Most psychotherapists would answer, "Of course not," but in light of our discussion of accommodating to the clients' frame of reference, is the answer so clear? One can easily conclude that this client is not ready for insight-oriented psychotherapy because he lacks understanding of, and motivation for, the psychotherapeutic process. On the other hand, if I enter his world, perhaps there is a way to make treatment happen. I might start, for instance, by clarifying that although I cannot find a girlfriend for him, maybe I can help him find a girlfriend himself. I would then ask him to tell me about his efforts to find a girlfriend so far (and while we are at it, about his family and social experiences). I would, if appropriate, refer him to community resources designed to facilitate socialization into the Deaf community. I might also make concrete suggestions to him about ways to improve his chances of developing relationships and role play with him various approaches to asking women out. In my terminology, our treatment goals would be to develop more appropriate social skills, decrease isolation, and improve mood and self-concept. In his terminology, our goal would be to find him a girlfriend.

Earlier, we raised the question of how one adapts psychotherapy to make it relevant and affirmative to a particular minority group, in this case, culturally Deaf people. The answer outlined here, as taken from the literature on counseling and psychotherapy with other minorities, is that, in a nutshell, one must be culturally self-aware as a hearing or Deaf person; one must have extensive knowledge of the Deaf community and of the history of Deaf-hearing relations; and one must have a broad array of skills, in particular competence in the different forms of signed communication.

Cultural self-awareness in hearing and Deaf people are explored further in the chapters by Lane; Hoffmeister and Harvey; Humphries; Harvey; and Glickman. To be culturally self-aware as hearing people certainly involves having knowledge of, and taking some distance from, the ideological positions commonly espoused by hearing people. Culturally self-aware hearing people do not, for instance, argue that deaf children should be denied access to either ASL or to other deaf people because such children have to learn to adjust to a hearing world. Nor do culturally self-aware hearing people seek, either economically, politically, or psychologically, to perpetuate the dependency of deaf people on hearing people so as to bolster their own sense of credibility and self-worth. Rather, culturally self-aware hearing people seek to empower deaf people to make their own choices. This certainly involves respecting the Deaf community and culture.

Culturally affirmative therapists certainly need to know the forms that oppression of deaf people has taken. Lane's work (1992; chapter 2, this volume), is an important resource to this end. Humphries (chapter 4, this volume) discusses Deaf–hearing interaction as it pertains to the emerging new Deaf consciousness. In my chapter, I outline what I believe to be common developmental stages deaf people pass through as they develop cultural self-awareness. The knowledge dimension discussed here certainly includes understanding Deaf worldviews, how culturally Deaf people commonly interpret many shared experiences, and which metaphors, themes, and stories are important in the culture. Therapists also need knowledge of the many barriers that have prevented deaf people from utilizing more extensively mental health services.

Four kinds of culturally affirmative therapy skills were discussed in this chapter. These were: (a) skills in language, nonverbal communication, and collaboration with professional interpreters (discussed further in Lytle and Lewis chapter 10, this volume); (b) skills in expanding and flexing clinical roles (discussed further by Zitter, chapter 8, this volume); (c) skills in collaborating with indigenous healers, helpers, community leaders, and paraprofessionals (discussed further by Wax, chapter 9, this volume); and (d) skills in selecting and designing culturally syntonic treatment interventions (an example of which, appropriate use of metaphor and stories, is discussed by Isenberg, chapter 7, this volume). Perhaps a core skill is the ability to incorporate all the previous to help deaf patients heal from the trauma of their oppression by hearing society. Harvey (chapter 6, this volume) discusses how he used his knowledge of trauma and oppression in Deaf people to facilitate the recovery of one deaf client.

There are many ways to adapt counseling and psychotherapy to the culturally different, but the danger of making cultural considerations salient or figural is that individual clinical considerations can become peripheral or ground. *Culturally affirmative therapy is the successful balancing of cultural and clinical considerations.* The introduction of cultural considerations into therapy addresses a past limitation, but the process of stressing culture over individuality may create an equally ineffective approach. One needs to consider both the cultural context as well as the individual resources and limitations of one's clients. We are never working, of course, with hypothetical deaf people but rather with particular individuals who may, or may not, fit into any particular theory. Culturally affirmative therapy involves this continuous, creative process of matching the most effective language and therapeutic approach to a particular person from a particular community at a particular moment in that person's life.

And there is yet another challenge. What if the culture with which one works is often itself oppressive in some way, be that authoritarian, racist, sexist, homophobic, or audist? Deaf people typically share all the other prejudices of the larger society. Many hearing people have been uncomfortable, for instance, with the importance many Deaf people give to their state and national beauty contests. I have sometimes been uncomfortable with what seemed to me to be an anti-education bias of some deaf people (although given their experiences with the educational system, it is easy enough to understand), and I know of deaf people who were impeded, in their pursuit of higher education, by the notion that in so doing they were betraying their community and becoming, in effect, hearing. Does cultural affirmation mean one adopts an uncritical attitude toward all aspects of the culture in question and does not challenge it for fear of being thought oppressive?

Ultimately, all counseling and psychotherapy is based on values and a particular vision of humanity. The challenge of culturally affirmative therapists is to balance an appreciation and love for cultural diversity with a commitment to a society that promotes what they view to be healthy human development.

REFERENCES

Abad, V., Ramos, J., & Boyce, E. (1974). A model for delivery of mental health services to Spanish-speaking minorities. *American Journal of Orthopsychiatry, 44*(4), 584–595.

Acosta, F., Yamamoto, J., & Evans, L. (1982). *Effective psychotherapy for low-income and minority patients.* New York: Plenum.

Anderson, G., & Rosten, E. (1985). Towards evaluating process variables in counseling deaf people: A cross-cultural perspective. In G. Anderson & D. Watson (Eds.), *Counseling deaf people: Research and practice* (pp. 1–22). Arkansas: Arkansas Rehabilitation Research and Training Center on Deafness and Hearing Impairment.

Andrade, S. J. (1978). *Chicano mental health: The case of Cristal.* Austin, TX: Hogg Foundation for Mental Health.

Atkinson, D. (1985). A meta-review of research on cross-cultural counseling and psychotherapy. *Journal of Multicultural Counseling and Development, 13,* 138–153.

Atkinson, D. (1987). Counseling Blacks: A review of relevant research. *Journal of College Student Personnel,* 552–558.

Baker, C. (1977). Regulators and turn-taking in American Sign Language. In L. Friedman (Ed.), *On the other hand: New perspectives in American Sign Language.* New York: Academic Press.

Baker, C., & Cokely, D. (1980). *American Sign Language: A teacher's resource text on grammar and culture.* Silver Spring, MD: T. J. Publishers.

Battison, R., & Baker, C. (1980). Introduction. In R. Battison & C. Baker (Eds.), *Sign language and the deaf community: Essays in honor of William Stokoe* (pp. vii–xi). Silver Spring, MD: National Association of the Deaf.

Bayer, R. (1981). *Homosexuality and American psychiatry.* New York: Basic.

Benderly, B. L. (1980). *Dancing without music.* New York: Doubleday.

Bernal, G., Bernal, M., Martinez, A., Olmedo, E., & Santisteban, D. (1983). Hispanic mental health curriculum for psychology. In J. Chunn, P. Dunston, & F. Ross-Sheriff (Eds.), *Mental health and people of color* (pp. 65–93). Washington, DC: Howard University Press.

Bienvenue, M. J., & Colonomos, B. (1985). *Introduction to American deaf culture: Rules of interaction* [Videotape]. Silver Spring, MD: Sign Media.

Bienvenue, M. J., & Colonomos, B. (1986). *Introduction to American deaf culture: Values* [Videotape]. Silver Spring, MD: Sign Media.

Bienvenue, M. J., & Colonomos, B. (1988b). *Introduction to American deaf culture: Identity* [Videotape]. Silver Spring, MD: Sign Media.

Bienvenue, M. J., & Colonomos, B. (1988a). *Introduction to American deaf culture: Group norms* [Videotape]. Silver Spring, MD: Sign Media.

Block, C. (1984). Diagnostic and treatment issues for Black patients. *The Clinical Psychologist, 37*(2), 54–71.

Boyd-Franklin, N. (1989). *Black families in therapy: A multisystems approach.* New York: Guilford.

Brown, P. (1973). *Radical psychology.* New York: Harper Colophon.

Brown, P. (1974). *Toward a Marxist psychology.* New York: Harper Colophon.

Chaplin, J. (1988). *Feminist counselling in action.* London: Sage.

Chesler, P. (1973). *Women and madness.* New York: Avon.

Cooper, D. (1970). *Psychiatry and anti-psychiatry.* London: Granada/Paladin.

Delgado, M. (1979). Therapy Latino style: Implications for psychiatric care. *Perspectives in Psychiatric Care, 3*(17), 107–112.

DeMatteo, A., Veitri, D., & Lee, S. (1986). The role of sign language interpreting in psychotherapy. In M. McIntire (Ed.), *Interpreting: The art of cross-cultural mediation* (pp. 183–206). Proceedings of the ninth national convention of the Registry of Interpreters for the Deaf. Silver Spring, MD: R.I.D.

Dolgin, D., Salazar, A., & Cruz, S. (1987). The Hispanic treatment program: Principles of effective psychotherapy. *Journal of Contemporary Psychotherapy, 17*(4) 285–289.

Foucault, M. (1965). *Madness and civilization.* New York: Vintage.

Frank, K. (1979). *The anti-psychiatry bibliography and resource guide.* Vancouver, British Columbia: Press Gang.

Freedman, P. (1994). Counseling with deaf clients: The need for culturally and linguistically sensitive interventions. *Journal of the American Deafness and Rehabilitation Association, 27*(4), 16–28.

Frishberg, N. (1986). *Interpreting: An introduction.* Silver Spring, MD: R.I.D. Publications.

Gannon, J. (1981). *Deaf heritage.* Silver Spring, MD: National Association of the Deaf.

Garnets, L., & Kimmel, D. (1991). Lesbian and gay dimensions in the psychological study of human diversity. In J. D. Goodchilds (Ed.), *Psychological perspectives on human diversity in America* (pp. 137–192). Washington, DC: American Psychological Association.

Garretson, M. (1980). Forward. In C. Baker & R. Battison (Eds.), *Sign language and the deaf community* (p. v). Silver Spring, MD: NAD press.

Glickman, N. (1983). A cross-cultural view of counseling with Deaf clients. *Journal of Rehabilitation of the Deaf, 16*(3), 4–15.

Glickman, N. (1984). The war of the languages: Comparisons between language wars of Jewish and Deaf communities. *The Deaf American, 36*(6), 25–33.

Glickman, N. (1986). Cultural identity, deafness and mental health. *Journal of Rehabilitation of the Deaf,* 20(2), 1–10.

Glickman, N. (1993). *Deaf identity development: Construction and validation of a theoretical model.* Unpublished doctoral dissertation, University of Massachusetts, Amherst.

Glickman, N., & Carey, J. (1993). Measuring Deaf cultural identities: A preliminary investigation. *Rehabilitation Psychology,* 38(4), 277–283.

Glickman, N., & Zitter, S. (1989). On establishing a culturally affirmative psychiatric inpatient program for Deaf people. *Journal of the American Deafness and Rehabilitation Association,* 23(2), 46–59.

Goffman, E. (1963). *Stigma: Notes on the management of spoiled identity.* Englewood Cliffs, NJ: Prentice Hall.

Gunnings, T., & Lipscomb, W. (1986). Psychotherapy for Black men: A systemic approach. *Journal of Multicultural Counseling and Development,* 14(1), 17–24.

Harvey, M. (1989). *Psychotherapy with deaf and hard-of-hearing persons: A systemic model.* Hillsdale, NJ: Lawrence Erlbaum Associates.

Helms, J. (Ed.). (1990). *Black and White racial identity: Theory, research and practice.* Westport, CT: Greenwood.

Herz, F., & Rosen, E. (1982). Jewish families. In M. McGoldrick, J. Pearce, & J. Giordano (Eds.), *Ethnicity and family therapy* (pp. 383–391). New York: Guilford.

Higgins, P. (1980). *Outsiders in a hearing world.* Beverly Hills, CA: Sage.

Hillard, A. (1985). A framework for focused counseling on the African-American man. *Journal of Non-White Concerns,* 13(2), 72–78.

Ho, M. K. (1987). *Family therapy with ethnic minorities.* Newbury Park, CA: Sage.

Ivey, A. (1991). *Developmental strategies for helpers: Individual, family and network interventions.* Pacific Grove, CA: Brooks/Cole.

Jackson, A. (1983). A theoretical model for the practice of psychotherapy with Black populations. *The Journal of Black Psychology,* 10(1), 19–27.

Jacobs, L. M. (1974). *A deaf adult speaks out.* Washington, DC: Gallaudet University Press.

June, L. (1986). Enhancing the delivery of mental health and counseling services to Black males: Critical agency and provider responsibilities. *Journal of Multicultural Counseling and Development,* 14(1), 39–45.

Keith-Spiegel, P., & Koocher, G. (1985). *Ethics in psychology: Professional standards and cases.* New York: Random House.

Kuhn, T. (1970). *The structure of scientific revolutions.* Chicago, IL: University of Chicago Press.

Laing, R. D. (1967). *The politics of experience and the bird of paradise.* Middlesex: Penguin.

Lane, H. (1984). *When the mind hears.* New York: Random House.

Lane, H. (1992). *The mask of benevolence: Disabling the deaf community.* New York: Knopf.

Laval, R., Gomez, E., & Ruiz, P. (1983). A language minority: Hispanic-Americans and mental health care. *The American Journal of Social Psychiatry,* 111(2), 42–49.

Levine, E. (1960). *The psychology of deafness.* New York: Columbia University Press.

Levine, E. (1981). *The ecology of early deafness.* New York: Columbia University Press.

Levine, E., & Padilla, A. (1980). *Crossing cultures in therapy: Pluralistic counseling for the Hispanic.* Belmont, CA: Wedsworth.

Marcos, L. (1976a). Bilinguals in psychotherapy: Language as an emotional barrier. *American Journal of Psychotherapy,* 30(4), 552–560.

Marcos, L. (1976b). Linguistic dimensions in the bilingual patient. *The American Journal of Psychoanalysis,* 36(4), 347–354.

Marcos, L. (1979). Effects of interpreters on the evaluation of psychopathology in non-English speaking patients. *American Journal of Psychiatry,* 136(2), 171–174.

Marcos, L. (1988). Understanding ethnicity in psychotherapy with Hispanic patients. *The American Journal of Psychoanalysis,* 48(1), 35–42.

Marcos, L., & Urguyo, L. (1979). Dynamic psychotherapy with the bilingual patient. *American Journal of Psychotherapy,* 33(3), 331–338.

Masson, J. M. (1988). *Against therapy: Emotional tyranny and the myth of psychological healing.* New York: Atheneum.

McDonald, H. (1986). *The normative basis of culture: A philosophical inquiry.* Baton Rouge: Louisiana State University Press.

McGoldrick, M., Pearce, J., & Giordano, J. (Eds.). (1982). *Ethnicity and family therapy.* New York: Guilford.

Meadow, L. (1972). Sociolinguistics, sign language and the deaf subculture. In T. O'Rourke (Ed.), *Psycholinguistics and total communication: The state of the art* (pp. 19–33). A compilation of papers presented at a special study institute held at Western Maryland College, June 23–28, 1971. Washington DC: American Annals of the Deaf.

Mindel, E. & Vernon, M. (1971). *They grow in silence.* Silver Spring, MD: National Association of the Deaf.

Myklebust, H. (1964). *The psychology of deafness.* New York: Grune & Stratton.

Nash, J., & Nash, A. (1981). *Deafness in society.* New York: Lexington.

Oler, C. (1989). Psychotherapy with Black clients' racial identity and locus of control. *Psychotherapy, 26*(2), 233–241.

Padden, C. (1980). The deaf community and the culture of Deaf people. In C. Baker & R. Battison (Eds.), *Sign language and the deaf community* (pp. 89–103). Silver Spring, MD: National Association of the Deaf.

Padden, C., & Humphries, T. (1988). *Deaf in America: Voices from a culture.* Cambridge, MA: Harvard University Press.

Pedersen, P. (1988). *A handbook for developing multicultural awareness.* Alexandria, VA: American Association for Counseling and Development.

Pollard, R. (Ed.). (1993). Special issue on psychology and deafness. *Rehabilitation Psychology, 38*(4).

Ponterotto, J. (1988). Racial consciousness development among White counselor trainees: A stage model. *Journal of Multicultural Counseling and Development, 16,* 146–156.

Rainer, J., & Altshuler, K. (Eds.). (1966). *Comprehensive mental health services for the deaf.* New York: Columbia University Press.

Rogers, C. (1967). The conditions of change from a client-centered viewpoint. In B. Berenson, & R. Carkhuff (Eds.), *Sources of gain in counseling and psychotherapy.* New York: Holt, Rinehart & Winston.

Sabin, J. (1975). Translating despair. *American Journal of Psychiatry, 132*(2), 197–199.

Schlesinger, H., & Meadow, K. (1972). *Sound and sign: Childhood deafness and mental health.* Berkeley: University of California Press.

Seleskovitch, D. (1978). *Interpreting for international conferences.* Washington, DC: Pen & Booth.

Stansfield, M. (1981). Psychological issues in mental health counseling. *R.I.D. Interpreting Journal, 1*(1), 18–31.

Stokoe, W. (1978). *Sign language structure.* Silver Spring, MD: Linstok.

Stokoe, W., & Battison, R. (1981). Sign language, mental health and satisfactory interaction. In L. Stein, E. Mindel, & T. Jabaley (Eds.), *Deafness and mental health.* New York: Grune & Stratton.

Stokoe, W., Casterline, D., & Croneberg, C. (1976). *A dictionary of American Sign Language on linguistic principles.* Silver Spring, MD: Linstok.

Sue, D. W. (1981). *Counseling the culturally different.* New York: Wiley.

Sue, D. W. & Sue, D. (1990). *Counseling the culturally different* (2nd ed.). New York: Wiley.

Sue, D. W., Bernier, J., Durran, A., Feinberg, L., Pedersen, P., Smith, E., & Vasquez-Nutall, E. (1982). Position paper: Cross-cultural counseling competencies. *The Counseling Psychologist, 10*(2), 45–52.

Sue, D. W., Arredondo, P., & McDavis, R. (1992). Multicultural counseling competencies and standards: A call to the profession. *Journal of Counseling and Development, 70*(4), 477–486.

Sue, S. & Morishima, J. (1982). *The mental health of Asian-Americans.* San Francisco: Jossey-Bass.

Sue, S., & Zane, N. (1987). The role of culture and cultural techniques in psychotherapy: A critique and reformulation. *American Psychologist, 42*(1), 37–45.

Szasz, T. (1963). *Law, liberty and psychiatry: An inquiry into the social uses of mental health practices.* New York: Macmillan.

Szasz, T. (1970). *Ideology and insanity: Essays on the psychiatric dehumanization of man.* Garden City, NY: Anchor.

Szasz, T. (1974). *The myth of mental illness: Foundations of a theory of personal conduct.* New York: Harper & Row.

Thomas, A., & Sillen, S. (1972). *Racism and psychiatry.* New York: Brunner-Mazel.

Torres, W. (1983). Puerto Rican and Anglo conceptions of appropriate mental health services. In K. Davis & R. Bergner (Eds.), *Advances in descriptive psychology* (pp. 147–170). JAI.

Torrey, E. F. (1986). *Witchdoctors and psychiatrists.* New York: Harper & Row.

Warfield, J., & Marion, R. (1985). Counseling the Black male. *Journal of Non-White Concerns, 13*(2), 54–71.

White, M., & Epston, D. (1990). *Narrative means to therapeutic ends.* New York: Norton.

Wilcox, S. (Ed.). (1989). *American Deaf culture: An anthology.* Silver Spring, MD: Linstok.

Chapter 2

Cultural Self-Awareness in Hearing People

Harlan Lane
Northeastern University

IRONY AND SELF-AWARENESS

The common credo of numerous professions serving Deaf children and adults can be expressed in these terms: "The proper management of the hearing-impaired child is a highly technical endeavor requiring intensive multidisciplinary intervention at the earliest possible time and continuing through the life cycle, involving the family, the school, and the workplace." The members of those professions might well call this credo a truism. Of course, hearing-impairment in childhood (as in adulthood) is a grave problem; "When deafness is total, it is a catastrophe," wrote a leading French otologist (Chouard, 1978, p. 21). Certainly there is a need for audiologists to take the measure of the impairment and, with therapists, to attempt to mitigate it and its consequences. Surely the family is affected and "the [habilitative] program should," in the words of a British educator of Deaf children, "provide a saturation service for the family" (Tucker & Nolan, as cited in Gregory & Hartley, 1991, p. 87). Who can doubt that Deaf children require a special education? Finally, counselors and others must indeed guide Deaf children's transition from special school to independent living and employment.

So much seems clear: Individuals suffer from illness and disability—hearing impairment is one example—and an enlightened society has highly trained professionals who intercede. On further thought, however, it is possible to see these truisms as claims. To call them claims is to imply that there could be other claims and that the people who make these statements have an interest in making them. Once that epistemological shift has been made—from taking the words as a description to taking them as a claim—numerous questions arise.

Who has the authority to make such claims, and how did they acquire it? What do they have to gain by making such claims? What is Deaf peoples' authority to make claims about themselves, and how do their claims compare with those of the authorities? If Deaf people were not characterized as individual victims but as members of a shared culture, how would that change the competent authority and the measures taken in their interest? What claims are made about Deaf people and their needs in other countries with other social structures? What claims were made in our country in earlier eras?

The critical perspective on statements of social problems by competent authorities has been called social irony (Gusfield, 1989). The irony lies in pointing out that the motives and consequences of the authorities' actions are different from what they claim. This perspective contrasts with that of the naive realist, who takes the statements of the social problem to describe accurately the characteristics of the problem itself. The social ironist knows that things can be seen in another way. He contrasts, for example, the campaign of technological intervention in the life of the Deaf child of hearing parents with the absence of such specialized intervention in the life of the Deaf child of Deaf parents. The social ironist points out that Deaf parents are not organized toward the solution of problems more than any other parents; they simply expect their child will acquire language, communicate with them, go to school and acquire a profession, and so on. Generally, they do not seek the services of the hearing establishment devoted to the social problem of hearing impairment. The social ironist calls attention to who made the claim of a social problem in the first place: It was the very professionals devoted to remedying the problem they claim exists. Whereas the realist believes that problems lead to solutions, the ironist believes that solutions lead to problems—in the sense that existing professional groups build consensus that social problems exist. In short, the ironist believes that social problems are constructed by interested groups in particular cultures at particular times.

A culturally self-aware person is a person who has accepted living in a permanent field of tension between naive realism and social irony. On the one hand, it is too taxing and immobilizing to hold up innumerable cultural premises for inspection, to try to make them appear strange, to affirm with the ironist, that can be seen in another way. Like the centipede who cannot move if it takes a critical posture on coordinating one hundred legs, the culturally self-aware person must dress, eat, speak, write, and interact most of the time as if the familiar ways of doing things were inherently given. On the other hand, what distinguishes the culturally self-aware person from the oaf is access to leisure, freedom from economic cares and from the imperative to move, which allow that person to imagine other worlds, to be a social ironist.

For a hearing person to ask, "Who are hearing people?" is to step out of the field of action and to hold basic premises up for inspection, making the familiar appear strange. There would be no culturally hearing or Deaf people, if everyone were hearing or everyone were Deaf. The cultural status of a hearing person exists only in juxtaposition to the cultural status of a Deaf person, and vice versa. Just as we discover our cultural status as hearing (or Deaf) people only by discovering the Other, so the hearing (or Deaf) child starts to become culturally aware when the child discovers the Other.

Deafness is not in itself a significant issue in the lives of culturally Deaf people. Hearing people have created deafness as an issue, as White people have created Blackness as an issue.

HOW SHALL WE CONCEIVE OF OUR HEARING STATUS

Thus I have tried to show that in order to answer the question, "Who are hearing people," we must answer the question, "Who are Deaf people?"

But the naive realist does not let us proceed and objects: "I don't need to reflect on Deaf people to compass what it is to be a hearing person. I just need to imagine what it would be like to lose my hearing or to recall times when I couldn't hear—because of the loud noise of a passing train, for example; then I'm grateful that I can hear music, the sounds of the birds, and (at least some of the time) my spouse."

One of the assumptions underlying this argument that bears inspection is the assumption that the senses and culture are separable; that one can subtract or add a sense and retain one's cultural status. There's nothing to learn: Deaf people are just like me except they can not hear. If the speaker knows, or knows about, people who do not hear but share his or her culture, that will reassure him that he's on the right track, as will people who do not see, do not walk, and so on. The realist has not considered a developmental perspective: Suppose I had grown up using primarily vision; how would that have affected my perception of the world, my language, my social relations—in short, my culture? Would it be the same thing as giving up hearing now? The answers lie in examining Deaf cultures, just what the realist declined to do at first.

Among the tools of the social ironist are inspecting other cultures and, because history is a form of travel, inspecting our own culture at other moments in time. If we want to grasp our cultural status as hearing people, it does not help to discuss people's sensory capacities with the presumption of culture unchanged. We need to encounter Deaf culture, its distinct values and mores, and its distinct worldview; and several chapters in this volume allow just that encounter (to the extent that text can provide it). The purpose of this chapter is to describe the forms that this encounter has taken historically, as another way of discovering the meaning of Deaf people, and therefore of hearing people.

In general, the recorded accounts of the encounter between culturally hearing and Deaf people rarely involve mere passersby. Instead, the hearing people who engage in these encounters are, typically, hearing children of Deaf parents or hearing "professionals." Professionals are self-selected, specifically trained, and have an abiding stake in this encounter. The central problem confronting hearing professionals is how to construe deafness in the first place. Not that this question is actively posed. On the contrary, like Deaf children who discover that they are Deaf and hearing children that they are hearing, fledgling professionals recognize only late, if ever, that deafness could well be construed in another way and therefore has been construed all along.

The way in which professionals construe deafness is not, for the most part, an individual matter. It is central to this analysis that there is a social structure in which numerous components conduce to the same end. For example, the aspiring teacher of Deaf children enrolls in a program of "special education" that links the approach to Deaf education with that of educating physically handicapped, blind, emotionally disturbed, and mentally retarded children. The faculty who elected to teach in that school; the decisions that invited, retained, and promoted them; the textbooks they write and use in class; and the certification standards for this graduate program all work together to insure that the aspiring teacher constructs and reinforces a certain conception of Deaf people. A similar sketch could be given, for, say, audiology, school psychology, and so on, and it can be shown that each of these subsystems interlocks in a larger cultural construction of Deaf people that is reflected in legislation, jurisprudence, allocation of state and federal funds, the presentation of Deaf people in the media, and so on. It is helpful in a discussion to isolate a subsystem for analysis, but it is important, when that temporary expository device has served its purpose, to re-enmesh the subsystem in the larger field of forces of which it is an inextricable part.

HISTORICAL MODELS FOR
THE CONSTRUCTION OF DEAF PEOPLE

I examine two models. One emerges from the more or less coordinated efforts of hearing professionals in several subsystems and various epochs to exercise reproductive control over Deaf people. The other underpins the efforts of Deaf people in various epochs to lay claim to and govern a place of their own. In each case, I am seeking the dominant claims, stated or implied, concerning the construction of Deaf people. However, many more questions arise in an historical examination of reproductive control and place for Deaf people. To what extent does a given group have the power to determine the public construction of deafness, and by laying claim to what legitimacy? Which social conditions favored or disfavored the influence of this group? Where did they get their money? Beyond their implicit construction of deafness, what were their key messages? What are the links between this group and others; what are its subdivisions?

REPRODUCTIVE CONTROL OF DEAF PEOPLE

Hearing efforts to regulate childbearing by Deaf people have a long history that extends to the present day. Prior to the Enlightenment, Deaf scions of wealthy families, especially women, were frequently sequestered in religious institutions. This not only ensured their chastity, it kept them out of sight: If one child were known to be deaf, other children would be less marriageable. Indeed, it was this practice of sequestering Deaf children in religious institutions in 16th century Spain that led Ponce de León to develop at the monastery of Oña the first recorded method of teaching the Deaf to speak (Plann, 1993). With the beginnings of education for Deaf people as a group in 18th century France, Deaf boys and girls were not only strictly segregated in schools (a common, if less rigorous, practice with hearing children) but also Deaf girls were sent on graduation to special asylums explicitly with the purpose of avoiding their circulation in society at large (Lane, 1984). Laws refusing primogeniture to deaf-mutes, laws restricting consanguineous marriage, and laws specifically prohibiting or discouraging Deaf marriage (Berthier, 1837) all had the effect of discouraging Deaf people from marrying and reproducing. Such laws reflected values in society at large and presumably reinforced efforts by hearing parents to discourage their Deaf children from marrying and reproducing.

"Marriages of Deaf persons in Ontario appeared to be comparatively rare, before the opening of the Ontario institution in 1870" (Winzer, 1993, p. 140). It seems likely that gathering scattered Deaf children in residential schools facilitated Deaf marriage, but many educators were vigorously opposed and urged celibacy on the pupils. Edward Miner Gallaudet, at one time president of the Conference of Principals of Institutions for the Deaf, urged in the *American Annals of the Deaf* that Deaf people chose hearing spouses or abstain from marriage entirely so that their "defect [would not] descend to offspring" (Gallaudet as cited in Winefield, 1987, p. 101). "Even after school provided Deaf individuals with a wider choice of marriage partners," Winzer (1993) wrote, "low marriage rates remained a characteristic of Ontario's Deaf population" (p. 140).

The overriding purpose of the highly successful movement for oral education of Deaf children that arose in the late 19th century was not enabling Deaf people to speak with their neighbors, shopkeepers, and the like, nor was the goal to facilitate their learning written English; the purpose was not primarily educational at all—it was to discourage reproduction by Deaf people by discouraging their marriage. In the heated debate over a Nebraska law, for example, that required the state residential school for the Deaf to use oral methods only, the president of the National Education Association weighed in with this support of oralism: Deaf people who sign "tend to segregate themselves from society—to intermarry. [They are] freaks, dummies" (Van Cleve, 1984, p. 209).

The movement to create day schools for Deaf children who would live at home and use spoken English in school, had similar primary aims. It began in Wisconsin shortly after the Milan Congress and was championed and funded in part by Alexander Graham Bell (Cf. Lane, 1984). Day schools, Bell told Wisconsin lawmakers, allow "keeping deaf-mutes separated from one another as much as possible" (Bruce, 1973, p. 393; Van Cleve, 1993). He warned of the dangers of Deaf congregation at the state residential school. An 1894 attempt by educators to expand the day school law and reduce class size to four or five Deaf pupils provided that "congenital deaf-mutes of opposite sexes shall be kept apart as much as possible and marriage between them discouraged" (Wisconsin Phonological Institute, 1894). The next major day school movement began in Chicago. The Chicago Board of Education similarly declared that day schools were valuable because they prevented Deaf intermarriage and the production of Deaf offspring (Van Cleve, 1993).

As John Van Cleve (1993) pointed out, these "day schools" were actually day classes in hearing schools, a forerunner of our contemporary mainstreaming. A question worthy of investigation is whether the desire to discourage Deaf intermarriage and reproduction was an important motive in the mainstreaming of Deaf children in our time as it was in the day school movement of the turn of the century. Granted, other forces were surely at play, forces such as budget reduction and the broader social movement of deinstitutionalization. Nevertheless, it is doubtful whether parents and legislators would have mounted a similar campaign if mainstreaming had been shown to increase Deaf intermarriage. Apparently, one of the hopes harbored by many parents who keep their Deaf children at home is that the child will not "marry deaf" and be "lost" to the Deaf community.

Hearing people have embarked on direct as well as indirect programs to restrict Deaf reproduction. In the 20th century, there have been movements in the U.S. and in Germany, for example, to sterilize Deaf people by law and to encourage Deaf people in voluntary sterilization. The legal initiative in the United States had limited success, but its well-publicized pursuit led untold numbers of Deaf people to abandon plans for marriage and reproduction or to submit to voluntary sterilization and untold numbers of hearing parents to have their Deaf children sterilized (Johnson, 1918). Alexander Graham Bell, head of the Eugenics Section of the American Breeders Association (later the American Genetics Association) laid the groundwork for such efforts in his numerous statistical studies and censuses of the deaf population in the U.S. and, especially, in his 1883 Memoir Upon the Formation of a Deaf Variety of the Human Race, presented to the National Academy of Sciences, in which he warned that "the congenital deaf-mutes of the country are increasing at a greater rate than the population at large; and the deaf-mute children of deaf-mutes at a greater rate than the congenital deaf-mute population" (Bell, 1883/1969, p. 40). Bell attributed the problem to sign language, which "causes the intermarriage of deaf-mutes and the propagation of their physical defect" (Bell, 1883/1969, p. 44). The Eugenics Section prepared a model sterilization law and promoted it in the nation's state legislatures; it called for sterilization of feebleminded, insane, "criminalistic," deaf, and other "socially unfit" classes (Lane, 1993, p. 287). By the time of the German sterilization program, some 30 states in the U.S. had sterilization laws in force. However, none of them specifically included deaf people.

It is difficult to find a rationale for Bell's actions and those of other advocates for reproductive regulation of Deaf people, if they are taken at face value. It seems likely that the Eugenics Section was aware that state legislatures would not include Deaf people in forced sterilization programs as required by their model law. Indeed, in the storm that raged over this issue, Bell disavowed any such aim, on the grounds that even "killing off the undesirables altogether, so that they could not propagate their kind . . . would diminish the production of the undesirables without increasing the production of the desirables" (Bell as cited in Winefield, 1987). Moreover, the tables of data in Bell's Memoir show that only 1% of the pupils in his sample had two Deaf parents; hence it was evident that if all Deaf couples in the U.S. stopped reproducing entirely, either through birth control or sterilization, there would be an insignificant reduction in the Deaf population of the U.S. For the same reason, it must have been evident to him and other advocates of day schools, oral education, and other measures to discourage Deaf socialization, that such measures—even if totally successful—would have a trivial impact. A statistical study of the deaf population conducted by E. A. Fay, Vice-President of Gallaudet College, (Fay, 1898) with funding from Bell, showed that there was no greater likelihood of a Deaf child if both parents were Deaf than if only one was and that Deaf married Deaf three fourths of the time no matter whether the partners attended manual or oral schools, residential or day schools. All this Bell and other eugenicists must have known.

Consequently, the purpose of the eugenics movement with respect to Deaf people, the measures aimed at discouraging their socialization, intermarriage, and reproduction, was not so much to achieve those goals, which were largely unachievable and would be ineffective if achieved. Instead, the purpose was to reinforce a certain construction of deafness, one that linked it in its defining features to impairments such as feeblemindedness and to a particular noninfirm establishment with its own authorities, legislation, institutions, and professions. Moreover, the eugenics campaign marked deafness as an important social problem requiring expertise, one that had been previously overlooked, much to the danger of society. In this respect, the claims making closely paralleled the movement to awaken society to the dangers of mentally retarded people in our midst. As psychologists and superintendents of institutions for the feebleminded stood to gain from the recognition of the newly discovered social problem of mild retardation, so a competent authority that stood to gain from the construction of deafness as newly discovered menace was the burgeoning organization Bell had founded, the American Association to Promote the Teaching of Speech to the Deaf (AAPTSD). So it is nowadays that police and other social agencies promoting stiffer penalties for drunken driving are unmoved by evidence that penalties are without effect because they are striving most of all to promote a construction of the drunk driver as criminal (Gusfield, 1982).

The construction of deafness that the eugenics movement sought to reinforce was never stated explicitly, but some of its properties can be inferred from documents such as the model sterilization laws and from recorded statements. Thus, on various occasions, Bell called it an "affliction" (Bell, 1898), a "calamity," and a "defect" (Bell, 1883). Wolfensberger (1989) pointed out that the feebleminded were said in this era to "need" institutionalization, bizarre and injurious treatments, and sterilization. An Indiana law, for example, provided for sterilization "if their physical and mental condition is improved by it" (American Neurological Association, 1936). Among the needs of the Deaf person in the implicit construction were: (a) the use of spoken language and nonuse of manual language, therefore, a need of professionals to teach spoken language; (b) a special education in very small oral classes for Deaf children located in mainstream settings, thus, a need of hearing professionals to teach orally; and (c) a need to desist from marriage and reproduction, or to have sterilization, so that they would not "hand down their affliction" (Bell, 1898). The claim of Deaf people's need for bizarre and injurious physical treatments from a professional establishment came later, beginning in the 1970s (Lane, 1992).

The eugenics movement as it concerned Deaf people worldwide has received regrettably little study. Horst Biesold (1993) investigated the sterilization and execution of Jewish Deaf in Germany during the Nazi era. The German sterilization law that went into effect in 1934 provided the following: "Those hereditarily sick may be made unfruitful (sterilized) through surgical intervention. . . . The hereditary sick, in the sense of this law, is a person who suffers from one of the following diseases . . . hereditary deafness" (Peter, 1934, p. 190).

The census of 1933 showed 45,000 "deaf and dumb" persons in a total population of over 66 million. An estimated 17,000 of these deaf Germans, a third of them minors, were sterilized. In 9% of the cases, sterilization was accompanied by forced abortion. An additional 1,600 deaf people were exterminated in concentration camps in the 1940s (Biesold, 1988; Higgins, 1993). As in the U.S., the medical profession was the certifying authority for forced sterilization. And as in the United States, such legislation may have been concerned more with constructions of social problems and the identification of competent authority than with measures for their practical resolution.

In 1992, researchers at Boston University announced that they had identified the "genetic error" responsible for the most common type of inherited deafness (BU Team, 1992; Gene that causes, 1992). The director of the National Institute on Deafness and Other Communication Disorders (NIDCD—one of the National Institutes of Health; 1989) called the finding a "major breakthrough that will improve diagnosis and genetic counseling and ultimately lead to substitution therapy or gene transfer therapy" (BU Team, 1992, p. 6). Thus, a new form of medical eugenics applied to Deaf people is envisioned; in this case, by an agency of the U.S. government. The primary characteristics of people with this type of inherited deafness are—in addition to deafness and its accompanying features such as manual language— facial features such as widely spaced eyebrows and coloring features such as white forelock and freckling (Fraser, 1976). For such characteristics to be viewed primarily not as human variation in physiognomy, coloring, and so on, but as a "genetic error," some of the common features are clearly construed as a disease or infirmity. Behind the director's claims of major breakthrough, improvements in diagnosis and genetic counseling, and potential for genetic engineering, are the implied claims, among them: (a) This variation is a disease and hence should be avoided; (b) society's interest in avoiding it outweighs any individual or group's desire to continue it; (c) medical research such as our institute supports has led to this achievement, and the public's investment in our research is justified in part by these developments; and (d) the competent authority in these matters is medical authority.

Because all forms of human variation are genetically determined but the genetic causes for only some of these are actively sought, the pursuit of such genetic causes tells much about how that variation is construed as a social problem. Currently, homosexuality, inherited deafness, and an alleged inferiority in the intelligence of African Americans are among the social problems for which genetic causes are actively sought by federally sponsored research. Research on the genetics of heterosexuality, hearing, and White intelligence, such as it is, reflects quite a different construction of those social groups.

Remarkably, the NIDCD explicitly addresses the problem of the construction of deafness in its strategic plan (National Institute on Deafness and Other Communication Disorders, 1989). It acknowledges that "[M]any deaf individuals believe that deafness is not a disorder but a culturally defining condition" (p. 40). Because the statement makes this a matter of individual belief among deaf people (whereas it is tenet of Deaf culture), and because the statement makes no mention of what hearing people believe, there is the implication that the authors of the statement and other such authorities have a different and perhaps more objective view of the matter. The statement goes on to say, however, that the NIDCD respects "the cultural integrity of deaf society" (p. 40). Which construction of deafness would allow the Institute logically to support eugenic measures for the prevention of hereditary deafness all the while respecting the cultural integrity of Deaf society? The Institute planners are willing to acknowledge, it seems, that there is a problem, but that is as far as they are prepared to go. Elsewhere in the report, the Institute's commitment to a single underlying construction of deafness is as clear as its name: It calls for genetic research to improve diagnosis, counseling, and gene therapy all with a view to the prevention of deafness. It is, of course, unethical to seek to prevent a "culturally defining condition." Is genetic counseling available for mixed race couples? For homosexual prospective parents? For which culturally defining conditions is it available?

One of the chairmen of the Institute's planning group recently told *The New York Times*: "I am dedicated to curing deafness. That puts me on a collision course with those who are culturally deaf. That is interpreted as genocide of the deaf" (Pride in a Silent Language, 1993, p. 22). Again, the main reason issues like gene therapy generate strong feelings and invite pronouncements by various leaders and organizations is not because of direct practical consequences; rather, they reveal underlying and conflicting constructions of deafness. Similarly, surgeons and audiologists in the lead to surgically implant young Deaf children are hostile to those children using signs or American Sign Language, not because of any evidence that ASL detracts from the child learning English (indeed, the available evidence points to the contrary) but because the child with a surgically implanted prosthesis is the archetype of a certain construction of deafness, whereas the signer is the archetype of a diametrically opposed construction. Thus to sign is symbolically to negate the construction of deafness that has motivated the surgery, the cost, and the efforts of the surgeons, audiologists, speech therapists, special educators, and others.

The construction of deafness as a social problem that has underpinned the long history of efforts to promote reproductive regulation of Deaf people has certainly changed in the course of that history as different claims-making groups have waxed and waned and as broader societal reflection on social problems has changed. Nevertheless, there are constant features. To articulate that construction is to adopt the language and social constructs of a particular era. In current terms: Among our society's problem groups are the disabled. One such disability is deafness. Deaf people miss out on a great deal of importance because they cannot understand spoken language and often cannot speak understandably. However, many deaf people can, with sufficient training, learn to speak and read lips. Sometimes surgery and technology can be helpful in mitigating their deafness. A caring society provides therapy, medical treatment, technology, and support groups for deaf people. It also attacks the causes of deafness so as to prevent it as far as possible.

DEAF PEOPLE'S YEARNING
FOR A PLACE OF THEIR OWN

A Place of Their Own is the title of a history of the Deaf community in the U.S. by John Van Cleve and Barry Crouch. Where is this place, so fundamental to the meaning of deafness that it can serve as the emblem of American Deaf history? Nineteenth Century Deaf leader Olof Hanson wrote: "Deaf people were foreigners among a people whose language they [could] never learn" (as cited in Van Cleve & Crouch, 1989, p. ix). Where is the land of the Deaf "foreigners"?

The land of a people is not purely a geographic matter. Hanson was born in Sweden, but Swedish people immigrated to the U.S. from several nations in Scandinavia, and many soon claimed the U.S. as their land. The land of the Jews is located where most Jews have never set foot. The land of Native Americans is not only the fragment of territory left to a particular tribe by law but (at least) all such reservations, however scattered. The land of the Deaf "foreigners" is, in the first instance, the network of residential schools for the deaf. For the members of Deaf communities everywhere have this singular property, that the vast majority—9 out of 10 in America—have hearing parents and can thus acquire Deaf language and culture only in a shared place. That Deaf Americans should feel they have a place of their own, that such a conception is needed to organize the prominent facts of American Deaf history, testifies to quite a different construction of deafness than the one based on disability spelled out earlier.

Van Cleve and Crouch attribute the very existence of the American Deaf community to the shared place that is the residential network. "It seems that deaf people came together and created distinct cultural units—communities—only in response to particular historical developments of the late eighteenth and nineteenth centuries, especially the growth of cities and the establishment of state-supported residential schools for Deaf children" (Van Cleve & Crouch, 1989, p. 1). Of course, the Deaf youngster who arrives at the residential school has a different perspective on the same facts, one captured by Edmund Booth's aphorism, when he said he felt "at home among strangers" (Schein, 1989). It is the importance of place for Deaf people, and the central role of the residential school as place, that explains why Deaf introductions require stating one's school; why the Deaf community favors voluntary segregation in residential schools, a fact so baffling to contemporary disability theorists; why Deaf people mount aggressive campaigns to block the closing of residential schools; and why the American Deaf community is so bitterly opposed to mainstreaming.

The central role of place in the minds and lives of America's Deaf people could not be satisfied by the residential network alone. For one thing, many of the residential schools were founded and directed by hearing people, and late in the last century those people used draconian measures to replace ASL with English and to impose hearing culture. Moreover, the Deaf young man or woman, having developed a deep sense of place at the residential school, then graduated and frequently lived apart from the school and its community (though many stayed on at the school or in the town). The search for a place apart from the residential school led to the establishment of Deaf clubs, tiny reservations of deafness across America, where Deaf people governed, socialized, and communicated fluently in ASL when the work day—often spent in the hearing world—was over.

We are very familiar with the desire of linguistic and cultural minorities to have their own place. Our television screens are awash in bloody images from the former Yugoslavia, where culturally diverse groups are at war over place. The desire of Jews worldwide to have their own place in Israel is a source of conflict. Our own nation was founded by Pilgrims who were "foreigners" in their own land and who yearned for a place of their own. We cannot doubt that the centrality of place goes beyond mere conditions favoring business success or religious tolerance and that it is an expression of the deepest wellsprings of the personal search for identity and an integral part of the social fabric that is culture. Therefore, the yearning for place is an important marker (language is another) that a group indeed has a distinct culture.

The significance of place is so central to the lives of America's Deaf people that a utopian vision of a Deaf place has taken material form from time to time. It was first put forth in the 1830s by recent graduates at the "Vatican" of the residential school network, the American Asylum for the Deaf in Hartford. They formed an association to purchase land from the federal government and voted in 13 members; however, employment scattered the group, and the project died. It is significant that the Deaf "father" of American Deaf education, Laurent Clerc, had advocated allotting some of the land granted the American Asylum by the Congress for the purpose of establishing a Deaf "headquarters." In the 1850s, the desire of American Deaf people for a place of their own surfaced once again, this time articulated by J. J. Flournoy among others; there was an extended debate in the *American Annals of the Deaf* and in Deaf organizations (Lane, 1984; Winzer, 1986). Similar utopian plans arose in the English (Van Cleve & Crouch, 1989) and French (Cf. Lane, 1984, p. 275) Deaf communities in the last century, and a Deaf utopia is the subject of a novel by American Deaf author Douglas Bullard (1985).

Bell understood that place was symbolic of and underpinned another construction of deafness, one antithetical to the one he was promoting and unfavorable to the interests he represented. In his 1883 *Memoir*, he warned that "twenty-four deaf-mutes, with their families, have already arrived [in Manitoba] and have settled upon the land. More are expected next year" (Bell, 1883/1969, p. 45). Therefore, he was profoundly opposed to Deaf place. It is likely that his opposition concerned constructions and symbols more than the role of the schools in Deaf reproduction because he knew that Deaf people who attended nonresidential schools intermarried at about the same rate, and because he was a bitter critic as well of the discussion of a Deaf utopia (Bell, 1883).

Flournoy not only promoted a Deaf land; he had been active in efforts to establish the Georgia School for the Deaf and, among many others, in the drive to establish a national Deaf college. Such initiatives touched a responsive cord throughout the American Deaf community. Numerous schools for the Deaf had been founded by Deaf educators when the movement arose to found the National Deaf-Mute College at mid-nineteenth century. The college was a further expression of the role of place in the American Deaf community, and it is in this light that the 1988 "Gallaudet Revolution" should be understood. It is significant that the four student leaders who sealed the gates to the Gallaudet campus and barred entry to administrators were Deaf children of Deaf parents, deeply imbued with a sense of Deaf community, and natively fluent in ASL. The most prominent student leader explained to USA Today the significance of the Revolution as it relates to the construction of deafness:

> Hearing people sometimes call us handicapped. But most—maybe all Deaf people—feel that we're more of an ethnic group because we speak a different language. . . . We also have our own culture. . . . There's more of an ethnic difference than a handicap difference between us and hearing people. (This protest, 1988, p. 11a)

The new Deaf president of Gallaudet sought to explain the difference in the underlying construction is these terms: "More people realize now that deafness is a difference, not a deficiency" (as cited in Gannon, 1989, p. 173).

It may be helpful if I, with a hearing person's perspective in the late 20th century, try to spell out this construction of deafness of which Deaf people's yearning and striving for "a place of their own" have been symptomatic and emblematic for centuries. There is a Deaf community in the U.S., a language minority with a distinct culture. Members of this culture are different from the majority in their physical organization as they are in their language, culture, and experience of the world, which arise in part from that organization. A caring society would provide interpreters, teachers, and other professionals who know their language and value their culture.

CONSTRUCTIONS OF DEAFNESS

Deaf leader Harvey Corson, former superintendent of the Louisiana School for the Deaf and former Vice-President of Gallaudet University, explained the historical shift in the dominant construction of deafness in these terms:

> As Deaf people, how we see ourselves and view the world, what we have learned and have been taught, have changed in profound ways. The center has shifted—from disability, to ability; from handicap to culture; from silent individuals to a vibrant community; from primitive gestures to sign languages; from invisible people to recognized individuals throughout history. (Corson, 1991, p. 5)

Of course, Dr. Corson does not mean that Deaf people have changed from silent individuals or that gestures have been replaced by sign language. What has changed is the construction of deafness internalized by many Deaf people themselves. Deaf people now recognize more widely that they speak a natural language, that they have a rich culture and heritage, and that they must pursue a political agenda in order to protect and extend that culture and heritage.

In announcing a change in construction of deafness within the Deaf community, Corson reminds us of the plea for a change in construction made by his French counterpart in 1853; addressing the Academy of Medicine at the start of its debate on mainstreaming and the best methods of educating Deaf children, the dean of French Deaf professors, Ferdinand Berthier, said: "You are concerned gentlemen with more than an ordinary medical question. This is a lofty issue of humanity and civilization which demands the full attention not only of doctors but also of teachers, philosophers, and scholars" (Berthier, 1853, p. 2).

Deaf people and organizations have been vehemently against day schools, oralism, and integration, but the authorities have not been concerned to hear those protests. To the extent that we hold a cultural construction of deafness, this disdain of the authorities for Deaf people's views on Deaf issues is ethically offensive. American values frequently require that the cultural group be consulted—certainly since the civil rights movements of the mid-20th century. But the precedent for the disability construction is not to consult with the concerned groups. Thus, it is not a practice to involve organizations of people with motoric impairment, mental illness or retardation, sensory impairment, and so on in educational, public health, and other policy issues. The consultative practices of our government are one index, therefore, of its underlying construction of the group. The Food and Drug Administration felt no need to hear from any member of Deaf culture when authorizing cochlear implant surgery on young Deaf children. Gallaudet President I. K. Jordan does serve on the 18-member advisory board of the National Institute on Deafness and Other Communication Disorders; however, his place is reserved by law for a person with a communications disorder, which he denies he has. Presumably, the members of the board do not ask, and he does not tell.

The "troubled persons industry" that deals with deaf people is itself torn with strife in the U.S. as elsewhere: Some advocate mainstreaming of deaf children, whereas others are vehemently opposed; some urge focusing on the important skills of speech and speechreading, whereas others cry that its a waste of time and crowds out real education; some urge surgically implanted cochlear prostheses to give the child the best chance at learning or using spoken language, whereas others affirm that this is needless and useless surgery on defenseless children.

There have been countless efforts to resolve or squelch these disputes since at least the 18th century. Such efforts generally appeal to shared goals and argue the means, or they focus on disputes about goals—for example, what is the purpose of Deaf education; is it not foremost to learn to communicate? Neither of these attempts at resolution or at outright ending of the debate has succeeded. "The question of methods is practically retired," proclaimed a leading educator of the Deaf in 1900 (Booth, 1900, p. 452). He was wrong.

I submit that the conflict that has polarized the professions and separated many hearing professionals from the Deaf people they claim to serve goes deeper than goals or means and arises instead from the disputing parties' understanding at the outset of what deaf means. As a social problem, deafness can be variously construed. Social problems are not just "lying there in the road, waiting to be discovered" (Gusfield, 1984, p. 38). They are instead constructed by particular cultures at particular times, in response to advocacy by interested groups.

THE CULTURALLY SENSITIVE PSYCHOTHERAPIST AS SOCIAL IRONIST

Most people entering the professional establishment serving the Deaf find their earlier acculturation to a disability construction of deafness reinforced. Even as civil rights movements and the social science research of recent decades has led professionals to pay lip service to a linguistic minority construction, the disability construction plays an ever larger role in the lives of Deaf children and adults, in the expenditures of government, and in the training of professional people. Without the disability construction, there is no reason for the treatment establishment, so that establishment is far from replacing it. In this context, the cultural self-awareness of the hearing professional begins with an epistemological shift. Instead of asking whether professional claims are true, the culturally sensitive psychotherapist (CSP) asks prior questions such as: Who is making those claims, in behalf of which goals, which presuppositions are embedded in the claim, and so on. That is, the claim itself is taken as the subject of inquiry. The historical perspective on the changing and competing constructions of deafness, from the eugenics movement to the cochlear implant movement to the Deaf President Now movement, is helpful in avoiding the trap of naive realism.

People in the professions serving the Deaf are trained to accept the naive realist interpretation of fundamental claims uncritically. That acceptance is symbolic of being "one of us"—rather like the Nicene Creed. Thus, the challenge of culturally sensitive psychotherapy consists of much more than merely learning about the culture of Deaf people and trying to use that knowledge on the job—to interpret body language appropriately, for example. The challenge of the CSP is to take a critical stance, the social ironist's stance, on as many claims as possible, and especially the axioms. It is axiomatic that hearing professionals are seeking to help their clients. Then the ironist asks, "How do the clients help the professionals?" It is axiomatic that it is a hearing world. Then the ironist asks, "How is our clients' belief that their deaf-world is legitimate counter to professional interests?" It is axiomatic that severe deafness is better than profound deafness. "Who introduced those terms, and what do they say about the abilities and inabilities of professionals and of Deaf people? When is less hearing helpful and to whom?" We are told that hearing-impaired professionals are playing a larger role in delivering services to Deaf people. The ironist asks, "Who defines that role, and what is its scope? Who introduced the term hearing impaired? Which groups are included within its compass and which groups excluded? Whose interests are served by those distinctions? How are they written into law and practice?" It is axiomatic that old-fashioned beliefs must give way to modernity. The ironist asks: "Whose interests are served by the application of technology? What else is being justified as modern, and why must it be justified?"

The social ironist thinks of claims making as a dramatic performance, artistically designed to interest audiences (Gusfield, 1981). Such irony exposes the forces that are at work, which are hidden because mystification serves the interests of the professions. However, mystification does not serve the therapeutic alliance. If the social forces that underpin claims making are ignored, therapists will act oppressively and clients will respond with their traditional adaptive responses to that oppression. If there is room for the linguistic minority construction in the therapeutic relationship, there is more possibility for culturally Deaf persons to use their authentic voice. Moreover, the nature and causes of the Deaf client's psychological condition and the psychological condition itself are claims that the CSP must view with irony or risk wasting time or worse. I have shown elsewhere, for example, that the psychological tests used with culturally Deaf people are inappropriate in language, content and norms, and are administered and scored with invalid procedures (Lane, 1992).

As part of their training, therapists endeavor to identify their own psychodynamics at work in responding to their clients. As a result, therapists are less judgmental and create a condition in which more of the forces at play on the patients can be discerned. In effect, therapists take an ironist's position on their own responses and claims. Instead of identifying X's behavior as, say, aggressive, the therapist asks, "Can the same behavior be seen in another way? If so, what way and why am I intimidated?" It is this posture that the CSP adopts with respect to his or her professional training and activities. The patient says, I engaged in behavior X because I felt Y, but the therapist knows that the motive offered may be a response to the behavior (and the need for an explanation) and not its cause. Similarly, when the CSP is told that a profession is responding to an emergent social need, he or she asks whether the possibility of a professional program created the perception of a social problem. The therapist asks to whom this claim was addressed, how it came to be made, what counts as evidence of the problem, and who stands to gain by the particular construction of the problem.

The significance of professional attempts at management of culturally Deaf people, whether by surgery, oralism, day schools, or genetic engineering, lies not in their objective efficacy but in their symbolic ability to reinforce the perceived legitimacy of the hearing professions engaged in those activities.

REFERENCES

American Neurological Association. (1936). *Committee for the investigation of eugenical sterilization. Eugenical sterilization: a reorientation of the problem.* New York: Macmillan.

Bell, A. G. (1969). Memoir upon the formation of a deaf variety of the human race. Washington, DC: A. G. Bell Association. (Original work published in 1883)

Bell, A. G. (1898). *Marriage: An address to the deaf* (3rd ed.). Washington, DC: Sanders.

Berthier, F. (1837). Lettre sur les difficultes au marriage des sourds-muets. [Letter on the difficulties in marrying encountered by deaf-mutes]. *Le Sourd-Muet et l'aveugle, 1,* 190–195.

Berthier, F. (1853). *Observations sur la mimique considerée dans ses rapports avec l'enseignement des sourds-muets.* [Observations on sign language in relation to deaf education.] Paris: Martinet.

Biesold, H. (1988). *Klagende Hände. Betroffenheit und Spätfolgen in Bezug auf das Gesetz zur Verhütung erbkranken Nachwuches, dargestellt am Beispiel der "Taubstummen."* [Crying hands: Victimization and the after-effects of the law for the prevention of genetically defective offspring, as presented in the case of deaf mutes]. Solms-Oberbiel: Jarick Oberbiel.

Biesold, H. (1993). The fate of the Israelite Asylum for the Deaf and Dumb in Berlin. In R. Fischer & H. Lane (Eds.), *Looking back: A History of Deaf communities and their sign languages* (pp. 157–170). Hamburg: Signum.

Booth, F. W. (1900). Editorial. *Association Review, 2,* 451–452.

Bruce, R. V. (1973). *Bell. Alexander Graham Bell and the conquest of solitude.* Boston: Little Brown.

BU Team Finds Genetic Cause of Waardenburg Syndrome. (1992) *Deaf Community News,* March.

Bullard, D. (1985). *Islay.* Silver Spring, MD: TJ Publishers.

Chouard, C.-H. (1978). *Entendre sans oreille* [Hearing without ears]. Paris: Laffont.

Corson, H. (1991, June). *Deaf history: Its role in understanding deaf experience and its contribution to deaf studies.* Address to the First International Congress on Deaf History, Gallaudet University, Washington, DC.

Fay, E. A. (1898). *Marriages of the deaf in America.* Washington, DC: Volta Bureau.

Fraser, G. R. (1976). *The causes of profound deafness in childhood*. Baltimore: Johns Hopkins University Press.

Gannon, J. (1989). *The week the world heard Gallaudet*. Washington, DC: Gallaudet University Press.

Gene that Causes Waardenburg's Syndrome. (1992). *The New York Times, 141*, B7,C2.

Gregory, S., & Hartley, G. M. (Eds.) (1991). *Constructing deafness*. London: Pinter.

Gusfield, J. (1981). *The culture of public problems: Drinking-driving and the symbolic order*. Chicago: University of Chicago Press.

Gusfield, J. (1982). Deviance in the welfare state: The alcoholism profession and the entitlements of stigma. In M. Lewis (Ed.), *Research in social problems and public policy* (Vol. 2, pp. 1–20). Greenwich, CT: JAI.

Gusfield, J. (1984). On the side: Practical action and social constructivism in social problems theory. In J. Schneider & J. Kitsuse (Eds.), *Studies in the sociology of social problems* (pp. 31–51). Norwood, NJ: Ablex.

Gusfield, J. (1989). Constructing the ownership of social problems: Fun and profit in the welfare state. *Social Problems, 36*, 431–441.

Higgins, W. (1993). La parole des sourds [What the deaf tell us]. *Psychanalystes, 46–47*, 189.

Johnson, R. H. (1918). The marriage of the deaf. *Jewish Deaf*, 5–6.

Lane, H. (1984). *When the mind hears: A history of the deaf*. New York: Random House.

Lane, H. (1992). *The mask of benevolence: Disabling the deaf community*. New York: Knopf.

Lane, H. (1993). Cochlear implants: Their cultural and historical meaning. In J. Van Cleve (ed.), *Deaf history unveiled* (pp. 272–292). Washington, DC: Gallaudet University Press.

National Institute on Deafness and Other Communication Disorders. (1989). *National Research Plan*. Bethesda, MD: National Institutes of Health.

Peter, W. W. (1934). Germany's sterilization program. *American Journal of Public Health, 24*(3), 187–191.

Plann, S. (1993). Pedro Ponce de León: Myth and reality. In J. Van Cleve (Ed.), *Deaf history unveiled* (pp. 1–12). Washington, DC: Gallaudet University Press.

Pride in a silent language. (1993, May 16). *The New York Times*, p. 22.

Schein, J. (1989). *At home among strangers*. Washington, DC: Gallaudet University Press.

This protest. (1988, March 15). *USA Today*, p. 11a.

Van Cleve, J. V. (1984). Nebraska's oral law of 1911 and the deaf community. *Nebraska History, 65*, 195–220.

Van Cleve, J. V. (1993). The academic integration of deaf children. In R. Fischer & H. Lane (Eds.), *Looking back: A History of Deaf communities and their sign languages* (pp. 333–347). Hamburg: Signum.

Van Cleve, J. V., & Crouch, B. (1989). *A place of their own*. Washington, DC: Gallaudet University Press.

Winefield, R. (1987). *Never the twain shall meet*: The communications debate. Washington, DC: Gallaudet University Press.

Winzer, M.A. (1986). Deaf-Mutia: Responses to alienation by the deaf in the mid-nineteenth century. *American Annals of the Deaf, 31* 29–32.

Winzer, M. A. (1993). Education, urbanization and the deaf community: A case study of Toronto, 1870–1900. In J. V. Van Cleve (Ed.), *Deaf history unveiled* (pp. 127–145). Washington, DC: Gallaudet University Press.

Wisconsin Phonological Institute. (1894). *Improvement of the Wisconsin System of Education for Deaf-mutes*. Milwaukee: Author.

Wolfensberger, W. (1989). Human service policies: The rhetoric versus the reality. In L. Barton (Ed), *Disability and dependency* (pp. 23–41). Bristol, PA: Taylor & Francis Falmer Press.

Chapter 3

Is There a Psychology of the Hearing?

Robert Hoffmeister
Boston University

Michael A. Harvey
Boston University
Gallaudet University

People make vocational choices for a variety of reasons—conscious and unconscious, rational and irrational, healthy and nonhealthy. This universalism is true for those who decide to enter any helping profession and, more specifically, for those who decide on a career of helping Deaf persons. Meadow (1981) noted that a hearing person's initial "missionary zeal" on entering the fields of working with Deaf people may productively fuel later accomplishments or may set the stage for eventual burnout.

As hearing students new to the "field of deafness," we study hard to learn the subject matter, about American Sign Language (ASL), the Deaf community, Deaf culture, and so on. We come to feel knowledgable and qualified to help Deaf persons, confident that we have something important to offer. We enter our respective professions with full gusto, with our hopes and dreams for a long and fulfilling career. Helping people is, after all, a noble profession.

Everthing seems fine until our bubble is burst. "Why so much hearing bashing from the Deaf community?" "Even many hearing people make me feel like I shouldn't be in the profession anymore!" We become angry. We become insecure. We question our motivations, our skills. We indeed question whether to remain in the field.

As hearing people, we may understand some of the dynamics behind hearing bashing as interwoven in a long history of opression of Deaf people by the hearing culture. And we remind ourselves not to personalize its content: "I certainly don't deserve to be called an oppressor just because of other hearing persons' behavior!"

This position has much merit. Why should a White person be blamed for slavery that happened more than 100 years ago? We should be innocent until proven guilty!

But nobody is completely innocent. We cannot help but incorporate and act out some of what we are continually exposed to in our culture. We are only partially successful at resisting the various "isms" that abound: sexism, racism, ethnocentrism, ageism, classism, and so on. At times, we, at best, unwittingly "oppress" our friends, lovers, and acquaintances in relatively benign and perhaps not so benign ways, and, in turn, those people oppress us.

An exploration of the the psychology of the hearing must include an analysis of our noble side, but not at the expense of acknowledging and understanding our "dark" side as well, our duality. In this context, our focus is not primarily to seek justice—who is right and who is wrong; who is the oppressor and who is the oppressed. We are both. There is a saying attributed to Mahatma Gandhi: "If you follow the old code of justice—an eye for an eye and a tooth for a tooth—you end up with a blind and toothless world." (cited in Johnson, 1991, p. 15).

The intent of this chapter is to take a hard look at the psychology of the hearing. The first part of the chapter examines some common reasons why we may initially become motivated to work with the Deaf. The second part of the chapter delineates common "relational postures" of hearing people toward Deaf persons, that is, predominate ways that we tend to perceive and behave toward Deaf persons. Each posture also implies ways that we perceive ourselves as hearing professionals.

In the third part of the chapter, we specifically address our attitudes and behaviors with respect to American Sign Language. We note that the continuing controversy regarding the importance of signed and spoken language is the central determinant that affects our relationships with Deaf people. Finally, the last part of the chapter describes what a collaborative relationship between Deaf and hearing people might look like. Some of the challenges to this collaboration are explored.

We base our conclusions on informal observations of our peers and on relevant literature. But our psychological examination is not only on those "others"; it must also necessarily include and be influenced by the psychology of the first author, as a hearing educator, and of the second author, as a hearing psychologist. For better or worse, we are all in this together. Hopefully, some of what is described will be generalizable to the reader and, to use a hearing metaphor, have "a familiar ring to it."

HOW DO PEOPLE BECOME INTERESTED IN WORKING WITH THE DEAF?

The first level of analysis is to describe some common reasons why we hearing people may decide to enter professions that are focused on the Deaf. This section describes seven such possibilities. Naturally, the categories are not exhaustive, nor mutually exclusive.

I Once Knew Someone Who Was Deaf: The Friend Decision

Probably the most common way to enter the field is through contact with a Deaf or hard-of-hearing person during childhood or early adulthood. Many professionals, for example, have grown up as a neighbor to a Deaf friend or had met a Deaf student in their schooling years. A relationship between a Deaf and hearing peer may be predominately one of dependency or it may be one of mutual exchange.

In a dependency relationship, the hearing peer chooses to befriend the Deaf peer but not necessarily the other way around. If the Deaf peer is in an integrated classroom and the children in the classroom are being taught sign language so that they may communicate with the lone Deaf peer, not all children will learn to sign equally well. Typically, as with people learning second languages, a small number of hearing students in the class will learn to sign rapidly and to some extent more fluently than most of the other students. Consequently, the Deaf student's decision to befriend particular hearing peers may be based more on their perceived capability of signing or interpreting than on whether the Deaf student wishes to befriend the hearing student per se.

Although this relationship may involve a high mutual exchange factor, it is ultimately built on dependency. The Deaf peer obtains an interpreter and a friend. It is the interpreting part of the relationship that makes for excessive dependency and that threatens to "pollute" the friend part of the exchange. Being in a position to control the language and the information flow between two parties puts the hearing student interpreter in a power-based role. Many times as children, the power is not consciously realized but is always there.

A mutual exchange friendship is the most difficult to arrive at between Deaf and hearing peers. As with all friendships, there must be some give and take, ups and downs, and positive and negative tensions. The Deaf person inevitably experiences circumstances probably not noticed by the hearing peer. For example, when a nonsigning hearing person attempts to converse with the Deaf peer, the actual conversation is often directed to the hearing peer who does sign. Phrases such as "tell him . . . " are signs of an imbalance within the conversational act. The challenge is to work out a mutually empowered way of handling such omnipresent temptations toward imbalances of power.

My Parents Were Deaf: The Parental Decision

Many children who have Deaf parents enter professions that are related to the Deaf. Many children of deaf adults (codas), report that they have always known that they would become, for example, an interpreter, a teacher of the Deaf, and so on. It is also not uncommon for extended family members to encourage a coda to pursue a career working with the Deaf because one is perceived to already possess the requisite skills. This was the experience of the first author, a coda.

Codas may believe that they possess a unique knowledge base about deafness and Deaf culture. As such, they may feel an ethical mandate to enter the field, as described later in this chapter. Other professionals attribute a special kind of wisdom to codas. It is not uncommon for professionals to defer to peers with Deaf parents based solely on heritage. However, this bestowal of knowledge may or may not be deserved. It is frequently an extension of what was bestowed to codas as children; many questions were asked of them as young children that were beyond their understanding, but people assumed they knew the answer just because of their contact situation with the Deaf (Preston, 1994).

This situation provides one with a sense of power and control. This sense is possibly similar to the continuation of power and control one felt as a child who may have functioned as an adult in situations with their parents. But it is a double-edged sword, for this power and control often exceeds the person's self-perceived capabilities.

Intrigue With Sign Language: The Language Decision

Another common entrance into working with Deaf persons is when one becomes enthralled with American Sign Language. This may have been the result of having taken a course in sign, from having attended a signed play, or from having met Deaf people in a bar or other social gathering. The second author of this chapter, for example, saw a Deaf adult sign "America the Beautiful" and found it to be captivating, an impressive display of the sign abilities of a Deaf person. Although he did not have the skills to judge whether the Deaf person was in fact a good signer as regarded by the Deaf Community, nevertheless, he became intrigued with ASL. He described ASL as a "totally beautiful language" and therefore entered one of the fields working with Deaf people.

Indeed, sign language has been described as having great artistry and a ballet-like presentation of the movements. Because American Sign Language is in a different mode and done with the hands and arms, the articulator is in plain sight. It is not fundamentally different than a spoken language sounding pleasant to the ear.

Some people enter the deafness field via the language decision as a result of having chosen ASL as one of a list of languages in college. Some may have a propensity for learning languages, and ASL presented another linguistic challenge. Others have found it difficult to learn spoken languages, but assumed that, because sign language is in different mode, they could more easily become proficient in this language. Although they soon learn that their assumption was false, nevertheless, some become captivated by ASL and therefore by Deaf culture.

This latter point deserves special mention. Because learning American Sign Language requires at least tentative exposure to the Deaf community, many ASL students find themselves getting more than they bargained for at the outset. They may become intrigued with Deaf culture, overwhelmed by it, and so on. There are many possibilities. As soon as the professional learns to carry on a conversation with a Deaf person using sign, then further complexities arise with regard to the hearing person's view of their signing ability, their knowledge about the community, and their role within this new group of people. This is described later in the chapter.

A New Challenge: The Professional Challenge Decision

Professionals may become attracted to the field of deafness as a result of working with a Deaf client who required more help than they were capable of providing. This challenge may spark a fervor to identify new theories and techniques that can help that new population. Our fervor may, in fact, have primarily altruistic origins, as described in a later category. However, it is our experience that those in the helping professions are frequently expected to know all facets of their areas and how to assist all types of people, including the Deaf. Consequently, what may begin as altruism may be replaced by narcissistically driven behavior: Namely, one helps a deaf client because "no one is going to stump me!"

Some professionals in this category may enter the field because they are bored in their present positions and see this as an avenue out of boredom. The professional has a new field to learn about and is rejuvenated. Here, the professional's decision is also narcissistically driven.

It must be emphasized, however, that there is nothing inherently negative about satisfying narcissistic drives. Indeed, narcissism is hypothesized to be an omnipresent component of all human drives (Kernberg, 1984). One's level of awareness and psychological intactness are important factors. However, the possibility of narcissistic need satisfaction becoming oppressive is real and is described in the following category.

The Deaf Need My Guidance:
The Dominant Colonialist Decision

Interest in the field of deafness sometimes has an "imperialistic flavor" to it. Deaf people offer new territories for the professional to conquer. One may even envision getting public recognition for new work in a new field. (We term this the "Noble Prize syndrome".) These professionals are able to gain power by working with the Deaf, power they would not have working with other hearing people. As an analogy, consider the case of a dominant colonialist, namely, a person who escapes from their own country and gains power over others by being in a position of political power.

The danger in the dominant colonialist posture is that one may devalue the opinions and sentiments of the Deaf community because they have become the object of one's narcissistic need gratification. Some, but not all, medical professionals display this view when confronted with conflicting views from Deaf people themselves. They discount the value of the opinion of Deaf people because of attributing their own medical opinion to be of a much higher order. Balkany (1994), for example, is an Ear, Nose, and Throat doctor (ENT) who wrote an editorial in the *New England Journal of Medicine*, actually stating that the Deaf community's opinion does not matter!

Identification With the Oppressed: The Outsider Decision

Many professionals have unresolved narcissistic wounds and identify with the problems of Deaf people. At a conscious or unconscious level, we attempt to "fill up" ourselves and resolve our pain by seeking to help Deaf persons cope with similar issues of oppression and rejection. Miller (1981), in *Drama of the Gifted Child*, eloquently described this common plight of therapists: "It seems to me that if we [therapists] can do anything at all, it is to work through our narcissistic problems and reintegrate our split-off aspects to such an extent that we no longer have any need to manipulate our patients according to our theories but can allow them to become what they really are" (p. 22).

The positive outcome of this decision is for one to learn that narcissistic healing can only be done at a personal level and in a mutually intimate relationship with another (Jordan, Caplan, Surrey, & Stiver, 1991). In this case, what begins as co-dependent behavior by the hearing professional eventually catalyzes that person to "heal thyself."

How Can I Help? The Altruism Decision

The word *altruism* is rooted in the Latin *alter*, which simply means "other." August Comte has been credited with coining the term and conceived of it as devotion to the welfare of others, based in selflessness. Is such behavior possible? Skeptics such as Machiavelli, Hobbes, Marx, and Freud would argue that humans are incapable of acting out of any other motive than their own self-interest. On the other hand, Emile Durkheim believed that altruism exists in every society (Behhah, 1973). Lerner (1995), in a widely circulated journal entitled *Tikkun*, coined the term *politics of meaning* to emphasize that a latent need of U.S. society is to shift the dominant discourse from selfishness to caring.

People in this category feel touched by the needs of an outsider group, such as the Deaf community. They see a need and view their ethical mandate as requiring them to help. It has been speculated that a propensity for altruistic behaviors may originate in the value placed on caring in one's family of origin (Oliner & Oliner, 1988). One learns to extend one's boundaries of concern beyond oneself. It was Hillel who asked: "If I'm not for myself, who will be for me? If I'm only for myself, what am I?"

May God Be With You: The Religious Decision

The initial public entrance into the world of the Deaf community was first proposed by De L'Eppe and Gallaudet, members of the clergy. The funds raised for various programs and other missionary functions were received through the auspices that the Deaf people known at the time needed to be exposed to the word of God. Most religions hold this underlying missionary perspective.

There is a significant number of hearing persons who enter the fields that work with Deaf persons through contact with a religious structure. A professional could actually be a minister or cleric or be influenced by some function within a religious framework. Almost every religion in the U.S. has a section devoted to the Deaf population. It is through these sections that many hearing professionals learn that Deaf people need to receive the word of God. As a result, such professionals become interested in pursuing careers focused on assisting Deaf people in a variety of ways.

Professionals who enter with the missionary perspective must take care not to impose paternalistic behavior that can result in oppressive outcomes. This perspective, in its attempt to instill religious values, may unwittingly lead some to ignore or even display disrespect of the values of the Deaf world and many of the individuals within it. As an example, the helper might focus on speech and hearing skills that would shine a negative light on the use of a signed language. In contrast, for many Deaf adults, the use of a signed language can not only expose them to the word of God but is a means of empowerment.

The origin of one's motivation to work with Deaf people is typically multide-termined. One may be influenced by several of the previous reasons or others that are not listed. One may empathize with the Deaf community's outsider status with respect to the hearing world and simultaneously view working with Deaf clients as a new challenge. Moreover, one's initial reasons for entering the field are not static. One may first have altruistic motivations but later revert to dominant colonialism, or the reverse. As is described later, one may initially be impressed by ASL, only to later invalidate it.

COMMON HEARING "RELATIONAL POSTURES" TOWARD DEAF PERSONS

The reasons why hearing professionals initially enter the field of deafness may or may not correlate with their eventual perceptions of Deaf people or their behavior toward them. Moreover, their original intent(s) typically evolve into habitual ways of perceiving Deaf people, of perceiving hearing "helpers," and of behaving toward hearing and Deaf persons. We refer to these patterns of perception and behavior as "relational postures" that hearing professionals have toward deaf persons.

As with the listing of initial decisions to enter the field, there is the risk of oversimplification, and there is certainly significant overlap between these postures. The intent is to provide a heuristic framework for analyzing components of how and why hearing people perceive and behave toward Deaf people in certain ways.

The Freedom Fighter Posture

Some hearing professionals view Deaf people as the victims of societal oppression and, as such, honor an ethical mandate to correct that oppression. They become "freedom fighters." The freedom fighter is focused on righting the wrongs of society that have been perpetrated on Deaf people.

Consider the case of children of deaf adults. Codas may be exposed to a number of circumstances in which the Deaf people in their young lives were subjected to extremely complicated and oppressive interactions by hearing people. The hearing child undoubtedly experiences a variety of emotions, such as empathy, compassion, helplessness, and guilt.

They may feel a false sense of power to correct the wrongs done to their parents. This sense of power, not necessarily conscious, sometimes leads to a variety of later behaviors. As one example, codas may be in the "business" of assisting other Deaf people to overcome societal oppression in order to ameliorate or resolve their childhood guilt. The positive outcome of this dynamic is that the work pursued by the coda can be on behalf of the Deaf, for whom and with whom they are working.

As an analogy, Eli Weisel had witnessed his father being murdered by Nazis. For reasons that he himself acknowledges as irrational, he felt responsible. Partially, as a result, he has dedicated the rest of his life to ensure that no other Jews can similarly be murdered.

In both cases, those adults who had much earlier helplessly observed their parents undergoing oppression no longer feel as much helplessness as a result of saving like-others. They master their childhood pain vis-à-vis persons who come to symbolize their parents, more technically termed *transference objects*.

The effects of feeling powerlessness as a child and/or observing the powerlessness of significant others may emerge at different times under differing circumstances. One may be outspoken and driven while at other times be the mediator or peacemaker. If, as children, we have been put in many stressful situations out of our control, we may seek to gain power and control as an adult in order to avoid a reenactment of childhood anxiety. In the specific case of codas, this stance may also be encouraged by other professionals who defer or accord them special expert status. Additionally, one may serve as a "bridge" between both cultures, often related to one's mediation role in childhood.

Of course, there are many freedom fighters who are not codas, much like there were many non-Jews—so-called "righteous Gentiles"—who fought Nazism. We use the example of codas to note the prevalence of that relational posture among this group. As another example, Gunther and Harvey (1995) interviewed a sample of interpreters about those psychological factors that affect the quality of their interpreting. It was found that many interpreters—codas and noncodas—sustain their motivation to remain in the field because of their committment to undo what they perceive as a wrong of society: an unequal balance of power between Deaf and hearing persons. They derive meaning from fulfillment of their ethical mandate to fight for freedom, for more equal participation.

It has been our experience that this posture accounts for at least one facet of many hearing professionals' involvement in the field. It is a double-edged sword, however, in that the freedom fighter posture may precipitate frustration and burnout when one has to accept limitations to change society (Meadow, 1981). Moreover, one may fight for Deaf persons' freedom while also operating from a variety of other relational postures, as described later. One, for example, may view both society and Deaf people as deserving blame. One may blur our boundaries while operating within freedom fighter posture.

The Pathological Posture

Our society honors those who work to "help" the less fortunate among us. Deaf people, like many other oppressed minorities, have always been considered to be of a lesser stock than hearing people. It is no wonder that to work with the Deaf as a career is enhanced, supported, and highly rewarded. Witness the number of times one has been told that it "must be very rewarding to work with deaf children."

With this relational posture, one believes that the Deaf need the help of a hearing person in order to function well in the hearing world and avoid the horrors that may otherwise befall them. This way of thinking leads people to construct approaches, to build theories, and implement techniques that will "help" Deaf people lead better lives. The implicit framework assumes that Deaf people's lives are somehow negative and need help from professionals. This posture persists, even though a Deaf person may be depicted as having tremendous skills. Marlee Matlin, for example, in the popular television series "Reasonable Doubt," must have a hearing cop as an interpreter who not only interprets but helps her solve cases, and most importantly, helps her to function in the courtroom.

This posture also accounts for what many professionals who work with Deaf people erroneously term as "the psychology of deafness." Indeed, there are four major texts in the field, one published as recently as 1994, with exactly that name (Levine, 1960; Marschak, 1994; Myklebust, 1960; Vernon & Andrews, 1990). The notion of a psychology of deafness is really more about the psychology of hearing professionals who work with the Deaf (Lane, 1992; Vernon & Andrews, 1993).

This posture also leads one to discount the Deaf culture and community. Many professionals who are charged with the responsibility to advise, consult, and guide Deaf children and adults are totally unaware of the cultural, linguistic, and personal practices of Deaf people. Almost all programs that train ENTs, audiologists, and speech and hearing professionals include information about hearing-impaired people; yet, to our knowledge, these programs do not typically employ Deaf professionals as faculty or even have advisory or policy boards that have significant number of Deaf professionals as members. Nevertheless, these programs graduate professionals who are certified or licensed by national and state organizations.

Almost every professional certifying body that is connected to the Deaf has no Deaf persons as part of their boards. National Institute of Health, Institute for the Deaf and Other Communicative Disorders, the American Medical Association, American Psychological Association, and American Speech Hearing and Language Association, all of which control vast numbers of researchers and practitioners in fields relating to the Deaf, rarely have Deaf persons on their boards or any mechanisms in which Deaf input could be received and heeded. This results in decisions that hinder instead of help Deaf people in their everyday lives. They proceed under their own set of values that in many cases can harm Deaf people (see Mather & Mitchell, 1994).

This pathological posture is supported by the dominant cultural view that to be Deaf is something less than desirable. The medical profession, as a prime example, established a specialty whose sole purpose is to figure out how to correct problems of the ear. If the medical profession is unable to correct the problems of the ear, we will need teachers who will help the Deaf learn about the world. Then for those Deaf persons who continue to have difficulty learning about the world, we have mental health professionals who will help the Deaf cope with or adjust to the hearing world.

This poses enormous circular problems. How do we understand the idea of coping with the world? The idea of coping suggests there is a set of behaviors that one can learn to reduce the stress in one's life. However, the stress is defined by the hearing professionals, not by Deaf people. The focus of coping results in enhancing those skills felt to be deficient, that is, speech clarity, hearing acuity, and so on. Again those deficits are defined by the hearing professional.

When we hearing professionals fail at enhancing these skills, the fault resides with the problem of deafness and not with the values the hearing professional holds to be true. We now have gone full circle and did not even have to include the Deaf person in our helping framework.

The current discussion regarding cochlear implants is an example of this circular process. Medical, audiological, and manufacturing interests lobbied the FDA to approve the use of cochlear implants with Deaf children. In spite of no real evidence that they work better than a good hearing aid, there have been thousands of cochlear implant procedures done on children to date. Yet, this is a surgical procedure that implants a foreign, untested body into the skulls of children. The engineers who design the cochlear implant, the physicians who perform the surgeries, and the audiologists who test the results carry on these dangerous procedures without any valid evidence that the procedures work and that they enhance the quality of life of the Deaf person.

This type of professional does not have the Deaf person's interests at heart. They are essentially only interested in tinkering with technology. These professionals tend to have no contact with adult Deaf persons and receive little or no input from the Deaf community. They operate on the value that what they do is right and not open to question. In fact, such people receive accolades for performing "miracles" with Deaf children. The media works to support this idea.[1]

Blame the Victim Posture

How do people who bear witness to oppression explain its occurrence? Rather than attempting to make the world more just, as in the case of the freedom fighter, professionals in this posture instead blame the victim. "The Deaf must deserve their lowly status." This stance is phenomenologically similar to the pathological posture.

Codas, for example, have spent much of their childhood bearing witness to such oppression. It is the first author's experience that some may resolve the resulting pain and rage by concluding that either their parents or their parents'

---

[1] In 1994 on "60 Minutes", in a show called "Miracle Workers," there was a portrait of the doctors who surgically implant cochlear implants. These are devices that function like hearing aids but are surgically implanted in the head, instead of inserted in the ear. To date, cochlear implants have been found to be no more effective than high-powered hearing aids.

friends may not have been very intelligent. This is based on listening to the hearing perspective of the Deaf person. The coda may turn this belief into oppressive behavior equal to or greater than the oppressive hearing people who generated it in the first place.

Some reactions to the Nazi persecution of the Jews provides an analogy. There are many Jews (and non-Jews) who criticize the Jewish victims for allowing themselves to have been slaughtered. "Somehow, it must have been their fault." In the case of rape victims, we often hear the sentiment that "she shouldn't have been in that bar in the first place", or "it was her fault for wearing those revealing clothes," and so on.

In the case of our views of Deaf persons, this oppressive behavior may be displayed in a variety of ways. We may perceive Deaf people as somehow lacking, that is, as "retarded" or as "lacking language." There are many other examples. The interpreter who mocks the Deaf person's poor signing skills; the teacher who does not think Deaf people should teach because their speech is not good enough; the professor who thinks that Deaf people should have tried harder to obtain English reading and writing skills equivalent to hearing people; the rehabilitation counselor who encourages Deaf people to accept low paying jobs because they are not motivated to obtain any better; and the psychologist who believes that Deaf people do not have the internal processes to explain how they function in different or difficult situations. Marschark (1994), for example, even suggested that Myklebust may have been right in his view of the Deaf person as being deficient; because they are Deaf, they will always need hearing people to reduce the deficiency.

Oppression, in the form of blaming the victim, may arise from attempts to resolve feelings of inadequacy and confusion when interacting with Deaf people. For example, a psychiatrist knowledgeable about the Deaf relates the following true story:

> A Deaf person requests a prescription for birth control pills from a psychiatrist. She complies and writes a prescription. The Deaf person goes to the pharmacy to fill the prescription. The hearing pharmacist is in a hurry; so, instead of taking the time to figure out what is needed, tells the Deaf person to go to room 510. Room 510 is the mental health clinic.

> The Deaf person, however, persists and tries to convey to the pharmacist what she needs by writing on a piece of paper. The pharmacist is flustered and becomes increasingly anxious. He therefore just waves the Deaf person away.

> By now the Deaf person is becoming upset. Yet the Deaf person goes to room 510, not knowing it is the mental health clinic. In the mental health clinic, the clinicians take care to speak loudly and with exaggerated mouth movements. They do not understand this young Deaf person's speech nor her "waving her hands." She becomes more agitated; because all she is looking for is to fill a prescription for birth control pills! The mental health professionals do not understand why a handicapped person is in their shop looking for birth control pills. They become confused and anxious.

> The mental health professionals then commit the Deaf person, without her consent, to an inpatient mental health ward. It took 3 days for the Deaf person to finally contact the psychiatrist who issued the prescription and get the matter straightened out.

The professionals, rather than admit their own communicative inadequacy, felt that the Deaf person should have been able to communicate through speechreading. The Deaf person was the problem, not that the professionals were unable to adequately communicate. The Deaf person, now labeled as "patient," was given a diagnosis. Unfortunately, this scenario of not accepting responsibility and not showing basic respect for adequate communication is all too common. It is one of the most oppressive, and, in a certain respect, emotionally abusive acts that could be imposed (Mather & Mitchell, 1994).

In the same framework, there are professionals who do not sign well enough to understand the Deaf person yet refuse to use an interpreter. Instead, they blame the Deaf person for communicative inadequacies. Typically, these are hearing professionals who have had difficulty learning ASL or have chosen to use one of the artificial signed languages called Manually Coded English (MCE). Knowing how to sign using MCE does not provide the professionals with the skills to understand many Deaf people. When confronted by Deaf people, such professionals may feel unappreciated while internally knowing they are not very skilled. But they do not attempt to learn ASL or its linguistic structure. As a result, they may attribute various deficiencies to their Deaf students— blaming the victim—based on their previous training, mostly if not altogether from hearing professionals (Lane, Hoffmeister, & Bahan, in press).

This attitude is most evident in the education fields where many teachers (9 out of 10) who work in the mainstream, or non-Deaf centered programs, have learned about the Deaf from books in university training programs and have almost no contact whatsoever with Deaf adults outside of school (Woodward, 1990).

Mather & Mitchell (1994) related the following circumstance that they considered to be a form of communication abuse:

> Hector, age 17, is a deaf boy who attends a mainstream high school program. He uses sign language and attends regular classes with an interpreter. He has shown particular talent in higher math and photography. Recently, Hector visited his school guidance counselor to discuss college applications. Hoping to practice his signing, the counselor, who has only rudimentary signing ability, chose *not* to request an interpreter. Moreover, he felt that the Deaf student "should be bright enough to make do without one."
>
> Without an interpreter, the counselor was unable to understand Hector's requests during the meeting. After several attempts to make himself understood, Hector became frustrated, reached for a pad of paper, and wrote, "LEARN MORE SIGN!" He left the counselor's office angry and frustrated and vowed not to return without an interpreter. (p. 118)

Many Deaf people have had enough of this type of behavior when they were growing up. As adults they tend not to be as forgiving of such professionals as they were when they were younger. The Deaf community's understandable rejection sets the stage for a recursive cycle in which the hearing professionals, rather than tolerate and "contain" the blame, instead do more of blaming the victim. They may complain that Deaf people are ungrateful; "they don't recognize the hard work that we do." The more the Deaf community becomes empowered to act against hearing persons' oppressive behavior, the more hearing professionals experience a loss power and control. As a result, they may overeact by continuing that oppression in an attempt to disempower the Deaf community.

Idealization and Betrayal Posture

In contrast to the pathological and blame the victim postures, many hearing professionals in the beginning stages of their involvement with the Deaf community, idealize Deaf people. On television and in the movies, Deaf persons are sometimes portrayed as idealized giants; giants whose skill and prowess are impossible for the average Deaf person to achieve. Marlee Matlin, a recent and popular example, is seen on prime-time television as a Deaf person who not only understands lipreading at 50 paces but can understand someone signing to her back. Idealization of target groups in the media is not restricted to Deaf persons; consider how women are portrayed in various centerfolds.

This idealization posture, however, sets the stage for hearing professionals to experience betrayal. The idealized image, by definition, is an unrealistic normative stereotype of a Deaf person. When Deaf people are unable to live up to hearing persons' unobtainable expectations, they are viewed as flawed: "This is not what Deaf people should be!" Hearing persons, now perceiving Deaf persons more realistically, may experience a kind of shattering of their "Walt Disney" image and then may experience feelings of being let down or betrayed. This progression from idealization to betrayal is similar to what has been documented in regards to marital partners who experience the shattering of their idealized images of each other, along with subsequent feelings of betrayal (Dym & Glenn, 1993).

There is another common reason that neophyte hearing persons may initially idealize Deaf people. Much of the information professionals have learned from Deaf persons has been through the American Sign Language classes that are so prevalent today. Through this format, we are in awe of a new world that opens up to us in regards to the Deaf culture and community. We are shocked to learn about their historical and present-day rampant oppression. We may uncritically accept whatever cultural generalizations our initial Deaf teachers make. We take what they say as gospel.

This scenario also sets the stage for betrayal. At this date, only some of Deaf cultural information has been verified as having sufficient generlizability, and much of it is still in the form of "cultural notes." As more and more information is collected and the cultural notes become verified, many times the students outgrow the expertise of their Deaf teachers. Students find out that the cultural information they had received from their Deaf teachers may in many instances be incorrect. They may feel duped, angry, and let down because they have been led to believe that all Deaf people think this way.

This juncture also has implications for one's continued motivation to learn

---

[2]"Good Enough" is a sign frame used by Deaf people in both literal and figurative contexts. In its figurative context, it means that a person has done just enough to get by.

ASL. Feeling betrayed by the heretofore "idealized object," we now feel abandoned, angry, and burned out. We become frustrated and alientated in our work environment. It may be at this time that our initial fervor to master ASL often wears off. Beginning signers may feel that after a few classes they have learned "good enough."[2] Intermediate signers do not make the next effort to move to the next step and learn ASL fluently. For example, it is not uncommon for hearing teachers in preschools to have limited signing skills but state that they know enough sign to interact with their Deaf students.

A hearing professional may now lament, "how could they [Deaf people] view me as just another hearing oppressor in their lives?" We may feel hurt, righteously indignant, and rejected. We are ruefully reminded of our outsider status. We come to feel betrayed when learning that the Deaf do not really want nor appreciate our help. And we are confronted with the well-documented cultural phenomena that no matter how proficient we become in ASL, the fact is that we will always been seen as outsiders. Our initial hopes are shattered.

Rather than wallow in feelings of betrayal, professionals must grieve this loss; that it is always the case that full adoption by an oppressed group (Deaf community) of a member from an oppressor group (hearing community) cannot happen. We need to let go of the hope of being adopted by Deaf people and not subtly demand inclusion as a requisite for providing services. Moreover, therapists and other community workers are confronted with the possibility that they someday may not have a place in working with Deaf people. We painfully acknowledge that we cannot depend on Deaf clients for our income and must reconcile that Deaf people may someday not ask us to provide services.

The Cognitive Dissonance Posture

Cognitive dissonance occurs when a person cannot reconcile two or more conflicting beliefs, behaviors, or both. Consider the case of a professional who is beginning to learn sign language. In the second author's experience, having recently graduated from a Clinical Psychology doctoral program, I felt very proud of myself; and, in fact, I felt sort of grown-up, particularly when others referred to me as Doctor. But how was I to reconcile self-pride with the fact that, after several months of study, I couldn't even correctly sign "Good morning, how are you?" to a Deaf person? "Is it signed this way or that way?" "I thought my facial expression was correct." Having been confronted with my novice status, I became confused and anxious.

This is a typical example of cognitive dissonance for many neophyte signers. In this case, the cognition "I am proud and competent" conflicted with the behavior "I can't even correctly sign 'good morning.'" This dissonance produced confusion, anxiety, and lowered self-esteem.

Cognitive dissonance, with its attended confusion and anxiety, may also arise from misinformation about deafness. As stated previously in the idealization posture section, the available information about Deaf people is not always from reliable sources. Hearing professionals are trained in two major ways: through sanctioned, bureaucratic programs focusing on deafness and from informal, nonsanctioned individual Deaf people throughout the world. To our knowledge, it is still rare to find Deaf professionals training hearing professionals in anything other than sign language within the sanctioned programs. Partially as a result, the people who provide the training for professionals to work with the Deaf, in most cases, do not adequately know the subject matter.

Consequently, hearing professionals gain critical knowledge through non-sanctioned interactions with Deaf persons. We earlier described how this situation may encourage us to idealize the Deaf peer/professional. But, more relevant to the present discussion, it may also cause intolerable levels of confusion. We become confused because of questioning what we had earlier accepted as unequivocal truths. For example, one sign language student lamented, "One Deaf leader told me . . . about Deaf culture; but the other Deaf leader said that he was wrong; still another person said . . . about Deaf people. Which is it?" In this case, the dissonance was experienced as a result of two pieces of conflicting information from valued sources.

Cognitive dissonance also reigns when hearing professionals' own behavior comes into conflict with what they learn about the values of the Deaf community. Many professionals set out in a career path with practices that are in conflict with what Deaf people believe to be right. As one clinician put it, "What I have been recommending for twenty years with my deaf patients no longer matches with what I have come to believe is correct."

There are two common examples of this conflict or dissonance. The first example is the different cross-cultural values placed on residential programming for Deaf students. Deaf people refer to residential schools in a positive light and feel that such schools contribute to their feelings of community. Moreover, Deaf people frequently lament that many of their peers who have been in the integrated setting are really much more isolated and traumatized than their peers who attend large day and residential programs for the Deaf.

That view, however, is counter to hearing society's views of public education. Mainstreaming or inclusion is often viewed as temporary and positive by hearing parents and hearing professionals. They see this isolation from Deaf peers and signed language either as a necessary less-than-optimal situation, or they go so far as to see it as good for the isolated Deaf child to try and have hearing friends. In this regard, the number of hearing friends one has sometimes can be seen as a measure of success by hearing professionals who encourage parents to feel this way (Hoffmeister, 1985; 1993; 1994a, 1994b).

A second common value conflict has to do with different cross-cultural views of mental health. Briefly, hearing professionals may be caught between their own beliefs concerning the criteria of emotional adjustment and those of Deaf people. If Deaf children throw temper tantrums and are constantly seeking isolation from hearing authorities (or parents) who are unable to communicate with them, is this an example of emotional maladjustment? If Deaf persons do something not expected within the hearing world—that is, discuss things very bluntly or give the impression that they are overly critical—does this provide evidence of "mental illness?" To both queries, many hearing professionals would respond "yes", whereas many Deaf people disagree.

Effects of Cognitive Dissonance

When we cannot internally reconcile two or more conflicting beliefs or behaviors concerning the Deaf community, we may react in a variety of ways that are potentially dysfunctional for ourselves and destructive to the Deaf community. Anxiety and deflated self-esteem are at the top of the list. As one clinician lamented, "Hearing that Deaf person lecturing us about how we're oppressors and what we've done wrong . . . pulled the rug out from under me!" Yalom (1989), an experienced psychiatrist in the hearing world, reflects on his own struggle, beginning when his new-found beliefs came to conflict with what he did in practice:

> How I long . . . for the certainty that orthodoxy offers. . . . Analysts seem more certain of everything than I am of ANYTHING. How comforting it would be to feel, just once, that I know exactly what I'm doing in my psychotherapeutic work—for example, that I am dutifully traversing, in proper sequence, the precise stages of the therapeutic process. But, of course, it's all an illusion. If they are helpful to patients at all, ideological schools with their complex metaphysical edifices succeed because they assuage the THERAPIST'S, not the patient's, anxiety (and thus permit the therapist to face the anxiety of the therapeutic process). The more the therapist is able to tolerate the anxiety of not knowing, the less need is there for the therapist to embrace orthodoxy. (p. 35)

Unfortunately, many professionals attempt to reduce their anxiety and assaults on their self-esteem by becoming angry at Deaf people. We may complain that the Deaf "do not want our help." We may feel that we have put in a great deal of time and effort into our careers and feel that Deaf people do not appreciate the good work that we do. Yet, we may continue to make decisions without even considering input from Deaf people. Or we become the professionals who search for that Deaf person who not only fits the stereotype (the needy deaf person, or [small d] deaf person who is not a member of the Deaf community) but who agrees with our perspective as hearing professionals.

Other professionals like hearing parents of deaf children may avoid Deaf people. Schlesinger and Meadow (1972) described the "shock, paralysis, withdrawal syndrome," referring primarily to hearing parents who first encounter Deaf people and sign language. Rather than tolerate and "work through" our dissonance between perceived self-competence and incompetent signing ability, we, sometimes literally, walk the other way when a Deaf person approaches.

More seasoned professionals may also avoid Deaf people. Although one's vocation may involve working directly with Deaf persons, there is an avoidance of contact in social or non job-related situations. Many professionals avoid contact with the Deaf community, using the rationalization that "I am too busy." Indeed, some separation of one's job and personal life is psychologically healthy and necessary to prevent burnout; and hearing professionals need to maintain healthy boundaries with the Deaf community. But avoidance of Deaf people is often in the service of anxiety reduction. In this case, professionals may withdraw from contact with persons who differ from their opinion and ignore any information that will conflict with the outcomes they view to be of high value, such as obtaining perfect English skills.

We stated earlier that one's reactions to dissonance may or may not prove dysfunctional and destructive. This section has focused only on negative outcomes. We later elucidate ways that one can make use of such dissonance as a way to develop healthy and respectful ways of working with Deaf people. It is important to emphasize at this point, however, that there is nothing detrimental or oppressive about experiencing dissonance per se. What potentially becomes unhealthy and destructive is when we do not have sufficient awareness and understanding of how such dissonance affects our motivations to be of assistance.

Confusion of Boundaries Posture

Sometimes professionals overidentify and seek to become totally integrated in the Deaf Community. What begins as the outsider decision does not evolve in complexity but becomes one's sole raison d'etre. Such professionals frequent Deaf clubs and Deaf social gatherings, not so much for enjoyment or for an opportunity to enhance their sign language abilities but because they feel they are part of the Deaf Community. Particularly as professionals become more skilled in sign, they may easily fall into this trap.

It is a trap for two reasons. First, as elucidated elsewhere in this chapter, hearing professionals typically do not become part of the Deaf community. Thus, this endeavor is bound to precipitate frustration and burnout, perhaps culminating with the professional leaving the field. Or that stance will lead to a sense of entitlement, thereby leading to becoming blameful or resentful of the Deaf community.

Secondly, as helpers, we have to be mindful of the negative effects of internalizing the trauma that any oppressed minority group, such as Deaf people, has experienced. This phenomena is referred to as *vicarious trauma*. For example, McCann and Pearlman (1990) noted that psychotherapists who work with trauma victims on a regular basis often experience the same trauma symptoms, including burnout and diminished functioning. Boundary regulation becomes particularly important in order to psychologically protect oneself. Gunther and Harvey (1994) found that interpreters frequently sustained vicarious trauma from interpreting situations in which a Deaf person was oppressed. The quality and intensity of the interpreters' responses were influenced by their degree of involvement with the Deaf community and transference acting out with respect to earlier emotionally laden experiences. Common vicarious trauma reactions included fear, anxiety, depression, anger, rage, guilt, shame, and lowered self-esteem. For example, one interpreter felt an overwhelming sense of guilt when the Deaf consumer was ignored during a meeting, even though his interpreting was flawless. The etiology of his guilt had to do with having witnessed his father abuse and ignore his sister during their childhood. In a transferential sense, the deaf consumer had become his sister.

Overidentification also may lead to feeling overneeded. As we gain the respect of the community, our own evaluation of our skills is naturally enhanced. As we come to feel needed, we may unwittingly come to rely on helping others in order to gain self-respect. Such co-dependent behaviors include taking on too many roles. Consider the example of an mainstream classroom interpreter who is sometimes the Deaf student's teacher, tutor, confidant, and counselor. Or consider interpreters who feel that they are so important to the students that they cannot take a personal day off to attend a friend's wedding. Their feeling is that, without their expertise, the students cannot succeed on their own (Nover, 1994).

At the other extreme of overinvolvement and overidentification, some professionals erect too rigid boundaries between themselves and the Deaf community. They put in 40 hours a week working with Deaf people but do not question their work, nor take much pride in it. Typically, this person does not sign very well and has difficulty communicating with Deaf adults and Deaf professionals. This inability to sign well may turn into a rigid pattern whereby all communication is conducted in a manner determined by the hearing professional. Many such persons use English-based signs and assume that "I can make myself understood." It is extremely disheartening for people who have been working with the Deaf for many years to admit they do not have the requisite language skills to be understood by, and to understand, most of the Deaf adults in the community.

We may engage in coalescing activities among themselves in order to gain support for our behavior and maintain our self-esteem. We may gather together in a hearing group that is clearly defined, that is, teachers who support signed English and resist learning ASL. We may informally get together to complain about Deaf people. Whereas it is necessary and healthy to form our own hearing support groups, it is detrimental to engage in groups in lieu of any dialogue or input from Deaf professionals or the Deaf community. This is analogous to the harmful effects of professionals who assist AIDS patients without requesting any input from the AIDS community.

There are many reasons why we may erect too rigid boundaries. We may silently or vocally ridicule Deaf people as in the blame-the-victim posture. We may become angry that "they don't act grateful" as in the pathological posture. There are many possibilities. As the second author illustrates later in this volume in chapter 6, "Utilization of Traumatic Transference by a Hearing Therapist," we may emotionally "numb out" in order to protect ourselves from becoming overwhelmed by Deaf persons' pain. Such "affective constriction" is a common vicarious trauma reaction.

THE LANGUAGE PARADOX

An analysis of the "psychology of the hearing" must specifically address hearing persons' attitudes and behaviors with respect to American Sign Language. The omnipresent debate and lack of acknowledgment regarding what role sign language and spoken language play and their importance to Deaf people are the central, overriding factors relating to the adequacy of all interactions between hearing and Deaf people. However, many times hearing professionals do not even understand the issue of communication and its importance. A hearing person's lack of American Sign Language skills is among the top topics that constantly cause damaging cross-cultural interactions and that cause Deaf persons to harbor acrimony toward hearing persons.

As stated in the first section of this chapter, for many hearing professionals, it was sign language that prompted entrance into the field. However, it has often been those very people who end up changing the language, not for the Deaf but for themselves. Hearing professionals changed from ASL-based education to oral education to make it easier for themselves in the latter part of the 19th century and then, in the mid-20th century, changed from oral to an English-based sign system not for the Deaf but for themselves. This is the central paradox or hypocrisy.

Many of us, except codas, have learned about the Deaf from books and university training programs. Yet in many texts, the fact that most of the Deaf community knows and uses American Sign Language is usually ignored, down played, or denigrated (Hoffmeister, 1993). This central issue then is often left to the individual discretion of professionals who make decisions about how to communicate with their Deaf clients and how to advise hearing parents to communicate with their Deaf children.

Although American Sign Language is taught to thousands of hearing college students, it is not a preferred language within the mainstreamed educational community for use by Deaf persons. It is not explicitly stated as such, but reference to ASL is usually through the use of the term *communication*. When researchers and professionals wish to refer to English, the more respected term *language* is used; but when they wish to refer to some signed form, they use the term communication. The use of the term language as a euphemism for English is misleading to new professionals who are not aware of the historical context. These professionals then may become indoctrinated to this usage and insidiously invalidate ASL in favor of English. Our own language influences our perceptions, as exemplified by the recent movement to use *African American* instead of *Black*, *woman* instead of *girl*, and so on.

To be able to sign covers a wide-ranging set of skills. To be able to sign can mean that a person is able to find a sign (the lexical frame) for each English word as it is spoken. Because there are not lexical signs for all the English words, many signs are created to fill this gap. This type of signing behavior falls under the heading of manually coded English (MCE). To understand MCE you must know English. This makes it easy for the professional but extremely difficult for the Deaf child or adult who is not that fluent in English. These professionals are able to sign or produce a visual form of English but are not understandable to most Deaf persons.

At the other end of the continuum is the person who learns ASL, the language of the community. This person is able to produce ASL in the language structure and forms of the people who use it. To reach real fluency in ASL, however, requires years of training and interaction with Deaf people. Much like non-English languages, one must be encased in the culture and community of users to become fluent. It is here that many professionals who work with the Deaf have difficulty. The time it takes to become a fluent user of the language may conflict with the time needed for career and family obligations. There are many professionals who are working with only a small number of hours dedicated to learning ASL.

Consider the situation of mental health professionals who provide clinical services for Deaf people. Those professionals who are known to have proficiency in sign language receive all the requests for information about the Deaf. Yet there is no systematic way to determine whether those who say they can sign can really sign well enough to perform at the level the job requires. But because the Deaf community has been ignored for so long and hearing people traditionally have not learned to sign, the new generation of professionals who allegedly sign are welcomed. This is especially true in rural areas away from major metropolitan centers.

Moreover, referrals regarding Deaf people are made because a clinician can sign, not because that clinician may have the expertise in the area of inquiry. Hence one begets honors from both Deaf and hearing communities for having expertise in the area of the Deaf. Once referrals begin to come in and solutions to many problems are found, some professionals may feel they know more than they have actually been trained to do. As one becomes more respected for helping Deaf clients, the feeling of having expertise is great.

There is a myth that to transfer information from one field to another, especially with the Deaf, all one has to do is add the sign language. This has been done within the area of psychological testing for the past decade. Yet this is full of pitfalls and errors. There is more than just the language issue that is in need of transfer (Hoffmeister, 1988). Cultural and individual backgrounds combined with the variety of Deaf persons make the "transfer" issue extremely complicated.

HEARING–DEAF COLLABORATION

How can hearing people help promote constructive dialogue across the Deaf and hearing communities? The beliefs, values, and attitudes of the Deaf community need to be delineated. To date the fields working with the Deaf have not taken the time to sufficiently find out what the average Deaf person believes to be true or helpful. It is ironic that in the past 100 years there have been very few surveys and almost no research of Deaf views that could lead to a cultural description of the community; there have been few, if any, surveys as to which beliefs the average Deaf person holds as to how the communities function and interact; and no surveys as to how the general beliefs about educational history, social history, and emotional history have influenced their lives (Kannapel, 1993; Rutherford, 1993).

Consequently, Deaf professionals must create a circumstance to review information that is disseminated to ensure its reliability and validity. Hearing professionals must ensure that the information we receive from Deaf individuals is information applicable to the community as a whole and not to individual circumstances. In short, we must share the goal of obtaining empirical, generalizable "truths."

The beliefs, values, and attitudes of the hearing community also need to be delineated. As Sue, Arredondo, and McDavis (1992) articulated in reference to the ethics of culturally affirmative therapy, therapists must actively engage in the process of becoming aware of their own assumptions about human behavior, values, biases, preconceived notions, personal limitations, and so forth.

However, as with the Deaf community, to our knowledge there have been no systematic studies or treatises on the psychological dynamics, or relational postures, of hearing persons with respect to the Deaf community. As a result, we witness still rampant oppression, including misuse of psychological tests and inappropriate psychotherapy that have been described in this text. The failure to examine the psychology of the hearing makes for a dangerous situation. This chapter is meant to be one step in rectifying that direction.

As we have described, hearing professionals need to examine those reasons that prompted us to enter the field and remain in it; and most importantly, we need to discuss what we do professionally with both Deaf professionals and other Deaf persons. It is a complicated process of acknowledging that one's original, often unconscious, relational postures with respect to Deaf people may not lead to optimal ways of helping. In therapy lingo, we need to "work through" why we are working with Deaf people. We can then remain in the field and do service to it.

The reader interrupts: "But why are you preaching that we hearing people need to work through anything? Maybe you do, but do not put that on me!"

As stated in the introduction to this chapter, there is a lot of merit to the frequently voiced comment, "I'm not an oppressor, and I'm tired of being convicted and executed as guilty, never to be proven innocent!" Although, on our better days, we understand hearing bashing by some Deaf community members as a necessary step in their equalizing the heretofore unequal distribution of power, it nevertheless does not feel good. In fact, it feels damn unfair!

Again, as earlier stated, in our opinion, we hearing professionals need to acknowledge that the content of hearing bashing has some truth for us, at least some of the time. Like it or not, we are members of a majority who have taken, and have been given, a lot of power to define the lives of Deaf persons. We inevitably incorporate at least cultural "baggage" that surrounds us. One is never not prejudiced. Like it or not, one is both a saint and a sinner, an oppressor and a liberator.

Alexander Solzhenitsyn said it best: "If only it were all so simple! If only there were evil people somewhere insidiously committing evil deeds, and it were necessary only to separate them from the rest of us and destroy them. But the line dividing good and evil cuts through the heart of every human being. And who is willing to destroy a piece of his own heart?" (cited in Zweig & Abrams, 1991, p. 176).

Awareness of our "evil or oppressor side"—what Jung termed *the shadow*—can help us not act on such impulses at any given moment. We recall watching one of our favorite Star Trek episodes in which Captain James T. Kirk was asked by an alien to kill another person in order to save his own life. He refused. The alien was puzzled and said, "But I thought you human beings were naturally killers!" Kirk, with his usual dramatic flare, replied, "Yes, humans are indeed killers; but we don't have to kill *today!*" Our challenge is not to oppress *today!*

Let us return to the question of how to establish constructive dialogue between the Deaf and hearing communities? An analysis of the worldviews of each group is insufficient. An adequate understanding of any relationship cannot be accomplished by simply understanding the individual participants, whether these participants are at the micro-level of a dyadic relationship as between a therapist and client, or at the macro-level of society as between two groups of people. As systems theory teaches us, "The Gestalt is more than the sum of its parts." Something else happens when two or more individuals interact; a quality emerges that cannot a priori be predicted. We can only speculate.

We now engage in that speculation, in a sort of "wishful thinking" about what a collaborative relationship with Deaf people might look like. Hearing professionals would not work for the Deaf but with the Deaf. Exchange of information and cross-cultural fertilization will enable both communities to understand their compatible and conflicting approaches to serving the Deaf population. There would be a discussion of real needs, an equal exchange of ideas and information, and a cross-cultural understanding of how hearing and Deaf decisions affect the Deaf community. Deaf people would have equal authority to determine policy and sometimes more authority, especially if the decisions will determine life circumstances of Deaf persons.

Easy to say but hard to do. The thorny issues and challenges are now only beginning to be more clearly defined, in part, because Deaf professionals and lay persons have become more empowered. The issue of power is one such "thorn." Although the situation is changing, all too often, the professional's power has been uncontested. Whatever decision the professional made was deemed right because there has been no sanctioning group to judge its equitibility. The hearing professional too often has been both the judge and jury. As we have detailed, one can become a power person in this business without ever having contact with the people one has power over (Hoffmeister, 1994a, 1994b).

Deaf and hearing professionals must co-create a mechanism for exercising a shifting balance of power. Much like any dyadic relationship, one person or side may hold more power at any given time. Each side must be able to change roles in order to accommodate the shifting contextual requirements. For example, many times the initial relationship between a Deaf and hearing professional is one of teacher–student: The Deaf person teaches the hearing person ASL. Complicated interactions may occur when the hearing student progresses and then begins to provide information to the teacher. This shift requires role flexibility on the part of both the hearing and Deaf person.

Other examples of shifting roles include a clinician who is providing treatment to a current or previous Deaf teacher; a vocational rehabilitation counselor who makes decisions regarding a Deaf client who was at one time his or her teacher; and a classroom teacher who is learning ASL from a former student. In each instance, power is redistributed, at least temporarily. The issue of dual roles for therapists is a complicated one and is discussed in the introduction chapter by Glickman (Chapter 1, this volume) and the chapter by Zitter (Chapter 8, this volume).

These forms of role switching can cause great dissension within the relationship and potentially creates a vulnerability in both parties not encountered before. For example, the hearing therapist who had earlier been taught ASL by his/her Deaf client may note that the now Deaf client is not progressing as quickly as anticipated. The result is role reversal with its inevitable discomfort. Both hearing and Deaf professionals must learn to judge whether they indeed can switch roles. A common impediment is when the hearing or Deaf person had earlier idealized the other and now must see each other in a different light and renegotiate the rules of their relationship.

As another common instance of the need for role switching is when Deaf people are either functioning in an "amateur" framework or are in a profession controlled by hearing people. This structure is typical. Many hearing professionals who are part of this structure should carefully examine how or if they are helping to establish the atmosphere and conditions that facilitate empowerment of Deaf people. Specifically, it is often helpful to establish structured dialogues to mediate cross-cultural conflicts and to point out to the administration when procedures are, perhaps without intent, discriminating against Deaf people.

The major impetus for the shifting of roles and power between Deaf and hearing persons has been Deaf empowerment. Deaf people have begun to become empowered and want rights, authority, and control of Deaf-related programs and institutions. The Gallaudet revolution (Deaf President Now Movement) of 1988 is a quintessential example. Although, at times, empowerment of Deaf persons has been occurring with the support of hearing professionals—ironically with the exception of the Gallaudet revolution—we often find this to be a difficult and confusing process. It is tough to acknowledge that, as a consequence of Deaf empowerment, the Deaf will want our job or at the very least, a share of our job's power. It is inevitably tough to relinquish power.

Part of what makes recognition or Deaf empowerment difficult and confusing at the professional level has to do with the issue of affirmative action. On the one hand, institutions and agencies are appropriately hiring more Deaf people, including at administrative capacities. On the other hand, hearing and Deaf professionals must take care not to hire unqualified Deaf employees simply to fill quotas. West (1993) stated, with reference to the African American community, that many African American people are left wondering if they are being hired based on merit or based on a quota. Affirmative action can empower as well as disempower an oppressed minority. To make matters more confusing, many Deaf people require training to understand various administrative roles and the role of culture within the professional roles.

There remain many unanswered questions. Who has the expertise to train qualified hearing individuals? What are the qualifications of hearing and Deaf persons who can, as objectively as possible, facilitate cross-cultural exchange? Who will sanction these individuals? Who will supervise the hearing people in the business? Will hearing people allow Deaf professionals to supervise them? With the Deaf empowerment on the rise, *can* hearing people work side by side with Deaf people? Can Deaf people begin to trust hearing people?

CONCLUDING THOUGHTS

Hopefully this chapter has provided some elucidation of our psychology; a mirror of sorts that shows us our internal experiences as we first entered and now remain in a field working with Deaf persons. We acknowledged our altruistic, pure side; our healthy and unhealthy narcissistic side; and our dark side, our need to control, pathologize, and blame. We then wondered how we can appropriately work with Deaf people in ever-shifting roles.

Is there a psychology of the Hearing? Of course not, just as there is no psychology per se of the Deaf (Chess & Fernandez, 1980; Lane, 1992). However, there are common psychological dynamics of oppression, as discussed in the introductory chapter, that seem to go with being a member of an oppressor majority as well as an oppressed minority. This chapter has outlined those attitudes, motivations, needs, and behaviors that we hearing persons, as members of the oppressor group, often display.

With this psychological mirror, we can acknowledge both our rational and emotional reactions to changes in the Deaf community. We can co-create a safe place or, in Winnicott's (1965) terms, a "holding environment," with other Deaf and hearing people in order to understand and "contain" our experience. In other words, we can support each other to feel and act in ways that are healthy for us as well as for those Deaf clients that we serve.

REFERENCES

Balkany, T. (1994). A brief perspective on cochlear implants. *The New England Journal of Medicine, 328*, 281–282.

Behhah, R. R. (Ed.). (1973). *Emile Durkheim: On morality and society.* Chicago: University of Chicago Press.

Chess, S., & Fernandez, P. (1980). Do deaf children have a typical personality? *Journal of the American Academy of Child Psychiatry, 19,* 654–664.

Dym, B., & Glenn, M. L. (1993). *Couples.* New York: Harper Collins.

Hoffmeister, R. J. (1985). Families with deaf members. In K. Thurman (Ed.), *Children of handicapped parents* (pp. 112–125). New York: Academic Press.

Hoffmeister, R. J. (1988). Cognitive assessment of deaf pre-schoolers. In T. Wachs & R. Sheehan (Eds.), *Assessment of developmentally disabled children* (pp. 51–74). New York: Plenum.

Hoffmeister, R. J. (1993). *Can bilingual/bicultural education of the Deaf survive special education?* Paper presented at the annual convention of American Instructors of the Deaf, Baltimore, MD.

Hoffmeister, R. J. (1994a). *Cross cultural misinformation: What does special educational say about the Deaf, Working paper 26.* Boston: Center for the Study of Communication and Deafness.

Hoffmeister, R. J. (1994b, October). *Metalinguistic skills in Deaf children.* Paper presented at the Post Milan Conference: ASL and English Literacy. Washington, DC.

Johnson, R. A. (1991). *Owning your shadow.* San Francisco: Harper.

Jordan, J., Caplan, A., Surrey, J., & Stiver, I. (1991). *Women's growth in connection.* New York: Guilford.

Kannapel, B. (1993). *Language choice–identity choice.* Silver Springs, MD: Linstock Press, Linstock Dissertation Series.

Kernberg, O. (1984). *Severe personality disorders.* New Haven, CT: Yale University Press.

Lane, H. (1992). *The mask of benevolence.* New York: Knopf.

Lane, H., Hoffmeister, R. J., & Bahan, B. (in press). *A journey into the Deaf world.* San Diego, CA: Dawn Sign Press.

Lerner, M. (1995). What is a politics of meaning? *Tikkun, 9*(6), 97.

Levine, E. S. (1960). *The psychology of deafness.* New York: Columbia University Press.

Marschark, M. (1994). *The psychological development of deaf children*. New York: Oxford University Press.

Mather, S., & Mitchell, R. (1994). Communication abuse: A sociolinguistic perspective. In B. Snider (Ed.), *Post Milan: ASL and English literacy* (pp. 89–117). Washington, DC: Gallaudet University Press.

McCann, L., & Pearlman, L. A. (1990). *Psychological trauma and the adult survivor: Theory, therapy, and transformation*. New York: Brunner/Mazel.

Meadow, K. (1981). *Deafness and child development*. Berkeley: University of California Press.

Gunther P. E., & Harvey, M. A. (1995). *Vicarious trauma of interpreting*. Paper presented at Breakout Two Conference. Charlestown, SC

Miller, A. (1981). *Drama of the gifted child*. New York: Basic Books.

Myklebust, H. (1960). *Psychology of the deafness*. New York: Grune & Stratton.

Nover, S. (1994, October). *Full inclusion for Deaf students: An ethnographic perspective*. Keynote address given at Inclusion?—Defining quality education for deaf and hard of hearing students, Washington, DC.

Oliner, S. P., & Oliner, P. M. (1988). *The altruistic personality: Rescuers of Jews in Nazi Europe*. New York: The Free Press.

Preston, P. (1994). *Mother, father deaf*. Cambridge, MA: Harvard University Press.

Rutherford, S. (1993). *A study of American Deaf folklore*. Silver Springs, MD: Linstock Press, Linstock Dissertation Series.

Schlesinger, H., & Meadow, K. (1974). *Sound and sign*. Berkeley: University of California Press.

Sue, D. W., Arredondo, P., & McDavis, R. J. (1992). Multicultural counseling competencies and standards: A call to the profession. *Journal of Counseling and Development, 70*, 477–486.

Supalla, T. (1995). *Charles Krauel: A profile of a Deaf filmmaker*. San Diego, CA: Dawn Sign Press.

Vernon, M., & Andrews, M. (1993). *Psychology of deafness*. New York: Longmann.

West, C. (1993). *Race matters*. Boston: Beacon.

Winnicott, D. W. (1965). *The maturational processes and the facilitating environment*. Madison, CT: International University Press.

Woodward, J. (1990). Sign English in the education of Deaf students. In H. Bornstein (Ed.), *Manual communication in America* (pp. 67–80). Washington, DC: Gallaudet University Press.

Yalom, I. D. (1989). *Love's executioner: And other tales of psychotherapy*. New York: Harper Perennial.

Zweig, C., & Abrams, J. (1991). *Meeting the shadow*. New York: Putnam.

Chapter 4

Of Deaf-mutes, the *Strange*, and the Modern Deaf Self

Tom Humphries
University of California, San Diego

His task was not simply one of moving toward the requisite largeness of soul and faith in the value of his experience. He first had to seize the word. His being had to erupt from nothingness. Only by grasping the word could he engage in the speech acts that would ultimately define his selfhood. Further, the slave's task was primarily one of creating a human and liberated self rather than of projecting one that reflected a peculiar landscape and tradition. His problem was not to answer Crevecoeur's question: "What then is the American, this new man?" It was rather, the problem of being itself.

—*Houston A. Baker, Jr. (1985, p. 245)*

In writing of the autobiographical acts of southern slaves, Houston A. Baker, Jr. described a process in which slaves began to talk and to write about themselves not as property but as human. The process is one of creating a self out of "nothingness" as Baker characterized it. Slaves could neither talk nor write about themselves except as it was done by the slaveowner. And in that sense, slaves did not exist. Existence, or being, came about only when slaves could begin to imagine for themselves a separate being from the one created for them by the slaveowner and to find the words to talk about themselves in this new way.

Deaf-mutes of the 19th and the first half of the 20th century had a similar task. Considered at different times in history in various parts of the world to be nonhuman, or at the least, incapable of that which constitutes humanness, deaf-mutes could testify to the difficulty of imaging (as well as imagining) oneself and one's entire subset of humanity into existence. Surrounded by powerful

99

ideas of others that they were less than human, how could deaf-mutes conceive of themselves as anything more. They were not beings in the sense that humans are beings, but rather, exotic life forms patronized, experimented on, and excluded by humans from human society.

The evidence of history tells us that people who hear and speak regard people who do not hear as speechless and voiceless in both the literal and figurative sense. In imagining Deaf people, others have, throughout history, both understood that deaf-mutes neither could say anything nor had anything to say. Deaf-mutes, in suffering this silencing by others, also suffered a denial or silencing of the self. Like illiterate slaves, for whom the only traditions of talk and writing available to them were those of the slaveowner who did not consider them as beings, the deaf-mute had only the traditions of people who hear to emulate.

To have the word, or rather, to have language and traditions of language use such as the ability to tell stories about yourself and, then, to use the word to create a self that is more than the distorted reflection of a hearing people is the task that deaf-mutes have faced in bringing us to this point in history where Deaf people are as confident and certain of their place in humanity as they have ever been.

Yet, this is not saying much. The modern age for Deaf people did not begin until the 1970s. The voice of Deaf people from earlier eras is different in important ways. For one thing, the voice of Deaf people of the modern age is one of cultural explicitness and self-consciousness and a centeredness around a signed language that is not reflected in previous images of the Deaf self. However, the level of tension within communities of Deaf people across the country reflect that, as always, there is no peace or serenity among ourselves about who we are. "What is American Sign Language (ASL)?" "What is Deaf culture?" "Am I Deaf or deaf?" Deaf people ask these pointed questions of each other, of scholars, and of themselves. There are no answers, of course, because the questions themselves are born of evolving images of self and self-representation.

To understand the transition of a Deaf self into modenity, one must trace the development of these images of self and figure out how to alter conventional interactional patterns between Deaf and hearing people that would rapidly become dysfuncitonal to some extent. This chapter attempts to explain the differing theories about Deaf people held by others and by Deaf people themselves and how hearing and Deaf people account for each other. The problem of coming to voice for Deaf people is also an important aspect of the transition and is explored. Questions of authenticity (what/who represents the true Deaf self), the growing need of Deaf people to compel others to listen, and an insistent on telling their own story rather than allowing others to tell their story back to them are all central to the emergence of a new voice for Deaf people. Differences between Deaf and hearing people's ideals and concepts of being (and well-being) are also important and are examined here.

And, finally, Deaf and hearing people's existence in proximity to each other in this new age is not without conflict. How are conflicts played out now that the rules are different? Conflict and coexistence are reflected in discourse that we find within each group and in the interaction between groups. This chapter offers some examples of ways of categorizing this discourse and closes with some considerations for how interaction may need to be shaped for Deaf and hearing people to work successfully together.

A THEORY OF SELF PROPOSED BY OTHERS

It is the nature of human culture that the entirety of the person is accounted for in some way and that there are explanations for variation from the configuration of the "complete" being. Thus, hearing Americans, and hearing peoples of many other cultures, account for Deaf people among themselves in terms of disability or dysfunction. This is the theory that was for many, many years the only one allowed to exist both among hearing people and Deaf people. Deaf people were what hearing people theorized they were. Their accounting of themselves was the accounting of others. The Deaf person's image of self was the image of the hearing person rendered—languageless, speechless, unhearing, cultureless, and *strange*. Strange, not in the sense of "weird" but, as Spiro (1990) indicated, unknowable:

> But if the members of any group G cannot meaningfully and intelligibly translate the cultural concepts of any other group into their own concepts, then for G, other groups are not only strange; *they are fundamentally and irreducibly strange* [italics added]. In short, for G, any other group is . . . wholly Other unknown because unknowable. (p. 52)

Deaf people were unknowable but not uncategorized and undefined. Theories of deaf people abound among people who hear. And in the failure to know, the impossibility to know, hearing people permitted no other theory that Deaf people might have had of themselves to compete. The first theories that Deaf people have had about themselves were those of others. (If Deaf people are Other for hearing people, then hearing people are most certainly Other for Deaf people.)

Because hearing people could not know us, we could not know ourselves. Because the concept of the self was so much a variation of the hearing self, there could be no Deaf self that was any different. How could any Deaf person have a self different than what was imposed? It was unimaginable. There were no other possibilities. Deaf people were just what hearing people said they were.

Like the forces that stripped African slaves of their language and religion, their image of being, and made them pieces of property by pure force of the White man's imagination, Deaf people's self was that imagined by the other. They were even strange to themselves. They identified themselves and described themselves just as the hearing people among whom they lived did. In what other voice could they speak except the hearing person's voice? What resistance is possible when one cannot imagine another self?

How difficult it must have been to Jean Massieu to "defend" his educability (Lane, 1984). How difficult it must have been for John James Flournoy (1865), who advocated for a deaf state in the 1850s, to tolerate the constraints of living a life like a hearing man (without hearing) while being denied a place among hearing men. How difficult it must have been for George Veditz in 1913 to try to convince an unheeding world that signed language was worth preserving. How difficult it must have been for generations of deaf-mutes to live the life of the strange.

THE DEAF-MUTE AND THE SELF: STRANGE BUT TRUE

If being defined by others made deaf-mutes' image of themselves into something exotic and unusual, something special in the sense that they were savants, then it was this very image that bound them together and led to competing images. For in marking deaf-mutes, society threw them together in groups. Out of these groups grew communities and from these communities came remembering. Once remembering began, a competing self began to form and grow. Remembering and reminding, selecting and creating, defining and redefining, remembering and reminding, it took on its own energy. Deaf-mutes in communities, large and small, took the strange and made it unremarkable.

To compete with an identity of languagelessness, deaf-mutes maintained "the sign language" and used it for everyday communication and to remember and remind. To compete with a society that openly discussed their undesirableness in the genetic pool, they procreated and recruited other deaf-mutes into their communities, rejoicing in each lost deaf-mute found and saved. Seeing themselves as incapable of *culture*, they raised their own children in a culture ever becoming richer and richer, stronger and stronger. Deeming themselves not worthy of learning, they never forgot the knowledge of their community from generation to generation. Thinking themselves incompetent to participate in the institutions of society (religion, art, sports), they formed parallel institutions, deaf clubs, athletic organizations, church missions, and literary societies. Being told they were afflicted, they healed themselves by embracing the *strange* and thus made themselves whole.

Hearing people, supremely self-confident in their images of themselves as complete and untouchable and equally confident of the incompleteness of deaf-mutes, were a powerful force. Ideas about the nature of "man," boosted by the sheer numbers of people who hear and a consciousness that could see no other consciousness, were constants in the lives of deaf-mutes. Deaf-mutes, overpowered, accounted for themselves in two ways: first as what hearing people said they were, and second as they were able to "invent" themselves over time and generations. If cultures are in some sense inventions, then hearing people invented themselves and deaf-mutes, deaf-mutes invented themselves and hearing people. Each had to account for the other.

What was the difference, then, between hearing people and deaf-mutes in this respect? The answer to this is that whereas hearing people accounted for themselves as complete and deaf-mutes as deficit, deaf-mutes accounted for themselves as complete and incomplete and for hearing people as complete. This is quite a difference. The deaf-mute self, in its duality, was a marvel of reconciliation. In the same sentence, deaf-mutes could both denigrate and praise their "sign language" (Padden & Humphries, 1988), talk of themselves as uneducated and unintellectual in very educated and intellectual ways, and feel alienated from community while building strong and vital deaf-mute communities. They knew themselves to be strange but could be true to a vision of themselves as unaffected, unmarked, and normal.

This is sometimes quite explicitly stated as in the following from a column called "Glimpse From the Past" that appeared in the January 1994 issue of the *NAD Broadcaster*, the house organ of the National Association of the Deaf.

From the Silent Worker, January, 1954, Vol. 6, No. 9, Page 11

We note, too, that there is frequent reference in the press, over the radio, and on TV, about "normalizing the deaf" by restoring them to society. All of this is well-meaning, of course, but it is getting rather monotonous, to say the least.

In the first place, the deaf are about as normal as the fellow next door. True, he may be able to enjoy life a bit more due to his hearing and his fluent speech, but we think the deaf individual can give him a close race for all-around happiness in the enjoyment of life. (p. 15)

In the second paragraph, there is a grudging admission that hearing people are better. But deaf people are normal. This kind of doublespeak has been a way of reconciling these disparate beliefs about the self and is quite common in Deaf people's talk. (Padden & Humphries, 1988). But reconciliation in talk does not necessarily mean a reconciliation in the self. It may be a way to explain the conflict of self, however, to allow the two views to coexist within the individual without ripping him or her apart.

THE MODERN DEAF SELF

The reconciliation continues among Deaf people of the 1990s. Competing accountings still coexist. Hearing people for the most part still hold to their accounting of deaf people as flawed. Some things have changed, however. There is some re-inventing going on that talks of the sign language as American Sign Language and a concession that, perhaps, it is a language after all. There is a sense that the communities of Deaf people might actually be rooted in culture and ethnicity.

Deaf-mutes are no longer "deaf-mutes" or "the deaf" but "Deaf people" just as "Negroes" are no longer "negroes" or even "Blacks" but "African American," and "girls" are no longer "girls" but "women." For Deaf people, there has been a great rejection of hearing people's accounting of Deaf people. The old dual accounting of incomplete/complete exists, but it is increasingly politically incorrect to acknowledge it. Deaf identity is now defined very sharply and debated in explicit terms. Individual by individual, we are deciding who is Deaf and who is not based on a new public, and as yet, fuild, prototype. Everyone who was Deaf before is still Deaf, but, nevertheless, we are putting each other to the test applying criteria of authenticity that are hard to pin down exactly but that are rigorously applied.

For example, is a deaf person who went to a hearing public school, transferred to a residential school for deaf children for the last 2 years of high school, learned ASL beginning at the age of 15, and is now a student at Gallaudet University *really* Deaf? Many Deaf people debate the answer to this. Another common question among Deaf people recently has been, "What is ASL?" We are asking what the sign language is and getting lots of different answers. Yet, with a few natural changes in vocabulary, the sign language continues to be used as it has been for generations. Why do we ask ourselves this type of question? It is as if a questioning and cleansing must take place before we can trust those things that we are. The modern Deaf self must search its collective memory and make sure that we have forgotten the self created by others and have remembered the "real" sign language and the "real" Deaf self.

When once the only public definitions of the Deaf self were those of doctors, audiologists, educators, and psychologists, now public definitions of the deaf self are those of anthropologists, ethnographers, and Deaf people themselves. The modern Deaf self is about identity, cultural identity but also about public face and otherness.

Public face is the way that we wish others to see and think of us. In "seizing the word," the writers of the slave narrators began to exert a public face that sprang from their own minds, not from the minds of others. Deaf people of the 1960s and 1970s not only began to redraw their public face in a different image but to do something equally important. They reached a stage that other peoples in similar situations had also encountered: "For black women our struggle has not been to emerge from silence into speech but to change the nature and direction of our speech. To make a speech that compels listeners, one that is heard" (hooks, 1990b, p. 337).

To compel listeners, yes. A self cannot exist if it is not heard. Deaf people have had to create voices, learn to hear their own voices, and now it remains to compel others to listen.

Perhaps it is too strong to say that deaf-mutes both literally and figuratively had no voice. Literally, many deaf-mutes could speak aloud. And, figuratively, there were individuals who "spoke out" in a voice that seemed lifted out of the modern age. What Massieu, Flournoy, Veditz, and some others had to say certainly resonate today (Padden & Humphries, 1988). But it cannot be denied that for the great majority of deaf-mutes, they could only speak of themselves and their social condition in the voice of the other, hearing people. This was the same as having no voice at all, or worse, of having a voice that belied one's own humanness. And even if they did speak in a different voice, it could not be heard.

The presence of a new and different voice and the dominance of this voice over the voice of the other has been an important change in Deaf people's lives. But it is an artifact of another change: Deaf people's relationship to otherness. To speak in the voice of the other, to possess a self that was the creation of the other, was the fate of deaf-mutes. But if deaf-mutes internalized the other and made it their own self-image, then what Deaf people are doing today is establishing a new relationship with the other. Much of the deaf–hearing tension that has sprung up over the past few years has been about control of institutions such as schools and colleges and social service agencies. But a great deal of the tension has been about who speaks for Deaf people and the type of self that is portrayed by this speech. The conflict that grows out of this struggle is, in turn, about separation of the self from other.

In the beginning, when Deaf people of the 1970s were trying to make sense of a new self-consciousness, there was a heavy reliance on changes in the way hearing people were talking about them. The subconscious knowledge that deaf-mutes had about themselves, that they were a cohesive and close-knit group of sophisticated signers who shared a history, began to converge with descriptions of them by others. Others began to talk about deaf-mutes as a language minority and as a community with an ethnic experience. The science of hearing people, notably linguistics and anthropology, began to talk about ASL as a language and Deaf people as a culture. Working with their own changing vision of themselves and hearing people's new theory of them, Deaf people's new self emerged. However, it was still in many respects the other who defined.

In the 1970s and part of the 1980s, it was still the researchers and the voice of researchers, most of them hearing, who defined Deaf people's image of self. Deaf people's relationship to the other was still the same as it always had been. Hearing people became caught up in the rush to redefine Deaf people. Scholars and nonscholars alike rushed to embrace the ideal of equality and equivalence between Deaf and hearing cultures, ASL and English, and Deaf person and hearing person. For hearing people, defining deaf-mutes in the way that they did was part of hearing people's process of self-definition (Lane, 1992). How could a Deaf self-definition not be influenced by the great power of this change among hearing people? Dominated for centuries by the voice of the other, Deaf people had no problem now in adopting the new language of the other in talking about themselves. Only now the other had adopted a new story, one that reflects the story Deaf people have always tried to tell themselves but have been unable to sustain without internal and external conflict. It remained for Deaf people to go one step further and recognize that true voice means not telling back the stories of others about themselves:

> No need to hear your voice when I can talk about you better than you can speak about yourself. . . . I want to know your story. And then I will tell it back to you in a new way. Tell it back to you in such a way that it has become mine, my own. Re-writing you I write myself anew. I am still author, authority. I am still colonizer, the speaking subject and you are now at the center of my talk." (hooks, 1990a, p. 343)

Thus, the modern Deaf self has come to this. Not stopping at the "telling back" of their story by hearing people, they have placed distance between the Deaf self and other. But it has not been easy, and confusion and tension still reign. Deaf people debate Deaf people about who we are and what we are. Deaf people dispute hearing people about who we are. The distance is necessary because the internalized other still remains within each of us, threatening to dominate once again.

DIFFERENCES

The differences between Deaf and hearing peoples' theories about each other are quite real, and not imagined. How do the competing accountings that Deaf people and hearing people have of themselves and Deaf people differ? A few of these differences are discussed here.

Ideals of Completeness

What constitutes completeness? For hearing people, Deaf people are incomplete beings. Through this cultural filter, Deaf people will always be one down on hearing people. Nowhere are these ideals so explicitly evident than in the languages of Deaf and hearing peoples. In translating from language to language, and in particular from ASL to English, meaning is attempted to be equated, and often it reveals the gap between perceptions and the realization that there are no equivalences. There is no word in English to refer to Deaf people that does not carry a meaning that is foreign to Deaf people themselves. The idea of disability or lacking something is so attached to the English words used for Deaf people (*deaf, hearing impaired, hard of hearing, communicatively handicapped*, etc.) that there is simply no escaping it. On the other hand, there is little possibility of translating Deaf people's name for themselves into English. *The people* or *us* may began to convey the meaning but lacks the richness of the true meaning of the sign (often translated as *deaf*) that Deaf people use for themselves. (Padden & Humphries, 1988).

The English names for Deaf people are tied by history and perception to ideas of incompleteness, and it is difficult for English speakers to totally change from using the word deaf to mean someone with a hearing loss to an alternate meaning of someone of a particular community and worldview. Deaf people have no such problem, except in the sense that they are aware that their sign for themselves (glossed as DEAF) has the meaning of "hearing loss" for many people. To actually denote this meaning in the sign, Deaf people have to establish a context, alter the sign itself to be a little more explicit, or change it to another sign that is more specific to the meaning of hearing loss such as signs glossed as DEAF (2 hands) or EAR-SHUT.

Further, to describe a Deaf person, English speakers have little recourse to other vocabulary. The most common phrase, "can't hear," assumes again a dysfunction. Less offensive, but still loaded, is "doesn't hear." This is not the way Deaf people think of themselves and, as a description, it only reinforces the opposing sensibilities of Deaf and hearing peoples.

The Value of Being

One of the most difficult perceptions that both Deaf and hearing people have to deal with is the nature of the *being* that is the Deaf way of being. Because hearing people begin with an ideal of incompleteness in regard to Deaf people, is Deaf people's world an equal one? Are Deaf people, instead, marvels of adaptation? Have they adjusted to their condition in amazing ways? Do they sign because they cannot speak? Are they examples of the plasticity of the human being? Have they risen from the ashes of hearing people? It is one thing to see Deaf people as incomplete beings; it is another to believe there are other possible worlds, of equal quality and value.

To come to being, the deaf-mute certainly had to wrestle with the notion that all being begins from a single prototypical hearing human. If this is the way being begins, then yes, Deaf people are the descendents of a hearing Adam and Eve. Yet, what if Deaf people are not descendents of a hearing Adam and Eve but taken directly from the clay itself? What if they sign because this is the language of their community, no more special or exotic than English to a hearing American? What if the Deaf self sees hearing people as *strange* in the same way that hearing people view Deaf people? What if Deaf people are as supremely confident of the originality of their biology as hearing people are? Two sets of views of what constitutes the nature of being Deaf reveal crucial difference between Deaf and hearing people. For hearing people, the characteristics of their theory of Deaf people, rooted in a theory of incompleteness, are:

1. Contrastive/oppositional (hear/don't hear, speaking/mute, complete/incomplete, self/other)
2. Pathological (having physical and developmental conditions, needing medical intervention or prosthetic intervention, behavior is related to condition)
3. Adaptive (sign, use prosthetic interventions, adapt resources, use special procedures, systems, and technology)
4. Esoteric (noble, special, think without language, visual world, miracles of adaptation, needing to be taught and brought to life)

These can be compared to views Deaf people have about themselves:

1. Contained (self-knowing, having community, whole, complete)
2. Marked/unmarked (one with Deaf people but immersed among others, at risk)
3. Descendant (recipients and transmitters of ways of being, language)
4. Experiential and aesthetic (having moral imperatives and value systems based on experience that define a good life for themselves and the children, possessing concepts of beauty and ethics defined by experience, abstract creators)

These differences reveal the difficulty that hearing people may have in overcoming a deep-rooted sense of unequal worlds when it comes to Deaf people.

The Concept of Wellness

Others may never completely be able to let go of an idea that there is no naturalness to being Deaf. For these people, the Deaf self will always be housed in a body that does not work, is not well. In this regard, the distance between how Deaf people view their bodies and how hearing people view Deaf people's bodies makes the Deaf self unknowable to people who hear.

Two ways to approach the concept of wellness that are very instructive in understanding the distance and difference between Deaf and hearing peoples are: (a) the competition for ownership of Deaf people's bodies and (b) the relationship of the pathology of the body to the self.

Who owns the Deaf person's body? Do hearing parents own it for the first 18 years at least? Do educators hold it in trust for parents for most of this time also? Do doctors and other medical intervention personnel such as audiologists and speech therapists own it more than Deaf people themselves?

We are all familiar with the artifacts of the competition for Deaf people's bodies. Speech and hearing science, surgical procedures, faith healing, immersion techniques such as oral and mainstream education, brain studies, and so on. At no time, even to the present, have Deaf people, as a group, been in control of their bodies. Individual Deaf people on reaching adulthood sometimes manage to take control sufficiently to preserve their bodies in an image of wholeness, and insofar as they are able to do this, they have hope of attaining and maintaining physical well-being. But do others even know that ownership or Deaf people's bodies is an issue?

If Deaf people have had difficulty with others owning their bodies more than they do themselves, they have had even more of a struggle formulating a self that is not an extension of this nonfunctioning body. Would a mentally ill Deaf person's illness disappear if he were not deaf? Are there unique sets of psychological phenomena that attach themselves to people who do not hear?

This debate over whether there is a "psychology of the deaf" (Lane, 1992) is not about whether there is a paradigm that we call a mentally "well" deaf person and another paradigm that we call an "ill" deaf person but how these concepts of wellness and illness interact with a pathology called a "hearing loss." In hearing people, concepts of wellness and illness are associated with socialization, heredity, trauma, and even brain chemistry. Women have had certain psychological attributes related directly to their biology. Gay men and lesbians have also had attributes associated with their biology. In women, their biology was thought to dictate emotions, moods, and sometimes mental illness. In gay men, the converse was thought to be true; a psychological condition caused biology to go haywire. In Deaf people, a biological condition is thought to dictate social behavior, personality types, moral development, and maturity development among other things (Lane, 1992).

For deaf-mutes, the self as given to them by others started out unwell. The self was that of a hearing person without hearing. A self that was made alien by virtue of being unable to hear speech and other sounds and ultimately, made uncentered by being marginalized by the people who controlled their bodies. The deaf-mute self could only be made well again by "adjusting" to the fact of a loss and the place others made for him or her in their society. The modern Deaf self struggles with marginality but is centered, sometimes subconsciously, sometimes consciously, in a complex and schematic knowledge of self and the world (D'Andrade, 1990) unimaginable to those who see Deaf people as disabled.

Thus, an understanding of centeredness and wellness in Deaf people can only be approached by hearing people when hearing people no longer see Deaf people as extensions of their own biological imperatives. An African American is not a non-White person, a woman is not a nonman, and a Deaf person is not a nonhearing person.

Ideals of Solidarity

The place of the other in relation to the self in deaf-mutes was sometimes so close that the two were confused as one. The modern Deaf self is more distant from others' models of the Deaf self. Solidarity, or the stressing of the same in the same but different approach to intercultural contact, may threaten the modern Deaf self that is not far removed from a self proposed by others at this point in history. What this means is that in intercultural interactions, there is sometimes a natural tendency for one party to break down differences, to asset sameness, to assume that despite cultural differences, underneath the skin, we are all the same. It is this assertion of the sameness that is threatening to the Deaf self because most Deaf people are still struggling with or can remember what it was like to be totally dominated and defined by others. As is often the case in interethnic interaction (Scollon & Scollon), 1982), distance, rather than solidarity, may be desired by Deaf people and demonstrated in very active ways including aloftness, avoidance, and hostility in encounters with hearing people.

This is evident in the growth of "deaf only" activity in the past decade. Retreats, conferences, caucuses, and other such attempts of Deaf people to get together with themselves to the point of explicitly excluding hearing people are symptomatic of a need to let Deaf people be Deaf people without worry of influence from or accommodation of hearing people's needs. Some see this as separatism, but it is far from that. Separatism is a particular ideology that is not normally reflected in these types of meetings except when separatism, itself, is the issue. These attempts for Deaf people to take their own counsel are not separatist activities but, rather, are strong acts of marking of distance between Deaf and hearing people that Deaf people feel are necessary to their well-being. That this offends many hearing people is an indication of the difference in perception of the goal of interaction between Deaf and hearing people.

Although hearing people may think that Deaf people's goal is to be included in society, it is more likely that Deaf people's goal is one of maintenance of boundaries between cultures and a search for accommodation that allows the Deaf person to remain true to the self. When acted out in dramatic ways such as deaf only gatherings of Deaf people, solidarity is challenged and distance becomes so real, that an uncomfortable tension arises. Solidarity between Deaf and hearing people that seems to be highly valued by hearing people and often sought in friendships, mixed marriages, cross-cultural counseling, and psychotherapy may not, in Deaf people's view, be a desirable or realistic goal given the nature of the history of dominance by the other in Deaf people's lives. This is not to say that strong relationships do not develop between Deaf and hearing people but that deference (discussed more fully in a later section), not solidarity, is the most likely path to successful and lasting understanding between Deaf and hearing people at this point in history.

CONFLICT AND COEXISTENCE

Given these differences and Deaf people's own internalization of these differences, conflict is a possibility and a reality both within Deaf people's community and with others outside the community. Coexistence between Deaf and hearing people rests very strongly on reconciling these differences. As was mentioned earlier, the deaf-mute self was built on the assumption that the necessary reconciliation would happen *within* the Deaf person. Deaf people had to find ways to explain things and talk about things that gave hearing people their due. Hearing people were for the most part unconscious of Deaf people's ingenuity in maintaining within themselves two wholly different theories and, thus, finding ways to maintain coexistence with hearing people.

But the modern Deaf self is less interested in maintaining this type of duality. Conflict is pushed outward into the space between Deaf and hearing people, and hearing people are asked to confront differences on a conscious level. The modern Deaf self does not make the differences go away.

There are many ways that Deaf and hearing people act out the fundamental conflict over self. Here is a sampling:

1. Naming of Deaf people. Should they be called deaf or hearing impaired? Is hard of hearing okay?

2. Differing views of competence to control own institutions. Examples: The fight for a Deaf president at Gallaudet University, the push for Deaf directors and superintendents of schools and organizations, Deaf majorities on Boards of Directors, the "of, by, and for the deaf" political movement.

3. Struggle over control of the lives of deaf children. Examples: How will they be educated? Which language? Which culture? Who will teach them? Should young children be surgically implanted with electronic devices?

4. Argumentation over status inequality of ASL/English and Deaf people's/hearing people's culture. Examples: Legislative proposals for official recognition of ASL, demands for ASL interpreting as opposed to signed English interpreting.

5. Discriminatory/reverse discriminatory practices. Examples: Job descriptions that favor Deaf people versus job descriptions that favor hearing people, "hearing people need not apply" attitudes, hearing people can't teach deaf culture percepts, "we would like to hire a Deaf person but we can't find any qualified for the job" rationales.

Many of the ways that Deaf and hearing people act out the conflict over the Deaf self are played out in specific kinds of language and talk:

1. Accusatory talk that includes oppressor/oppressed, colonizer/colonized, powerless/empowered visions of blame and of "us" versus "them."

2. Challenge talk that tests the other's belief system. Example: "If you had a pill that would make you hearing, would you . . . . ?" "If you think it's okay to operate on deaf children to make them hearing, then it must be okay for Deaf people to operate on their hearing children to make them deaf."

3. Routinized expressions of problematicity or "griping" about the other. Examples: Complaints about lack of competence in ASL or in English, or "Deaf people have no tact," or "How will you get a job if you don't learn English?" or "You don't understand Deaf people."

Much of this conflict comes about because subordination and status inequality are not tolerable to a rising middle class of Deaf people. As the middle class of Deaf people grows, and it was quite small until the middle of the 20th century, so does the ideals and expectations of the group, thus increasing the likelihood of conflict. As more and more hearing people become aware of the changing status of Deaf people, there is much more possibility of conflict because many do not accept the underlying assumptions about language and culture that are the foundation of the new Deaf self.

Deaf people have to a large extent always maintained parallel lives while living with others (Padden & Humphries, 1988). But this has been quite a subconscious process, and coexistence in the past was built on Deaf people's acquiescence and accommodation to the self-imagining proposed by hearing people. With Deaf people less and less likely to accommodate and the modern Deaf self still in the process of imagining itself, some new models of Deaf–hearing interaction will inevitably evolve.

INTERACTIONAL CONSIDERATIONS

Earlier it was mentioned that solidarity, or the emphasizing of the sameness of Deaf and hearing people, threatens the new Deaf self. Yet there is a need to find some commonality or mutual knowledge of the other between Deaf and hearing people so that successful interactions can take place. Everyone wants to know which interactional pitfalls to avoid.

The establishment of difference is a strong current in Deaf–hearing interactions at this point in history. Everyone wants to see a difference. All of us want descriptions of how Deaf people's culture is different. In fact, difference is demanded. An example, for years there was a strong push in research on ASL to find that it was very different from English (in word order, for example). If this difference could not be found, then ASL was not a language, but bad English. The fact that ASL has basically the same word order as English (as do many other languages) has taken a long time to finally be accepted.

For another example, Deaf people have felt compelled to emphasize that their world is visual whereas hearing people's word is auditory. Deaf people see, hearing people hear. There is little to actually say about this difference, but there *must* be a difference.

The reason for this insistence that there must be a difference is because the old deaf-mute self is very much a presence in U.S. society. In order to legitimatize the new Deaf self, difference must be clear and must be articulated in ways that differences between other groups may not have to be. It was said earlier that to seek sameness, commonality, or solidarity in intercultural interaction between Deaf and hearing people may not be a realistic strategy at this particular time in Deaf–hearing relations.

The obverse of solidarity in discussions of interethnic communication is deference (Scollon & Scollon, 1982). Deference, a type of politeness system that recognizes the autonomy of Deaf people (and hearing people for that matter) and assumes a low power differential between Deaf people and hearing people, seems to be the type of interactional strategy that is better suited for the context in which Deaf and hearing people find themselves today. Increasingly, over the past decade, Deaf people have found ways to tell hearing people to "back off," to stop defining Deaf people, and to stop tampering with Deaf people's bodies. They have not always been polite about it. But the sentiment, regardless of how strongly it has been expressed, has been clear: Distance is needed.

This is not to imply physical distance but a distancing of wills, self-images, and voice. There needs to be an acknowledgment in the interaction that there is little power differential between the two parties to the interaction as well. The relationship of hearing people to deaf-mutes was one of dominance and acquiescence, one of great power on the part of hearing people and powerlessness on the part of deaf-mutes. Status equality is one way to reduce power differential. In intimate kinds of interactions, such as teaching, counseling, or psychoanalysis involving Deaf people as the student or the client/patient, control of the context of the interaction may be one of the ways that Deaf people try to attain status equality.

There are several ways that Deaf people may attempt to gain control. One of these is to control the placement of "the problem." Gone is the old deaf self taking responsibility for communication failure or misunderstanding of purpose. The problem is not that the Deaf person is deaf (and, thus, having problematic communication, language, and psychological profiles). The problem instead is the hearing persons lack of ASL fluency, lack of understanding of Deaf culture, lack of experience with Deaf people, lack of knowledge of how hearing people oppress Deaf people, or lack of solutions that work for Deaf people.

Another way might be to control language use. By insisting that the communication used in the interaction be in ASL, the sense of comfort and ease is shifted to the Deaf person and the burden of second language communication or reliance on a sometimes less than fluent ASL interpreter is shifted to the hearing person. If there is to be a struggle with language equality, let the hearing person, not the Deaf person as in the past, make the effort and try to maintain a sense of power while doing so.

Controlling language use is most commonly seen in Deaf people's attempts to have hearing people learn ASL rather than some signed English system, in attempts to have ASL as the primary language used in meetings and conferences, in pushes for interpreters to use ASL, and in attempts to require that teachers and therapists be fluent in ASL. But it is also evident when Deaf people choose not to adapt their signing or communication style in an attempt to be understood by hearing people. The decision to stay with ASL and normal conversational style in ASL rather than code switch to a contact language or to use speech involves a new relationship between Deaf and hearing people. It implies that there is no longer a basis for it always being the Deaf person who adapts his or her language in a communicative interaction between a Deaf and hearing person.

Related to this is the high expectations of an interpreter in terms of being able to move between ASL and English without the Deaf person having to adapt his or her language use. Control of language use has taken on such an edge that many hearing signers and interpreters find themselves, to their acute embarrassment, being judged on their ASL competence using a more exacting standard. Pressure to be competent in ASL or use an interpreter who is competent in ASL is very much a part of the landscape between Deaf and hearing people at this point in history.

Yet another way to achieve status equality (and sometimes skew it in favor of the Deaf person) is to control the moral high ground in the relationship. One of the side products of the emergence of the modern Deaf self is that hearing people are supposed to and, in fact, may actually feel guilty for the way that Deaf people have been and are treated in society. A sense of moral superiority, whether real or imagined, is a very powerful weapon in the hands of many Deaf people. In some contexts, Deaf people may try to achieve control by relying on the hearing person's feeling that hearing people deserve whatever Deaf people want to dish out at this point. This makes Deaf people feel confident that they can get away with "bashing" hearing people. Indeed, hearing people have a problem of knowing when and how to challenge Deaf people's bashing and their sometimes incorrect and ideologically suspect statements about hearing people in general.

Historically, hearing people have held the moral advantage because of the "good works" that they do with people who do not hear. Every deaf-mute knew that everything that hearing society made available to them was an act of kindness. Harlan Lane (1992) referred to the "mask of benevolence" behind which hearing people have injured Deaf people while professing to "help" them. Another way to look at this, however, is in the way that hearing people make themselves morally superior by being the ones who are helping. To share or even to claim the moral high ground, Deaf people speak often in the language of the oppressed minority. The discourse between Deaf and hearing people at this time seems filled with such phrases as "discrimination," "oppression," "inequality," and more recently "audism" (Humphries, 1977). Once the moral high ground shifts, the interaction takes on a different context, and control is attainable for Deaf people.

What do we do now? To change the context of the interaction and to attain some equality of control, both parties in the interaction need to view the interaction as an intercultural interaction. This involves placing the problem in the context of the different languages, communicative intents, and worldviews involved in cross-cultural discourse, not in the Deaf person or the hearing person. Neither Deaf people nor hearing people are necessarily skilled at intercultural interactions, and so in formal relations such as teacher–student, counselor–client, or therapist–client, it may be up to the professional to obtain the sensitivity and skill required to avoid breakdowns in intercultural communication.

It is possible that controlling the context of the interaction between Deaf and hearing people is more likely to produce results intended or hoped for my Deaf people just because Deaf people may feel more in control of possible outcomes. Solutions proposed by others are often not possible solutions in the eyes of Deaf people (Padden & Humphries, 1988). For Deaf people, ownership of the solutions may be more important for the moment than the actual results. An argument can be made that this is the way it should be, that this is the stage of the process of coming to voice in which Deaf people happen to be. Gaining control may be paramount at this particular time in history.

In summary, the strength of relationships that need to be built between Deaf and hearing people depend largely on several things: acknowledgment of differences; deference to each other's need for autonomy; acknowledgment of a struggle to find a new balance of power after a long history of inequality; a new paradigm of control in cross-cultural relationships, especialy in regard to language and communication; and, finally, the modern Deaf person's ability to see hearing people as having solutions that don't remind them of or return them to the deaf-mute life of the past. It is this last aspect that is crucial. Deaf people have to choose to believe and trust in the possibility that hearing people may be able to help them without couching the help in a defunct ideology of the strangeness of Deaf people.

COMPETING ILLUSIONS

Is Deaf culture an illusion, an extension of the pathology, an adjustment to being without hearing? It is easy to dismiss "culture" as a delusion of Deaf people. After all, the whole idea of culture and of a modern Deaf self can be made moot by the elimination of the hearing loss, can it not? Perhaps, but as we approach genetic selectivity, are we not each of us possibly moot? The biomedical discourse of the past that describes not a whole Deaf people, but a suffering deaf-mute people is a much more terrible delusion than any image Deaf people might create for themselves. Only through control of the image of the self can Deaf people make the *strange* normal.

REFERENCES

Baker Jr., H. A. (1985). Autobiographical acts and the voice of the southern slave. In C. T. Davis & H. L. Gates, Jr. (Eds.), *The slave's narrative* (pp. 242–261). New York: Oxford University Press.

D'Andrade, R. (1990). Culture and personality: A false dichotomy. In D. K. Jordan & M. J. Swartz (Eds.), *Personality and the cultural construction of society* (pp. 145–160). Tuscaloosa: University of Alabama Press.

Flournoy, J. J. (1856). Mr. Flournoy to Mr. Turner. *American Annals of the Deaf and Dumb, 8,* 120–125.

Flournoy, J. J. (1858). Reply to objections. *American Annals of the Deaf and Dumb, 10,* 140–151.

Glimpse from the past. (1994, January). *NAD Broadcaster, 16*(1), 15. Silver Spring, MD: National Association of the Deaf.

hooks, b. (1990a). Marginality as site of resistance. In R. Ferguson, M. Gever, T. Minh-ha, & C. West (Eds.), *Out there: Marginalization and contemporary cultures* (pp. 341–343). Cambridge, MA: MIT Press.

hooks, b. (1990b). Talking back. In R. Ferguson, M. Gever, T. Minh-ha, & C. West (Eds.), *Out there: Marginalization and contemporary cultures* (pp. 337–340). Cambridge, MA: MIT Press.

Humphries, T. (1977). *Communicating across cultures (deaf/hearing) and language learning.* Unpublished doctoral dissertation, The Union Institute, Cincinnati, Ohio.

Lane, H. (1984). *When the mind hears.* New York: Random House.

Lane, H. (1992). *The mask of benevolence.* New York: Knopf.

Padden, C., & Humphries, T. (1988). *Deaf in America: Voices from a culture.* Cambridge, MA: Harvard University Press.

Scollon, R., & Scollon, S. (1982). *Narrative, literacy and face in interethnic communication.* Norwood, NJ: Ablex.

Spiro, M. (1990). On the strange and the familiar in recent anthropological thought . In J. W. Stigler, R. A. Shweder, & G. Herdt (Eds.), *Cultural psychology: Essays on comparative human development* (pp. 47–61). New York: Cambridge University Press.

Veditz, G. (1913). *The preservation of the sign language* [Film]. Silver Spring, MD: National Association of the Deaf.

Chapter 5

The Development
of Culturally Deaf Identities

Neil S. Glickman
Mental Health Unit for Deaf People
Westborough State Hospital
Westborough, MA

Given the dominance of the medical–pathological model of deafness, what process must Deaf people undergo in order to understand themselves not as disabled people, but as people who are culturally different? What are the elements of a culturally Deaf identity and how might it develop? Because I am not deaf, and certainly not culturally Deaf, I have tried to answer these questions in two ways: firstly, by developing a broad understanding of how self-affirming cultural identities develop in other oppressed minority communities, including those I belong to; and secondly, by paying close attention to what culturally Deaf people themselves say about their identity. As a hearing person, my perspective is that of a sympathetic observer of Deaf culture.

In the introductory chapter, I presented an overview of cultural and racial identity development (C/RID) theory. In this chapter, I present a model for how I believe culturally Deaf identities develop in deaf people. I begin by citing the remarks of a prominent oral educator of deaf children because these remarks demonstrate just how central identity concerns are to deaf educators. Indeed, the oppressive positions these educators have taken regarding identity in deaf children have made them the traditional nemeses of the organized Deaf community. Next I review briefly the only major work by a Deaf author to address explicitly and in detail the issue of identity development in Deaf people. I then cite some prominent spokespersons for Deaf culture, culling from their remarks what I take to be the organizing themes around which Deaf identities develop. Finally, I present the model for how I think cultural deafness may develop.

Identity and Deaf Education

The comments of Leo Connor (1972), then President of the Alexander Graham Bell Association for the Deaf, illustrate the context in which the struggle of deaf people for self-definition has occurred. Connor's address was remarkable for the frankness with which he acknowledged how central questions of identity were to the famous controversy over methods in deaf education. Connor noted:

> Whether the deaf child grows up to be deaf or can live his life with a hearing loss is really what the education of deaf children is all about. It is why there is so much heat and seriousness about this question of teaching methodology. We are not debating a method for classrooms; we are deciding as an administrator or an educator or as parents whether a handicapped child shall be a member of a deaf subculture or a hearing impaired person whose philosophy and life objectives are as wide as those of the rest of the human race. (p. 524)

Connor described a "Bill of Rights" for deaf children. One of these rights was that "every deaf person must live and develop in the mainstream of society" (p. 524). This was an explicit call to inculcate a hearing identity in deaf children:

> This is the crux of my credo and hope: that every deaf child should understand and be understood by the hearing world not as a deaf person, but as a human being who has a hearing loss. (p. 524)

> I believe that deaf persons must have identity norms like everyone else and that schools and society have, up to the present, created a subculture for the deaf which feeds upon its own frustration and satisfactions. (p. 525)

> We should hope and work for the day when there is no subculture of the deaf but rather differences which are acknowledged, understood, and accepted by everyone, including the deaf. (p. 525)

In making his case for oral education, Connor was aware of strong opposition from the Deaf community. To undermine this opposition, he made the astonishing claim that Deaf people are too "biased" to define their own identity. The following is a classic statement of oppression: "If physicians are asked not to treat their own family because of close emotional ties, mental health experts know even more how biased can be the perspective of a handicapped person who tries to define his own social identity" (p. 525).

Connor's comments are useful but not in the manner he intended. He clearly sought to inculcate what we call a culturally hearing identity in deaf children. This is interesting because hearing people do not typically think of themselves as being a group or as having a common identity. Yet Connor and the Bell Association have had the problem of needing to teach deaf children to think of themselves as hearing children, albeit as hearing children who cannot hear, and thus they have had to identify formally what it means to be hearing. To this end, they value English over American Sign Language (ASL), speech over sign, association with hearing peers over that with deaf peers, and use of hearing aids and other technological devices for "fixing" a hearing loss. All of these values come to represent what it means, culturally, to be hearing. Even when deaf people do not share these values, they often define themselves in relation to them. Talk to any person born deaf, and one will generally find well-formed opinions on these topics.

Schowe's Identity Crisis in Deafness

There has been only one text devoted to identity issues in deafness per se. Schowe's (1976) *Identity Crisis in Deafness* is, as it is subtitled, "a humanistic perspective," a set of reflections by an educated deafened man on the meaning of deafness. Schowe made a number of observations relevant to this study.

Schowe described three "patterns of adjustment" to deafness that can be reconceptualized in terms of Deaf identity development. The first adjustment pattern refers to Deaf people who reject the hearing world and immerse themselves in the Deaf community. The second pattern is composed of people who reject the Deaf world and aspire to live comfortably in a hearing society that rejects them. Schowe referred to these people as "marginal." The third pattern refers to Deaf people who find commonalities among Deaf and hearing. In the Deaf Identity Development (DID) model to be outlined, the first pattern corresponds to the immersion stage, the second to the culturally marginal stage, and the third might be an early formulation of the bicultural Deaf identity.

Schowe speculated that the second pattern is the least healthy. He believed this pattern is characterized by self-hatred as well as idealizing normal standards. "In the case of the deaf, what they hate is their own deafness and all of its common manifestations, such as the manual mode of communication" (p. 54). The idealizing of normal standards is manifest in an obsession with developing good speech. Schowe also noted that the appeal of oralism is precisely this idealizing of the "normal":

> It must be understood that the oral (speech) teacher's rationalization of his position is very persuasive, especially for hearing parents of a deaf child who grasp eagerly for anything which contemplates eventual "normality" for the child. Many "oral" teachers disparage the deaf society as a walled off "island of manualism." It is their purpose, they say, to prepare the deaf child to "become a first class citizen in society at large rather than in a deaf society alone." (p. 56)

Although Schowe disparaged oralism, it is unlikely he would be considered culturally Deaf by contemporary standards. He was at best ambivalent about ASL and the Deaf community. He seemed to advocate chiefly for versions of sign language modeled on English: "The sign language may have some peculiarities of grammar and syntax which can be profitably studied, but any attempt to set up the deaf with an independent language of their own would be disastrous educationally and socially" (p. 132).

Schowe's "humanism" appears to make him uncomfortable with the idea of Deaf culture and community because it is the "universals" among people that tend to interest humanists. On the one hand, he understood the way oralism oppresses Deaf people, and he understood the appeal of sign language and Deaf society to Deaf people. On the other hand, he seemed to conceptualize the Deaf community just as the oralists do, as a ghetto cut off from humanity. The many examples he gave of poor English writing by Deaf people seem to make the point that sign language and Deaf culture corrupt the ability of Deaf people to communicate. In addition, his own flowery and self-consciously "literary" prose seem to mark a boundary between himself and ordinary Deaf people.

Schowe's work was written in the mid-1970s, just as the new constructions of deafness began to emerge. There has been little attempt to follow up on the detailed attention he gave to the issue of identity in deafness.

Contemporary Discussions of Deaf Culture and Identity

The most profitable place to find references to Deaf identity is in discussions of Deaf culture. It is useful, therefore, to review what some of the more prominent Deaf people have said about Deaf culture, especially as it pertains to identity. From my reading and conversations with Deaf people, three themes seem central to such discussions. First, Deaf people view themselves primarily as culturally different rather than disabled. Deaf people have a sense of community, of "us" and "them" and sometimes "us versus them." Secondly, fluency in and respect for ASL is critical. Deaf people often feel ambivalent about English (or whatever the dominant spoken language of their community is), on the one hand recognizing its importance for successful navigation in the larger society and on the other hand resenting it as the imposed language of domination. A similar ambivalence is found with regard to speech. Thirdly, Deaf people have strong feelings about the education of deaf children especially as regards (a) the place of sign and kind of sign in the school program; (b) mainstreaming versus residential placements; and (c) the degree of Deaf involvement in, and control over, the administration of these and other programs for deaf people.

Deaf People Understood as Culturally Different

One of the earliest presentations of a culturally Deaf viewpoint is Jacobs (1974). He described Deaf people as a minority group. Like many culturally Deaf people, he compared Deaf people to racial and ethnic minorities and not to other handicapped people. He also alluded to what we now understand as different kinds or stages of Deaf identity:

> The first factor to think about is the fact that Deaf persons constitute a minority group. Therefore, they are subject to the same problems that other minority groups face...The majority also has the melting pot, or manifest destiny concept of minority group persons—that all of them have to be the same. Thus, the Indians have their "white fathers," the Blacks their "whiteys," the Chicanos, their "gringos," and the deaf, their "hearies." (p. 61)

A frequently cited early work is Padden (1980, 1989). She presented a common culturally Deaf understanding of hearing loss:

> Being Deaf usually means the person has some degree of hearing loss. However, the type or degree of hearing loss is not a criterion for being Deaf. Rather, the criterion is whether the person identifies with other Deaf people, and behaves as a Deaf person. Deaf people are often unaware of the details of their Deaf friends' hearing loss, and for example, may be surprised to learn that some of their friends can hear well enough to use the telephone. (Padden, 1989, p. 8)

Padden also called attention to the importance ascribed to the label used to describe deaf people. As with other minority groups, the label the community uses is different from the label used by the majority culture:

> In hearing culture, it is desirable to distinguish between degrees of hearing loss. "Hard-of-hearing" is more valued and indicates that the person is closer to being hearing and is more capable of interacting on an equal basis with other hearing people. However, "deaf" is viewed more negatively and usually carries the implication that the person is difficult to communicate with, or may not speak at all. Thus, a deaf person is more likely to be avoided if he calls himself "deaf." But among Deaf people, the distinctions between hearing loss are not considered important for group relations. "Deaf" is not a label of deafness as much as a label of identity with other Deaf people. A person learning to interact with other Deaf people will quickly learn that there is one name for all members of the cultural group, regardless of the degree of hearing loss: Deaf. In fact, the sign DEAF can be used in an ASL sentence to mean "my friends." . . . Calling oneself "hard-of-hearing" rather than by the group name is interpreted by some Deaf people as "putting on airs," because it appears to draw undue attention to hearing loss. (Padden, 1989, p. 13)

In the anthology (Wilcox, 1989) from which Padden's article is reprinted, there are a number of articles by Ben Behan from his column in a Massachusetts newspaper, *Deaf Community News*. These columns reflect, often in a humorous way, many values associated with cultural deafness. In one article (Behan, 1989a), "A Night of Living Terror," Behan related a series of nightmares. First, it was Halloween Night, and upon answering the door, he discovered to his horror a trick-or-treater: "As I opened the door and glanced down at the kid, I couldn't believe my eyes. I screamed, dropped the bowl, and ran back into the house bolting the door shut behind me. The kid was dressed like a hearing person" (Behan, 1989a, p. 17).

Then begin the series of bad dreams. First Ben dreams that his girlfriend is signing in English. Then he dreams he is in a classroom with an incompetent sign language interpreter who turns his articulate ASL into garbled English and makes him the object of scorn and mockery by his class. Next he dreams he has become 65 years old, and he returns to Gallaudet College only to find that institution is inaugurating yet another hearing president. Then he dreams he has been forced to undergo a cochlear implant to improve his hearing. Finally, the worst nightmare of all, he dreams he becomes a hearing person.

In another article, Behan gave a proud, Deaf-affirmative self-definition: "Now I am not trying to deny my deafness. I am proud to be deaf! So proud that I feel there is a need to erase the pathological (disease) viewpoint of deafness" (Behan, 1989b, p. 30).

Behan reaffirmed this self-definition elsewhere when reflecting on Alexander Graham Bell. (Behan, 1989e) To proponents of oral education of deaf children, Bell is a hero for his fierce opposition to sign language and championing of oral/aural education. To culturally Deaf people, Bell is an historical villain for precisely the same reason. Most outrageous for them is Bell's attempt to get a law passed to forbid intermarriage among Deaf people. Bell saw such intermarriage as leading to the creation of a defective deaf race.

In this same anthology, Kannapell (1989) noted that Deaf people can act either Deaf or hearing. There is a sign for hearing-acting deaf people that is equivalent to the concept of "Oreo" in the Black–White context:

> If a deaf person behaves like a hearing person, other deaf people will sign "hearing" on the forehead to show "he thinks like a hearing person." Thus, he is on the fringe of the Deaf Community, depending on his/her attitudes. Conversely, if a deaf person behaves like a deaf person, other deaf people may sign "strong deaf," or "fluent ASL" which means that the person is culturally deaf. Thus, he or she is admitted to the core of the Deaf Community. (Kannapell, 1989, pp. 24–25)

Kannapell argued that cultural Deafness requires not only skill in ASL but also the requisite beliefs, values, and experiences:

> However, I want to emphasize that the knowledge of ASL alone seems not to be enough to qualify a person to be in the core of the Deaf Community. Everything else—shared common experiences, and cultural beliefs and values which are attached to ASL—also seem to be important requirements for admittance to the core of the Deaf Community. A deaf person who is in the core of the Deaf Community is considered to be "culturally deaf." (Kannapell, 1989, p. 25)

Higgins (1980), a hearing sociologist with Deaf parents, portrayed Deaf people as "outsiders in a hearing world." He considered the Deaf community and Deaf identity as phenomena parallel to those in other "outsider" groups. In his chapter on identity, Higgins' central theme is that Deaf people are ambivalent about their deafness. On the one hand, Deaf people are usually content to be deaf, and they find meaning, purpose, identity, and social fulfillment in the Deaf community. On the other hand, they face prejudice, discrimination, and stigmatization that they recognize to be major barriers in life:

> While membership in the deaf community is based on identification with the deaf, membership in the community supports and strengthens deaf people's identity and adjustment to deafness. A sense of wholeness and belonging is achieved within the deaf community which is lacking within the hearing world. Because life within the community is fulfilling, there is rarely any overwhelming desire to hear. I suspect that deaf people who are not members would be more concerned about their hearing losses than those who are. However, members live within a hearing world where deafness is a drawback. Therefore, for very practical reasons, members would enjoy being able to

hear again. It would help them navigate better in a hearing world! As members, though, they embrace their deafness. . . . As are other outsiders, the deaf are ambivalent about what makes them outsiders. (Higgins, 1980, p. 171)

Higgins' focus on ambivalence may reflect his own feelings as a hearing child of Deaf parents, or it may reflect his failure to differentiate between different stages in the process of becoming Deaf. His notion, for instance, that Deaf people would like, for practical reasons, to be hearing does not seem to me accurate as a generalization. It very much depends on identity development.

Yet Higgins is aware that Deaf people affiliate to different extents with the Deaf community and that this degree of affiliation dramatically affects their self-concepts as Deaf people. Higgins focused on the facts of hearing and speaking as the primary means by which Deaf people establish the boundaries between Deaf and not-Deaf, us and them. Thus for him, whether or not a Deaf person speaks well or has much residual hearing is very important in determining his or her degree of acceptance by other Deaf people. Yet other commentators discussed here have said that it is a person's attitude toward his or her deafness and the manner in which he or she behaves as a Deaf person that is far more important in determining acceptance by other Deaf people.

One of the fullest discussions of Deaf identities and group membership is in a videotape series on Deaf Culture (Bienvenue & Colonomos, 1988b). The video presentation takes the form of a talk show with culturally Deaf people on a panel and in the audience discussing identity. The Deaf people on this tape made the following points:

1. The most important aspects of a culturally Deaf identity are the attitude of total acceptance of oneself as Deaf, skill in ASL, knowing the social rules of the culture, and growing up in a Deaf residential school.

2. Culturally Deaf people do not ask or care about decibel loss, and, for some, doing so may even be construed as rude. However, many students in mainstreamed programs do ask about degrees of hearing loss.

3. Native Deaf children (that is, Deaf children from Deaf families) pass on the culture to their peers.

4. The label "hearing-impaired" connotes a negative, hearing-identified identity. Deaf graduates of mainstreamed programs use it. It is also used by Deaf people when interacting with hearing people because Deaf people perceive that hearing people seem to expect it.

5. There are various avenues through which hearing people can join the Deaf community, but they cannot be core members of the culture.

Padden and Humphries (1988) provided one of the richest accounts of the differences between how Deaf and hearing people construct the meaning of deafness. For instance, hearing people rely on the metaphor of "silence" for understanding deafness. Hearing people see deafness as an absence or a loss and assume Deaf people's lives are empty. Deafness, however, is usually not total, and even when it is, Deaf people use signed or gestured equivalents of many sounds and have their own way of making sense of sounds.

Padden and Humphries gave some comical examples of the struggles Deaf people have when attempting to make sense of the seemingly bizarre meanings that hearing people attribute to sounds. They described Deaf men discovering that hearing men often urinate inside the rim of the toilet bowl, rather than into the water in the center, to avoid making conspicuous noise. They described a Deaf woman who, knowing that hearing people are not offended by the sounds of coughing or sneezing, assumed they would also not be offended by the sound of passing gas and discovered to her horror that this was not true. They wrote, "A college student discovered one day in a cafeteria line than an unrestrained belch led the hearing people around him to draw conclusions about his socioeconomic class" (p. 98). Deaf people can fall into hysterics describing to each other these and other bizarre and incomprehensible practices of hearing people. Deaf people are aware of these sounds, but they may think about them differently. Their world is not silent, but full.

Padden and Humphries described the Deaf culture as having a "different center." The difference is that deafness is valued. Consequently, culturally Deaf people do not want to be thought of as hard of hearing or hearing impaired, and hearing people mistakingly insult them when they use these euphemisms. The phrase "a little hard of hearing" means to hearing people a slight hearing loss. To culturally Deaf people it means the opposite: mostly Deaf, but a little like hearing people. Telling someone he or she thinks like a hearing person is not a complement. This negative conceptualization of hearing is seen in the way that oral deaf people, those construed to be most like hearing people, are understood:

ORAL[1] recalls many extreme stereotypes; our friends gave us two: MIND RICH and ALWAYS PLAN. ORAL individuals are stereotypically represented as members of the establishment, as coming from hearing families that are inflexible about their children's behavior. As the belief goes, the richer the family, the more likely the family will embrace oralism (MIND RICH). The second stereotype portrays a typical ORAL person as one who actively tries to pass as hearing, and must be alert to every possible situation in order to pass successfully (ALWAYS PLAN). In its strongest connotations, ORAL means one who "cozies up to the opposition" and uncritically embraces the world of others. (Padden & Humphries, 1988, pp. 51–52)

Padden and Humphries described "learning to be Deaf" as fundamentally different depending on whether the Deaf child is born into a Deaf or a hearing context. In the former, Deafness is assumed from the start of life as given, normal and, natural: "The child uses Deaf to mean 'us,' but he meets others for whom 'deaf' means 'them, not like us.' He thinks Deaf means 'friends who behave as expected,' but to others it means 'a remarkable condition.'" (p. 17).

For this deaf child of deaf parents, deafness is discovered when he or she encounters the hearing world outside the home. Suddenly, hearing views of deafness impinge:

---

[1]Words in uppercase letters are English glosses for ASL signs. *Glosses* are tags for signs, not exact translations.

The child "discovers" deafness. Now deafness becomes a prominent fact in his life, a term around which people's behavior changes. People around him have debates about deafness, and lines are sharply drawn between people depending on what position they take on the subject. He has never thought about himself as having a certain quality but now it becomes something to discuss. Even his language has ceased to be just a means of interacting with others and has become an object: people are either "against" signed language or "for" signed language. In the stories we have collected from Deaf children of Deaf parents, the same pattern emerges over and over: "deafness" is "discovered" late and in the context of these layers of meaning. (Padden & Humphries, 1988, p. 18)

For the deaf child born into a hearing family, or acquiring deafness early in life, deafness right away signifies a terrible difference. Here, deafness becomes infused with the meaning hearing people ascribe to it. The deaf child in a hearing family lives in a world of isolation and disability, without even the basic tools of language for making sense of his or her condition:

For Tony, being deaf meant being set apart from his family and friends; he was "deaf" and had an "illness." In contrast, Sam, the Deaf child of Deaf parents, thought of being "Deaf" not as a consequence of some event, but simply as a given. For Sam, "Deaf" was not a term used to refer to him personally, but was just a normal way of describing himself and everyone he met. (Padden & Humphries, 1988, p. 20)

From Padden and Humphries' work, we can surmise that "becoming Deaf" or developing a Deaf identity differs depending on whether one is fortunate enough to be born to a Deaf family. Deaf children of hearing parents begin, more or less, with hearing constructions of deafness, whereas Deaf children of Deaf families begin with Deaf constructions.

At the core of Deaf identity, then, is the same construction that all self-af-firming minorities share: a sense of community, of peoplehood. Because one can talk about becoming Deaf, not in the sense of losing one's hearing but in the sense of joining a community, it is possible to study cultural identity develop-ment in Deaf people.

The Importance of American Sign Language

Before the study of ASL and Deaf culture took off, Deaf people's defense of sign language occurred often in the context of discussions of deaf education. Jacobs (1974), for instance, was resolute in his disdain for the oldest nemeses of the Deaf community: proponents of oral education. Commenting on the Alexander Graham Bell Association for the Deaf, he wrote:

The policy of this organization is repugnant to me for I feel that the group is the epitome of the imposition of the values and will of the hearing majority upon a Deaf minority. The comparatively few oral successes, about whom the *Volta Review* has printed glowing testimonials, do not make up for the many Deaf victims who have fallen by the wayside. Nor is it noted that the few successes achieved are despite, not because of the system. (pp. 97–98)

Jacobs made an impassioned defense of "manualism," the teaching of Deaf children with sign language. Jacobs and many others said that if the Deaf community has one core value, it is this passionate defense of sign language.

Padden (1989) described several Deaf cultural values. A central value is respect for American Sign Language. She noted: "An . . . important goal [of Deaf people] is the acceptance and recognition of their history and their use of signing as a means of communication" (p. 7).

Padden and Humphries did not discuss Deaf identity development per se, but they talked about the "changing consciousness" of Deaf people and of how Deaf people "learn to be Deaf." As with all minorities, how Deaf people view themselves is rooted in their sociohistorical circumstances. The increasing self-empowerment of Deaf people is reflected in changing consciousness of what it means to be Deaf. Central to this change is a new understanding about ASL.

Before linguists "discovered" American Sign Language, there was no formal name for it. ASL was merely "the sign language" or "manual communication." Similarly, Yiddish was often referred to as "Jewish language." The new consciousness of ASL as a full language has helped Deaf people no longer to feel embarrassed by and ashamed of their "gesturing" but instead to feel pride in their rich and complex native language. Deaf artists have always used sign language creatively, and the major literary form of Deaf culture has been its "oral" tradition of storytelling. Contemporary Deaf artists, however, create Deaf poetry with a conscious awareness of the grammar of the language. They make "plays on signs" and puns with a linguistic understanding of what they are doing. This new appreciation of ASL is very connected, according to Padden and Humphries, to how Deaf people see themselves.

The centrality of ASL is also discussed in the videotape series on Deaf culture (Bienvenue & Colonomos, 1985, 1986, 1988a, 1988b; and in chapter 4 by Humphries, chapter 2 by Lane, and chapter 10 by Lytle & Lewis, this volume). Contrasted to the positive importance that Deaf people assign to communication in ASL is the ambivalent, and at times hostile, feelings deaf people show toward spoken communication in the dominant hearing language. One cannot sign in ASL and speak in English at the same time. This is one reason why speech is sometimes devalued among culturally Deaf people.

Another reason is because hearing educators of deaf children have been so focused on enabling deaf children to speak. Padden noted the radically different meanings given to speech by culturally Deaf and culturally hearing people:

> Mouthing and the use of speech represent things to Deaf people. Since speech has traditionally been forced on Deaf people as a substitute for their language, it has come to represent confinement and denial of the most fundamental need of Deaf people: to communicate deeply and comfortably in their own language. Deaf people often distrust speech communication for this reason. (Padden, 1989, p. 10)

Padden noted that changes in the identity of deaf people are often reflected in a changing attitude toward speech:

> As an example of a conflict, a deaf person may value her speaking ability and may have always spoken when communicating with other people. But now she learns

that speaking does not have the same positive value with Deaf people that it has with hearing people. Even though some Deaf people can hear some speech, and some speak well themselves, speaking is not considered usual or acceptable behavior within the cultural group. The deaf person finds that she must change the behavior that she has always considered normal, acceptable and positive. (Padden, 1989, p. 12)

Higgins (1980) noted that the more integrated one is within the Deaf world, the less one is concerned with living up to hearing standards regarding speech, hearing aids, and other matters: "Membership may decrease hearing-impaired people's desire to improve their speech and lip reading abilities. From a sense of belonging within the Deaf community comes less of a desire to be like hearing people, which means to be able to hear and speak" (p. 172).

Language issues are often at the core of struggles by oppressed minorities (Glickman, 1984). Fluency in ASL, along with skill in adapting communication strategies (such as turning one's voice on or off), are important markers of identity in Deaf people.

Attitudes Toward Deaf Education

Before the modern Deaf awareness movement, Deaf people's concerns with education took the form primarily of a defense of manualism and an attack on oralism. Jacobs (1974) was especially vehement in his attacks on proponents of oral education, although he also called the defenders of total communication to task for their own paternalism:

The educators supporting the pure oral method seem to be much more blatantly paternalistic than the others, possibly because most of their deaf subjects fail to measure up to their rigid specifications in oral skills, and they are unable to communicate with them manually and get to know them better as worthwhile individuals. Indeed, one is given to believe that these teachers have found manual communication too complicated and time consuming to learn, so they have taken the easier road out by compelling deaf children to come all the way over the hurdle of their handicap, to learn their own communication modes. The others, who tolerate total communication, are not as offensively paternalistic as the oral method proponents, but they still regard manual communication as a secondary language and have been guilty of being paternal in their actions. (p. 25)

Deaf people initially embraced Total Communication as a manual program but in recent years, have become concerned about the dominance of signed English within these programs. As the linguistic sophistication of Deaf people has increased, calls for support of signing or manualism have changed into calls for support of ASL specifically. However, concern about the nature of the communication in deaf programs pales before concern about the far greater threat of the rise of mainstreaming and the decline of opportunities for all but the multiply handicapped deaf child to attend any deaf residential program. Recent commentary by deaf writers frequently focuses on two themes: (a) a criticism of mainstreaming as a practice that isolates rather than integrates deaf children, and (b) a call for the establishment of deaf educational programs (day or residential) that are genuinely bicultural.

Behan's (1989c) criticism of mainstreaming expresses common concerns. Traditionally, the Deaf school is the major arena for socialization of Deaf children into Deaf culture. The rise of mainstreaming is of concern to Deaf people not only because it dramatically threatens the continued existence of Deaf culture but also because mainstreaming is seen as a violation of the Deaf child's right to clear communication and interaction with peers. Behan condemned the practice of mainstreaming and criticized hearing educators and policy makers for never consulting with the Deaf community before they put such practices into place.

TBC News, the newsletter of The Bicultural Center, a Deaf advocacy organization (based in Riverdale, Maryland, until its closing in 1995) became an important forum in which Deaf people and hearing supporters express views on topics of importance to the Deaf community. Mainstreaming was frequently criticized in these pages (see issue number 70, for example). Bilingual education programs in self-contained Deaf environments were proposed as solutions. Bienvenue (1993) answered the question, "What is Bi–Bi education?" as follows:

> The most important thing to realize is that Bi–Bi education is not simply another method of education. It is a philosophy. When a school makes a commitment to Bi–Bi education, it is a commitment to respect the language and culture of deaf children in the classroom, in the hallways, in the cafeteria, at the board meetings and parent conferences and throughout the education experience of the child. The Bi–Bi philosophy respects the right of deaf children to acquire a natural language in which they can achieve native fluency—for deaf children in America, that language is ASL. A Bi–Bi school provides an environment where children are enculturated in American Deaf Culture. The Bi–Bi philosophy also strongly supports the need for deaf children to develop second-language proficiency in written English, as well as to develop an awareness of the larger American culture to which most of their parents belong. (p. 2)

Genuine bilingual education programs would require a greater degree of control by Deaf persons in the education of deaf children than one typically sees. Like other minorities, Deaf people frequently argue that programs that serve their community need to be staffed and run by community members. The problem, of course, is that the hearing parents of most deaf children do not necessarily welcome the idea of their children belonging to the Deaf community. The future identities of these children, how they will see themselves as relating to the Deaf and hearing worlds, is precisely the core issue of controversy. Nonetheless, from the culturally Deaf vantage point, for Deaf empowerment to occur, Deaf people need to be in prominent positions where they are able to influence policy and services that effect deaf people. Behan (1989d) argued in a paper titled, "The War is Not Over," that the successful "Deaf President Now" movement at Gallaudet University in 1988 should be extended and the following four demands made regarding Deaf education:

> 1) that 50 percent of the teachers be Deaf 2) that American Sign Language and Deaf culture be an integral part of the curriculum 3) that at least 50 percent of the school board be Deaf; that we be empowered to make decisions regarding the policies implemented by the Department of Education regarding the education of Deaf children; 4) and that we have DEAF SUPERINTENDENTS NOW! (Behan, 1989d, p. 190)

Deaf people express strong feelings about the education of deaf children, and in recent years, these three topics seem to be prominent in such discussions: (a) the place of sign and the kind of sign in the school program; (b) the desirability of mainstreaming verses self-contained deaf programs; and c) the degree of Deaf involvement in, and control over, the administration of these and other programs for deaf people. I believe the process of identity development in Deaf people is reflected in the changing positions taken on these issues.

Deaf Culture: Summary

For people in the Deaf community, deafness has a social rather than an audiological meaning. To be Deaf is to be a member of a special group, to claim one's culture and community as one's own. In contrast, hearing people prototypically understand deafness as a tragic medical disability, and they believe that the successful hearing-impaired person is the one fully integrated into the hearing world and not one constrained to live within the presumed confines of a Deaf ghetto. The process of Deaf identity development must involve a movement from a more hearing-like construction of deafness to a Deaf one.

The content of Deaf identities will be determined by a Deaf person's attitude toward the themes that are "figural" for Deaf people. The literature reviewed here suggests that the defining theme of Deaf culture is respect for American Sign Language and the belief that Deaf children must have full access to it from the beginning of their lives. Additional key cultural concerns are:

1. A social–cultural rather than medical–pathological understanding of deafness;
2. Respect for the Deaf community and culture and for the idea of Deaf people affiliating with their own;
3. "Healthy paranoia" toward hearing people and resentment of hearing paternalism;
4. A devaluation of speech, lip reading, and the use of hearing aids; and
5. A basic belief in the rights and abilities of Deaf people to control their own lives.

THEORY OF DEAF CULTURAL
IDENTITY DEVELOPMENT

The psychological processes underlying cultural identity development are probably the same across minority groups. That is, the member of a minority experiences some state of alienation from his or her community that is interrupted by the "discovery" of oppression. He or she then becomes immersed in this community, falling in love with everything pertaining to it, and becoming angry with the larger society. The minority person then enters a period of reflection where his or her vision of what it means to belong to this community enlarges. A final stage of biculturalism, which often includes a commitment to political action, is then achieved. Lately, it has been suggested that there is really no end state to this process. Rather, one can "recycle" through these stages at higher levels of sophistication throughout one's life (Ponterotto, 1988).

Within these broad parameters, the unique experience of each minority group creates particular cultural identity development issues. There are a number of special considerations that must shape our understanding of how culturally Deaf identities develop in Deaf people. First, we must ask: To which deaf persons does this model apply? Is this model relevant only to people born deaf or "early deafened," or can it apply to late-deafened people as well? Of what importance, if any, is actual degree of hearing loss? Is the model relevant only to the roughly 5% of deaf children born into deaf families; and if so, would this include oral deaf families? What about deaf children born into families with activist, pro-Deaf hearing parents? Deaf/deaf people, of course, also differ with regard to gender, race, ethnicity, sexual orientation, and so on, and one would want to know how these other differences interact to form a cultural identity.

The model presented here is hypothesized to be most relevant to people who are born deaf or become deaf early in life and have a hearing loss severe enough to require special education services. People with mild-to-moderate degrees of hearing loss or people who lose their hearing after adolescence usually remain "hearing identified." Their entire social world is composed of hearing people. Their language is the language they have used all their lives, that of the dominant society. For them, deafness is almost always a tragic loss, a seriously incapacitating disability (Luey & Per-Lee, 1983). Although late deafened people may experience some change in their attitude toward deafness (increasing acceptance, for instance), it is unlikely they will develop a primary cultural affiliation with the Deaf community and come, thereby, to view their deafness as a positive cultural difference. There are exceptions, of course.

The second special consideration in designing a model of cultural identity development for deaf people is that because they become deaf at such different ages and in such different environments, it is necessary to postulate several beginning points for cultural identity development. The four cultural orientations that are described and that are presumed to be developmentally related stages may all constitute initial stages in specific circumstances.

Thirdly, unlike most racial and ethnic minorities, most deaf people are born into families that do not share their cultural orientation—that is, in this case, they are hearing. They must be socialized into the Deaf experience by peers or nonrelated adults at school age or later, not by family from their earliest years. This certainly makes the acquisition of a culturally Deaf identity more difficult, but this is not a unique or insurmountable problem. The task for these deaf children is comparable to those of children of color by White families or to gay and lesbian young people who are usually raised by heterosexuals.

Fourthly, deaf children born into hearing families cannot be said to begin life as culturally hearing. They are more like African American children adopted by White parents than African American children in African American families.[2] But there is a difference here also. White families that adopt African American children presumably want these children and are psychologically prepared to raise them. Hearing parents are commonly devastated by the discovery that their baby is deaf and go through a predictable grieving process (Vernon & Andrews, 1990). The idea that they will need to learn another language to communicate to their own child is another unwelcome piece of news. But for this reason and because deaf children are commonly raised in linguistically inaccessible environments, deaf children can be thought of as culturally marginal within their own families, and the concept of cultural marginality (Stonequist, 1937) must assume a prominent place in any theory of Deaf identity development.

Fifthly, C/RID theories are traditionally most relevant to people with some college education or at least people with the cognitive abilities to care about abstract issues such as identity, rights, and the place of one's group in society. Actual empirical studies of cultural identity, such as the work of Helms (1990), are inevitably performed on a sample of college students. This raises the issue of the relevance of such models not only to the majority of early-deafened people who do not go on to college but also to grassroots members of any minority community. In addition, there is virtually no research on the interplay of gender, race, ethnicity, sexual orientation, and other differences in the formation of cultural identity for any minority group, much less for Deaf/deaf people.

The model that follows builds on the logic of models of C/RID that have been outlined in chapter 1 of this volume but has been modified to take into account the special considerations of deaf people described previously.

Stage 1: Culturally Hearing

Although Stage 1 is called culturally hearing, it is meant to apply primarily to a subset of deaf people, those deafened after adolescence, the period during which identity normally begins to consolidate. It is not meant to be a stage of identity development through which all deaf people pass but rather one that grows out of a particular experience of deafness. The notion of "cultural hearingness" may, however, have psychological relevance for a broad spectrum of deaf people.

Late-deafened people have already established hearing identities and, prior to their hearing loss, typically are uninformed about deafness and the Deaf community. Either through illness or accident, their hearing declines. The loss may be gradual or sudden. It is usually unexpected and most unwelcome.

Deafened adults inevitably experience their deafness as a powerful loss. Luey and Per-Lee (1983) described the stages of adjustment to this loss common among deafened people. The stages include shock, denial, anger, guilt, depres-

---

[2]This point was first clarified for me by Betty Colonomos of The Bicultural Center in Riverdale, Maryland.

sion, and adaptation. They noted that deafened people may experience pressure from peers and from professional people to "accept" their deafness, something far easier said than done:

> After experiencing all these stages, some people expect that they will be rewarded by experiencing a happy final stage called acceptance, and that all will be well. In many cases, deafened persons are under pressure to "accept" from family and friends who are tired of watching them grieve. In fact, it is not realistic to expect total acceptance, and it is likely that discussion of acceptance in the literature and by professionals has contributed greatly to people's feelings of inadequacy. (p. 13)

If hearing people unfamiliar with deaf people normally construe deafness in a highly negative light, then deafened people who are attitudinally hearing may find their hearing perspectives hardened by their own bitter experience of being deaf. For instance, deaf people are often stereotyped as isolated, lonely and sad, and as people unable to communicate effectively. These hearing projections of what it must mean to be deaf are, in fact, commonly the experience of deafened people for whom deafness comes to mean the loss of meaningful connection to other people and the world. Their own painful experience is salient for them, and the vibrant language and society of Deaf people is inaccessible and invisible.

Deafened people are usually culturally hearing. But what characterizes a culturally hearing identity? The idea is paradoxical because hearing people do not think of themselves as hearing. Of course, they know they can hear, but it does not occur to them to conclude that this fact makes them a cultural group. "Hearing" is essentially a category used by Deaf people to signify the "other." It has the kind of meaning for Deaf people that "White" has for racial minorities and "straight" has for gay men and lesbians. Hearing people only become conscious of being culturally hearing through exposure to the world of Deaf people. If they are sensitive and receptive, hearing people discover through this exposure that hearing does not just mean "can hear" but more importantly means, "a group of people who have a relationship with the Deaf community."

Because hearing people only exist as a group from the point of view of Deaf people, how can one think about hearing people having a distinct worldview and identity? One can only learn about hearing identity by talking with Deaf people. Janet Helms, the African American psychologist who developed the first instrument designed to measure White identity, remarked with irony at a presentation at the 1990 American Psychological Association convention that she did not grow up with the intention of becoming an expert on White identity. It is simply easier for African American people to conceptualize what it means to be White because from their vantage point, the ramifications of Whiteness are more obvious. Similarly, women may understand the male sex role much better than men, and gay and lesbian people may have insights into heterosexual behavior that heterosexuals lack. In all these cases, it is typical for the majority people to deny that their group identity is significant whereas the minority people experience on a daily basis the many implications of social group membership. These differing constructions of reality are not a matter of intelligence or insight but simply of social position. It is only from the audience that one can take in the whole stage.

Deaf people, then, can help us understand what it means both to be hearing and to think like a hearing person. The main elements of a hearing identity are the particular ways in which deafness and the ramifications of deafness are understood. First and foremost, deafness is constructed to be a medical disability. The ambivalence we find in marginal Deaf people about the meaning of deafness is not present in the culturally hearing. For them, the idea that Deaf people have a culture is foreign, ludicrous, unknown, or a dangerous threat to what they take as common sense. No other viewpoint about deafness is seriously entertained by the culturally hearing. Deafness is, purely and simply, a terrible tragedy; a profound loss or absence; an unrelenting source of pain, shame, and isolation.

To argue that culturally hearing people understand deafness purely as a pathology is not to say that they cannot, in some way, come to terms with being deaf if they lose their hearing. Some may adjust by approaching the Deaf world and progressing through the subsequent stages of Deaf identity. A prominent example of a deafened person who came to terms with deafness by entering the Deaf world is King Jordan, the first and current deaf president of Gallaudet University. Another is B. M. Schowe who, as is previously mentioned, wrote the only text to date on identity issues among Deaf people (Schowe, 1976). For most deafened people, especially those deafened late in life, adjustment or adaptation occurs entirely within a hearing frame of reference.

From a hearing perspective, what might this adaptation look like? Luey and Per-Lee (1983) described adaptation as the ability to acknowledge deafness as a reality and to pursue rehabilitative options. These include developing skill in lipreading, fingerspelling, and basic signs and in the use of telecommunication devices such as TDD's as well as television decoders. Many people can think of elderly relatives whose hearing has declined and who refuse to consider wearing a hearing aid. Conversely, the willingness to wear hearing aids, when they can help, reflects adjustment. The ability to discuss one's hearing loss easily, without shame, and even with a sense of humor, also shows adjustment. Deafened people who have accepted their deafness may even be able to call themselves deaf, but the word has solely an audiological meaning. They generally see no reason to affiliate with the Deaf community, and the Deaf community would see no reason to take them in as some of their own.

It follows that for the culturally hearing person, anything connected with the Deaf world (sign language, Deaf groups and organizations, validation of Deaf culture and history) represents not only the acceptance but the glorification of one's limitations. The Deaf community, if it is seen at all, is understood stereotypically. Deaf people are presumed to be lonely, isolated, and intellectually and socially inferior. This stereotype becomes a negative reference point, what *not* to become. Deafened people may resist strongly any suggestion that it is possible to view deafness in a positive light. They may experience this idea as a threat to their self-concept as hearing people who cannot hear.

Nash and Nash (1981) discussed "ordinary knowledge and the meaning of deafness." The construction of deafness that we are calling culturally hearing is called by Nash and Nash the normal and commonsensical understanding of deafness that the hearing majority holds. For the uninformed hearing person, deafness is, of course, a disability. It is absurd and ludicrous, from the hearing point of view, to frame it in any other light. Naturally, culturally hearing people believe, one wants to help those unfortunate deaf people make maximal use of what residual hearing or speech abilities they possess. Concomitantly, with a stance that enables them to imagine themselves to be social reformers, these culturally hearing people may plea for greater tolerance and understanding of the deaf from the society at large. The oral perspective, Nash and Nash noted, is essentially an extension of this commonsensical (hearing) view and thus possesses an intuitive appeal to hearing parents of deaf children. Nash and Nash (1981) wrote that "what seems to be most important to Oralists is that their understanding of what society is like not be changed by the presence of a deaf person. This is reasonable from their point of view" (p. 29).

It is unfortunate for deaf children that the oralist position has so much intuitive appeal. It reinforces the hearing perspective that hearing parents already possess, whereas appreciation of the Deaf viewpoint, the realities of being Deaf as Deaf people see it, requires a radical reorganization of meaning. The culturally hearing deaf person maintains this hearing perspective. In fact, if this conception of deafness is implicit for hearing people who have no reason to think about deafness, it can become manifest, salient, or otherwise "hardened" for the deafened person for whom these ideas have emotional appeal. To the extent that culturally hearing people, whether or not they have a hearing loss, become advocates for this perspective, it becomes possible to speak of "militant hearing" people and to appreciate the well-known Deaf leeriness of professional helpers, many of whom share this ideology and militancy.

"Cultural hearingness" may have a psychological reality for many deaf people beyond those who are late deafened. Because the dominant society is culturally hearing and so many educational and medical/mental health professionals work unquestioningly from this perspective, it is easy for deaf people to incorporate this "hearing voice" even as they struggle to define an alternative. Deaf people have heard countless times the cliche, "After all, it's a hearing world out there," which has been used to legitimize the oppression of Deaf people. The sign THINK-HEARING could fairly be translated as "culturally hearing" in the sense described here.

Deaf people, then, have a psychological image of what it means to be hearing, and they define themselves partially in relationship to this image. In psychoanalytic object-relations terminology, one might think of the culturally hearing person as an internalized "object" or representation of the other. It may be useful in psychotherapy with Deaf people to help them explore what the culturally hearing voice in their heads tells them about themselves. Chances are this voice is one that conveys a message of pathology: "You are sick. You are impaired. You are pitiable. You need help."

In summary, the culturally hearing identity, which prototypically would be found most often among late-deafened people, is conceptualized as having the following features:

1. Deafness is understood solely as a medical pathology, never as a cultural difference.
2. Medicine and technology are looked to for ways to help deaf people become full members of hearing society.

3. Hearing people are assumed to be more healthy and capable than deaf people. The deaf person strives to be hearing in attitude, behavior, worldview, communication style, and so on.

4. Deaf people are stereotyped as socially awkward, isolated and lonely, less intelligent, and so on. The deaf person strives to be different from these stereotypes. He or she strives to avoid contact with other deaf people.

5. The deaf person strives to overcome the barriers imposed by deafness. The successful deaf person is the one who is fully functional within hearing society without support services and without sign language.

6. Hearing deafness professionals (counselors, teachers, audiologists, doctors, etc.) are sought for advice and direction. They are presumed to be wise, informed, and benevolent.

7. Educational and social policy will most easily align with oralism. Use of residual hearing, speech training, speech reading, and mainstreaming are positive values. Grouping deaf children together is seen as "segregation," and exposing them to deaf adults who possess positive Deaf identities as role models is seen as "contamination," likely to detract from their enthusiasm about joining hearing society. Sign language is disparaged.

Stage 2: Culturally Marginal

Culturally hearing was described as a stage of identity development most relevant to late-deafened people. Cultural hearingness, however, is conceptualized here as a construct relevant to a broader spectrum of deaf people. This is to say that people who are deaf from early childhood form some conception of what it means to be hearing and define themselves, as Deaf people, in relation to this construct. This is most true for the majority of deaf children raised in hearing families. In spite of this, and in spite of the ferocious efforts of many educators of deaf children, the latter do not begin life as little hearing people. Deaf education, in both oral and Total Communication varieties, has tried to inculcate hearing identities. What it generally produces is marginal identities. What it should be producing is bicultural identities.

In this model of Deaf identity development, there are really three Stage 1s, depending on the age of onset of hearing loss and the context in which the deaf person is raised. Culturally marginal is Stage 2 for deafened people who begin to explore the social world of Deaf people. However, it is Stage 1 for the majority of deaf children who are raised in hearing families. It may be Stage 2 for a Deaf child of Deaf parents, who begins life with a bicultural identity but whose educational and social experiences cause him or her to lose connection with the Deaf world.

Culturally marginal deaf people do not, by definition, have a well-formed prior identity. There is no identity to shatter. Rather, they exist in a state of identity confusion and cultural marginality from the beginning. Although the oppression of African American people is real and powerful, African American children are nonetheless generally raised by African American families who love and cherish them and who transmit to them, through language and other means, some cultural tradition. Most deaf children are raised by hearing parents who, lacking any model of deafness as a cultural difference and lacking exposure to successful culturally Deaf adults, are often understandably devastated by the discovery of deafness in their child. The idea that they will have to learn another language to communicate with their own flesh and blood, a language that most in the larger society do not know, may well add insult to injury, but this "crazy" idea may become more reasonable when they discover how much more easily deaf children respond to sign than to speech. Nonetheless, the deaf child in a hearing family is often raised with minimal exposure to ASL and imperfect exposure to English. Without a solid language system, the child lacks the major tool needed for relatedness with others and embeddedness in some familial/social context. The child also lacks the major tool needed to think about himself or herself abstractly and therefore to form an identity. This child is both socially and psychologically marginal. The social marginality may be manifest in the absence of full and easy membership in any social group. The psychological marginality may be manifest in identity confusion, poorly differentiated internal representations of self and object, and a variety of emotional and behavioral disorders.

Stonequist (1937) described cultural marginality as a social phenomenon. It refers to people who are on the margins of two or more social groups. Stonequist also believed, however, that culturally marginal people have distinct psychological traits. These traits include ambivalence, excessive self- and race-consciousness, inferiority complexes, hypersensitivity to perceived injustice, and compensatory reactions such as egocentrism and aggression.

The central trait of ambivalence is evident in marginal deaf people through their relationship to the Deaf and hearing worlds. Hearing people are likely to be openly admired and emulated and secretly envied and resented. Deaf people are openly disparaged whereas the marginal deaf person nevertheless finds himself or herself most happy and comfortable in their midst. These conflicting attitudes shift constantly. The themes of deafness and hearingness are emotionally charged.

Another way to conceptualize marginality is to use the language of contemporary psychodynamic developmental theory (Horner, 1984). Marginality as a psychological process emerges out of disturbances in the process of attachment, symbiosis, and separation–individuation of the infant in relation to its primary caregiver, usually the mother. When development proceeds normally, the personality of the child becomes structured through the internalization of mental representations of the self and the object or other.

According to Horner, the kind and severity of psychopathology that develops depends on how and when the breakdown in the development of early object relations occurs. She noted, "It should be readily apparent that the earlier the interference with the processes involved in object relations development, the more serious the psychopathology" (p. 26). Thus, failures in establishing primary attachments to mother result in psychoses or psychopathic personalities; failures in the development of symbiosis and separation–individuation result in severe personality disorders, particularly borderline and narcissistic disorders; and developmental failures after the establishment of identity and object constancy result in less severe neurotic disorders.

People who have written about the psychology of deafness have speculated on how the child's deafness and the reactions of parents and the hearing world typically affect on the child's development. Usually the child's deafness is viewed as having a multitude of destructive ramifications. Various problems emerge either because of problems seen as inherent in deafness or because of inadequate ways in which people in the child's "ecology" (Levine, 1981) respond to the child.

In the deafness mental health literature, the psychological level (i.e., the psychological problems deaf people are alleged to have) is generally emphasized, whereas the sociocultural level (i.e., the ways in which hearing people typically respond to Deaf people) is minimized. The result has been a portrait of deaf people as deviant, maladjusted, and incapable of benefiting from insight-oriented therapies.

Certainly the strongest refutation to all of this literature on the alleged pathologies of Deaf people is the regularly cited superior performance of Deaf children of Deaf families, raised biculturally, on virtually every measure of mental health and educational and vocational achievement (Mindel & Vernon, 1971; Schlesinger & Meadow, 1972). This superior performance demonstrates that deafness per se need not become pathological. Rather, the inept and oppressive responses of hearing people to Deaf people either create various forms of maladjustment or impose a pathological viewpoint on psychologically healthy Deaf people.

As much as one may want to reject completely these notions of psychopathology in Deaf people, any clinician who regularly works with Deaf people has to recognize the relevance of these models to some of the clients he or she sees. A clinician can acknowledge the long history of inappropriate evaluation and treatment of Deaf people by hearing mental health professionals. He or she can also affirm Deaf culture and strong culturally Deaf identities. Nonetheless, the practicing clinician repeatedly sees Deaf clients with multiple neurological and other disabilities, severe emotional and behavioral problems, and extremely dysfunctional families. The question then for the mental health clinician who wishes to affirm deafness is how to think about and treat these various forms of pathology without joining and fostering further oppression of Deaf people.

This is where the concept of marginality becomes useful. The cultural marginality Deaf people face can be viewed as *isomorphic* (parallel) to the various kinds of psychopathology emerging from disturbances in psychosocial development that result from placing a deaf child in an unprepared hearing context. Marginality on the cultural level refers to lack of clear embeddedness in a social context, and this can manifest psychologically by the lack of clearly differentiated internal representations of self and object and by consequent disturbances in interpersonal relationships. By understanding the disturbed deaf person as experiencing some variant of cultural marginality, one immediately situates the deaf person in his or her social context. The environmental impact becomes more salient, the nature of the oppression of Deaf people is highlighted, and most importantly, the path is charted for movement away from marginality to the desired goal of appropriate social embeddedness and relatedness.

In this framework, joining a cultural community is seen as isomorphic to establishing selfhood and intimacy with other people. A culturally informed psychotherapy would need to work simultaneously on the psychological and cultural levels. On the one hand, from a psychodynamic standpoint, the clinician helps the client develop and internalize positive self- and object-representations. On the other hand, the therapist helps his or her client to establish a cultural identity vis-à-vis the Deaf and hearing worlds. It is here that an understanding of how Deaf cultural identities develop becomes useful. Marginality can thus be conceived of as both a psychological and a cultural phenomenon. Treatment interventions need to occur on both levels simultaneously.

Culturally marginal deaf people may function at very different levels in society. The least pathological manifestation of cultural marginality would be identity confusion in an otherwise healthy person. With sufficient language and intelligence, these high-functioning marginal deaf people can verbalize the existential question, "Am I Deaf, hard-of-hearing, or hearing? Where do I belong?" They may seek counseling for help resolving this identity confusion or help achieving satisfactory interpersonal relationships. In cases when a marginal client's development is normal, he or she may simply need to explore his or her relationship to two or more cultures. In cases when a client's marginality also reflects disturbances in the development of self, the therapeutic task is more complex.

The more pathological manifestations of marginality would be seen in deaf people with characterological or behavioral disorders. In public-sector clinical settings, a therapist typically sees a subset of lower-functioning deaf people who have multiple neurological, emotional, behavioral, and family problems. Lacking sufficient language skills and usually having below normal intelligence, these people have difficulty verbalizing their confusion. Instead, they behave in ways that are immature and socially inappropriate for both Deaf and hearing cultural contexts. They may have tantrums or aggressive outbursts. They may be belligerent and demanding in interpersonal situations. Commonly, they lack the social skills needed to maintain employment. They may be sexually inappropriate, and they may abuse illegal substances. Not surprisingly, the families of these clients have often not found a healthy way of accommodating the deaf family member, and family dysfunction becomes evident (Harvey, 1989). Although one cannot repeat strongly enough that there is no inherent psychopathology associated with deafness, the hearing world is generally so poorly prepared to nurture deaf children that cultural and psychological marginality is all too common.

One sees this also in Deaf education. Marginality in deaf people has been reinforced by both oral and Total Communication educational programs and even more dramatically by mainstreaming. The failure of deaf educators and mental health professionals to take Deaf culture seriously has had profound and tragic consequences for deaf children. It is primarily the limitations of deaf education that make marginality such a relevant theme for Deaf people.

Deaf Education and the Fostering of Cultural Marginality.   In the past 30 years, there have been two major changes in the education of deaf children in the U.S. The first change is the decline of oralism and the resurgence of the combined signing and oral method, now called Total Communication. The second change is the decline of the Deaf residential school and the increase in mainstreaming of deaf children in hearing educational settings.

Behan (1989c) called Total Communication a "total farce." He pointed out that Total Communication in practice has meant that teachers speak and sign at the same time, a practice more accurately called Simultaneous Communication (Sim. Com.). The signing that is used is almost always one of a number of artificial systems that have been invented to model English manually. These systems (Signing Exact English, Seeing Essential English, Linguistics of Visual English, and Sign English) grossly distort the grammar and semantics of ASL and are therefore resented by many in the Deaf community.

Total Communication actually seems to represent an ambivalent attitude toward ASL and Deaf culture. ASL is included in theory, but really it is simply tolerated when coming from students and not used as the formal language of instruction. Although Deaf culture may be acknowledged, a clear Deaf-affirmative view, which must include a significant number of culturally Deaf teachers and staff, is still the rare exception. The graduates of Total Communication programs, although they have signing abilities, may well be ambivalent and confused about their deafness. In other words, they may be culturally marginal as deaf people.

The passage in 1975 of PL94–142, the Education for All Handicapped Children Act, has fostered the practice of mainstreaming deaf children. The law called for a free, individually tailored, appropriate education, in the "least restrictive environment," for all handicapped children (National Center, 1984). The problem has been that the hearing people who implement this act generally interpret least restrictive environment to mean a regular classroom. Sending a deaf child to a Deaf residential school, the place where traditionally the majority of deaf children were socialized into Deaf culture (Stokoe, 1989), now is often seen as the more restrictive option.

In addition, in many states, including Massachusetts, responsibility for paying for the education of handicapped children has shifted from the state to the local area. Now the hearing bias in favor of mainstreaming is reinforced powerfully by the economic incentive of financially strapped communities to save money. Between the legal mandate to find the least restrictive setting, interpreted as the hearing setting, and the economic mandate to find the least expensive setting, which is almost always a nonspecialized program, deaf children are far more likely to be placed in regular classrooms than they were 10 years ago. The language input the child gets in this minimally accessible environment is likely to be highly confused.

The hearing view of mainstreaming is that it facilitates integration of deaf children into hearing society. The culturally Deaf view of mainstreaming is that it constitutes isolation for deaf children and a serious threat to Deaf culture. This culturally Deaf view is exemplified in a common play on the sign for mainstreaming. The normal sign has the five fingers of both hands wiggling and merging together from the shoulders to the center chest. The idea is to represent blending. The play involves changing the five fingers of one hand to one finger that is merged and then pushed down by the five fingers of the other hand. This changes the sign's meaning to connote oppression.

When marginal deaf children come from a Total Communication or mainstreamed program, their socialization as Deaf people may have to wait until they are college students or adults and discover the Deaf community. In the meantime, their orientation toward communication is likely to reflect this educational background. They are likely to have confused ideas about communication, in particular about how, when, and whether a deaf person should speak and sign simultaneously. The marginal deaf person is unlikely to know ASL, unlikely to have good judgment about which communication styles are normative in which contexts, and is unlikely to value ASL as a full language in its own right.

In summary, it is proposed that most deaf children born into hearing families first develop marginal identities. These identities are reinforced by Total Communication and mainstreaming programs as well as by oralism. These identities are characterized by some of the following:

1. Poor communication skills in both English and ASL. The inability to adapt communication for reasons of cultural appropriateness in a variety of settings.

2. Social behavior that is inappropriate for both Deaf and hearing communities.

3. Difficulty establishing and maintaining intimate relationships with either Deaf or hearing people. A deep, all-pervading sense of isolation and often bitterness.

4. Confusion regarding identity.

5. A sense of fitting in nowhere, being between worlds, and nowhere at home.

6. Shifting loyalties toward Deaf and hearing people. Sometimes the person feels most comfortable among other Deaf people, and other times he or she is uncomfortable being with other Deaf people. The person idealizes hearing people and strives to be like them but also feels anger and resentment toward hearing people. Although anger can be present, it is the changing, unstable affect and attitude that is more characteristic.

7. Searching for an elusive middle ground, especially as regards communication. Marginal deaf people are likely to value simultaneous communication (speech and sign simultaneously) and signing in some variant of English. Some bicultural deaf people may also value simultaneous communication, and the difference is likely to be that marginal deaf people *actively disapprove* of ASL and signing without speech, whereas bicultural people can value many communication strategies and adapt as circumstances warrant.

Stage 3: Immersion in the Deaf World

In Black Identity Theory, pre-encounter is followed by encounter, the confrontation with what Helms (1990) called "the identity shattering something." No separate encounter stage is conceptualized for this model of Deaf identity development. There are two reasons for this. First of all, even in Black Identity Theory, it is difficult to determine what distinguishes this stage from pre-encounter on the one side and immersion on the other. Encounter is a transitional stage, difficult to describe on its own terms. In Deaf identity development, it would refer to the "moment" of discovery of one's Deafness. This is likely to be a time of confusion, emotional volatility, and rapidly changing opinions. The volatility of the stage makes it difficult to operationalize reliably. Subjects may show marginal identities at one moment and immersion identities the next.

Secondly, those Deaf people moving into immersion from marginality are not so much rejecting a prior identity as forming an original identity. They may literally, for the first time, have a language for thinking about themselves. I believe this makes the process of encounter for these Deaf people different than for those who have a clear prior identity. It is probably more accurate to speak of late-deafened people, who previously were culturally hearing, as having an "encounter" when they discover the social meaning of deafness than for marginal deaf people who are emerging out of a culturally and linguistically confused wasteland.

Other theories of C/RID have given us the essential outlines of the immersion stage. It is characterized chiefly by anger, especially toward the dominant groups in society; uncompromising rejection of everything pertaining to the majority society; an exuberant love affair with everything pertaining to the minority culture even while sharp distinctions are made as to what does, and does not, represent the minority viewpoint; dichotomous thinking ("You are one of us or one of them, good or bad"); and political militancy.

What would a Deaf-immersion identity look like? To extend the other models of C/RID to the Deaf experience, one would expect a person in this stage to seek, by definition, immersion into the Deaf world. In other cultural contexts, this stage could take the political form of separatism or nationalism. In fact, there have been historical instances of calls for Deaf states. Padden and Humphries (1988) described the attempt of John James Flourney, a Deaf property owner in Georgia in the 1850s, to establish a separate Deaf state. The matter was discussed earnestly, pro and con, in the letters to the editor of the *American Annals of the Deaf and Dumb* from 1856 to 1858. According to Padden and Humphries, although most Deaf leaders opposed the idea (for what, after all, would they do with their hearing children?), the idea nonetheless captured their imagination. Deaf leaders entertained seriously the idea of purchasing large tracts of land to sell to Deaf settlers at low rates. Even the editor of the *Annals* supported this more scaled-down Deaf separatist vision. In recent years, a Deaf writer (Bullard, 1986) wrote a novel, *Islay*, about a Deaf man who establishes a separate state for Deaf people. Again, although not a practical reality, the idea resonates.

Behan (1989e) discussed Alexander Graham Bell's attempt to prevent the forming of a Deaf "race" by prohibiting intermarriage among Deaf people. Behan abhorred that idea but responded favorably, in a manner that would have terrified Bell, to the notion of a Deaf race: "To me that's great! Imagine us being called a 'race' instead of 'handicapped.' Yeah! Imagine saying to yourself: 'I am a member of the Deaf race'" (p. 85).

Deaf people with immersion identities want to surround themselves with everything they think is Deaf. As with members of other minorities, however, these Deaf notions of deafness may be stereotypical. This is not a personal, integrated identity, but something one latches onto. It is like a new suit of clothes one tries on before it is tailored to fit one's individual body. In this stage, the person determines the right and wrong ways to be Deaf and labels anyone who does not fit his or her ideal as "hearing-minded." It is a stage of "unreasonableness." People who use their voices, sign in English, marry or associate with hearing people, or wear hearing aids can be rejected cavalierly.

One would expect an immersion stance to be most evident in those issues traditionally of most concern to Deaf people: communication, the meaning of deafness, the interaction between Deaf and hearing people, the control of Deaf institutions. Two of the four student demands of the Gallaudet strike were for the selection of a Deaf president and the increase in Deaf representation on the Gallaudet Board of Trustees to 51% (Gannon, 1989). These demands had to do with the symbolic and real control of this premier Deaf institution. Along with this, one would expect Deaf people with immersion identities to want all Deaf schools and programs to be run by Deaf people and to believe that Deaf people should be taught, counseled, ministered to, and so on, primarily, if not exclusively, by Deaf people. Hearing people would be reduced to a much less central role in Deaf people's lives, and in the visions of some may be excluded entirely.

The medical–pathological model of deafness would be rejected firmly. Deafness is understood solely as a cultural difference, rather than as a disability. The problems Deaf people have are caused by hearing people controlling their lives and not by the limitations of not being able to hear. The proper language for Deaf people is ASL, and English may be rejected as the language of the oppressors. There is no reason for Deaf people to speak, even in hearing contexts, and simultaneous use of speech and sign, along with any sign code that imitates English, would be rejected as anything from insensitive to a gross violation of Deaf values. Hearing aids are a very visible symbol of the imposition of hearing values, and one would expect Deaf people in this stage to discard their hearing aids just as the American colonists discarded the tea that symbolized British tyranny. The idea of curing deafness through cochlear implants or other medical procedures would be considered the equivalent of cultural genocide.

The dominant emotion of this stage is anger. Hearing people, however well meaning, may find themselves the target of this anger. This writer can remember lifting weights in the Gallaudet gymnasium alongside Deaf undergraduates and having trouble gaining access to the universal weight machine. The message I felt at the time was, "This is our space. What are you doing here?" Sign language students who are hearing commonly share stories about their difficulty gaining access to the Deaf world and about this or that Deaf person who, to their mind, treated them rudely. Perhaps hearing people expect to be greeted as saviors, but Deaf people pick up quickly on paternalism, and their angry reaction can be swift and hurtful.

This writer does not mean to suggest that these immersion views are not legitimate. They are necessary and health affirming and as legitimate as those of any other minority. As frustrating as it can be for hearing people to interact with Stage-3 Deaf people, there may well not be enough angry Deaf people rocking the boat. In addition, hearing people, like Whites and other majority groups, collectively "have it coming." Hearing people need to be challenged to understand how our behavior, even if we believe ourselves well intentioned, has been oppressive to Deaf people. Nonetheless, there is an uncompromising quality to the thinking and behavior of minority persons in this stage that is, in the end, a limitation both for them and for their cause. Ultimately, it is a multicultural world, not a hearing world, and separatist visions, however necessary in the short run, do not advance our collective humanity.

In summary, the immersion stage is characterized by the following:

1. Immersion into the Deaf world. An enthusiastic and uncritical embrace of everything Deaf.
2. Idealization of the Deaf world and disparagement of the hearing world.
3. Either/or thinking, such as the tendency to believe Deaf can do no wrong and hearing can do no right, and a rigid definition of *true* cultural Deafness while writing off others as hearing impaired or hearing minded.
4. The reversal of traditional hearing values: ASL is superior to English. Deaf people should never use their voices. Signing and speaking simultaneously is never appropriate. Only Deaf people should run Deaf programs or teach or counsel Deaf people.
5. Generalized anger, but especially directed at hearing people. A readiness to confront hearing people for perceived injustices.
6. The early part of this stage (in the Black Identity Theory this is called immersion) is characterized by being more anti-hearing than pro-Deaf. Positive Deaf values are defined by their opposition to traditional hearing values rather than by what works for Deaf people. The late part of this stage (in the Black Identity Theory this is called emersion) is characterized more by the attempt to define a Deaf-affirmative vision rather than being antihearing per se. As one progresses through this stage, one's vision of affirmative Deafness grows and becomes more inclusive. One becomes more concerned with supporting other Deaf people than with attacking hearing people.

Stage 4: Bicultural

A bicultural Deaf identity is proposed as the final stage of Deaf identity development. In this stage, a person affirms Deafness as a cultural difference and feels a profound connection with other Deaf people. At the same time, the strengths and weaknesses of both Deaf and hearing people are recognized, and the person has a personal and balanced perspective on what it means to be Deaf. In the same way that African Americans can reach the point where they know how to reject racism without rejecting White people, so can bicultural Deaf people reject hearing ethnocentrism without rejecting hearing people.

For deaf people who begin life as culturally marginal, becoming bicultural can represent the final stage of identity development. Deaf children raised in Deaf families, however, are usually bicultural from childhood. They are born into a world where deafness is the norm, communication in sign is a given, and where one learns how to interact with hearing outsiders just as racial minorities learn how to interact with White outsiders. Schein (1989) quoted Jacobs:

I was born Deaf of Deaf parents who had an older Deaf son. Therefore, my family was entirely Deaf, and we lived in a world of our own, where manual communication was the order of the day. I grew up in a loving atmosphere and never knew any deprivation of communication; my parents knew my wants, and I knew just how far I could go without bringing their wrath down on my head. The conversation was full and interesting at the dinner table. I learned all the facts of life at appropriate times. I attended a residential school as a day pupil. My only communication difficulties arose when I began doing business with the outside world, but I thought nothing about them because I had observed my parents' methods of overcoming these barriers. I merely followed the same road—that of employing a pad and pencil to convey my wishes, and attempting to read lips at first, then offering the pad and pencil to the other party if I failed to understand him. (cited in Schein, 1979, p. 123)

How would the identities of Deaf children of Deaf parents develop given that they probably are bicultural from the beginning of life? One hypothesis is that they experience relatively little change in identity compared with Deaf children of hearing parents. Another hypothesis is that depending on their educational and social experiences, they may move "backward." That is, the encounter with the hearing orientation of Deaf educational programs as well as the larger society may confuse and marginalize them or may make them more radically Deaf. This issue can not be researched until there is a tool for measuring Deaf identity, and hopefully the Deaf Identity Development Scale (DIDS), to be described shortly, may prove useful in this regard.

Which kinds of institutions have been created by people with a bicultural Deaf identity, and what are the positions espoused by such institutions? One model was exemplified by The Bicultural Center, a Maryland-based organization of Deaf and hearing people dedicated to affirming the equality of Deaf and hearing cultures. The newsletter of The Bicultural Center, TBC News, was designed "to provide Deaf activists and their supporters with a forum for the exchange of ideas." Articles in TBC News routinely defined and defended Deaf culture, interviewed strong Deaf leaders and culturally sensitive hearing parents of Deaf children, cited some of the more egregious examples of hearing paternalism and oppression of Deaf people, and advocated for bilingual approaches to Deaf education and more Deaf control of Deaf schools and programs.

The Bicultural Center was also distinguished by offering a model program of instruction in ASL as opposed to the Sign-English-based instruction usually offered by schools claiming to teach sign language. Similarly, its model of interpreter education was based on the kinds of sophisticated instruction in interpreting one finds in prominent schools of foreign language interpreting, and not on models of transliteration (spoken English to sign English and vice versa) commonly taught in sign language interpretation programs.

People associated with The Bicultural Center were sometimes characterized as radicals. This was unjust, to my mind, as the positions advocated by The Bicultural Center were really quite moderate compared with the wide range of stances taken by minorities. They did not advocate for the superiority of ASL, for the expulsion of hearing people from Deaf people's lives, or for the complete eradication of speech and speech-reading training from Deaf education. They did not advocate that Deaf people should live in communities completely separate from hearing people. Nor did they say that English was irrelevant to Deaf people. These would indeed be radical positions more representative of Stage-3 immersion consciousness. Instead, they simply took seriously the notion of equality between Deaf and hearing cultures. The fact that The Bicultural Center could be stereotyped as radical demonstrates, I believe, the degree to which hearing people and hearing consciousness have framed the terms of the debates about deafness.

The main components of a Bicultural Deaf identity would appear to be as follows:

1. Clear cultural pride as a Deaf person while recognizing that both Deaf and hearing people have strengths and weaknesses.
2. Some feeling of comfort and skill in both Deaf and hearing settings. There may still be a preference for either one. The feeling of being at ease, if not at home, in both worlds.
3. An appreciation and respect for English and ASL as distinct languages of equal value and conversational abilities in both languages.
4. The ability to recognize and oppose hearing paternalism and other forms of Deaf oppression while maintaining friendly alliances with hearing people who are judged to be trustworthy allies.
5. A deep and personal sense of what it means to be Deaf.

Within these parameters, some questions are hotly debated among bicultural Deaf people. Is it ever appropriate to sign and speak simultaneously? Although mixing the languages is generally opposed, there are Deaf and hard-of-hearing people who prefer this mode of communication, and there can be a conflict between support for cultural values and support for the preferences of individual Deaf people. How much importance should be given to speech, speech reading, and amplification in the education of Deaf children? What role should interpreters have in the Deaf community? What is the best way to give Deaf children exposure to English? In which ways can hearing people be meaningfully and helpfully involved with Deaf people? What does a Deaf person look for in a hearing ally? What should be the relationship between hearing parents of deaf children and Deaf adults? How broadly should culturally Deaf be defined, and can one even, in some circumstances, consider oral deaf people to be culturally Deaf?

Although it is inappropriate for a hearing person to attempt to answer these questions for Deaf people, it has been my observation that culturally Deaf people differ on these points and that the answers change depending on the time and circumstances. For instance, the question of whether hearing people who can sign should sign for themselves or use interpreters when making presentations to mixed Deaf and hearing groups has met different responses in recent years. Not too long ago, it was considered inappropriate for hearing people not to use interpreters, but recently it has been considered insensitive to use interpreters. Sociohistorical developments have an impact on the definitions of cultural Deafness that are posed. To the extent the Deaf community feels secure, such notions tend to broaden, and to the extent it feels attacked, such notions narrow. Bicultural Deaf people, more secure in their personal identity as Deaf people, may define cultural Deafness more broadly than Deaf people in the immersion stage. They may include, for instance, those highly educated Deaf people who respect ASL but prefer to communicate with signing closer to English, something not usually acceptable to someone in Stage 3. At the same time, certain thresholds probably would not be crossed by a bicultural Deaf person. Any notion that English is superior to ASL, for instance or that Deaf people are best thought of as handicapped, would be impossible to reconcile with cultural Deafness.

A bicultural Deaf identity would, therefore, likely include the following component:

6. The ability to appreciate and affirm different visions of positive cultural Deafness. For instance, a bicultural Deaf person might strongly identify with Deaf culture while preferring to sign in Pidgin Sign English or even to speak and sign simultaneously. Sensitive and respectful to Deaf culture, these bicultural individuals nonetheless know when to turn off their voices and code switch into the best ASL they can produce.

Deaf Identity Development: Summary

The theory of Deaf identity development outlined here is based on other models of C/RID applied to the particular circumstances of Deaf people. This model is unique with regard to these other models of C/RID in two respects:

1. Several beginning points are hypothesized depending on the circumstances in which one becomes deaf. The only true pre-encounter identity, in the sense in which this term is used in Black Identity Theory (Helms, 1990), is the culturally hearing identity, and this is most applicable to late-deafened people. These people may adjust to their deafness while maintaining an entirely hearing cultural perspective, or they may attribute new meaning to their deafness after encounters with Deaf people.

The vast majority of deaf people have hearing parents, and I have hypothesized that they first develop marginal identities. By contrast, Deaf children of Deaf parents probably grow up with bicultural identities, but they may progress backward for a time if they are marginalized or radicalized by experiences with deaf education.

2. The concept of marginality is more important to DID than to other models of C/RID. Several levels of marginality are proposed, ranging from existential confusion in otherwise mentally healthy people to severe emotional and behavioral disorders. Cultural marginality is conceptualized as isomorphic to psychological marginality. This implies that treatment methods would also need to be multilevel.

A highly controversial issue in the C/RID literature concerns the extent of heterogeneity of outcome for the "final" stage of identity. Put simply, the controversy swirls around the question: Is the "most advanced" or "most healthy" cultural identity necessarily one involving significant identification with the Deaf community? Could a culturally hearing deaf person also be mentally healthy? This question is very politically charged. Certainly, Deaf militants (Deaf and hearing people with immersion identities) would like to believe that cultural identification with the Deaf community is a prerequisite for mental health, but a recent rethinking of Black Identity Development by one of its major proponents, William Cross (1991), implies that one must evaluate the beliefs of these militants cautiously.

Cross reconceptualized the initial pre-encounter stage to allow for a "Euro-centric" rather than "Afro-centric" identity, and he argued that there is no necessary relationship between these kinds of cultural orientations and mental health. However, if one considers the gay and lesbian context and conceptualizes Stage 1 as being "in the closet," then there is clear evidence that Stage 1, "closeted" identities are correlated with emotional and psychological adjustment problems

(Garnets & Kimmel, 1991). Is cultural-identity development in deaf people more similar to such development for African Americans, where there need not be an association with mental health, or to such development for gay men and lesbians, where apparently there is such an association? Ultimately, this is an empirical question that cannot be answered until there is some valid and reliable instrument to measure cultural identity in deaf people that can be administered to a sample of Deaf and deaf people along with measures of psychological adjustment.

Theoretically, this model certainly suggests that whatever the final outcome or however broadly bicultural comes to be conceptualized, the process of cultural-identity change for Deaf people must involve some movement through an immersion stage of overly close and uncritical identification with what are perceived to be true culturally Deaf values. The model hypothesizes that people who have integrated their deafness in a healthy way into their larger identity must, at some point, have experiences something akin to an immersion period. This is proposed to be true even if these people later establish some distance between the core Deaf community and themselves and even if they later prefer the company of like-minded hearing people.

In other respects, the logic of Deaf identity development is the same as that of other models of cultural and racial identity development. Identity change occurs through the attribution of positive meaning to one's membership in a minority community. Initial constructions of minority identities tend to be extreme and radical, but, if circumstances allow, more moderate and balanced identities tend to develop. The issue of circumstances is important, because minority identity development cannot be conceptualized apart from the reactions of the larger world. Extreme circumstances create extreme viewpoints. To help any minority person develop from immersion to biculturalism, a therapist needs to demonstrate awareness of the oppression the client has experienced. The therapist needs to be able to validate the client's anger while simultaneously encouraging a broader vision of minority–majority relations.

Finally, as with other models of C/RID, it is assumed that a Deaf person can "recycle" through these stages throughout his or her life, reaching ever more complex understanding and integration of his or her emotional experience (Ivey, 1991). Again, circumstances bear on whether and how one becomes "reradicalized."

Table 5.1 presents a summary of the Deaf identity development model.

TABLE 5.1
Theory of Deaf Identity Development

Stage	Reference Group	View of Deafness	View of Deaf Community	Emotional Theme
Hearing	Hearing	Pathology	Uninformed & stereo-typed	Despair, Depression
Marginal	Switches	Pathology	Shifts from good to bad	Confusion & conflict
Immersion	Deaf	Cultural	Positive, non-reflective	Anger/"in love with Deafness"
Bicultural	Deaf	Cultural	Positive, personal, integrated	Self-acceptance & group pride

ASSESSMENT OF CULTURAL IDENTITY
IN DEAF PEOPLE

Therapists working with deaf people need to know something about the cultural identity of their clients. One way to learn about this is simply to ask relevant, probing questions. Indeed, the ability to raise these kinds of questions may suggest to one's deaf clients a high degree of sensitivity to, and awareness of, Deaf cultural issues. When the therapist raises these questions, the client may feel relieved that here is a person who is knowledgeable and informed and with whom it is safe to explore these subtle issues. Questions that may be useful as part of this process are listed in Appendix A.

The author has begun the process of developing an instrument designed to measure cultural identity in deaf people. This instrument, the Deaf Identity Development Scale, is described elsewhere in detail (Glickman, 1993; Glickman & Carey, 1993). The DIDS is a 60-item instrument, based on the Deaf-identity-development model presented in this chapter, which was developed first in English and then translated into ASL and videotaped. The ASL translation was validated. The DIDS was then administered in both English and videotaped ASL to 105 Gallaudet University students. The English version was also administered to 65 members of the Association of Late Deafened Adults-Boston (ALDA-Boston). The results are presented in the works cited previously. Based on these results, the DIDS has been revised and improved, and this new version is presented in Table 5.2. This new version has not yet been validated or normed, and no claims are being made at this point with regard to its validity, reliability, and utility. In addition, a new, ASL-videotaped translation has not yet been done and is necessary before this instrument can be best used with many culturally Deaf people. The instrument is presented here in the hope that it will be worked with, evaluated, and further revised until a suitable measure of cultural identity in deaf people is obtained.

Table 5.3 is a list of the DIDS items organized by scale. This will help in scoring the instrument. Scoring the DIDS for individual subjects is easy. The item responses are converted to a numerical scale as follows: SD = 1; D = 2; DK = 3; A = 4; SA = 5. To score the instrument, one simply takes the mean score for each scale. For example, one subject, a White sophomore at Gallaudet, born deaf, who has deaf parents and a family income of between $30,000 and $40,000, who began signing at age 2, who attended a signing residential school, and who used both the English and ASL version of the instrument scored as follows: hearing scale mean = 1.14; marginal scale mean = 1.38; immersion scale mean = 3.21; bicultural scale mean = 3.92.

What do these results mean? Without a completely validated instrument and normative date, accurate conclusions cannot be drawn. In the absence of a finished instrument, one can only make inferences based on what the DIDS scales appear to measure in reference to the theory on which it is based. The subject just described appears to be culturally Deaf[3] with a more bicultural than

---

[3]Culturally Deaf is defined operationally as scoring highest on either the immersion or bicultural scale.

TABLE 5.2
My Feelings About My Deafness

The purpose of these sentences is to find out about your feelings and thoughts about being deaf.

This research is in both English and ASL. You can read the English sentence and then respond or you can watch the ASL sentence and then respond. The English and the ASL mean the same.

Please do not write your name on these papers. Please answer honestly. There are no right or wrong answers. What is important is *what you* think and what *you* feel. Please try to respond to every sentence.

There are 60 sentences. On the videotape, there is a 7-second pause between sentences. Please try to answer quickly. Do not take more than a few seconds per sentence.

Your job is to circle how much you agree or disagree with each sentence. After each sentence, there are five choices:

SA: Strongly Agree   A: Agree   DK: Don't know   D: Disagree   SD: Strongly Disagree

Please circle the response that best matches how you think and feel.

Example

Most deaf people are happy.	SA	A	DK	D	SD

If you *strongly agree* with this sentence, circle SA. If you *agree*, circle A. If you *don't know*, circle DK. If you *disagree*, circle D. If you *strongly disagree, circle SD.*

1. I enjoy both Deaf and hearing cultures.	SA	A	DK	D	SD
2. I don't know how I feel about deaf people.	SA	A	DK	D	SD
3. Deaf people should only use ASL.	SA	A	DK	D	SD
4. Deafness is a terrible disability.	SA	A	DK	D	SD
5. I support Deaf culture, and I value many hearing ways.	SA	A	DK	D	SD
6. Deaf people do not need hearing aids.	SA	A	DK	D	SD
7. I feel sorry for deaf people who depend on sign language.	SA	A	DK	D	SD
8. It's hard for me to make friends.	SA	A	DK	D	SD
9. American Sign Language and English are different languages of equal value.	SA	A	DK	D	SD
10. There is no place for hearing people in the Deaf world.	SA	A	DK	D	SD
11. I call myself "Deaf."	SA	A	DK	D	SD
12. I don't like it when deaf people use sign language.	SA	A	DK	D	SD
13. I don't know whether I accept or reject the Deaf community.	SA	A	DK	D	SD
14. I want to help hearing people understand and respect Deaf culture.	SA	A	DK	D	SD
15. I don't know whether to call myself "hearing impaired" or "Deaf."	SA	A	DK	D	SD
16. Only deaf people should teach deaf children.	SA	A	DK	D	SD
17. Sometimes I love being deaf, and other times I hate it.	SA	A	DK	D	SD
18. Deaf people should marry hearing people.	SA	A	DK	D	SD
19. Hearing people don't help deaf people.	SA	A	DK	D	SD
20. When I see deaf people use sign language, I walk away.	SA	A	DK	D	SD
21. I can change between ASL and Sign English easily.	SA	A	DK	D	SD
22. Neither deaf people nor hearing people accept me.	SA	A	DK	D	SD
23. I am satisfied with what the Deaf world has to offer.	SA	A	DK	D	SD
24. I am always alone.	SA	A	DK	D	SD
25. I don't understand why Deaf people have their own culture.	SA	A	DK	D	SD

26. I have both deaf and hearing friends.   SA   A   DK   D   SD

27. Hearing people do not understand nor support Deaf ways.   SA   A   DK   D   SD

28. When I am with hearing people, I remember that I am   SA   A   DK   D   SD
    proud to be Deaf.

29. The focus of deaf education should be teaching deaf chil-   SA   a   DK   D   SD
    dren to speak and lipread.

30. I feel angry with hearing people.   SA   A   DK   D   SD

31. Deaf people need hearing aids to help them communicate   SA   A   DK   D   SD
    normally.

32. If one signs, it is best to speak while signing.   SA   A   DK   D   SD

33. I don't know whether I'd rather fall in love with a deaf per- SA   A   DK   D   SD
    son or a hearing person.

34. I seek out hearing friends who respect and value the Deaf   SA   A   DK   D   SD
    community.

35. I feel at home in the Deaf community.   SA   A   DK   D   SD

36. I don't know whether to think of my deafness as something SA   A   DK   D   SD
    good or something bad.

37. I feel comfortable with my child being either deaf or hear-   SA   A   DK   D   SD
    ing.

38. It is best for deaf people to communicate with speech and   SA   A   DK   D   SD
    lipreading.

39. Hearing people communicate better than deaf people.   SA   A   DK   D   SD

40. Teaching deaf children to speak is a waste of time.   SA   A   DK   D   SD

41. Sometimes I wish the Deaf community accepted me more,   SA   A   DK   D   SD
    but other times I'm glad I'm not a full member.

42. I only socialize with hearing people.   SA   A   DK   D   SD

43. It is wrong to speak while signing.   SA   A   DK   D   SD

44. I have thought a lot about what it means to be a proud,   SA   A   DK   D   SD
    strong, Deaf person.

45. I want to socialize with other deaf people, but often they   SA   A   DK   D   SD
    embarrass me.

46. I would like to have an operation that would give me full   SA   A   DK   D   SD
    hearing.

47. Although I have many hearing friends, I sometimes still feel SA   A   DK   D   SD
    angry with hearing people and hearing society.

48. Hearing counselors, teachers, and doctors who specialize   SA   A   DK   D   SD
    in treating deaf people can give me the best advice.

49. I feel comfortable with both deaf and hearing people.   SA   A   DK   D   SD

50. Only deaf people should run deaf schools.   SA   A   DK   D   SD

51. I feel good about being deaf, but I involve myself with hear- SA   A   DK   D   SD
    ing people also.

52. I can't trust hearing people.   SA   A   DK   D   SD

53. Sign language should be based on English.   SA   A   DK   D   SD

54. I call myself "hearing impaired."   SA   A   DK   D   SD

55. Learning to lipread is a waste of time.   SA   A   DK   D   SD

56. I don't know what the best way to communicate is.   SA   A   DK   D   SD

57. Deaf people should only socialize with other deaf people.   SA   A   DK   D   SD

58. I do not feel comfortable with either hearing or deaf people. SA   A   DK   D   SD

59. It is important to find a cure for deafness.   SA   A   DK   D   SD

60. My hearing friends will fight for deaf rights.   SA   A   DK   D   SD

TABLE 5.3
DIDS Items Organized by Scale

Hearing Scale

4. Deafness is a terrible disability.
7. I feel sorry for deaf people who depend on sign language.
12. I don't like it when deaf people use sign language.
18. Deaf people should marry hearing people.
25. I don't understand why Deaf people have their own culture.
29. The focus of deaf education should be teaching deaf children to speak and lipread.
31. Deaf people need hearing aids to help them communicate normally.
38. It is best for deaf people to communicate with speech and lipreading.
39. Hearing people communicate better than deaf people.
42. I only socialize with hearing people.
46. I would like to have an operation that would give me full hearing.
48. Hearing counselors, teachers, and doctors who specialize in treating deaf people can give me the best advice.
53. Sign language should be based on English.
54. I call myself "hearing impaired."
59. It is important to find a cure for deafness.

Marginal Scale

2. I don't know how I feel about deaf people.
8. It's hard for me to make friends.
13. I don't know whether I accept or reject the Deaf community.
15. I don't know whether to call myself "hearing impaired" or "Deaf."
17. Sometimes I love being deaf, and other times I hate it.
20. When I see deaf people use sign language, I walk away.
22. Neither deaf people nor hearing people accept me.
24. I am always alone.
32. If one signs, it is best to speak while signing.
33. I don't know whether I'd rather fall in love with a deaf person or a hearing person.
36. I don't know whether to think of my deafness as something good or something bad.
41. Sometimes I wish the Deaf community accepted me more, but other times I'm glad I'm not a full member.
45. I want to socialize with other deaf people, but often they embarrass me.
56. I don't know what the best way to communicate is.
58. I do not feel comfortable with either hearing or deaf people.

Immersion Scale

3. Deaf people should only use ASL.
6. Deaf people do not need hearing aids.
10. There is no place for hearing people in the Deaf world.
16. Only deaf people should teach deaf children.
19. Hearing people don't help deaf people.
23. I am satisfied with what the Deaf world has to offer.
27. Hearing people do not understand nor support Deaf ways.
30. I feel angry with hearing people.
35. I feel at home in the Deaf community.
40. Teaching deaf children to speak is a waste of time.
43. It is wrong to speak while signing.
50. Only deaf people should run deaf schools.
52. I can't trust hearing people.
55. Learning to lipread is a waste of time.
57. Deaf people should only socialize with other deaf people.

Bicultural Scale

1. I enjoy both Deaf and hearing cultures.
5. I support Deaf culture, and I value many hearing ways.
9. American Sign Language and English are different languages of equal value.
11. I call myself, "Deaf."
14. I want to help hearing people understand and respect Deaf culture.
21. I can change between ASL and Sign English easily.
26. I have both deaf and hearing friends.
28. When I am with hearing people, I remember that I am proud to be Deaf.
34. I seek out hearing friends who respect and value the Deaf community.
37. I feel comfortable with my child being either deaf or hearing.
44. I have thought a lot about what it means to be a proud, strong Deaf person.
47. Although I have many hearing friends, I sometimes still feel angry with hearing people and hearing society.
49. I feel comfortable with both deaf and hearing people.
51. I feel good about being deaf, but I involve myself with hearing people also.
60. My hearing friends will fight for deaf rights.

---

immersion identity. This means this person feels a positive affiliation with the Deaf community as well as some comfort and ease with hearing people. A clinician might also make a qualitative analysis based on individual items endorsed by the subject. For example, if the subject "strongly agrees" with the statement, "When I am with hearing people, I remember that I am proud to be deaf," this can be inquired into and discussed.

There are many possible uses of such an instrument. An important research project would be to determine whether there is any correlation between cultural identity and mental health. Such a project would involve giving a sample of subjects both the finished DIDS and a measure of personality and psychological adjustment appropriate for deaf people. Should cultural deafness, as expected, be correlated with positive indications of mental health, the implications for the entire field of deafness would be revolutionary.

One might also want to research whether different counseling or therapy approaches work differently with Deaf people who possess different kinds of cultural identity. For example, under which circumstances would it matter if the counselor is deaf or hearing? Is group therapy more useful with Deaf people with high immersion identities? Which therapeutic strategies help marginal deaf people move beyond marginality?

Deaf people develop culturally Deaf identities in a manner analogous to how other minority persons come to think of themselves as culturally distinct. In all the work on cross-cultural and culturally affirmative counseling, cultural identity is considered vitally important. Minority persons who are culturally self-aware care passionately about identity. Therapists who can comfortably show expertise and sensitivity on these cultural identity concerns, including self-awareness and comfort with their own cultural identity, are well on their way to becoming effective therapists with culturally different people.

Appendix A

Assessment Questions for Cultural Identity

Questions that can be useful in assessment of Deaf cultural identity in deaf people are listed in this appendix. Of course, one needs to select and phrase questions in such a way that they match the intelligence and verbal sophistication of clients. Questions such as these need to be asked with great sensitivity and in the context of a respectful relationship. They touch on emotionally loaded themes and should not be raised unless the questioner demonstrates an attitude of genuine support.

1. When did you become deaf?
2. Are any family members deaf? How did your parents feel about your deafness? Tell me about communication in your home.
3. What kind of school programs did you go to? How do you feel about these programs now? How do you feel about oral education, Total Communication, bilingual education, mainstreaming, and Deaf residential schools?
4. When you were a child, how did you think about your deafness? Have your views about your deafness changed? How? Can you describe the process?
5. How did you find out about the Deaf community? What was the process of discovery like for you?
6. When and how did you learn to sign?
7. How do you prefer to communicate? Do you feel there is a right way for Deaf people to communicate? How do you communicate with hearing nonsigners? How do you feel about sim. com., Sign English, PSE, ASL, and using your voice?
8. Do you call yourself "Deaf," "deaf," "hard of hearing," "hearing impaired," or something else?
9. In terms of the Deaf and hearing worlds, where do you fit?
10. In which ways do you feel comfortable/uncomfortable in the Deaf world?
11. What do you like and dislike about being deaf?
12. Have you ever felt angry with hearing people? Would you tell me about that? When did you feel most angry? What makes you feel most angry? How have your expressed/shown your anger?
13. Have your feelings about hearing people changed? How?
14. How do you feel about hearing professionals who work with Deaf people (doctors, audiologists, teachers, counselors/therapists, rehabilitation counselors, interpreters) generally? What have your experiences with these professionals generally been like?

15. How do you decide whether a hearing person can be trusted to support you as a Deaf person? What helps you trust and feel comfortable with hearing people?
16. Under which circumstances, if any, do you think hearing people should (a) teach deaf children, (b) counsel or provide therapy to deaf people, (c) run Deaf programs, and (d) teach sign language?
17. What role, if any, do you think hearing people should take in the Deaf world? (How can hearing people be helpfully involved with Deaf people?)
18. What does Deaf Power or Strong Deaf mean to you? What does Deaf Culture mean to you? How do you decide who is culturally Deaf?
19. Tell me how you feel about this statement, "It's a hearing world, and Deaf people must fit into it."
20. Do you believe that deafness is a disability or handicap?
21. If you could take a pill to become hearing, would you? How do you feel about this question? Would you prefer your children to be deaf or hearing, or does that matter?
22. How do you feel about Deaf people marrying or having relationships with hearing people?
23. What is most central to your Deaf identity?
24. Is there anything else about your Deaf identity that I haven't asked about?

REFERENCES

Behan, B. (1989a). A night of living terror. In S. Wilcox (Ed.), *American Deaf culture: An anthology.* (pp. 17–20). Silver Spring, MD: Linstok.

Behan, B. (1989b). Notes from a "seeing" person. In S. Wilcox (Ed.), *American Deaf culture: An anthology* (pp. 29–32). Silver Spring, MD: Linstok.

Behan, B. (1989c). Total communication, a total farce. In S. Wilcox (Ed.), *American Deaf culture: An anthology* (pp. 117–120). Silver Spring, MD: Linstok.

Behan, B. (1989d). The war is not over. In S. Wilcox (Ed.), *American Deaf culture: An anthology* (pp. 189–192). Silver Spring, MD: Linstok.

Behan, B. (1989e). What if . . . Alexander Graham Bell had gotten his way? In S. Wilcox (Ed.), *American Deaf culture: An anthology* (pp. 83–87). Silver Spring, MD: Linstok.

Behan, B. (1989f). Who's itching to get into mainstreaming? In S. Wilcox (Ed.), *American Deaf culture: An anthology* (pp. 173–178). Silver Spring, MD: Linstok.

Bienvenue, M. J. (1993). Bi-Bi: The cure for deaf education. *TBC News.* No. 58, 1–3.

Bienvenue, M. J., & Colonomos, B. (1985). *Introduction to American Deaf culture: Rules of interaction* [Videotape]. Silver Spring, MD: Sign Media.

Bienvenue, M. J., & Colonomos, B. (1986). *Introduction to American Deaf culture: Values* [Videotape]. Silver Spring, MD: Sign Media.

Bienvenue, M. J., & Colonomos, B. (1988a). *Introduction to American Deaf culture: Group norms* [Videotape]. Silver Spring, MD: Sign Media.

Bienvenue, M. J., & Colonomos, B. (1988b). *Introduction to American Deaf culture: Identity* [Videotape]. Silver Spring, MD: Sign Media.

Bullard, D. (1986). *Islay.* Silver Spring, MD: T. J. Publishers.

Connor, L. (1972). That the deaf may hear and speak. *The Volta Review,* pp. 518–527.

Cross, W. E. (1991). *Shades of black: Diversity in African-American identity.* Philadelphia: Temple University Press.

Gannon, J. R. (1989). *The week the world heard Gallaudet.* Washington, DC: Gallaudet University Press.

Garnets, L., & Kimmel, D. (1991). Lesbian and gay male dimensions in the psychological study of human diversity. In *Psychological perspectives on human diversity in America*. Washington, DC: American Psychological Association.

Glickman, N. (1984). The war of the languages: Comparisons between language wars of Jewish and Deaf communities. *The Deaf American, 36*(6), 25–33.

Glickman, N. (1993). *Deaf identity development: Construction and validation of a theoretical model*. Unpublished doctoral dissertation, University of Massachusetts, Amherst.

Glickman, N., & Carey, J. (1993). Measuring deaf cultural identities: A preliminary investigation. *Rehabilitation Psychology, 38*(4), 277–283.

Harvey, M. (1989). *Psychotherapy with deaf and hard-of-hearing persons: A systemic model*. Hillsdale, NJ: Lawrence Erlbaum Associates.

Helms, J. (Ed.). (1990). *Black and white racial identity: Theory, research and practice*. Westport, CT: Greenwood.

Higgins, P. (1980). *Outsiders in a hearing world*. Beverly Hills, CA: Sage

Horner, A. (1984). *Object relations and the developing ego in therapy*. New York: Aronson.

Ivey, A. (1991). *Developmental strategies for helpers: Individual, family and network interventions*. Pacific Grove, CA: Brooks/Cole.

Jacobs, L. M. (1974). *A Deaf adult speaks out*. Washington, DC: Gallaudet University Press.

Kannapell, B. (1989). Inside the Deaf community. In S. Wilcox (Ed.), *American Deaf culture: An anthology*. Silver Spring, MD: Linstok.

Levine, F. (1981). Insight-oriented psychotherapy with the deaf. In L. Stein, E. Mindel, & T. Jabaley (Eds.), *Deafness and mental health* (pp. 113–132). New York: Grune & Stratton.

Luey, H. S., & Per-Lee, M. (1983). *What should I do now? Problems and adaptations of the deafened adult*. Washington, DC: National Academy of Gallaudet College.

Mindel, E. & Vernon M. (Eds.). (1971). *They grow in science*. Silver Spring, MD: National Association of the Deaf.

Nash, J., & Nash, A. (1981). *Deafness in society*. New York: Lexington.

National Center for Law and the Deaf. (1984). *Legal rights of hearing-impaired people*. Washington, DC: Gallaudet College Press.

Padden, C. (1980). The Deaf community and the culture of Deaf people. In C. Baker & R. Battison (Eds.), *Sign language and the Deaf community* (pp. 89–104). Silver Spring, MD: National Association of the Deaf.

Padden, C. (1989). The Deaf community and the culture of Deaf people. In S. Wilcox (Ed.), *American Deaf culture: An anthology* (pp. 1–16). Silver Spring, MD: Linstok.

Padden, C., & Humphries, T. (1988). *Deaf in America: Voices from a culture*. Cambridge, MA: Harvard University Press.

Ponterotto, J. (1988). Racial consciousness development among White counselor trainees: A stage model. *Journal of Multicultural Counseling and Development, 16*, 146–156.

Schein, J. (1989). *At home among strangers*. Washington, DC: Gallaudet University Press.

Schlesinger, H., & Meadow, K. (1972). *Sound and sign: Childhood deafness and mental health*. Berkeley: University of California Press.

Schowe, B. (1976). *Identity crisis in deafness*. Tempe, AZ: Scholars.

Stokoe, W. (1989). Dimensions of difference: ASL and English based cultures. In S. Wilcox (Ed.), *American Deaf culture: An anthology* (pp. 49–60). Silver Spring, MD: Linstok.

Stonequist, E. (1937). *The marginal man: A study in personality and culture conflict*. New York: Charles Schribner's Sons.

Vernon, M., & Andrews, J. (1990). *The psychology of deafness: Understanding deaf and hard-of-hearing people*. New York: Longman.

Wilcox, S. (Ed.). (1989). *American Deaf culture: An anthology*. Silver Spring, MD: Linstok.

Chapter 6

Utilization of Traumatic Transference by a Hearing Therapist

Michael A. Harvey
Boston University
Gallaudet University

"My family is hearing, and they don't sign."

If I had a nickel for how every time I have heard this sentence from deaf clients of hearing families, I would be a rich man. Sue's story was no different.

I nodded my head in the best sympathetic, supportive manner I could muster. Out of as much clinical habit as a trusted conversation opener, I commented that it must have been tough and asked her to tell me more. However, Sue, perhaps also out of habit, responded that it was no big deal and that she had "gotten used to it." Born profoundly deaf, she had become numb to missing the day-to-day (oral) conversations among her mom, dad, and three brothers during her childhood. She was now 42 years old.

Unfortunately, I, as her therapist, had also become numb to that motif. Like many newcomers to the field of deafness, I was initially shocked to learn about many deaf persons' experiences of communicative isolation within their hearing families of origin. But gradually and insidiously, their stories of pain became the routinized expectation, the norm.

Luckily, some event typically breaks this spell and forces me again to fully acknowledge the devastating effects of communicative isolation within one's family. Either I witness its effects directly while interviewing a deaf-member hearing family. Or I observe the effects indirectly when a deaf person reacts with anxiety to to present-day "transference objects": when a particular individual(s) triggers childhood-based anxiety. In Sue's case, that affective trigger occurred at work.

As an assembly worker at a high-tech corporation, her job was solitary and routinized. She had performed essentially the same functions for more than 20 years and fully expected to remain at this position until retirement. Although Sue was underemployed and admitted to feeling bored, she found comfort in what she described as her self-made cocoon. In her cocoon, she was safe. She was shielded from the hoards of hearing people who surrounded her.

Not so today. Her boss had scheduled a department meeting.

A few hours after that meeting, Sue arrived for our appointment looking ghost white and more pale than I had ever seen her since beginning treatment 3 months earlier. After some hesitation, she vaguely alluded to "feeling emotional during the day." But it soon became clear that the meeting had been the focal point. Whereas her affect and tears showed her pain, her tentativeness showed her fear of exploring it with me; or perhaps she wasn't even sure how to discuss it. After her tears had subsided, her countenance became vacant and expressionless. She matter-of-factly listed her work schedule that day, fell into her chair, and became sullen.

"Sue, could you tell me exactly what happened at the meeting in the present tense, as if it's happening now?"

Her face instantly regained its expression, but this time, was marked by jagged folds on her forehead and clenched teeth. Slowly and methodically, she moved time backward and relived the scene.

> One by one each person is entering the room; they say something to me that I can't understand. All of them sit down around the meeting table and continue their banter, sometimes laughing, and other times exchanging knowing glances at each other. They are talking to each other, some laughing, some looking serious, others looking pressured. I am sitting at the corner of the table. Bill, a coworker, says something to me. I think he's asking me how my work was going today. But he has a moustache, and it's tough to lipread him. Now my boss is coming in, and he's talking to Bill, Larry, George, and Alice. They laugh about something. People are laughing more.

At this point, Sue's signing became noticeably more erratic, and her arms and legs began to shake. Her tears returned and quickly exploded into loud sobs as she held on to the sides of the chair, as if for dear life. Her helplessness and terror are what Herman (1992) described as the salient characteristic of a trauma reaction.

I thought of Sue's initial comments to me that "it's no big deal that my family doesn't sign." Her initial efforts to avoid painful thoughts or feelings are indicative of *affective constriction*, another salient characteristic of a trauma reaction (DSM–IV, 1994; Herman, 1992). Now, however, the department meeting triggered her to re-experience isolation, desperation, and terror in full force—affects that she had defensively split off from her consciousness.

Did the department meeting symbolize or resemble an earlier distressing experience? When I asked Sue to recall similar experiences to the department meeting, she predictably revisited scenes of eating with her family at the dinner table. Again, I asked her to imagine and recite a typical interaction, as if it was happening in the present.

She shut her eyes.

> Mom, Dad, George, Tom, and Greg are sitting down at their seats. I sit down last at the seat by the toaster. Tom is excited about something, I think about school. He is laughing and yelling something at George that I can't understand. My dad interrupts, and his face looks serious. I think it's about money or the car or something. He's angry about something. I wish he didn't have a beard, and he's talking too fast. I wish I could understand them! Now Greg is pointing his finger at George and saying something. I wish I could understand them!

With her hands clenched in the air, she slowly signed: "I feel like I'm drowning in ice water."

Although her experience of "drowning" at the dinner table had occurred well over 30 years ago, I was struck by its similarity to her description of the meeting at work.

> The department meeting: "One by one each person is entering the room; they say something to me that I can't understand. . . . I am sitting at the corner of the table. Bill says something to me. . . it's tough to lipread him."

> The dinner table: "Mom, Dad, George, Tom, and Greg are sitting down at their seats. He is laughing and yelling something at George that I can't understand."

It seemed that Sue was not only coping with the inadequate accommodations at work, conditions that would normally cause anxiety and frustration, but was also experiencing affective intrusions from the past; while at work, she reexperienced her much earlier sentiment of drowning at the dinner table.

THE TRAUMA OF CHILDHOOD CONVERSATIONAL ISOLATION

Is sustained conversational isolation traumatic for a deaf child? McCann and Pearlman (1990) noted that an event is considered traumatic to an individual if it (a) falls outside the range of ordinary human experience, (b) exceeds the individual's perceived coping abilities, and (c) significantly disrupts the individual's psychological functioning.

Perhaps the most ambiguous criterion to satisfy is whether sustained conversational isolation falls outside the range of ordinary human experience. On the one hand, it can be argued that this experience is very much part of the ordinary, or prevalent, experiences of many deaf persons who grow up in hearing families (see Sussman, 1976; Vernon & Andrews, 1993). Indeed, I, like many clinicians in the field of deafness, even expected this sentiment from Sue in regards to her nuclear family: "If I had a nickel for . . ."

However, to the extent that language-based communication with family members and significant others is a cross-cultural norm and fulfills a universal human need, the absence of such communication is extraordinary. In fact, the DSM–IV (1994) defined a traumatic stressor, at least in the case of child sexual abuse, as involving "*developmentally inappropriate* [italics added]. . . experiences without threatened or actual violence or injury" (p. 424). As Herman (1992) put it: "Trauma is extraordinary not because they occur rarely but rather because they overwhelm ordinary adaptations to life" (p. 33).

In terms of whether sustained, childhood conversational isolation exceeds one's coping abilities and causes a disruption of psychological functioning, the field of deafness has unequivocally answered affirmatively. Inadequate communication with significant others during one's developmental years severely impedes all facets of psychosocial development (see Lane, 1984; Mindel & Vernon, 1987; Moores, 1982; Schlesinger & Meadow, 1972).

It is my contention that the quintessential trauma for many of the deaf clients we see in psychotherapy is conversational isolation.

COMMON TRAUMA RESPONSES

The many observed human responses to trauma fall into three main categories. These are called *intrusion, constriction,* and *hyperarousal* (Terr, 1990). Traumatized Viet Nam veterans, for example, may experience intrusion in the form of "flashbacks", constriction via "numbing out", and hyperarousal by their persistent readiness for combat (Laufer, Frey-Wouters, & Gallops, 1985).

Consider the following commonly observed posttrauma reactions of deaf clients in treatment:

1. Intrusions: reexperiencing the traumatic event. Deaf clients frequently report reexperiencing in hearing groups those affects that had been associated with earlier experiences of isolation (Harvey, 1993). For Sue, the inadequate accommodations within her work environment were symbolic of earlier inadequate accommodations within her family. These environmental triggers served to flood her with anxiety.

2. Constriction: avoidance of stimuli associated with the trauma. When avoiding external stimuli in order to reduce anxiety, one may shun hearing persons. When avoiding *internal stimuli,* one may "shut off" certain anxiety-provoking feelings or thoughts. Sue shielded herself by "not trying to think about my feeling lost when hearing people don't include me." In regards to her family, she had held on to the belief that feeling left out was no big deal.

3. Hyperarousal: increased autonomic reactivity. As described in earlier publications (Harvey, 1989), deaf clients appear keenly aware of the adequacy of communication in particular environmental contexts. They may react in a passively resigned or an assertive manner (Harvey, 1982). In addition to the obvious healthy necessity of attending to communication accessibility, such vigilance may also be related to childhood traumatic sequelae for many deaf clients in treatment. Again in Sue's words, "The dinner table horrors make me stay on guard for it happening again."

The reader will recognize these reactions as indicative of post traumatic stress disorder (*DSM–IV,* 1994).

A CAUTIONARY NOTE

Is assisting deaf clients in treatment to acknowledge possible trauma and posttrauma reactions validation of a common experience or just another pathological label? As we know, the history and current status of deaf persons is replete with cases of misdiagnoses, overpathologizing (Vernon & Andrews, 1993), and other acts of defamation promulgated by hearing persons. Why is this act different from all other acts?

Here, it is important to emphasize that, by definition, posttrauma reactions represent normal adaptations to abnormal conditions (Terr, 1990). For a deaf client to acknowledge the markedly debilitating effects of childhood conversational isolation, he or she ipso facto, acknowledges its oppressive aspects. And to acknowledge that one had to cope with oppression, one comes to validate oneself as a survivor. This dual process of bearing witness and self-affirmation is the "stuff" that makes for empowerment.

In marked contrast are the many deaf clients who internalize their oppression in the form of shame. I recall one deaf male adolescent who was fluent in ASL but shamefully admitted to having poor ASL skills. After careful questioning, it became clear that his self-evaluation was based on his difficulty understanding the school interpreter. That so-called interpreter, however, had taken only three sign language classes! His healing began only after he had labeled—had beared witness to—the oppression within the educational environment.

The healing process must also include parents. It is easy to forget that many hearing parents are affected by society's "audist" bias (Lane, 1984) and profoundly grieve when their child is first diagnosed as deaf. Parents are simply a microcosm of society's overt and covert vilifying of differences. Again in case of Sue's parents, the medical profession had taught them to implicitly shield Sue and themselves from the seemingly overwhelming pain of acknowledging deafness; they would discuss it only in a perfunctory and superficial manner. The diagnostic crisis thus metasticised to become a debilitating trauma for all parties.

MANAGEMENT OF COUNTERTRANSFERENCE

The proper use of any therapeutic technique is predicated on the therapist being able to adequately achieve empathic attunement with the client, even to sense what the client dismisses as, in Sue's words, no big deal. This rather formidable task depends on the adequate management of countertransference. Specifically, a hearing therapist may have difficulty empathizing fully with a deaf client's affective experiences of communicative isolation with (a) hearing persons outside of the session, or (b) the therapist himself or herself within the session.

Isolation in the Hearing World

Here, the therapist must fully acknowledge and mirror the traumatic impact of communicative isolation that had pervaded a deaf client's early (hearing) family experiences as well as more present-day isolation that routinely occurs among most hearing persons. In my case with Sue, however, far from fully appreciating the impact of that trauma, I initially only paid lipservice to it. Similar to many therapists who routinely hear these stories, my first internal reactions to Sue's recollections of her familial conversational isolation were, at best, desensitized and, at worst, discounting or nonempathic.

Why does this countertransference reaction commonly occur among therapists? The answer becomes clear now that we have properly elevated the impact of sustained communicative isolation to the level of oppression or trauma—essentially to make it a "big deal." What is directly traumatic for a client may be *vicariously traumatic* for a therapist. Stated differently, Jung (1966) used the metaphor of an "unconscious infection" to describe the traumatizing effects of working with people in psychological pain.

McCann and Pearlman (1990) outlined common posttrauma reactions that therapists themselves exhibit when working with trauma victims/survivors. They noted alterations with psychological and interpersonal functioning, including intrusive thoughts or images and painful emotional reactions. For example, my initially blase stance with Sue is indicative of affective constriction, a classic sequelae of trauma. In a different vein, I, too, experienced short-term affective intrusions in the form of ruminations and nightmares, following my elicitation of Sue's anxiety at her department meeting. Sue's trauma had obviously restimulated similar earlier distress for me.

Therapists must adequately deal with their vicarious trauma reactions in order to adequately provide a "holding environment" (Winnicott, 1965) for clients' pain and suffering. In particular, therapists who work with deaf clients must monitor the contagion effects of bearing witness to their frequent reports of experiential detachment in the hearing world. Left unchecked, these vicarious trauma reactions may irrevocably pollute the therapeutic interaction and block the attainment of a meaningful empathic connection with deaf clients. In this case, the hearing therapists may unwittingly negate the deaf clients' sense of solidarity in the Deaf community and ultimately pathologize their experience of being outsiders in the hearing world.

Isolation in the Session

Similarly, therapists must adequately deal with their countertransference to deaf clients' experiential detachment in the treatment session. Here the phenomena of traumatic transference and traumatic reenactment (Terr, 1990) become relevant. In other words, when a deaf client has been traumatized by hearing persons, that client will likely reexperience and/or act-out that trauma with the hearing therapist.

Traumatic transference and reenactment come in different forms. In another publication (Harvey, 1993), I described how a deaf client's decision to see a hearing therapist may reflect traumatic reenactment characterized by idealization. Here, the client views the therapist as an omnipotent and omniscient parental figure with a corresponding defective sense of self. The therapist is both idealized and viewed as unavailable. This idealizing transference reaction often relates back to early childhood experiences of feeling isolated and devalued; the child attempts to mitigate that trauma by idealizing the unavailable, hearing parental figure.

Herman (1992) discussed a similar phenomenon where hostages come to view their captors as their saviors and to fear and hate their rescuers: "The repeated experience of terror and reprieve, especially within the isolated context of a love relationship, may result in a feeling of intense, almost worshipful dependence upon an all powerful, godlike authority. The victim may live in terror of his wrath, but she may also view him as the source of strength, guidance, and life itself" (p. 92).

During my initial session with Sue, for example, I asked her, "Why did you choose me as your therapist?" She replied that she would never consider working with a deaf clinician because "they don't know as much; but hearing therapists know what to do." On exploration, it became clear how Sue had similarly idealized her parents in order to defend against feelings of anxiety and insecurity. Although she seldom could adequately follow what her parents were saying, she at least took comfort in "how smart they must be."

Here, the countertransference challenge was to resist the temptation of seeking validation from Sue. It feels good to be needed, maybe even to be idealized. However, it is particularly important for therapists of the dominant culture who work with oppressed minorities to work through our narcissistic problems and be relatively free from the hope that our clients might emotionally fill ourselves up (Miller, 1981).

Managing my countertransference remained relatively easy as long as we were discussing Sue's traumatic transference of idealizing me or her experiences of feeling traumatized by those hearing persons *out there*. It became less comfortable, however, when we began to focus on what it was like for her when I, on occasion, did not understand her ASL or when she did not understand mine.

During one session, I either accurately noticed or imagined a slight but perceptible scowl on her face when she had difficulty understanding me. I wondered whether I was being oversensitive. I thought of how many times my dad would correct my grammar growing up. In the middle of a discussion—perhaps when I was telling him about something exciting that had happened at school—he would admonish me for a grammatical faux pas. To this day, I may feel trepidation when deciding on the correct choice of saying *I* or *me*.

I could similarly get defensive with Sue; I could apologize for my ASL skills. Or I could get a bit self righteous—maybe even angry—and defend how I have practiced, continue to practice, but will never be perfect. "ASL is not my native language, you know!" But these private scenarios reflected my countertransference and were sentiments that I would have liked to have shared with my father. They did not belong in the treatment session.

It is impossible to prevent countertransference, for it inevitably and often quite insidiously intercedes in treatment. Rather, the task is to recognize the effects of countertransference, to analyze its origins in one's own family, and to prevent it from polluting the therapeutic interaction. In 12-step lingo, we are all, in a sense, "in recovery."

USE OF TRAUMATIC TRANSFERENCE AND REENACTMENT

Just as it is impossible to prevent therapist countertransference, it is impossible to prevent client transference. Consider the commonly observed case of a deaf client experiencing negative traumatic transference reactions of devaluing a hearing therapist. This reaction is easy to understand when that hearing therapist is, in fact, cross-culturally incompetent, that is, not proficient in ASL and ethnocentric. In this case, the client's negative perceptions of the therapist are accurate. But it is not the complete picture. This situation triggers not only present-day affects of disappointment and rage, but also trigger heretofore unavailable, split-off affects related to previous experiences of oppression.

That culturally incompetent therapist inevitably, at best, is unable to use these client perceptions as an opportunity to facilitate therapeutic gains. At worst, such therapists inadvertently retraumatize deaf clients. Either way, the therapist's conduct is unethical and he or she must be held accountable.

However, a competent therapist is not immune to receiving the wrath of a client's negative transference. Although that therapist may even be natively proficient in ASL, knowledgeable about Deaf culture and self-aware, he or she may nevertheless be perceived by the deaf client as deficient or incompetent. By definition, transference is a distortion of reality, stemming from one's previous conflict-laden relationships. However, it does not necessarily impede treatment. That therapist can utilize traumatic transference to facilitate emotional gains.

A competent hearing therapist offers a unique opportunity for a deaf client: namely, to reenact and work through in vivo in the session early experiences of traumatic oppression. Perhaps this is what hearing therapists can do best. As an analogy, although it is often preferable for female survivors of (male) rape to work with female therapists, a male therapist nonetheless can provide a unique context for recovery. Provided that the male therapist is appropriately sensitive and competent and provided that a solid alliance is established, he can facilitate an emotional working through of the sexual assault. The female client benefits from a "corrective experience" of transferentially rebuilding trust in men. Resolution of the negative traumatic transference with a male therapist complements the benefits gleaned by working with a female therapist.

Consider another case of a gay client who devalued himself as a result of internalizing the perceptions of significant straight, homophobic role models. Feeling accepted by a straight therapist represented a corrective experience for this client. It allowed the therapeutic relationship to uncork the shame and rage against straight people that he had suppressed. And most importantly, the straight therapist, a symbolic (transferential) oppressor, validated the client's hurt and rage with a different effect than would have been possible from a gay therapist. As the client said during the last stage of treatment, "I knew I could count on my gay friends to say I'm okay . . . but hearing it from this straight guy felt more special."

Let us return to Sue. After some thought, I became aware of my own proclivity to emotionally react to Sue criticizing my signing as if she was my father criticizing my grammar. Given that I got my countertransference under control, it was now time to make therapeutic use of Sue's transference reaction to me; to use it as a window for us to examine and modify how she empowered hearing people at her own expense.

What did her scowl mean? What was she trying to say?

When I asked her how she felt when I didn't understand her signing, or vice versa, she instinctively tried to take care of me: "I know that you sometimes ask me to repeat things. It's all right. Don't worry about it."

Repeated questioning yielded the same results. But I sensed, on a nonverbal level, that Sue had much more to say; perhaps sentiments that she dared not reveal to me, and even to herself. I imagined her years of irritation, her squelched rage and her hopelessness, all buried under layers of defenses. Her defenses, exemplified by "it's no big deal . . . don't worry about it", shielded her from that pain, the trauma that had threatened to overwhelm and immobilize her as a child.

But, like many others, her posttraumatic pain had not remained buried but continually threatened to surface and disrupt her present-day functioning. My hope was that we would excavate it together.

I asked her just to pretend—to make believe—that she was at least a wee bit angry or frustrated with me.

Again, her nonverbal reactions were the most visible responses to my request. She squirmed in her seat, glanced at the window but then made and sustained eye contact with me, as if to test the waters before jumping in. "Can I trust him?" "Will he negate my pain like the others?" "Can this hearing person possibly understand my experience?" "Will this hearing person devalue my cherished language, ASL?" "Will this hearing person understand me as Deaf?" I imagined these and other questions swarming around in Sue's head. After some initial awkwardness, she rose to the task. Her signing was clear and deliberate: "Frankly, I don't always understand you."

Having made that declaration, her countenance vacillated between fear and anger. She made a motion to apologize, but I opted to interrupt her.

"Please continue, and stop being so nice," I quipped.

An awkward laugh. "Okay, you asked for it," she mused. Then a deep breath before she let me have it!

"You sign okay; I understand you most of the time. But your signs are sometimes sloppy. And your expression, can't you show more expression? You're soooo hearing!! It's frustrating. I'm tired of hearing peoples' sloppy signs. I'm tired of it, fed up!!"

Her once slight scowl became a glaring dagger. "You sit there so smug, probably thinking about your hearing clients. Looking forward to seeing *them!*"

Once she began, she did not want to stop. Certainly, this was not the time to justify my signing ability nor to address the topic of other clients. It was a time to allow and encourage Sue to verbally confront a hearing authority figure without recrimination. Most likely, she had never had this opportunity before, and it was long overdue.

I simply remained seated with her and waited. Seeing no offensive reaction from me, she continued to unleash her fury. It continued for several moments. Then came what had been hidden from both Sue and me; her face softened a bit and became somber. Her signing became a bit slower and smaller. After a pause, she continued:

"I need you to understand me, you know? Sometimes I get scared, you know, that you don't know how I feel. That you don't get it. That you nod your head but just pretend to understand (uses the "empty yes" sign). That you patronize me like other hearing people do."

Now she looked down at the floor. Soon, renewed tears signaled that she was finally tapping into her pain; it had been buried beneath her rage.

"I feel so misunderstood, so cut off from you."

Her words were poignant remnants of the trauma that she has sustained with hearing persons, beginning with her parents. I became the hearing parent, the hearing boss, the hearing oppressor. All of her previously unavailable feelings now filled the room. Although I had hoped for this moment and had privately predicted it, I nevertheless was a bit shaken. The awesome power of one's soul never ceases to humble me.

How does a hearing therapist utilize traumatic enactment to facilitate a healing experience for a deaf client as opposed to actually causing additional psychological injury?

There are two requirements for a positive outcome. The first requirement echoes what has already been mentioned in this chapter and volume. The therapist must be cross-culturally competent to work with deaf persons: have proficiency in ASL, have knowledge about Deaf culture, have the ability to use culturally syntonic interventions, and have self-awareness.

In regards to Sue's criticism of my signing ability, I have gotten feedback from deaf colleagues that my signing skills are quite adequate, although not at the level of a native signer. In spite of the limited times when Sue and I had to ask each other to repeat phrases, we both acknowledged that our communication was, for the most part, full and unencumbered. In my judgment, I was not, in fact, retraumatizing her.

The second requirement is for the hearing therapist and client to cocreate a safe environment that fosters indepth and uncensored dialogue regarding the trauma-based feelings that the client may reenact toward the therapist. The client must be able to fully and safely express, examine and process the resulting overwhelming and often terrifying emotions. Indeed it is the very absence of the sense of human connection with a trusted, nurturing other that isolates and, in large part, makes childhood trauma so destructive in the first place. Herman (1992) stated that "helplessness and isolation are the core experiences of psychological trauma. Empowerment and re-connection [italics added] are the core experiences of recovery" (p. 197).

Whereas trauma negates and dehumanizes the victim, the therapeutic alliance bears witness, affirms, and restores the victim's humanity. Again to cite Herman: "The fundamental premise of psychotherapeutic work is a belief in the restorative power of truth-telling" (p. 197). I would add another premise: the belief in the restorative power of reexperiencing old wounds that are both catalyzed and validated by a nurturing other.

My relationship with Sue became a catalyst for her to recall and reexperience traumatic memories of conversational isolation. As expected, the wounds that she felt from me she had also felt from many others. Slowly and tentatively, we began to explore and label the components of her present-day pain with others and with me; her fear, detachment, anger, rage, self-depreciation—in short, those feelings that she had also experienced as a child, those same feelings that she had earlier dismissed as no big deal.

Her childhood was also full of picnics and sports outings, her family's favorite outdoor activities. Sue had often reminisced about the pure gaiety of these events. Sadly, because of our work, those memories lost their purity; but what they lost they gained in fullness and accuracy. For example, during one session, as we examined her experience when my signing was not clear, Sue recalled for the first time a particular picnic on a sunny, warm, breezy day: "It was almost perfect," she mused, "except that I could not stop staring at my brothers talking 'mumbo-jumbo' while continually thinking 'I feel so misunderstood, so cut off from you.'"

Not coincidentally, those were the very words she had used to describe how she felt with me.

As Sue more fully recognized and experienced her repeated ordeals of isolation, she could grieve. Or perhaps more accurately, she could continue the process of her grieving by moving forward from the denial stage. Yes, there were many beautiful parts of her childhood—a loving family, two dogs and a cat, and even the honor of being the neighborhood champion at tetherball. But there were also the traumatic parts—seemingly long periods of feeling alone while among hearing people, constantly guessing what her parents and brothers were voicing and feeling ashamed that she was an "oral failure" and that she could not speak and speechread well enough to make her parents proud.

After exploring how her emotional reactions with her coworkers and me had been colored by traumatic transference from her family of origin, we were able to forge these insights to become a kind of psychological "safety net", one that would prevent her from becoming affectively flooded and "drowning." The concept of transference was no longer abstract and removed but became an important part of Sue's repertoire to help her separate her childhood pain from present-day pain. In her words, "It's tough enough coping with communication problems with people at work without feeling like I'm with my family all over again."

Sue and I had been working together for almost 1 year. One day, she stomped into my office, looking more enraged than I had ever seen her. Apparently, the personnel office at her company had just announced a reduction in interpreting services due to fiscal constraints and other corporate realignments. Her boss had assured her that there was nothing to worry about, that everyone in her department would speak slowly, and that she did not have to attend the "unimportant meetings."

Posttraumatic fear was no longer her first response. Her rage now predominated as she clenched her fists in the air as if toward her boss: "He can't do this! It's not fair!" Perhaps realizing that she was on unfamiliar ground, she abruptly reverted back to sinking in her chair and lamenting that "there's nothing I can do," her old response that she was forced to practice so many times as a child. But she then recovered with more anger, then more retreat, and more anger. Finally, after vacillating between those extremes, she arrived at a place of empowerment. She made eye contact with me, slowly and simply said, "I don't deserve this anymore."

Coincidentally, the legal system had recently agreed that she did not deserve such restrictions anymore. The American Disabilities Act (ADA) had just been passed.

Sue had contacted an attorney, learned about the ADA and arranged a meeting with her boss. During that meeting, she calmly and lucidly explained the criteria of reasonable accommodations to her boss and gave him the name of her attorney should he wish further clarification. She thanked him for his time, warmly shook his hand, and bid him a good day.

Two weeks later, her company managed to procure the funds for increased interpreter services, as well as notetakers, visual alarm systems, and a TTY.

CONCLUDING THOUGHTS

In this chapter, I have attempted to illustrate the potential benefits of a hearing therapist helping a deaf client to work through traumatic transference factors in treatment.[1] This construct helps make sense out of the subtle relational dynamics that invariably influence and shape the therapeutic relationship, albeit in different forms and with varying degrees of intensity, regardless of the model of intervention, duration of treatment, or other contextual factors. In the case of Sue, she had denied her pain and rage with me, her hearing therapist, as she also had done with significant hearing persons in her life.

Understanding how traumatic transference factors contribute to a client's dysfunction opens up possibilities for intervention. But only one of many such possibilities is to discuss the transference with the client. The advisability of this approach naturally depends on the particular context and warrants clinical judgment. Sue was insightful, self-motivated, and articulate—attributes that lend themselves to the use of such insight-oriented approaches. Moreover, she had the financial means to engage in a longer term therapeutic contract than would have been possible in many managed health care contexts.

I often think back to when I first met Sue, particularly to reminisce how I seemed to be under a "spell" of emotional deadness to her childhood pain of conversational isolation. I remain indebted to Sue for helping me "break that spell" and to understand it as affective constriction, secondary to my own vicarious trauma. It was only then that I could become more open to vicariously experiencing her pain and to increasing my understanding of what her pain means.

How often I relearn this basic dialectic of conducting therapy: to affectively experience the inner psychological life of a client, without censure or interpretation and to cognitively make theoretical sense of it. Sue and I were able to absorb the emotional impact of her childhood and present-day terrors of drowning, understand its traumatic implications, and then further her recovery.

---

[1]Although Deaf clients also experience traumatic transference with *Deaf* therapists, descriptions of these dynamics are beyond the scope of this chapter.

I am not, however, positing that all deaf persons who come from hearing, nonsigning families are necessarily survivors of trauma. The occurrence of posttrauma reactions is multidetermined, depending on an individual's psychological makeup and on other available support systems. I am, however, openly speculating about the prevalence of such trauma and its implications for assisting deaf-member families.

As Sue and I came to appreciate, it indeed is "a big deal."

REFERENCES

American Psychiatric Association (1994). *Diagnostic and Statistical Manual of Mental Disorders IV.* Washington, DC: Author.

Harvey, M. A. (1982). The psychological effects of frustration on the advocate. *Deaf American, 34,* 14–15.

Harvey, M. A. (1989). *Psychotherapy with deaf and hard of hearing persons: A systemic model.* Hillsdale, NJ: Lawrence Erlbaum Associates.

Harvey, M. A. (1993). Cross cultural psychotherapy with deaf persons: A hearing, white, middle class, middle aged, non-gay, Jewish, male, therapist's perspective. *Journal of the American Deafness and Rehabilitation Association, 26*(4), 43–55.

Herman, J. L. (1992). *Trauma and recovery.* New York: Basic.

Jung, C. J. (1966). Psychology of the transference. In R. S. Hull (Ed.), *The practice of psychotherapy (Vol. 16, Bollingen Series;* p. 58). Princeton, NJ: Princeton University Press.

Lane, H. (1984). *When the mind hears: A history of the deaf.* New York: Random House.

Laufer, R. S., Frey-Wouters, E., & Gallops, M. S. (1985). Traumatic stressors in the Vietnam War and Post-traumatic stress disorder. In C. R. Figley (Ed.), *Trauma and its Wake (Vol. 1,* p. 238). New York: Brunner/Mazel.

McCann, L., & Pearlman, L A. (1990). *Psychological trauma and the adult survivor: Theory, therapy, and transformation.* New York: Brunner/Mazel.

Miller, A. (1981). *Drama of the gifted child.* New York: Basic.

Mindel, E. D., & Vernon, M. (1987). The impact of deaf children on their families. In E. D. Mindel & M. Vernon (Eds.), *They grow in silence: The deaf child and his family* (2nd ed., p. 93). Boston: Little Brown.

Moores, D. F. (1982). *Educating the deaf: Psychology, principles and practices* (2nd ed.). Boston: Houghton Mifflin Co.

Schlesinger, H., & Meadow, K. (1972). *Sound and sign: Childhood deafness and mental health.* Berkeley: University of California Press.

Sussman, A. E. (1976). Attitudes towards deafness: Psychology's role—past, present, and potential. In F. B. Crammette & A. B. Crammette (Eds.), *VII World Congress of the World Federation of the Deaf* (p. 128). Washington, DC: National Association of the Deaf.

Terr, L. (1990). *Too scared to cry.* New York: Basic.

Vernon, M., & Andrews, M. (1993). *Psychology of deafness.* New York: Longman.

Winnicott, D. W. (1965). *The maturational processes and the facilitating environment.* Madison, CT: International University Press.

Chapter 7

Storytelling and the Use of Culturally Appropriate Metaphors in Psychotherapy With Deaf People

Gail Isenberg
University of Vermont

In the last several years, those in the field of psychotherapy and psychology have actively used metaphor, storytelling, and narrative as viable techniques in affecting change in clients. Major influences in this area include Milton Erickson and "indirect hypnotherapists" and contructivists such as Michael White and David Epston. One reason for the growing interest in therapeutic metaphor and storytelling modalities is to provide therapists a way in which to work with clients who "seem stuck," are "resistant," thought of as "noncompliant," or otherwise unable to respond to traditional direct treatment approaches (Lankton & Lankton, 1989). Some have found this work to be more respectful of clients. The work of Milton Erickson has been described as moving from the "psychology of pathology" to a "psychology of potentials" (Mills & Crowley, 1986, p. xvii). Clients are believed to bring their own internal resources and potentials to therapy. Therapeutic metaphor and storytelling are techniques with which to tap into this unconscious store of experience, feelings, and thoughts, to help facilitate new learnings and meaning-making.

Constructivists have argued that it is not the event that is significant but rather the meaning we make of it. Bateson, as reported by White and Epston, stated "that it was not possible for us to have an appreciation of objective reality." We understand these events by the "network of premises and presuppositions that constitute our maps of the world" (White & Epston, 1990, p. 2).

As psychotherapists work with culturally diverse clients, it becomes increasingly evident that treatment techniques be flexible in addressing and adapting to those premises and presuppositions influenced by culture. This may be another reason for the appeal of therapeutic metaphor and storytelling:

> The logic of an analogy can appeal to the conscious mind and break through some of its limiting sets. When analogy also refers to deeply engrained (automatic and therefore functionally unconscious) associations, mental mechanisms, and learned patterns of behavior, it tends to activate these internal responses and make them available for problem solving. (Erickson, Rossi, & Rossi, 1976, p. 225)

Psychologists and psychotherapists who are familiar with clients' cultural experience and worldview are able to utilize this understanding via metaphor. Storytelling is important because it provides one means of connecting with the worldview of one's clients and "accessing resources" within their frame of reference. When therapists can draw on culturally common experiences and express them symbolically, it "guarantees that a client will have some personal meaning to attach to the imagery. The universality of the symbol multiplies the number of probable associations the client is likely to make" (Lankton & Lankton, 1983, p. 128). Metaphors that attend to clients and their cultures also foster a therapeutic "joining" via a shared perception.

STORYTELLING IN CHILDHOOD

Through the ages, storytelling has been valued by cultures throughout the world. Stories not only are a source of entertainment but are used as metaphorical tools that enable us to think in a more complex and abstract manner. They are "active ways of affirming basic beliefs of the group. The stories are instructions, which go beyond simply recalling the past and teach about how one's life should be conducted and what must be valued" (Padden & Humphries, 1988, p. 33). They help children understand who they are in the context of their family, culture, and heritage. Children are told stories in a variety of ways by different people in their world. Parents may tell a story about their own childhood experience to provide a coping strategy to their children. "I remember when I was in the third grade. It was very difficult for me too. But you know what helped me? . . . " They are told stories about themselves at a younger age. "When you were a baby, you used to sit and watch people around you for hours. You were so calm and patient. One day when you were only. . . ." Children not only learn about their behaviors at an early age, but, depending on how the story is told, they discover how they are perceived by others. They can begin to develop a sense of self.

In a larger context, children learn about the values of their families and culture through stories. These may be through personal histories of people they know and care about, or they may be fables that incorporate aspects of cultural heritage that are often presented as metaphorical fables. As Pearce, cited, in Mills and Crowley (1986), stated:

Fantasy is the inner world of the child. It is also the natural, innate process through which the child learns to make sense of the world outside himself. Indeed, fantasy is viewed by some as a genetic, biological function with a time clock of emergence that is necessary for healthy child development. (p. 36)

Attending to these stories allows children to learn in both concrete and abstract manners that facilitate a more complex understanding of their environment.

DEAF CHILDREN OF HEARING PARENTS WITH LANGUAGE BARRIERS

Although there may very well be several groups of children falling into this category, the focus of this chapter is on a large subset of deaf children who have experienced language barriers while growing up within their families. In their research examining the developmental problems of deaf children with hearing parents, Schlesinger and Meadow found hearing mothers "less flexible, less approving, more didactic and more intrusive than mothers of hearing children" (cited in Maher, 1989, p. 214). Henggeler and Cooper (1980), in their study of 15 deaf children of hearing parents and 15 hearing children of hearing parents, found:

Hearing mothers of deaf children interacted less extensively with their children, were less responsive to their children, used more directive control strategies and fostered behavior on the part of their children that may lead to a rigid concept of self and an interpretation of reality that is concrete and matter of fact. (cited in Maher, 1989, p. 214)

The children tended to view the world in a concrete, right-and-wrong manner. They knew what they were supposed to do and not to do, but they did not necessarily understand why. By not being able to communicate with parents, other family, and cultural group members, deaf children miss out on important information identifying who they are within the culture, their heritage, and the values of the larger system within which they live. This information is often passed on through stories and metaphors that deaf children with communication barriers are not told.

An art therapist working with Native American children, two of whom were deaf, observed the deaf children to paint pictures depicting Native American life in a Hollywood-like stereotypical fashion. This included pictures of teepees and breech clothes. Neither child used either the form of shelter or clothing they had painted. These children were of different tribes living on their respective reservations, yet their only cultural reference source was from television. The art therapist reported that few if any members of their cultural group were able to communicate with these young boys. They were never told of their ancestors, metaphorical stories that conveyed cultural values, or simple stories of their own earlier years. Thus, these two deaf Native American children seemed lost within their own communities. The isolation many deaf children feel from their families and the hearing culture at large cuts off their access to information for awareness of social and cultural norms and expectations (Gough, 1990).

DEAF CULTURE VALUING STORYTELLING

As with many other cultures, Deaf culture has a strong storytelling, "oral" tradition. In their book *Deaf in America: Voices From a Culture,* Padden and Humphries (1988) shared stories from Deaf culture to present both the group's history as a way of "repeating and reformulating the past for the present" (p. 38) and to teach the "wisdom of the group to those who do not have Deaf families" (p. 38). Many of these stories touch on shared experiences, such as feeling left out and isolated at the dinner table while hearing relatives talk among each other. "When I ask what they are talking about they only respond, 'Oh, it's nothing, not important.'" This almost universal story, highlights the importance communication has for Deaf people, not just as a means of exchanging information but as a metaphor for connection.

Another common challenge, as pointed out by Padden and Humphries (1988), for Deaf people living among those who can hear "is to figure out complicated meanings attached to various sounds," (p. 99) particularly noises emanating from the body. Deaf people learn that coughing and sneezing are socially acceptable sounds. Yet they can find themselves confused and embarrassed should they generalize this acceptance to belching or flatulation when around hearing people.

A reoccurring theme within Deaf culture is having to coexist with hearing people. This theme is expressed through stories, both literal and metaphorical, serious and funny. An example of this theme is presented in the following joke:

> A Russian, a Cuban, and a Deaf man were on a train. The Russian pulled out a bottle of vodka and began to drink it. When the vodka was half drunk, the Russian threw the bottle out the window. He said to the Cuban and Deaf man, "It doesn't matter; in my country we have plenty of vodka." The Cuban, then, took out a huge cigar and began smoking. After he had smoked part of it, he threw it out the window. He then said to the Russian and Deaf man, "It doesn't matter; in my country we have plenty of cigars." The Deaf man thought for a moment, then grabbed the Russian man and threw him out the window. He then grabbed the Cuban man and threw him out the window. "It doesn't matter," he said. "in my country, we have plenty of hearing people." (anonymous)

This joke was translated from ASL to English, and although it may well be funny "in Deaf," it might not be "in Hearing." Via humor, it validates anger toward hearing people experienced by many Deaf people. Another important reason this joke resonates for Deaf people is that it presents them as another "nationality," like Russians or Cubans.

Stories and humor about everyday deaf experiences provide a sense of connectedness with others and facilitate the development of a cultural worldview. A deaf man who grew up in a small rural community takes great pride in telling the stories he has learned about his family and community. Although unsure where he learned these stories, he believes they were retold to him by his older deaf sister and deaf playmate living within the neighborhood. Alhough his parents are hearing, there was adequate communication to pass on his family history. This father of three has thrived in his hearing/deaf community.

> Stories told by the members of a culture about their origins, whether they use religious
> or fantastic motifs, are creations of meaning about the culture's existence. They
> reaffirm the present by instilling meaning into the past. (Padden & Humphries, 1988,
> p. 26)

Deaf culture is rich with stories and poetry that tell of its heritage and values
that provide a sense of connectedness. By being able to communicate with
parents from their own culture, these children learn through stories "that there
are ways of being Deaf" (Padden & Humphries, 1988, p. 38). Like their hearing
counterparts within other cultures, they are able to make meaning of their world
in a complex interactive manner.

STORYTELLING AND METAPHORS IN THERAPY

Metaphors and storytelling are familiar therapeutic tools when working with
hearing children and adults. Milton Erickson, Lankton and Lankton, and Mills
and Crowley are a sampling of therapists who have discussed the value of
storytelling in therapy. Brown (1991) stated that "all learning, in a real sense,
depends on having a story in mind" (p. 123). He continued: "Stories can be
used to achieve rapport, give advice, increase self-awareness, stimulate motivation, reframe or redefine a problem" (p. 244).

Storytelling in therapy, as with children at home, can be a vehicle that helps
clients learn about themselves while thinking in a more complex manner.
Lankton and Lankton (1983) found metaphors to be more effective than logical
thought: "While conducting a massive mental search for related associations,
the mind brings together the common symbols and elements of a new perceptual
framework by entertaining the metaphoric theme" (p. 80). Knowing that
stories and metaphors are powerful therapeutic tools when working with
hearing people and recognizing that Deaf culture has historically valued storytelling, it seems reasonable to apply this technique to deaf clients.

With limited access to the hearing world, clients who are deaf often enter
therapy thinking the issues they present are unique to themselves. Many worry
they are "crazy." Inadequate communication inhibits comparisons between
deaf individuals and hearing people at large. Isolation can be experienced
within the deaf community as well. Like those who are hearing, clients who are
deaf worry about the stigma of having an emotional problem. Deaf clients do
not always disclose their problems to deaf friends. I have had several clients who
have refused to seek support from their friends for fear that others in the deaf
community would "hear" about it. For whatever reason, some deaf clients
become so isolated, they do not realize the commonalty of their life experiences
both happy and painful. It has not been uncommon for deaf clients to ask,
"Other deaf people feel the same as me?" or to say, "I never knew other deaf
had the same kind of problem. I never talked to others about this before." By
failing to utilize a support network, deaf clients enter therapy with limited
understanding of how common or unique their problems are.

PSYCHOEDUCATIONAL APPROACH TO STORYTELLING

Using a psychoeducational approach to storytelling, deaf clients are provided information relevant to their situation. They can also learn how their problems relate to hearing and/or deaf people.

Many deaf clients I have worked with have disclosed a number of incorrect assumptions about hearing people. Among these have been the belief that hearing people do not suffer from anxiety, depression, or other emotional problems. Relationships are negatively affected when clients react to hearing people based on faulty assumptions. Lack of communication between deaf clients and the hearing people in their lives only reinforces these presuppositions. It is difficult to encourage deaf clients to check out their assumption by talking directly with the hearing person they may be in conflict with. This is particularly true when language barriers exist. Psychoeducational stories can address this issue. Rather than directly explain to clients their erroneous assumptions, a story can help them recognize how their assumptions about others may be problematic. The following is an illustration of such a story.

Life Experience Story (Deaf-Related)

> I once knew a male client, suffering from anxiety, who apologized for his loud heartbeat. I thought I had misunderstood and asked him to repeat. He again said he was sorry for his loud heart. I obviously looked confused, so he explained that he had once seen someone playing a big bass drum. He could not hear it but felt the vibrations of the instrument in his stomach and chest. Hearing people told him that bass drums were very loud. He learned from this that loud noises produced vibrations that could be felt. Likewise he assumed that vibrations in his stomach and chest meant "loud noise." There were times when this man became anxious. When this happened, he was nervous. His breathing became shallow and fast, and his heart began to beat faster and stronger in his chest. Because his anxious heart beat felt the same as the bass drum within his chest, he believed that he was producing a loud noise. He was sure that hearing people would be able to hear his heart. This made him even more nervous and worried. The more anxious he became, the louder he thought his heart became. He would look at hearing people around him and interpreted their behaviors, whatever they might have been, as being bothered by his loud, thumping heart. His anxiety quickly evolved into serious panic attacks. He became so concerned about his loud heart and possible hostility from those who could hear that he seldom left his home.
>
> I was the first person he had been able to communicate his fear to. As he sat in my office, becoming increasingly anxious about his loud heart, he felt compelled to apologize for what he thought was an annoyance to me. When I finally understood his concern, I let him know of the auditory limitations of hearing people and told him that no one could hear his heartbeat. It took several attempts to explain what hearing people could and could not hear before he believed me and was able to let go of his incorrect assumption. Once he did this he began to relax and have a soft, quiet heart.

This story serves many therapeutic purposes. First, it addresses anxiety that may be experienced by deaf clients regarding interactions with hearing people including hearing therapists. Deaf clients may be more open to acknowledge feelings of discomfort within therapy following a story such as the one just mentioned than if hearing therapists were to directly question clients about their feelings. New clients have responded to direct queries regarding their feelings with "Fine, no problem" or "OK." However, when told a story similar to the previous one, deaf clients have been able to state how they either identify with or differ from the feelings addressed. "Me too, feel nervous around hearing people"; "I never thought hearing people could hear my heart, but I do feel uncomfortable at times with hearing people"; "Not scared, angry"; or "Yes, I'm a little scared about having a hearing counselor: maybe you will not understand deafness."

A second purpose for telling this deaf experience story is to present an example of how assumptions acted on without first checking to see if they are accurate can have negative consequences. It is doubtful that many deaf people assume hearing people are capable of hearing others' heartbeats. However, many clients do make assumptions that result in unpleasant behaviors, feelings, and thoughts that bring them to therapy. This story provides a model from which clients can see how assumptions can result in unhappiness, whereas those that are acknowledged and checked out can be resolved in a satisfactory manner. Indirectly, deaf clients are told that by examining their thoughts/assumptions, they too might feel better resulting in a soft and quiet heartbeat.

A third purpose for telling this story is to let deaf clients know that hearing people have limitations, for example, they cannot hear heartbeats. Although an unusual and extreme example, it is a subtle message reminding deaf clients that those who can hear have limitations and abilities just as deaf people do. It also lets clients know that therapists have limitations as well. They do not magically know what is happening inside clients. Rather, clients need to tell therapists what they feel and think in order for the therapeutic relationship to succeed. In the story, the deaf man would have continued feeling anxious had he not told the therapist about his belief that she could hear his heart. Only by opening up to her were they both able to work through the problem to reduce his anxiety.

Finally, this was a story with a deaf central character. Clients who believe they are isolated in their feelings often benefit from knowing they are, in fact, not alone. Just as it is important for children to feel a sense of connectedness through stories, so too can it be said for deaf clients. A story that incorporates another deaf person provides the knowledge that others with whom they can identify have gone through similar experiences and feelings. By accomplishing this, stories can: (a) demystify a client's particular problem, (b) provide a sense of connection with others, and (c) change an attitude of hopelessness to one of hopefulness. "Others have felt as I do now, and they were able to work it out successfully. Maybe I can, too".

Not all stories need to have deaf central characters. The issues presented by clients may be universal ones that do not necessarily require identification with other deaf people. Problems presented in therapy by deaf clients are often common to those clients who can hear. Telling a story that parallels clients' therapeutic issues rather than being deaf specific may be more appropriate.

An adult deaf male client came to me asking for hypnosis to eliminate his tinnitus. He had previously tried a number of different therapists and therapies to help rid himself of the constant ringing in his ears. These past attempts met with initial success and eventual failure. The client found fault with his past therapists and their techniques. He had a tendency to externalize both responsibility for cure and blame for failure. Hypnosis had become the new "cure" to rid him of his problem. Not wanting to repeat the previous pattern of failure as well as address the issue of having the client take responsibility within therapy, I shared with him a the following story about a person who wanted to go to graduate school.

Life Experience Story (Not Deaf-Specific)

> This person felt she was smart enough to succeed in graduate school, so she applied to the college of her choice, feeling confident they would accept her. Although she was a capable person, her application was weak, particularly in the area of test scores. She discounted this admittance criteria and was sure the university staff would recognize her aptitude in other ways. Well, she was not accepted. She then waited and applied to four schools the following year. Again her test scores were not very good. Again she felt, although less sure the second time, that admissions officers would know that she was a worthwhile candidate for graduate school. Again she was turned down by all four institutions. For a while after, she felt rejected and blamed the school personnel for failing to accept her. She wanted others to magically recognize her abilities and help her achieve her goals. Not long after this second group of rejections, this person found herself becoming angry, at first with others but then at herself. Like a light turning on, she understood that she could not expect a magic cure to her problems. She needed to accept responsibility and work to succeed. So she did. She practiced her test-taking skills, improved her resume, and worked together with others to prepare her application for school. She applied to three schools the third time. After all of her effort, she was successfully accepted by one graduate college. She knew that the only magic involved in achieving her goal was that of her own effort. Others may have assisted her, but she was the one responsible for her success.

As with the first story, this one tried to convey several messages. The first was a positive suggestion acknowledging the client to be an intelligent capable person who can succeed. The second message conveyed was that there would be no magical cure for the tinnitus that plagued the client. Third, although the client would receive assistance by his therapist, responsibility for therapeutic success was in part his. Fourth, there was the possibility that even after working hard, he may not experience complete success, for example, elimination of tinnitus. Just as the woman in the story was only accepted by one of the three schools she had last applied, the client may find that his tinnitus would not disappear.

Several weeks after telling this story, the client reported that his tinnitus had improved slightly but that he knew there was no magic cure. He seemed ready to accept both the strengths and limitations of the therapist, as well as his own responsibility for the process of adjustment to his medical problem.

METAPHORICAL STORIES

Gerrig and Gibbs, cited in Brown (1991), believed the purpose of metaphor is "communication, particularly in situations where new meanings are being developed" (p. 131). They pointed out that metaphor is goal directed:

> Metaphors are experienced as a gentle and permissive, not a confrontive or demanding way to consider change. At one level, a metaphor is "just a story" that doesn't require any response, but at another level, it stimulates thinking, experiencing, and ideas for problem resolution. (Lankton & Lankton, 1989, p. 2)

A metaphorical approach to therapy encourages patients' own individual responses and creativity rather than prescribing some externally imposed solution (Zeig, 1980).

Using metaphorical stories with deaf clients can achieve the same objectives as they do with hearing clients. Although it was once believed that deaf people could not process abstract information, one has only to watch the stories and poems of deaf culture to know this to be only a myth. As with psychoeducational stories of life experiences, metaphorical stories may or may not be deaf specific. The following two metaphors, one nondeaf specific, the other relating to deafness, are examples of how to encourage clients to work toward change and examine the process of doing so.

Metaphor (Nondeaf-Specific)

I knew a woman who wanted to learn how to knit. She had recently learned a new skill and could spin wool into yarn. However, she didn't know what to do with the beautiful yarn she was making. This woman belonged to a special group of people who were spinners, weavers, and knitters. Each of the members of this group had different strengths in different areas. Many of the members were skilled knitters. So the woman, who didn't even know how to hold a pair of knitting needles, asked for help. One of the group members agreed to teach her to knit. The very first thing taught was how to hold the needles. The teacher was very emphatic about the "proper" way to hold needles and yarn. The left hand was directed to hold its needle stationary while the right hand, with yarn trailing over and under several fingers would manipulate its needle and yarn with simple finger and wrist action. The teacher, had herself, learned this technique from her mother who assured her, was the correct way in which to successfully knit. The woman obediently practiced what she had been shown. At first, her fingers were awkward and clumsy. Her knitting was uneven and rough. The woman thought, "I will never learn this skill." Before long, however, she found her hands, fingers, and wrists becoming comfortable with needles and yarn.

Not long after she had begun learning how to knit, she was observed by another member of the group. This person, also a skilled knitter, watched the novice practice what she had been taught for a few moments and then said, "You shouldn't hold your needles like that. Let me show you the right way to knit." This woman then pulled out her own knitting, slowly and patiently demonstrating a different way to knit. Both left and right hand seemed to move together in and out. Her right index finger and thumb controlled the path of the yarn around the needles. It was very different from the method taught by the novice's teacher. This woman was obviously very skilled; her knitting flowed evenly and swiftly. However, when the novice tried this new technique, she again felt awkward and uncomfortable. It was as if her hands had to relearn to knit. What confused the woman was how this second skilled knitter was so sure that her technique was the most correct. Her teacher had said the same thing, yet they knit very differently. It was clear that both knitters made beautiful sweaters, scarves, hats, and mittens, but both indicated that their method of knitting was the only right way. The woman practiced both techniques and eventually became comfortable with each, however, she found that she preferred one way of holding the needles more than the other. It was a better fit for her.

As she became more comfortable with her skills, she would watch other knitters in the group. She found that almost everyone held their needles and yarn a little differently from the others. They all made beautiful clothes, yet she heard many say that their way was the only correct way to knit. Now, this was a very smart woman. As she looked around at the different group members, she finally understood that there really was no one "right" way to knit. In fact, there were many ways to create beautiful garments with yarn and needles. What is important is that you feel comfortable with your own technique and skills.

A while later, the woman developed a problem with one of her hands and was unable to knit the way she had been taught. Although now a skilled knitter herself, she found it painful to hold the knitting needles as her teacher had shown her. The woman worked hard trying different ways to manage both needles and yarn with her hands, until she successfully developed a new way that truly "fit" for her.

This metaphor is often told to clients who believe there are only one or two ways to deal with issues they present in therapy. They look to therapists to provide them with the "right" answer in which to solve their problems. This story conveys the notion that, whatever the difficulty, there may be many strategies to use to resolve it. It also suggests that it is clients who need to decide which strategy or stratagies/skills are a good fit. Other imbedded suggestions within this metaphor include: (a) the group or groups with which clients belong may have members with skills they may want to observe and learn from; (b) clients are considered smart and capable of synthesizing whatever skills learned in therapy to best fit their needs; (c) therapists do not have all the answers but can provide new skills and learnings to clients; and (d) should clients be confronted with a new challenge, they may very well be able to adapt skills learned in therapy to help resolve it in a healthy positive manner.

This particular metaphor has been told to both men and women. Although traditionally a craft done by women, many men are skilled knitters. If a client has difficulty relating to knitting as a metaphor, it can easily be changed to another, more appropriate one. Other crafts or hobbies such as wood working, gardening, or cooking can be substituted for knitting. Any activity that requires learning, practice, and mastery can be used as a metaphor. The story is a metaphor for itself in that there are no single right topics/skills from which to draw on. What is important is that the metaphor stimulate thought and connections within the clients' own experience in order to develop new learnings.

There are times when therapists may want a metaphor to relate directly to deaf experience. An example of this occurred with a deaf woman who was struggling with interpersonal skills. She found it particularly difficult to communicate her feelings and was frustrated with the slow uncomfortable learning process. This client had lost her hearing at the age of 5 of unknown etiology. Although educated in an oral environment, as an adolescent, she learned pigeon sign language and, as an adult, communicated using both modes simultaneously. The following story was told to her.

Metaphor (Deaf-Specific)

Do you remember learning how to sign? I know a man who took sign language classes to help him communicate with people with whom he was close. He wanted to improve communication between himself and others. It did not take long for him to find out that communicating with his hands was more difficult than he had expected. His fingers were stiff and awkward. He felt self-conscious trying out new vocabulary with what he thought were clumsy hands. He was so uncomfortable there were times when he almost quit. Communicating in this new way was difficult, and he wasn't sure it was worth it. But he also knew that if he wanted to communicate with the people he cared about, in an open and clear way, he needed to continue to practice and learn. So that's what he did. It took awhile, but not as long as he first thought, before he began to feel more comfortable. When first beginning to learn sign, he needed to concentrate and be aware of his every move, fingers, arms, hands, mouth, face, and other parts of his body. But as he practiced, and time went on, the signs became a part of him, flowing out of his body smoothly, and with ease. As you know, people sign differently. You may have noticed how some people communicate with quick crisp signs, whereas others have large flowing sign movements. Although people are expressing similar thoughts and feelings, they do it in a way that matches who they are. This man was to do the same thing. As he became a more fluent and skilled communicator, he noticed how his signs matched his personality. People who had, in the past, had a difficult time understanding him, now received his communication easily. It wasn't that he signed pleasant thoughts all the time. In fact, occasionally he needed to let someone know something unpleasant. But because he was able to communicate clearly, others appreciated and respected him. When he takes the time to look back at those first awkward efforts, he is pleasantly surprised at how far he has come using this new language, comfortably, smoothly, and clearly. This man, finds himself teaching others to sign and to learn a new language. And when they look uncomfortable and awkward, he tells them, "It's normal to feel clumsy and unsure when you are learning a new skill. Just keep practicing, and you will feel increasingly more comfortable with this new language."

As with the man in the story, it took great effort and practice for the client to become comfortable communicating her feelings with those who were close to her. The use of sign language as a metaphor for communicating feelings incorporated the experiences of this particular deaf client. As a postlingually deafened person who learned sign later in her childhood, she could identify with the man in the story, remembering her own struggles, frustrations, and eventual success while learning a new language. Unconsciously, the story conveys the message that she is learning another new language, that of expressing feelings to others. Although she may again experience the awkwardness of acquiring a new skill, she has the capacity to succeed in therapy, as she has done in the past with sign language.

"The therapeutic metaphor must evoke both the imagistic familiarity of the literary metaphor and a relational familiarity based on a sense of personal experience" (Mills & Crowley 1986, pp. 64–65). The reason this metaphorical story was successful with regard to this client was because she could relate her deaf experience, on an unconscious level, to that of the character in the story. A person deaf at birth, born into a deaf family in which American Sign Language is the primary language, may not find this particular metaphor relevant to his or her life experience. Just as hearing people tend not to consider their own speech and language development, prelingual deaf people born into signing deaf families tend not to think about their sign language development. This demonstrates the importance of knowing how clients perceive their individual deaf experience when preparing therapeutic stories. Knowing the etiology, age of onset, family of origin, and mode of communication preference as well as communication development are all important factors to consider when creating a metaphorical story for deaf clients.

CLIENT AS STORYTELLER

Storytelling within therapy does not necessarily need to be limited to therapist as narrators. Clients can be storytellers as they share their life experiences, troubles, and learnings in therapy. White and Epston (1990) pointed out:

> Stories are full of gaps which persons must fill in order for the story to be performed. These gaps recruit the lived experience and the imagination of persons. . . . persons give meaning to their lives and relationships by storying their experience and that in interacting with others in the performance of these stories, they are active in the shaping of their lives and relationships. (p. 13)

In therapy, deaf clients can be asked to narrate their life stories as a way to clarify for both therapists and clients an understanding of past experiences. This can be done by simply asking clients to tell a story about a particular event, person, and so on. Another strategy would be to ask clients to bring awards earned, special gifts from others, mementos from places visited, and/or family photos into therapy sessions and tell stories about the items. Visual and tactile cues, such as photos and special items, can by particularly helpful as story catalysts. Pictures can rekindle memories, both positive and negative, about recent and remote experiences that allow deaf clients to process feelings and make new meanings about themselves and others. Being able to touch an object, like a special gift, can foster a metaphorical element to the deaf clients' story.

Dreams, too, can generate material for a client's story. An example of this was provided by a client who came to therapy to work on marital issues. Married to a hearing man, the deaf woman felt exploited in several ways including language. Her husband never learned to sign, although he had promised to do so. The client financially supported her husband for many years. Her feelings about her relationship, husband, and self were presented in therapy through the story of a dream she had experienced.

The Freedom Dream

> A place where I often dreamed of being. It was in the middle of winter, and I rented a log cabin up north in the Adirondack Mountains. The log cabin was located in the deep, thick pine tree forest covered with white snow and a crystal-white, iced lake was nearby the cabin.

I found myself standing at the end of the dock covered with white snow watching an eagle flying over the lake. There was another animal, it was a white-tan wolf sitting near the dock looking at me while I was awed by the free creature exploring over the mountains.

For a while, the wolf was observing me while I was feeding live mice to the eagle sitting on the post of the dock. I also gave the wolf some raw red meat. I sat down on the dock peacefully examining the eagle and wolf eating their food. In my dream, I figured that I wished I was an eagle because the eagle is able to fly free where ever it wants to go and for the wolf, the same freedom I longed for.

This dream-story provided a great deal of information regarding the client's feelings and thoughts about herself and helped clarify her goals and aspirations. This story allowed us to address her desire to be free. We were also able to examine other metaphorical images within the dream-story. For example, we explored the similarities and differences between the eagle and wolf, the meaning of her feeding these "free" animals, and who might be represented by these different images. Although in our work together we did not pursue altering the dream, we could have. The client could have been asked to change the dream-story in a way that would have been more satisfying to her. Allowing her to create solutions or alternatives metaphorically might help in shaping her "real" life story.

Many deaf clients would probably prefer to use visual and tactile items as storytelling cues, but it is important not to assume that these would be the only items used. Depending on etiology, age of onset, and other aspects of a person's deafness, clients may use significant and special auditory cues, for example, a song, musical instrument, chimes, and so on, to tell about themselves. Stories may be of sounds not heard anymore or heard only by others. They may be about grieving what has been lost, celebrating a memory, or making a curious reference to the hearing world. Clients should be encouraged to use whichever cuing items that help them tell their story.

Clients as storytellers can also be used to resolve therapeutic issues. By utilizing positive interests, hobbies, skills, and/or leisure activities, clients can develop stories as a technique to help themselves. One such example is drawing. *Cartoon Therapy*, developed by Mills and Crowley (1986), facilitates a clear communication of clients' problems and allows them a vehicle with which to resolve it in a creative and satisfying manner. Young clients utilize their cartoon characters as "fully developed living metaphors that can act as a symbolic alternative for working through fears, anxieties, and conflicts" (Mills & Crowley, 1983, pp. 209–210). In a variation on a theme, a male deaf client, having difficulties relating to coworkers at his place of employment, was discovered to enjoy drawing cartoon-like characters. He was asked to draw a cartoon strip that began to tell the story of a recent negative interaction on the job. He was directed, for homework, to draw the beginning of the strip telling how the confrontation began and developed. In subsequent therapy sessions, different scenarios were discussed and worked through until a more satisfying ending was developed. He was then asked to complete the cartoon strip with the preferred ending. He was encouraged to try out these newly developed conflict resolution strategies within the real life experience. By using his artistic abilities, we were able to draw on the client's creativity while working on a problem he had previously considered unresolvable.

SUMMARY

As with hearing people, storytelling is a useful indirect therapy tool for deaf clients. Deaf people, like those who hear, enjoy receiving as well as telling stories. Storytelling carries with it the possibility of obviating client resistance that can occur with more direct therapeutic approaches. This was illustrated by the deaf client who was willing to accept the limitations of hypnosis and reduce external blame for past unsuccessful interventions to "cure" is tinnitus after being told a parallel story in which the main character recognized the role of self-responsibility to achieve goals.

Stories are, at times, more palatable to clients than are other therapeutic strategies. It is not unusual for deaf clients to sit back in their chair when I sign "I want to tell story," or "That remind me story, about . . . ." Although "Once upon a time . . ." may be a powerful indicator that a story is about to be told to hearing people, the phrase does not translate easily into sign language. The former signed story introductions have been found to be more effective when working with deaf clients.

When developing stories, whether psychoeducational or metaphorical, it is important that clients have a "sense of identification with the characters and events portrayed" (Mills & Crowley, 1986, p. 65). Providing a connection between clients and others, via story character, reduces feelings of isolation. Many deaf clients have responded to stories told to them in therapy with, "You mean other (deaf/hearing) people have same experience/feeling?" As clients connect to a story and character, those feelings of isolation change to one of shared experience that can result in normalizing issues presented in therapy. Referring to the beginning of this chapter, storytelling in therapy can educate deaf clients about others in their environment, provide an opportunity to understand themselves in a more complex way, and as an indirect technique obviate defenses that may occur as a result of more direct therapeutic approaches.

In creating a therapeutic story, therapists need to consider and utilize information about clients' interests, skills, and significant life events, as well as understand how their deafness has been integrated into clients' sense of self. Most deaf clients I have worked with have not come to psychotherapy to discuss their adjustment to deafness. Rather, they have come to work through the same issues/problems that hearing clients present, for example, marital or relationship difficulties, substance abuse problems, parenting issues, low self-esteem, anxiety, depression, and so on. Although deafness is rarely the presenting issue, it is a vital element of clients' sense of who they are that should be considered by therapists. This is particularly true when using storytelling in therapy sessions. What may be a terrific metaphor for hearing clients may seem alien to those who are deaf. The same is also true for clients within deaf culture. Stories that have been successful when working with adult deafened clients may foster feelings of distrust and a belief that therapists lack sufficient understanding and empathy by those clients prelingually deaf. Someone who has lost their hearing due to physical abuse and lives as a "hearing-impaired" person may have a different experience from one who grew up in the "Deaf World" surrounded by those in deaf culture. In order to provide clients with the connections they need to identify with a therapeutic story, therapists should consider the clients' life experience and cultural identity.

It has been assumed, in this chapter, that therapists are able to communicate clearly with their deaf clients. If this is not the case and therapists use interpreters to facilitate communication, then it behooves therapists to not only understand deaf culture but also the nuances of sign language. Those therapists who have been taught how to develop therapeutic metaphors for hearing people incorporating homophonic and other auditory techniques to present unconscious suggestions need to examine visual cues and sign "puns" that can be adapted to accomplish the same objective. Working with an interpreter or other person who is a fluent signer while creating stories will produce better chances of client identification and therapeutic success than ignoring this important communication mode.

Storytelling as a therapeutic technique is not only a viable tool but can be very effective when working with deaf clients. This chapter has discussed several ways in which storytelling can be applied to psychotherapy with this particular population. Deaf culture, like other groups, uses storytelling to instruct and develop meaning about its existence. Because many deaf people experience isolation within their hearing families and often lack the opportunity to know the stories of their heritage, they present themselves in therapy feeling alone with their problems. Storytelling in therapy can provide comfort, a shared experience, and new ways of viewing problems as well as creating possibilities for their resolution. Storytelling in therapy has proven to be a successful technique with hearing clients. I have found it to be a viable and very satisfactory tool to use when working with deaf clients.

REFERENCES

Brown, P. (1991). *The hypnotic brain*. New Haven, CT: Yale University Press.

Erickson, M., Rossi, E. L., & Rossi, S. I., (1976). *Hypnotic realities*. New York: Irvington.

Gough, D. (1990). A transition program for hearing-impaired students: Their perceptions of the process of change. *Journal of American Deafness and Rehabilitation Association 24*(1), 12–22.

Henggeler, S., & Cooper, P. (1980). Deaf child–hearing mother interaction: Extensiveness and reciprocity. *Journal of Pediatric Psychology, 8*, 83–95.

Lankton, S., & Lankton, C. (1983). *The answer within*. New York: Brunner/Mazel.

Lankton, S., & Lankton, C. (1989). *Tales of enchantment*. New York: Brunner/Mazel.

Maher, T. F. (1989). Psychological development of prelingual deaf infants. *Clinical Social Work Journal, 17*(3), 209–222.

Mills, J. C., & Crowley, R. J. (1986). *Therapeutic metaphors for children and the child within*. New York: Brunner/Mazel.

Padden, C., & Humphries, M. (1988). *Deaf in America*. Cambridge, MA: Harvard University Press.

White, M., & Epston, D. (1990). *Narrative means to therapeutic ends*. New York: Norton.

Zeig, J. K. (1980). *A Teaching Seminar with Milton H. Erickon*. New York: Brunner/Mazel.

Chapter 8

Report From the Front Lines: Balancing Multiple Roles of a Deafness Therapist

Sherry Zitter
Westborough, MA

Susie is sitting defiantly in her elderly parent's living room, refusing to leave. Her parents, on the phone to my office, tell me nervously that the crisis worker wants to send the police to force her back to her residence. "We don't want that," they say tearfully. "But we can't handle her here. What else can we do?"

It is 9:00 p.m. on a weekday evening. Susie is a mentally retarded, intermittently assaultive deaf woman in her 40s who uses visual–gestural (V–G) communication. No one can communicate clearly to her: not her family members, the residential staff on duty, or the crisis worker. She has assaulted another resident and walked the 3 miles in the rain to her parents' home, where she would rather live. No interpreter is available until morning.

If I stop at her parents' house on my way home, maybe I can draw and mime enough to get through to Susie, to explain that she must leave voluntarily or risk being dragged out by the police. However, I also risk our therapeutic relationship if she feels I am intruding or associates me with those who force her away from her parents. If I don't go, Susie has no communication and is not given a choice about controlling her fate tonight.

What's a therapist to do?

The previous example[1] encapsulates of some of the typical dilemmas—ethical, clinical, linguistic, cultural—that therapists working with deaf adults[2] face on a daily basis. Factors such as severe lack of appropriate resources, service providers with grossly limited communication skills, and a system that expects us to be all things to all deaf people conspire to create situations where our roles and responsibilities are far from clear.

As hearing therapists doing cross-cultural work with deaf populations, we seem to be asked to do many contradictory things at once: maintain high productivity to protect our programs; take the time to do culturally sensitive work; develop measurable, reimburseable treatment plans; expand our roles to fill in the gaps for needed and missing services; and keep clear professional boundaries while actively advocating for community needs. The task of sorting out when and how we should intervene in "nontraditional" ways can be daunting. The amount to be done can easily feel overwhelming, and it is crucial to remember that we cannot and should not "do it all."

In this chapter, I look at the real world of therapists who work with deaf people in a public sector agency. Such therapists must possess a range of assessment and intervention skills that would humble any "regular" therapist who actually understood our field. I discuss typical challenges with which we are faced in our daily work and describe the four-dimensional model I use to help me decide when to remain a "pure" therapist and when and how to flex my role in a way that supports client rights, dignity, and empowerment. Such decisions must be made in the political context of one's agency and one's state, the ethical context of one's profession, and the cultural context of the Deaf community.

Expansion of one's therapeutic role may include developing nontraditional treatment plans involving therapist tasks like case management, advocacy, education, crisis management, and independent living skills development and justifying these nontraditional functions in client-centered, "objective"behavioral terms that satisfy agency and insurance company mandates. They must also include the self-care and personal limit setting necessary to avoid burnout. Without careful assessment, expansion of role only as appropriate and needed, and full understanding of the demands of the system, effective therapy can be impossible.

As you read on, Sarah's story and three other examples of deaf clients are presented. The first part of the chapter uses these vignettes to illustrate a multidimensional model for therapeutic decision making, through the assessment and treatment process. The end of the chapter widens the focus to ethical considerations, creative treatment plan development, and juggling the competing demands of clients, agencies, and selfcare.

Sarah went to a deaf residential school and loves being Deaf. She just graduated from Gallaudet University last spring and is working at a good job in a bank. She has chosen to move to a big city, where there is a large Deaf community and two Deaf clubs.

---

[1]Each case description is a composite of several clients, and all names and identifying information have been disguised.

[2]Although many similar problems are faced with deaf children and with hard-of-hearing or late-deafened people, so many issues and approaches are different that I focus this chapter on prelingually deafened adults.

> Sarah called me on the TTY and told me she wanted help with how to handle an ex-boyfriend, who wouldn't leave her alone. She asked how long I had known sign and about my training. She wanted to know if my agency would accept her insurance from work and asked for directions.

Deaf people come to therapy with a wide range of expectations and functioning levels. At one end of the range, a well-informed Deaf person like Sarah, with good life skills and social skills, wants to work on a well-defined problem. Serving this person is easy: The client and I understand and agree on my role as a pure therapist and on the role of a client. She does not need other kinds of help from me. This type of client is also in the minority.

More frequently we see the tragic results of a sociopolitical system that denies deaf children basic communication, quality education, and access to a community. We also see the products of a medical community saving premature babies earlier and earlier, babies who grow up with multiple neurological and organic deficits associated with their deafness.

This motley collection of clients has extremely diverse needs and problems. One group includes impulse-disordered clients, some referred from the courts for mandated treatment whose behavior is not labeled criminal only because their lack of comprehension in any language system renders them incompetent to stand trial. Others are withdrawn, socially inept clients who could be mentally retarded, geographically isolated, chronically mentally ill, or simply extraordinarily language-deprived.

Most people with these types of backgrounds have no concept of why they are in a therapists's office, and it might take months to explain it to them fully—if indeed this can be done. Their agendas may include wanting to get out of the office and never come back; feeling they finally have a friend in the world—for an hour a week; wanting to enlist the therapist's help in getting a TTY, cigarettes, or money; or getting rid of the referring provider whom they feel is "telling them what to do."

Clients such as Sarah and Susie have very different skills and deficits in crucial arenas, which greatly affect our roles as therapists in what we can offer, and indeed what we sometimes must offer. These parameters also define somewhat the degree of success we might realistically expect from therapy.

> Jack is in his 60s, severely hard of hearing, and tries to hide the fact that he cannot read basic English sentences. He dropped out of public school at age 16 to work alongside his dad in the family carpentry business. In the last 10 years, many of his dad's steady customers have died. Since his dad died a year ago, Jack doesn't get many jobs anymore.

> Jack doesn't know of any other deaf people in his rural midwestern county and doesn't even know services for deaf people like himself exist. When he becomes increasingly depressed and withdrawn, his daughter somehow finds my name and drives him the 3 hours to my office for an evaluation.

Jack is unaware of the existence of other deaf people or of sign language. His isolation from a Deaf community, geographic lack of resources, and ignorance of the purpose of therapy are problems we often encounter. How these interact with his depression, and some possible ways to help him, are discussed in the following section.

> **Peggy** is a wiry 24-year-old, deaf since birth. Her alcoholic father physically abused her and her hearing sisters when they were young. She was completely mainstreamed, without interpreters, until college. Extremely bright and a skilled lipreader, she earned excellent grades despite this lack of support services. Her family was proud of treating her "no different than anyone else."
>
> Arriving at National Technical Institute for the Deaf (NTID) knowing no sign, Peggy dropped out after 2 years. In the winter of her sophomore year, she was raped by a deaf man in the parking lot of a local deaf club. Worsening substance abuse and two psychiatric hospitalizations made keeping up with her classwork impossible.
>
> Peggy is bristling with anger over what hearing and deaf people have done to her. She has no friends (except her pot dealer) and has been fired from several jobs for angry outbursts. Under stress, she will sometimes self-abuse. She finds it extremely hard to trust anyone.
>
> Peggy's nonsigning therapist of 2 years has just moved away. Although Peggy reluctantly set up an appointment to see me next week, she does not really want to go to a deaf program and does not want help from anyone anyway.

How do we help deaf clients who hate their own deafness? What is our role? If Peggy wants a therapist who knows nothing about deafness, is this her right? How do her upbringing, her various traumas, and her personality disorder impact her clinical, cultural, and communication needs, and how does this inform my role as her therapist? How can the local crisis team, emergency room, or hospital unit be used as back-ups if they have no knowledge of deafness? These questions are explored as Peggy's story unfolds.

Using the four composite clients described previously as examples, I first discuss the therapists' role with each through a multidimensional assessment model. Four basic areas of *communication, clinical, cultural,* and available *resources* are assessed. I then look at exactly what we do differently with deaf clients and why. The assessment model guides when and how our roles must expand from traditional therapy and when such expansion could be disempowering or otherwise inappropriate.

Finally, I address the areas of our jobs that require more than assessing each client in his[3] unique environment. Agencies, insurance companies, and the Deaf community itself need to be dealt with in specific ways. We make complex decisions about our roles in a small community where client and therapist have more interaction than in the larger culture. We have to fulfill agency and insurance requirements for therapy to be approved and reimbursed. We struggle with drawing lines against higher and higher demands of us.

---

[3]When the use of the pronoun *he* or *she* is necessary for the sake of clarity, I wish to avoid both the awkward *he or she* and the practice of designating the therapist *she* and the client *he,* which I believe carries with it many unconscious gender-specific implications. I simply alternate the two pronouns throughout the text.

The latter section considers the ethical implications of various stances with clients and focuses on how to set therapeutic goals that the client *and* the agency can accept: goals that are concrete, doable, and clinically and culturally appropriate. It shows that clinical and culturally Deaf viewpoints are not at odds but must work together to provide effective treatment. Suggestions are offered about how, in an age of shrinking resources and managed care (some of us in Massachusetts call it "mangled care"), one can juggle the agency demands of more paperwork and higher productivity with the imperatives of case management, advocacy, and multiple agency involvement that we face daily on the front lines with deaf clients.

Alas, the task of doing culturally appropriate therapy with deaf people is not as "simple" as learning sign language, although we know that learning sign language is far from simple. We need to draw on a full range of abilities integral to working with disadvantaged, disempowered, and culturally different people. We need clear models and guidelines to make good decisions and justify them to those without experience in this complex field. This chapter is a start to providing such models and guidelines.

Culturally Appropriate Assessment and Treatment of Deaf Clients: A Multidimensional Model

This section presents an approach that evaluates client strengths and deficits in four areas and uses the resulting assessment as a guide for effective and appropriate intervention. I first explain the model, then demonstrate its use through stories from the introduction, and finally show how treatment decisions flow from each assessment.

THE MODEL: COMMUNICATION, CLINICAL, CULTURAL, AND RESOURCES DIMENSIONS

Four dimensions are explained (Fig. 8.1) that are helpful in conceptualizing how much and where therapists can or must intervene. On each dimension, the left side symbolizes the most limitations, serious concerns, or lack of resources. Clients on this end would require a great deal of intervention and support. The right side represents the greatest skills or resources and the least amount of intervention or case management necessary.

Most clients are somewhere between these two extremes, and it is this complex combination of skills and challenges we assess as a starting point for intervention. This helps determine how to intervene most effectively and no more than necessary.

Looking at Fig. 8.1, our goal is to help clients move from left to right on each scale, increasing their autonomy and sense of empowerment. As much as possible, we want clients on the left side to move *from being done for, to doing with, to doing independently.*

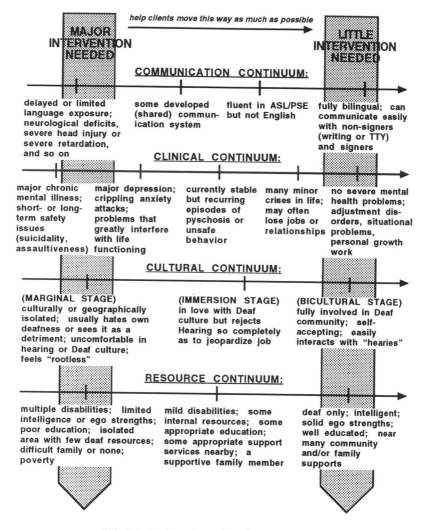

FIG. 8.1. The four dimensions for assessment

Each continuum is explained in more detail later, by showing where each of the four case examples might be placed.

Communication Continuum

Without communication, no therapy is possible. Yet the deaf clients we see exhibit a wide spectrum of communication styles and abilities. Exposure to sign, quality of education, lipreading skill, and cognitive or organic limitations are but a few of the factors that shape a deaf person's communication, as depicted in Fig. 8.2.

At the extreme left of this dimension is Susie (see arrow), whose communication is V–G, concrete, and often idiosyncratic. Also on this end are people who, due to organic problems (such as mental retardation, brain damage, head injuries, and AIDS dementia) or language deprivation, have no common linguistic system with more than a few close others. Such clients have a most daunting task negotiating society and need the most immediate intervention and long-term linguistic training to increase their abilities to feel empowered in their own lives.

Next is Jack, who has picked up some sign as an adult and has a few lipreading skills, but does not really have a reliable way to communicate with either hearing or deaf people. He speaks in grunts, catches a few words on people's lips, and fakes his way through the rest. Unlike many people to the left on this scale, Jack is painfully aware that he is missing a lot. If a therapist can penetrate his discouragement and belief that he has no other communication options, such a client could become quite motivated to learn other ways to communicate.

Another person in this area of the scale could be a fluent English reader and writer, who has no effective way to communicate with Deaf or hearing except by pen. A person who had been language deprived for decades but has been in a language-rich environment with Deaf staff for several years and is beginning to communicate clearly, expressively and receptively, would move from the left side of the scale to Jack's position. Any of these folks would need some communication training and supports in the linguistic aspects of daily living—with the goal of becoming as independent as possible.

Someone comfortable in a widely used manually coded English (MCE) system would fall in the middle of this scale. Such a client could be sophisticated in use of interpreter services or may need skills training.

Sarah, who is fully bilingual in sign and English (the right end of the scale), needs no linguistic support from a therapist. She can make her own TTY and relay calls to get information or set up services. She can talk with deaf people easily, code switching as necessary.

Peggy, like Sarah, can read and write well in English, enabling her to access hearing services independently. She can sign in MCE, so she can talk to a limited range of deaf people. Whether she learns ASL or not, in order to be fully bilingual, depends largely on clinical issues and is discussed later.

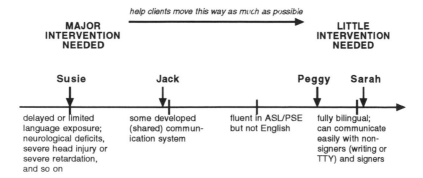

FIG. 8.2. Communication continuum.

The communication assessment helps therapists know how best to talk with each client at the beginning and whether an effective linguistic system exists to communicate with significant others. It informs us of whether temporary or long-term supports are needed for a client to function well linguistically. It gives us a sense of his emotional experience around being understood or comprehending others.

Clinical Continuum

One of the most important parts of our job is evaluating if someone is safe enough not to hurt herself or others. Aside from this, we often have the complex task of giving each person a diagnosis and developing a treatment plan in just a few sessions. In the next section, I detail some ways in which clinical assessment with deaf people can be different. At this point, I focus only on where various types of clients are placed on this dimension (see Fig. 8.3).

On the extreme left are mentally retarded (MR) clients like Susie, whose impulsiveness and/or language deprivation contribute to frequent behavioral problems. Other MR clients could be anywhere on this dimension, depending on their behavioral and clinical level.

Someone with a major mental illness could be in the middle of the spectrum if stable on medications and solidly supported by a good residential and day situation. However, if the same person has ongoing delusions, hallucinations, assaultiveness, suicidal tendencies, or frequent crises from the stress of daily living without sufficient community support, he would be at the far left end of the scale, needing more focused case management interventions. (These could range from setting up psychopharmacological consults to advocating for more appropriate programming.)

Sarah, at the far right end of the spectrum, presents with no major psychological problems, and is clear about therapy goals and motivated to change. Peggy, who has a personality disorder, could be in the middle of this scale or could be at the far left, with chronic suicidal attempts or dangerous impulsivity,

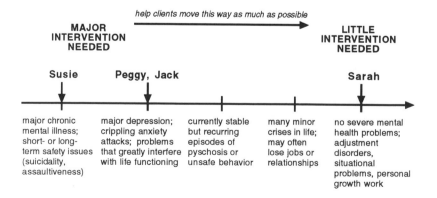

FIG. 8.3. Clinical continuum.

depending on many other factors. From what has been described so far, one would put her between the left and the middle.

Jack is depressed but not suicidal, and is still able to function in many areas. He would be toward the left of the scale but closer to the middle than Peggy.

The further to the left on this dimension a client falls, the more active intervention is needed by a therapist, both in the office and with other resources. A client who falls more to the right tends not to need as much case management, and the client and therapist can focus more easily on pure therapeutic work.

Cultural Continuum

A strong cultural identity often is believed to be inextricably linked to good mental health. One cannot be ashamed of who one is and feel good about oneself at the same time. Each of us with a stigmatized identity must make our peace with who and what we are, as opposed to the stereotypes of society, in order to fully accept ourselves. Cultural acceptance, although intertwined with good mental health, is considered here as a separate dimension in order to focus more deeply on assessment and intervention in this vital area. As shown in Fig. 8.4, I use the cultural identity categories developed by Glickman (chapter 5, this volume).

Susie has little awareness of Deaf or hearing cultures. She has some understanding of who is deaf and who is hearing, but this information has no meaning for her. She is low-functioning marginal, on the left side of the scale. Peggy is self-hating, knows or likes few other deaf people, and would be high functioning but quite marginal, even more toward the left. Jack, who does not know about or live near a Deaf community, is also marginal and would need assistance if he wishes exposure to Deaf community resources.

Sarah, who is secure in her own deafness and has a strong tie to the Deaf community is on the right end of this scale.

The cultural dimension, then, measures one's feeling about one's own deafness and cultural ties to the Deaf community.

Resources Continuum

This dimension includes an assessment of four types of resources: internal personal resources; external personal resources; social and community resources; and social and community pressures.

INTERNAL PERSONAL RESOURCES
intelligence
ego strengths such as insight, maturity, and judgment
understanding of therapy process, psychological mindedness
past successes with problem solving and view of self as resourceful

EXTERNAL PERSONAL RESOURCES
education
job
advocacy skills
social skills
family support

SOCIAL AND COMMUNITY RESOURCES
nearby Deaf community and deaf organizations signing service providers, accessible
services

SOCIAL AND COMMUNITY PRESSURES
discrimination on the basis of deafness
discrimination due to other "differentness" such as ethnicity, mental retardation,
cerebral palsy, lesbianism, and so forth
poverty, lack of money

The resource continuum (see Fig 8.5) looks at different "layers" of resources
to identify those available to each client for support as therapy progresses. Some
of the elements of this dimension are considered in the *Diagnostic and Statistical
Manual IV* (*DSM–IV*) Axis IV (What are the stressors on this individual?) and
Axis V (How well does she function?). Increasing a client's awareness of various
internal and external resources may help the client use the resources more
effectively.

Susie has limited intelligence, little education, and few ego strengths. She
has no understanding of therapy. She is a hard worker and wants to appear "like
everyone else" and so tries to act mature; these are strengths that can be drawn
on to help her through crises. However, she has little judgment or insight.
Unfortunately, she has gotten her way often through acting out, so her problem-solving approach leans in that direction.

A person with multiple disabilities affecting how she thinks (neurological or
organic problems, retardation, thought disorders) has less emotional resources
to cope with the stresses of oppression and prejudice. More toward the left side
of this dimension, people such as Susie may require more support and advocacy
politically.

A person who is deaf and blind, or deaf and has cerebral palsy, is viewed by the
able-bodied and able-ist world as having little potential or value. The extra
challenges of illness or disability can require frequent doctor's appointments and
contact with multiple agencies. Exponentially more time may be needed to fight
for different types of access or search for providers sensitive to this cluster of issues.

When a deaf person, such as Sarah, is intelligent and well-educated, comfortable with who she is, and has a community close by for support, the daily

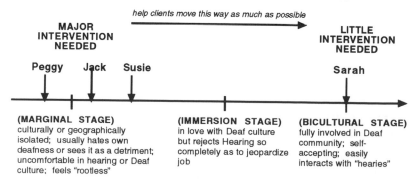

FIG. 8.4. Cultural continuum.

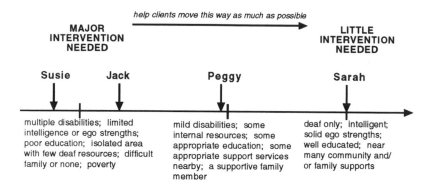

FIG. 8.5. Resource continuum.

stresses of an ignorant hearing world are easier to cope with. Sarah has a high level of ego strength and knows what she wants from therapy. Sarah has also had the luxury of choosing me out of five signing therapists in her city.

Certainly, Sarah and I would explore how she feels about having a hearing therapist (and that there were no Deaf therapists to choose from). Certainly issues of discrimination may arise in our therapeutic work together. But Sarah does not need my help to find resources or a sense of community. She would be on the right end of this scale.

Peggy is intelligent, well-educated, and lives near many deaf resources. She has little judgment or insight. Peggy feels misunderstood by everyone and views herself at the mercy of other people. Her family is not a support, and people in her life react negatively both to her deafness and her personality disorder. She would be placed on the middle of this scale.

Jack's intelligence is average, although certainly diminished by an inadequate education and ineffective communication. His judgment is intact, and he demonstrates maturity. He has no understanding of therapy but some sense of himself as a problem solver. However, all the education and self-advocacy skills in the world wouldn't solve access issues for Jack, who lives in an area without interpreters, or for someone who lives in a state where the nearest signing therapist is 4 hours away. Our role as therapists sometimes must expand when there is nobody else to pick up the slack. Jack would be placed toward the middle left of this scale.

I use the resources continuum to highlight which internal, external, and community supports each client has available. I draw on these to help him with the current situation, or I can offer various community supports when he is ready.

As we use these four dimensions to assess each client's skills and deficit areas, we can develop a fuller understanding of our therapeutic roles with each individual. By evaluating communication skills, clinical strengths and difficulties, and cultural self-esteem, we can see whether immediate intervention is needed for safety and which approaches in each area may work best for this individual. By assessing the client's support systems, including other providers, we can clarify which tasks can be done independently by the client, which can and should be referred to others, and which must be done by us. We can see naturally where expansion of the therapeutic role is appropriate and necessary in order for therapy to happen—and also where such expansion would be inappropriate, overprotective, and self-serving. We can create a vision with clients of increasing independence as services fall into place, as we show them how to do things with us, and then as they learn to do things independently. Each therapist and client must build a unique construct in which therapy takes place: a structure where client's strengths, needs, and dreams are validated and where realistic goals are set together that create a sense of movement toward greater independence, competence, and self-esteem.

HOW TO ASSESS CLIENTS ON EACH DIMENSION

This section demonstrates how to use each dimension for assessment that leads to effective, culturally appropriate intervention. Assessment questions are provided for each dimension and summarized in an appendix at the end of the chapter, to be used as guides when thinking about specific clients.

Linguistic/Communication Considerations

> Susie is at her hearing sister's wedding shower. She gestures and chatters away to one of her sister's friends, who knows no sign and has no idea what Susie is saying. The friend is looking more uncomfortable by the minute. When she turns away to join another conversation, Susie blissfully continues signing and making sounds.

> Jack takes the intake form from the receptionist at my agency, nodding as if he understands her instructions. He sits down and pretends to read it. When she asks if he wants some coffee, he nods. He doesn't drink coffee, so when it appears, he's embarrassed and doesn't know what to do. He wants to ask where the rest room is, but assumes he won't be able to understand the explanation, so he just shifts uncomfortably in his chair.

A common communication system between therapist and client is essential to forming a relationship and assessing anything else. Unfortunately, as we have all experienced, such common ground is sometimes difficult to find. The first step upon meeting a new client is to assess her communication, which involves more than code switching to match the client's preferred mode as closely as possible.

As I greet a new client in the waiting room, I notice how he introduces himself: whether he is a fluent or awkward fingerspeller, whether he uses his voice while signing, how comfortable he is with using his body and facial expressions for inflection. As I show him to the office or offer him something to drink, I notice if and how well he seems to be understanding me (remembering that the high anxiety inherent in a first appointment may often impede understanding more than usual).

Even without stressful situations, some clients produce different linguistic styles than they are most comfortable receiving. This can range anywhere from clients educated orally, who sign to hearing people in English but understand

ASL better, to linguistically deprived people who have had to mime their way through life to be understood. Many such persons have a much more highly developed expressive linguistic system than receptive. They are used to reading body language and facial cues, but not formal signs, and often use specific signs expressively that they cannot recognize visually. With such clients, the usual premise that receptive language develops faster than expressive does not hold. It is therefore not always true that clients can comprehend signs that they have used expressively.[4]

If a client and I fall into an easy rapport, with little struggling to understand or be understood, we can linguistically relax and concentrate together on the problems that brought the client into therapy. When that familiar tight feeling in my stomach tells me communication will be a torturous process for both of us, communication becomes the first mighty hurdle to be overcome before assessment or treatment can begin.

Connecting to the client—whether emotionally or through communication—is the task of the therapist. It is crucial to convey to the client that it is my responsibility to adjust to her communication needs rather than the other way around. (This may seem obvious, but I have seen therapists correcting clients' sign! Such an approach detracts considerably from establishing rapport.)

There are wonderful trainings by deaf professionals about how to match idiosyncratic language systems of deaf clients, and a full discussion of these techniques is neither my specialty nor within the scope of this chapter. One's basic attitude of total respect and taking responsibility to understand can be communicated easily. Using an interpreter and/or a relay interpreter when communication is a struggle is an immediate and concrete way to get across the message that one takes the need for clear communication seriously.

A family member is sometimes instrumental initially to interpret idiosyncratic "home" signs. There are clinical risks involved in meeting with the client along with a family member he may view as oppressive. However, if communication is not happening with a client who has been isolated from the Deaf community, I sometimes take that risk in order to establish basic communication. If I decide to do so, I let the client know (through miming, drawing, or use of a calendar) that the family member will only be present one or two times to help me understand him, and then we will meet alone.

Communication Assessment Questions

If communication is a struggle, other issues are helpful to consider:

1. At which age was this person exposed to meaningful communication (if at all)? Knowing the client's linguistic history—at which age he was first exposed to which communication methods, how much exposure or deprivation there has been—helps the therapist sense a client's potential for language growth. In the absence of

---

[4]Thanks to Bill Huston, director of Northern Essex Community College's interpreter training program (Haverhill, Massachusetts), for helping me understand this vital distinction.

compromising factors such as retardation or brain damage, even much older deaf people can benefit from a language-rich environment such as a day program run by Deaf staff. In the many areas where this is unavailable, a one-on-one Deaf tutor could be utilized beneficially.

2. How is this person used to communicating? What is her natural communication style? Is it primarily linguistic or alternate methods (such as tantrums when angry, working when lonely, withdrawing when depressed?)

A chronic behavioral disorder cannot be properly diagnosed until a person has a way to communicate wants and needs with those around him: Often behavioral difficulties lessen considerably in a program with Deaf or fluently signing hearing staff, or as language grows.

3. Is either receptive or expressive language considerably stronger than the other mode?

4. Can the client communicate (and if so, how well) over phone line with TTY, relay, or amplified handset? Would she be able to get across a message or ask for help this way in a crisis?

(Note: The list of assessment questions for each dimension is repeated in Appendix A.)

Answers to each of these questions may raise more questions, but gathering such information will begin to pull together a clearer picture of each person's linguistic skills and needs.

Clinical Considerations

Peggy is shouting unintelligible sounds in the emergency room as I arrive. I have been called from my office to assess this client I haven't met yet—indeed, I had hoped to meet her for a scheduled appointment next week under calmer circumstances. When I begin to sign to her, she screams something that sounds like "no sign language" and "burn in Hell." I immediately stop signing and ask orally if I can talk to her. She turns her face away and refuses to look at me.

Susie is sitting on her parents' sofa with arms crossed and jaw set, stating with her body language that she's not leaving their apartment. If pushed to do something she doesn't want, her next step is typically to break glass and threaten to hurt herself with it.

As therapists, our most immediate responsibility is to determine if a person is at risk to himself or to others—even if a common communication system has not yet been established. This decision must sometimes be made in a crisis situation, where client's and caretaker's agitation or escalating dynamics between them can blur both communication and clinical assessment.

If a therapist determines a client may be at risk for suicide or self-injury, this opens up a host of problems, from crisis workers untrained in deafness (who may be the gatekeepers for hospital placement) to the inherent disempowering of a client by placing him unwillingly in a hospital, if this be necessary.

Other clinical issues, less urgent but just as important to determine the direction of successful therapy, include doing a thorough mental status exam, checking for signs of thought disorder or personality disorder, and understanding this client's worldview or cognitive set: What is her opinion about why things happen in her life the way they do?

Clinical Assessment Questions

As a therapist assesses each client along the clinical dimension, questions to consider include:

1. Is the client at risk to hurt himself or others?
2. Does the client show evidence of a personality disorder or a thought disorder?
3. If the person feels disempowered, where do the feelings of disempowerment stem from?

(Understanding where a person experiences lack of empowerment in the past or present helps a therapist know how to help the empowerment process take place. Most acting out behavior is at least partially rooted in feeling trapped, disempowered, helpless, or ignored.)

4. Which cues in the present seem to trigger inappropriate behavior? Where could the particular form of behavior (self-mutilation, throwing things, running away, sexually inappropriate behaviors, etc.) have been learned?
5. Is there a trauma history (or symptoms of a possible trauma history), particularly physical or sexual abuse?

(Disclosure of trauma often takes months, if not years, of building therapeutic alliances. Some clients do not even remember traumatic events until a great deal of trust and safety has been established in therapy. Deaf children, often unable to communicate clearly to adults, are particularly vulnerable targets for abuse. The astoundingly high percentages of female and male victims of childhood abuse is probably even higher in the deaf population. Therefore, our deaf adult clients are likely to have a high rate of childhood abuse histories.)

6. How does this person's communication style change—if it does—during a crisis or a temporary psychosis?

When in crisis, any of us could have more trouble processing information. Notice if a deaf client changes her signing style when upset. I remember a client with schizophrenia who signed more English-like when having an episode. The focus on endings seemed to organize his thoughts, or maybe he was more anxious and reverted to the type of "language" production that had been expected of him in school. However, he had trouble understanding if I matched him and signed back in English! He responded better if I continued signing to him as I always did.

7. Which interventions seem to "fit" with this person? Can she reality test? Understand cause and effect? Show insight?

As one overlaps one's knowledge about the person's communicative and clinical needs, a picture of both necessary and useful interventions emerges. Although common elements of respect and choice, containment and safety are always present, particular clinical and communication patterns require unique responses.

For example, a client with a personality disorder who refuses interpreter services might need to be told that the evaluating psychiatrist needs the interpreter to understand the client better and that the client can choose not to watch the interpreter if he prefers. A V–G client with a behavioral disorder might need far more time and attention to be sure she understands before setting firm limits than one fluent in ASL. The intervention section details these types of decisions in case discussions.

Cultural Considerations

> When I write down my name for Jack and show him my name sign, he looks embarrassed and waves my hands away, mumbling something that sounds like "I talk. Not that stuff."

> Peggy's self esteem has been built partly on her lipreading skills. She does not want to admit that signing makes things easier for her. She associates ASL with the "mean" deaf people who ignored her and one who raped her. She can accept me signing in rigid MCE with all the endings, and says "What?" with a puzzled expression if I miss an English tense.

What do therapists do when clients want to communicate orally, but this does not seem an effective means of communication for them? Obviously, we match our clients' communication styles initially, but then what? If they reject using sign language (or whatever would be most effective for them), is part of the therapeutic process to help them discover and feel OK about whatever means of communication works best for them, rather than forcing themselves into the mold others expect of them? I would contend that it is. (See the story of Peggy's and Jack's treatment in the next section for a fuller discussion of this issue.)

Language and culture, as well as self-esteem and cultural pride, are intertwined, in some ways inseparable. As one assesses each client's language, it is instructive to notice whether she introduces herself in a culturally Deaf way, if he exhibits awareness of the local Deaf community and resources, if she has a name sign or shows sophistication about use of interpreters. Aspects of Deaf culture I would notice in a first interview might also include a client making reference to or questioning me about mutual acquaintances in the community; questions about deaf programs at which I had worked previously; blunt (from a culturally hearing perspective) questions about my hearing status, marital status, deaf family members, or motivation for working with deaf people; and hugging or expecting a hug as a typical goodbye gesture within the community, perhaps even at the close of a first meeting.

Cultural Assessment Questions

Some questions to consider when evaluating a client's cultural self-image and resources are:

1. In which stage of Glickman's cultural identity model (see Glickman, chapter 5, this volume) would this person be?

2. When did this person first meet another deaf/Deaf person? What was the context? What messages about deafness did he get and from whom?

3. If the client is in Glickman's marginal stage, what exactly does the person feel and think about the Deaf community and Deaf culture? Has she experienced ridicule or rejection from deaf people—in school, Deaf clubs, or other situations—and generalized this experience to all deaf people? If the client's feelings toward deafness are negative, are the feelings rigid or do they seem open to change with education and exposure?

Resource Considerations

Susie might have handled her mild retardation far differently in a family that had the ability to provide structure and not tolerate aggressive behavior.

Jack's view of himself as dependent on others and incapable contributed to his nosedive into depression after his father's death.

Peggy's superior intelligence enabled her to finish 2 years of college at NTID, despite her struggle to learn sign at age 18, her trauma history, and her personality problems.

Clients come to our offices with a unique mix of internal and external resources and gaps. What they are born with (intelligence, native personality, neurological functioning) and what they are given and earn (family, money, education, job) combine to form their worldviews and develop their ego strengths. Assessing these internal and external resources helps us to focus on the quality of the hand each client has been dealt, and to expect from her as much as she can do and no more. It helps us explain to a client at his own level of intellectual and emotional understanding what his strengths and weaknesses appear to be. It helps with developing an alliance and drawing from strengths to problem solve together. Yet there is a larger sphere of resources to notice as well:

"How can a deaf person drive safely?"

"Can't you just read my lips?"

Hearing people either seem to think deaf people can do nothing or expect them to act just like "hearies"—or both! Deafness is invisible. Hearing people own and run the majority of resources (financial, educational, political) in the world. It has been a struggle for the Deaf community to come of age politically, to work together for the right to the adaptations necessary to participate fully in work and society.

Society and community provide resources—but can also be a source of discrimination. Susie bears the double oppression of deafness and a mental disability to which many react with fear and lack of respect. Jack lives far from a supportive Deaf community and the appropriate services that could help him grow. Clients have different sets of skills and resources to support them through the therapy process and through life. Helping them learn which resources are available and what discrimination they may face increases empowerment and independence.

Resource Assessment Questions

1. What is this person's level of intelligence and maturity? What are her ego strengths, both at this moment and in general?

2. How well does he understand the process of problem solving and of therapy? How much confidence does he have in himself? If his confidence is low, can the therapist find in his history examples of successes, of skills, and can he take in these examples to modify his self-perception?

3. Which supports does the person currently have in her life (family members, friends, neighbors, priest, doctor) even if they are not deaf or do not sign?

People who care and have an ongoing relationship with a client may be able to encourage her to take risks and try new things, or may be the ones who sabotage any new growth, unless they are brought into the therapy process.

4. What are the stressors (Axis IV) in this person's life currently? Is he unemployed? Has she recently lost a loved one through death or divorce? Has he recently been diagnosed with a new illness or disability, or is he dealing with a progressive one?

5. Which community resources (both Deaf and nondeaf supports) are available in the local area? Do they cost money? Are they mandated to be accessible through federal ADA legislation? What is the referral process? Is there a waiting list? Can a therapist advocate (or help a client advocate herself, or both) for a hearing agency to pay a deafness provider to give services if this fits the client's needs better? (I have been pleasantly surprised at how quickly managed care plans that rarely refer out have been willing to pay me privately to see a Deaf client.)

6. What is the client's general level of functioning (Axis V)? What is her level of behavioral control, social skills, education, vocational functioning? How much is he able to advocate with the therapist's support and guidance, and how much does the therapist have to do this for him? Does she understand what advocacy is, what her rights are as a deaf person and as a U.S. citizen in general? What can he learn about his legal rights and how to access them?

7. Which disabilities or differences (Cerebral palsy, AIDS, Jewishness, lesbian-ism, etc.) does the client have, besides deafness, that might cause oppression or discrimination? How aware is she of how these differences affect her life and how to constructively manage these pressures?

This section has examined some of the common dilemmas for therapists in the communication, clinical, cultural, and resource arenas. I have reviewed a set of evaluation questions for each area (repeated in Appendix A) to focus on each client's strengths and need areas.

With these four types of assessment in mind, let us now turn to the sample cases and consider what we know about them and how this leads to clinically and culturally appropriate treatment planning.

ADVENTURES IN INTERVENTION

This section pulls together what has been discussed about each composite case study. Sarah's case need not be discussed further, as it represents therapy with a high–functioning Deaf client, in which a clinician could remain comfortably in an unexpanded therapeutic role. Each of the more complex examples demonstrates how multidimensional assessment leads naturally to effective, culturally appropriate interventions. For each client, the assessment focuses on what we need to know in the current situation. Following each assessment is a treatment plan, including a crisis plan if needed. Final discussion highlights ways the therapist's role must at times expand to include tasks such as advocacy, case management, crisis intervention, and community networking.

Assessing and Intervening With Susie

Susie, the mentally retarded and assault-prone woman who is refusing to leave her elderly parents' home, will likely be dragged away by the police if I do not stop by to explain her choices to her. But would my involvement contaminate our treatment and make me appear to be the enemy?

Assessing Susie on each dimension will guide my intervention strategies.

Assessment

Communication Issues.   Susie was hardly exposed to any sign until adulthood. When I began working with Susie 3 years ago, her lack of proper schooling combined with her mild retardation had produced a woman with many V–G skills and little formal ASL.

Throughout childhood, Susie observed her father communicating by hitting or throwing something when upset or angry. Susie learned to do the same. Language is not her natural medium to express feelings or wishes. Stronger expressively than receptively, she relies on body and facial cues to learn the feelings of others. We should not expect her to be able to use formal thought and language to modulate her actions in the near future.

When Susie is upset, her ability to understand becomes severely limited. Crises are times to lower expectations of communication; many of us unconsciously raise them instead. To get through to Susie effectively in a crisis, one would expect to give her multimodal V–G: to mime, draw, and engage her in a role play if possible to give her the best possible chance of understanding through her emotional pain.

Clinical Issues.   Over the years, Susie has learned primarily to get what she wants through disruptive behavior. She has experienced that whoever is the loudest, strongest, and most stubborn has the best chance at limited emotional and financial resources.

To Susie, not being able to live with her parents seems unfair and arbitrary. Her struggle to move in with them has ruined several placements and resulted in hospitalizations in the past, due to self-abusive or assaultive behavior. Although she recompensated quickly, freedom there was limited, and she does not want to return.[5]

---

[5]This is a major advantage. Assaultive clients who find the hospital reinforcing can be more difficult to keep calm, because there is no deterrent and indeed a reward for losing control.

Retardation in itself is not a problem clinically—some retarded people hold long-term jobs and lead peaceful and productive lives. But Susie's background and inability to develop abstract thinking, even when exposed to sign, limits her ability to envision future consequences if she acts out. She often feels disempowered, and the only power she has experienced is threatening or assaulting to get her way.

However, Susie is in touch with concrete reality and has no apparent delusions or hallucinations. Money and food are incentives for her; this may be valuable in the current crisis.

Solving this situation well must involve presenting Susie with options, where she does not feel forced, or she will only become more stubborn.

Cultural issues. In Glickman's terminology, Susie is low functioning and emotionally marginal. Susie has never felt a sense of Deaf community. She is much less concerned with whether someone is deaf or signs than with how much attention people pay to her or how often they do what she wants. She has not yet learned to feel empowered through being understood.

Resource Issues. Susie has few ego strengths to help her make well-informed choices. She is retarded and uneducated. She does feel positively about therapy and has some investment in others seeing her as mature, not babyish.

Susie's Northeast state has many more deaf resources than the average. However, she has already lost three placements due to unsafe behavior that traumatized other residents. Her current residence, with minimally signing staff, is not optimal but is the best option available for both communication and behavioral control. If she loses this placement as a result of the current crisis, where would she go? It would certainly meet less of her needs.

Susie has essentially no common communication system with her parents. They are scared of her, and thus reinforce her behaviors unintentionally by giving in to keep her calm. When she signs to them, they often nod "yes" without understanding her—so she has asked to move in with them and gotten nods from them both! Susie is unable to grasp that they do not understand what she is saying. In two family meetings with an interpreter, they were unable with my support to tell Susie directly that she cannot live with them. This ongoing lack of clarity is a major stressor and has kept her unable to accept reality and move on with her life. In the current crisis, Susie's parents could inadvertently undermine any authority who is present.

Summary. In reviewing what we know about Susie on four dimensions, relevant to the present situation, we find:

Linguistically, she will need multimodal V–G: receptively, at minimum, and ideally interactively for any hope of getting through to her. If I decide to intervene, I should prepare some drawings and simple mime approaches to communicate most clearly.

Clinically, Susie relates to familiar people who have gratified her with attention in the past. Tonight, this includes her residence staff, her parents, and me. She needs to feel in control, not forced, or she will use aggression as her way to feel powerful. She is unable to abstract and predict future consequences, but is in touch with reality. Showing her two clear choices may get through to her. She likes money and food and might be won over by offers of either. She does not like going to the hospital.

Culturally, Susie would not respond better to a deaf person than a hearing one. Susie's experience over time of a specific person who has been helpful and paid attention to her would be the most helpful at influencing her behavior.

There are no signing resources except me until morning. If her parents let her stay overnight, Susie is so concrete that she would feel she had won a battle. This would strengthen her resolve to stay put. Behaviorally, it would reinforce her refusal as the way to get what she wants. Her parents, besides being unable to help, would probably detract from any intervention.

If the police drag Susie away and she becomes assaultive in the process, she may or may not lose her residential placement. Her lesson would certainly be that "might makes right"—reinforcing her determination to be even more stubborn or aggressive next time around.

Interventions

Crisis Plan.   The emergency worker, residence staff person, and I worked out a plan with the knowledge and resources at our command. Despite the risk that Susie might see me as an authority or "the enemy," I would go to her parents' home and communicate her choices to her, serving the role of her ego: I would lay out the choices for her and try to support her in making the one she would like the best.

The residence staff person on duty (who only knew a few signs, but whom Susie liked) would meet me in the parking lot outside Susie's parents' apartment building. She would go into the apartment first and ask Susie to go with her for ice cream, one of her favorite treats, on the way home. If Susie refused (we thought she would), the staff person would ask her parents to go with her down to the lobby, so I could talk to Susie alone in the apartment. (Susie had never hurt herself when alone, always in front of others for effect.)

After just a few minutes, I would go into the apartment, looking worried and upset. I would pace back and forth, wringing my hands, telling Susie I was scared and did not want the police to come. In as few signs and gestures as possible, I would plead with her to go with the staff person instead of the police. I would take out a picture I had already drawn of Susie driving with staff in a van to the ice cream store and home, and a different one of Susie in a police car and then in a hospital, and point to them as the two choices (see Fig. 8.6).

I would take a "one-down" position with Susie, communicating to her not that I was angry or an authority, but that she and she alone had control over how this scene would turn out—and that I was terrified she would make an awful choice.

As we carried out our plan, things went smoothly at first. After Susie refused to go home with the staff person, her parents reluctantly agreed to go with the staff person to the lobby. When I entered the apartment, Susie at first would not look at me, her eyes downcast as if expecting to be yelled at. When I ignored

FIG. 8.6. A visual presentation of Susie's choices.

her, my body language and face expressing anxiety and worry, she became puzzled and then intrigued. She began sneaking peeks at me talking to myself: "OH NO, POLICE, DON'T WANT, NO! HOPE (fingers crossed, praying to God) SUSIE, GO HOME SOON, NO POLICE, NO HOSPITAL, HOPE, PRAY. . . "

When Susie began making longer periods of eye contact, I started to talk directly to her, pleading with her, worry in my face, leaving it all up to her. I showed her the pictures of the two choices she had. She tore the pictures up. I mimed trying to stop the police and being unable to do so.

When Susie remained adamant that she would not budge, I made my body language elaborately clear that I had given up. My face fell in disappointment, my shoulders sagged forward in defeat, and I shrugged and said goodbye. As Susie continued to look stubborn, I turned and dragged my feet slowly toward the door. I turned and made one last plea to the powerful woman in whose hands the decision rested: "PLEASE NO COP, NO HOSPITAL PLEASE." She set her jaw and I walked out, leaving the apartment door open invitingly, and waited in the hall. I hoped that once Susie had lost her audience, she could think again about her choices and make a conscious decision.

After 2 or 3 minutes, Susie stood up and slowly walked to the door. I looked at her, my face carefully neutral so as not to indicate in any way that she had made the "right" decision or had been manipulated. She asked where her dad was, and I pointed downstairs to the lobby. She indicated that I should walk down the stairs with her. When she saw her parents and the staff person, she signed "ICE CREAM?" and the staff person nodded, her face also neutral. Susie hugged each of her parents in turn and walked out with the staff person to get ice cream, and from there went calmly back to her residence.

Discussion. I decided to intervene, and how I wanted to intervene, based on my evaluation of Susie on each dimension. Her long-term positive relationship with me and lack of other effective communication options made me decide to take the risk of getting involved. Her communication style and personality style determined how I presented her options to her.

Luckily, this situation turned out positively. Had Susie continued to refuse to leave the apartment, her staff person and I would have said goodbye and left well before the police came, to minimize any concrete associations between us and the police. The elements of clear communication, a known person she trusted, and empowerment of her to make a choice without pushing created the most likely environment to succeed; but success was by no means certain.

Long-Term Issues. As soon as possible, a case conference should occur to develop a plan to prevent or minimize the chances of this type of incident happening again. The plan should include what to do if this happens again, and who should do it. This helps clarify my clinical role and how I am and am not willing to "flex" my role in future crises.

As clinicians in the deafness field, we often find ourselves in the following "Catch-22" situation: Crisis services are at best partially inaccessible to our clients, they can sometimes make a situation worse through inappropriate and insensitive interventions. If we do not expand our roles to become crisis workers at times, our most vulnerable clients get hurt when they are the least able to deal with it. If we do act as crisis workers, we are in a sense "enabling" the emergency care system to remain inaccessible and not make the adaptations it should, such as interpreters on beeper for mental health crises and ongoing trainings on deafness for new and experienced crisis workers.

A major purpose of a followup case conference would be to put the crisis team and the Department of Mental Retardation (DMR) on notice that I will not take this role again; that I expect them to implement alternate plans to be ready for Susie's next after-hours emergency.

The case conference could also strengthen Susie's behavior plan, with Susie giving input beforehand rather than attending, due to her limited understanding. Her frequency of her favorite reinforcement (seeing her parents) could increase with safe behaviors and be reduced if she went AWOL.

Other systems interventions would also be important to improve this situation long term. A task force should be formed of deafness providers to urge the DMR to hire a coordinator of deaf services statewide and some signing case managers. The residence needs to be reminded (again) of the importance of regular communications classes—not standard ASL classes but training with a (preferably Deaf) person skilled in visual–gestural communication and in helping staff become comfortable using the natural gestures they already know and "playing charades" with Susie. Such interventions take time and energy, but they would benefit far more clients than Susie and make all of our jobs easier.

Expansion of Therapist Role.   The story of Susie illustrates the role of a therapist when a crisis occurs, communication is limited, and a client's residential placement may be in jeopardy. It points out how a clinical crisis assessment cannot be done in isolation, without considering Susie's communication limitations and needs. It shows how I can expand my role without tainting it, and how I can maximize empowerment for a client in crisis through presentation of clear choices.

Assessing and Intervening With Jack

Jack has been brought to therapy by his daughter because he is becoming more depressed and withdrawn since his father's death and the lack of carpentry business. He has no effective means of communication nor awareness of a Deaf community or culture. He lives a few hours from my office (the closest Deaf service) and has no idea what therapy is for.

Assessment

Communication Issues.   Jack was educated rurally by teachers who knew little about the special needs of a deaf child and tried to "treat him like everyone else." He is used to getting by with as little communication as possible, pretending he understands, and isolating himself as a coping mechanism. He is understood by familiar hearing others better than he can understand them. His public school education clearly was not enough for Jack to develop a full linguistic system or to abstract easily. He is functionally illiterate, a fact he tries to conceal, and cannot use a TTY.

Because language modulates affect and increases impulse control, future orientation, and ability to plan and feel capable in one's life, part of my initial history taking always includes finding out as much as possible about a client's linguistic history: either from the client, from family, or from a referring provider. If I can learn at which age he was first diagnosed as deaf, his degree of loss, and how much exposure or deprivation there has been vis-à-vis various communication methods, it helps me sense the client's potential for language growth. In the absence of compromising factors such as retardation or brain damage, even older deaf people can benefit from a language-rich environment such as a day program run by Deaf staff. In the many areas where this is unavailable (or in Jack's case, where his higher vocational functioning might make him inappropriate for existing day program populations), a one-on-one Deaf tutor could be utilized beneficially. It is essential for a therapist to assess whether language deprivation is contributing to presenting symptoms, and if so, to make the necessary referrals or do the advocacy to help a client's communication expand.[6]

A first step, where possible, is to refer the client to a Deaf Independent Living Skills (ILS) program or multiservice center for a full communication evaluation. Even if this is an all-day trip to a neighboring state, the information gained about exactly which type of training is needed—and the evidence available in the report to advocate for funding ongoing language training (sometimes for staff/family as well as client)—can be extremely beneficial.

A good communication evaluation can point out issues such as: differences in expressive/receptive skills in various modes, strengths and weaknesses in communication strategies, and idiosyncracies in style and nonstandard use of standard signs. Clear recommendations can be made about which type of linguistic training is needed, which credentials/background are needed to work with the client effectively, and what communication strategies at home and at work would be the most useful. Such professional testing recommendations can also be used to advocate for funding for communication training by demonstrating its necessity.

Clinical Issues. My only nonstandard method in exploring Jack's symptoms is my approach to communication. I ask him about suicidality or assaultive wishes through a combination of speaking, lipreading, drawing, and miming. He is surprised by and appreciative of my efforts to be understood and assures me he will not hurt himself or anyone else.

Consistent with depression, Jack has been withdrawing from his usual activities and social contacts. He has been eating less and is becoming apathetic about his business. His depression may have been brought on by loss of his father and his changing work situation.

My sense from what Jack's daughter has told me is that he has no history of a thought disorder. Ruling this out directly may be difficult due to our limited abstract communication. I could try to draw and act out the idea of him seeing or hearing people that others don't see, but this might only puzzle Jack. If he draws any conclusion at all, it could be that I am crazy!

Jack does not seem to have chronic mental illness or to be a danger to himself or others, but he does have signs of clinical depression. Because his depression seems to be a reaction to situational stressors following his father's death, there is a good chance of it lifting fairly quickly with appropriate supports.

Jack's disempowerment around his business faltering comes on top of a lifetime of partial communication and extreme isolation from others like himself—which has been a long-term trauma for Jack. Such daily "faking it"

---

[6]If, however, the problem is that staff or family are "signing impaired"—that the client has a linguistic system common to other deaf people but is acting out or depressed partly because no authority in his life can communicate competently with him—then I am obligated to tell providers and agencies directly that this situation is unacceptable and advocate for change. Not to do this contributes to the presenting problem.

can damage self-esteem and create hopelessness and passivity.

However, before I plunge him headlong into the Deaf community, I need to be aware that such a sudden change could also be traumatic for Jack. I must move slowly—linguistically, clinically, and culturally—to open up choices for him and then allow him to make his own choices freely, even if his choice is to go with what is familiar and limited.

Cultural Issues.   Raised in public schools, Jack has been isolated from other deaf people and has no concept of a Deaf community. He views himself as handicapped and defective. Any sense of pride related to his deafness, when he feels it, comes from successfully faking his way through a brief interaction and seeing someone say in amazement, "He understands me so well!"

Jack has never had an extended or positive interaction with another deaf person. However, he has no special negative feelings toward deaf people and may be open to meeting them and learning about Deaf culture if he can move at his own pace and not feel forced.

Resource Issues.   Jack's probably average native intelligence has been severely compromised by language and educational deprivation. Due to this, his insight and sense of himself as capable have been impaired, although he has fair judgment and maturity.

Jack is very dependent on his daughter for daily tasks like bill paying and making appointments. He also appears emotionally dependent on her, although it is hard to tell how much this could change as his depression lifts. His daughter expects to care for him for the rest of his life. Neither knows about specialized services for deaf people. Both of them may be receptive to more training and greater independence for Jack, if resources are found that are not too distant.

Jack's small-town community could also be a resource. They have known him for a long time and have a philosophy of "taking care of their own."

Summary.   Because Jack doesn't have a comfortable communication system, one would have to use a combination of speaking, gestures, miming, and drawing in a carefully respectful way, so he does not feel looked down on. His depression seems situational, but this situation can be used as an opportunity for change and growth. Jack has some maturity and judgment, although he feels passive about problems in his life. Before he can begin to consider making choices, he needs to understand that he indeed *has* choices and learn some decision-making skills. He has little experience with deaf people but no strong negative feelings toward them. He has an involved daughter and a hometown community that might be helpful, but the nearest deaf services are 3 hours away.

Interventions

Short-Term Issues.   Using my assessment about Jack's communication, I would begin by doing simple psychoeducation about depression: its causes and symptoms, what helps it resolve. I would present the material in a variety of modalities—speaking with support from drawings and mime, with great respect and simplicity. I would constantly put the burden of communication on myself: Was I clear? Did I explain well or was I confusing? Now, can you explain the pictures to me so I know I taught you OK? (I would never say: "Is that clear?" or "Do you understand?" He would most likely feel pressured to fake understanding and give me the "empty yes.")

If appropriate, I might ask his sister to join us, for two reasons. If I ask Jack to explain our plan to his sister, I could get a sense of how well he has understood me and how well I have understood his communication needs. Such a meeting would also invest his sister in the treatment process and encourage her assistance in monitoring his depressive symptoms and in helping him to follow a daily routine and eat and sleep better. I would discuss the idea of this meeting with Jack first to be sure it would not threaten our alliance.

In the world of short-term treatment, many of us are pressured to refer clients to a psychiatrist immediately. I tend to resist this trend, unless it is absolutely clear to me that medication is indicated: For example, when psychosis or major depression with a biological base is present.

Jack's depression is likely situational, related to his father's death and subsequent lack of work, the core of his identity. Antidepressants often do not help situational depressions, and many have unpleasant side effects that could be hard for Jack to communicate. If his depression lifts from environmental changes and therapeutic interventions alone, I would avoid the risk of him starting on medication and being left on it long term due to lack of deafness-aware doctors in his area. If depression persists, I would refer him after 1 month to a psychiatrist for a medication evaluation.

I would immediately begin making Jack aware of the range of options he has for communication, vocational, and ILS evaluations and encourage him to take advantage of them, stressing that after the evaluation he can either accept or turn down what is recommended. With his permission, I would refer Jack to a case manager, who could refer Jack for the evaluations—preferably one who specializing in deaf clients and could travel to his home.

If waivers were needed to service someone out of our area, I would ask the case manager to get these. If there were no case manager, I would make the referrals and get the waivers myself (asking his sister to do as much as possible but filling in where my expertise was needed), because therapy is crucial for Jack, and evaluations must occur to provide evidence for the need for services. Because Jack lives at such a great distance, I might offer him less frequent 2-hour appointments or try to make my appointments on the same dates as his evaluations, unless one lasted all day.

Such an expansion of therapeutic role can take a lot of time. What am I giving up if I spend 1–4 hours by phone or letter making referrals or obtaining the needed waivers to serve him? I am not writing the letter to advocate for another client's housing. I am not finishing that guardianship evaluation report for another 2 weeks, later than a case manager would like it. I am writing briefer progress notes and shortening my phone calls, telling those I work with regularly that I "only have a minute today."

What do I give up if I do not do this? Not only would Jack not be served in our area, where the deafness access lies, but I would lose the chance to set an inter-area precedent, so that future deaf clients from Jack's area could more easily access services. If this is *not* the first time I or another deafness clinician has gotten such a waiver, the process may be considerably shortened by knowing who to contact on the state level for approval. If it is the first time, Jack's sister can be asked to do much of the calling and letter writing, using me as "coach" for each step.

Because immediate work activities may be key to lowering Jack's depression and the rehabilitation process for new clients is slow, I would expand my role early on to suggest some immediate vocational or volunteer opportunities to explore. I would talk to Jack about asking his sister to help him find more work in town. Rather than running a business on his own, Jack might find it easier to work under another carpenter, giving him a mentor and possibly forming a bond that he lost with his Dad's death. Or he might volunteer in some ongoing way that gets him out of bed each day with a purpose and a schedule: doing grocery shopping for elderly neighbors or "handyman" types of jobs in their homes, with his daughter as a go-between. The success of such a plan could determine how realistic it is for Jack to stay in his hometown and find a meaningful daily routine, as well as to clarify whether medication is needed.

Over time, Jack could learn from an ILS counselor how to take the bus from his home to my office. Ideally, Jack could also be referred to ongoing ILS training to develop minimal written English and TTY skills to conduct his communication independently. If this service is unavailable or if he cannot develop such skills, a case manager or interpreter available periodically for calls or letters is needed for full independence.

Through ILS or vocational resources, Jack may be introduced to items of independence such as a flashing doorbell or smoke alarm and a bed vibrator. These useful devices can promote his acceptance of and pride in himself as a deaf person. Through these agencies, Jack could be introduced to a deaf carpenter, shown how to use an oral interpreter, and given a tour of the highest level vocational workshop that services deaf clients. If he makes a good connection to another deaf person in the process, possibly that person could show him around the city or take him to visit the Deaf club. This spectrum of options will begin to open up his world slowly, without pressure.

Communication Strategies which Shape Treatment.   Besides using natural gestures frequently with Jack as I talked, I reinforced his use of gestures expressively. If he said a word and I did not understand, I might look puzzled but offered a gesture to clarify. If he agreed, I repeated the word and accompanying gesture for emphasis. Over time, Jack began to use natural gestures more and more freely, and found that others (both hearing and Deaf) understood him better this way. This secondary reinforcement caused him to use more and more gestures and increase his comfort level with using his body to communicate. With this experience, he might be more receptive to learning sign language later on.

Long-Term Issues.   As time goes on, Jack will need to be given a choice about moving to the city, where resources for him are plentiful, or staying near his daughter and his familiar surroundings. I would spend some time drawing and discussing these choices with him and helping him make up a pictoral list of "pros" and "cons" of each, from his perspective. I would ask his various providers and his daughter to talk with him as well, reinforcing the consequences of each choice. He must be free to choose either, but an informed decision can only be made after true exposure to both settings and talking through the positives and negatives for him of each choice.

Expansion of Therapist Role.   Jack is an isolated man who has functioned moderately well in his life, despite no effective communication system, and is now situationally depressed. What is my role with him in this case? I am clearly far more than a traditional therapist. I advocate for services, open new avenues of communication, network with existing services to connect him with his options, and "give advice" about all sorts of community involvement, both hometown and Deaf, usually considered outside the therapeutic realm.

What must we consider ethically when evaluating a possible expansion of therapeutic role?

My view of psychotherapy, modeled after Maslow's (1968)[7] hierarchy of needs, is that clients must have certain basic needs satisfied before meaningful psychotherapy can happen. If clients are not safe, fed, clothed, and sheltered, these problems must be their first priority—and therefore ours as therapists. Figure 8.7 shows my conceptualization of a therapeutic hierarchy of needs.

One of our jobs as responsible therapists is to assess where each client is on this hierarchy of needs and to help her progress to higher levels. A client who does not have money to eat will probably not be motivated to do relaxation exercises to combat her depression. A client who is homeless will not necessarily see the importance of learning not to hit people. Clients who grew up isolated from meaningful communication have missed a key to feeling love, connection, and support, components of healthy self-esteem. We not only need a common communication system with our clients but should try to insure they have meaningful communication in their daily lives with others.

Of course, someone other than a therapist should address meeting a client's basic needs. But if services are not currently accessible and no family or friends are competent to help, I contend a therapist ethically and clinically must do this work, because no other therapeutic work can be accomplished until such issues are resolved, or at least under way. These tasks can be written into a treatment plan as teaching advocacy skills, reducing anxiety, or any other legitimate, honest way in which this advocacy work relieves a client's presenting symptoms. Advocating with a client rather than for a client increases feelings of empowerment and a sense of therapeutic teamwork.

In order to holistically treat Jack's depression, I must look at him as a whole person—including not only his psychiatric symptoms but the social, political, and cultural climate that fosters and exacerbates them.

Eventually, I will help Jack do some decision making about a major life choice: whether to embrace the new options he has been exposed to or choose his old, familiar way of life with additional supports. No one ethically can make

---

[7]Maslow, a social psychologist, believed basic needs such as food, shelter, and clothing had to be met before people could focus on progressively higher goals such as relationships and self-actualization.

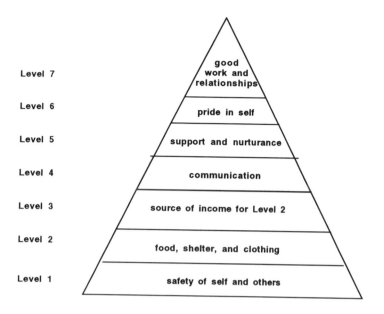

FIG. 8.7. A therapeutic hierarchy of needs.

this choice for him. However, as his therapist, I feel morally obligated to facilitate his access to options and to hone his decision-making skills, so he can be empowered to make the best choice for himself.

Assessing and Intervening With Peggy

Peggy is an intelligent, bitter, and furious deaf woman who currently is in the emergency room, out of control with rage. She has never met me and does not want anything to do with me or with sign language. How do I assist in assessing her and keeping her safe without alienating her?

Assessment

Communication Issues.   Peggy did not learn to sign until she arrived at NTID. She uses her voice along with English-word order Pidgin Signed English (PSE), leaning toward MCE with many prepositions and endings. She is a skilled lipreader and writes and reads English easily.

When calm, Peggy prefers to be simultaneously talked and signed to in English (Simultaneous Communication, or Sim. Comm.). She is uncomfortable communicating with ASL users. When agitated, she may reject any manual communication.

Clinical Issues.   Peggy grew up with an alcoholic and abusive father, was raped by a deaf man, and is abusing alcohol herself. Her rage at the world—deaf and hearing—and her suspiciousness and inability to connect with people have been exacerbated by her untreated rape and substance abuse. She isolates and is impulsive, putting her at risk for a third suicide attempt.

If Peggy is suicidal due to acute paranoia, antipsychotic medication may alleviate a good deal of the danger. Such medication may legally be administered by injection in most states without client/guardian permission if the client is at risk. Such a forced procedure, however, would further disempower an already agitated and disempowered client. If possible, convincing her to take medication orally and sitting with her until it begins to take effect is a far preferable alternative.

Peggy is clearly enraged but may not be about to hurt herself or anyone else. Because she has typical symptoms of a personality disorder, the mental health system can easily get annoyed with her and either discount her pain or slap her into restraints with a sedative to get rid of the irritation she arouses.

Peggy's sense of disempowerment stems partly from her rape, but it may have many other layers: an academically gifted oral teenager thrust into the world of Gallaudet, where her speaking and lipreading skills were suddenly not valued; and a young child who was physically abused in unpredictable ways and pushed to be a "pretend hearie" who, no matter how hard she tried, could never be quite that.

It is unclear at the moment what may have precipitated the current situation (more on that later!). For now, we can only speculate that some event triggered her trauma history. Peggy has scant resources for dealing with being flooded with feeling or for dealing with a system that treats her disrespectfully.

Cultural Issues.   Peggy's self-esteem has been built partly on her lipreading skills. She does not want to admit that signing makes things easier for her, and denies that a signing therapist might be of more value to her than a nonsigning one. She associates ASL with mean and violent deaf people who ignored her and raped her.

Peggy is not only totally hearing in her outlook, she has lumped all deaf people together as unfriendly snobs, rapists, and the cause of many of her difficulties. Because her emotional "memory" is not well developed, she does not have a long-range view of her problems and only remembers the very recent past, blaming all her feelings of frustration and disappointment on her NTID experience. Peggy hates her deafness and has no desire for deaf or even signing friends. Because of her rage and lack of insight, these feelings will not easily change.

Resource Issues.   Peggy is very bright but has few ego strengths at her disposal and little belief in herself. She has some college education. She lives in an area with many deaf resources, although she is not yet emotionally in a place to take advantage of them. She probably has inherited a tendency toward alcoholism, a grave disability.

Summary.   Peggy initially needs to be matched somewhat rigidly in terms of communication: When she is under stress and not signing, matching her orally may lower her anxiety. (However, introducing myself using Sim. Comm. would let her know I know sign and allow her to make the choice.) She has been told all her life that she should be able to get by without any sign. I need to demonstrate that I have no such expectation and that I respect however she chooses to communicate.

Clinically, Peggy appears to have symptoms of Post Traumatic Stress Disorder (PTSD) and is likely to expect criticism and feel intruded on, even with the gentlest approach. How much of her rage and suspiciousness was a biological predisposition and how much a result of her many traumas is not clear. But these tendencies have settled into a personality style that pushes people away, confirming her self-hatred, increasing her isolation, and leading her to suicide attempts. Attempts at self-medicating through drugs and alcohol only makes these problems worse.

Peggy has little sense of herself as powerful in the world, always blaming others for her feelings and situation. She is bright and knows her rights. But it was a culture shock to find herself in the midst of the NTID world. Used to being reinforced and praised for the ways she did *not* act like a deaf person, suddenly her context was turned upside down, and she was probably judged for how much she *could* act like a deaf person. In this context, she came up very short, having to learn sign from the start. Her usual coping mechanism of excelling academically may have been much harder here, and her usual denial of her deafness was challenged up and down. She responded by becoming more "anti-Deaf" and by drinking and smoking marijuana more and more.

Interventions

Crisis Plan.   My first task was to observe if Peggy was able to calm down and talk, or seemed as if she was escalating and might hurt herself or someone else. Peggy would have the greatest likelihood of calming down if she could feel both contained and in charge of what would happen next. Any intervention that made her feel controlled would probably make matters worse, especially because she had never met me.

In the emergency room, I decided simply to sit quietly with Peggy, not demanding interaction but lending her support with a steady presence. If she clearly did not want me to stay, I would empower her by leaving the room when she asked (no matter how rudely), thus putting myself in a one-down position and helping her feel in control of one part of her situation right now.

In fact, Peggy did demand that I "Get out!" and I complied, staying close by so I could hear that she was not hurting herself. I returned in a few minutes and orally asked her respectfully, "Can we talk?" She screamed, "No!" and I left again. The second time, she sighed and said "OK." I thanked her and slowly moved into the room, taking a chair across the room from her, where either of us could get out the door without being blocked in. The emergency room staff, relieved that I was handling the situation and busy with others, allowed me to take all the time I needed.

The best chance of maintaining safety without the need for physical inter-vention is to promote empowerment and personal responsibility, so often stripped from clients (especially deaf clients!) during times of crisis. Often clients voluntarily take medication and recompensate enough to go home, perhaps with a therapy appointment tomorrow or some additional medications as needed. If power must be taken out of a client's hands for safety reasons, I try to structure the hospital or respite stay to be as communication accessible and as brief as possible.

As Peggy became willing to answer a few questions, I could see that she was quite paranoid and appeared to be in the midst of a mild psychotic episode. She could fleetingly understand that if she stayed calm, she might not need to be hospitalized, but her paranoia made it hard for her to believe this, and she could not remain calm.

As we talked, I slowly incorporated a few natural gestures into my speech. Peggy made no protest and seemed to understand better. At one point, she did not understand a word I said, and I purposely repeated the word along with the sign and immediately said, "Oh! I'm sorry! I forgot—no sign language."

Peggy said, "That's OK, you can sign." I instantly thanked her in Sim. Comm., explaining how hard it was for me to talk without signing. She responded by Sim. Comm. as well, and our conversation flowed more easily after this.

However, Peggy's continuing psychosis and extreme paranoia made me judge that she was unsafe to return home to her apartment. I explained to her that she was not thinking clearly, and that an antipsychotic medication might help. I encouraged Peggy to consider the 24-hour observation bed in the emergency room, which could be used to avoid hospitalization as long as a person contracted for safety.

Peggy became enraged and agitated at the idea of not returning home. Despite my best efforts, she was unable to consider these alternatives and escalated dramatically, throwing objects and screaming. She was unable to recompensate and was restrained by two attendants, whom she bit and scratched in her fear and fury. She was then given a shot of medication to help her calm down. Before the injection, I tried to explain to her, through her agitation, what it was and what it was for. I felt helpless, sorrowful that this had happened, and upset that her hands—her means of communication—were tied to the bed for safety.

The psychiatrist on duty did not interview her directly but on the strength of my evaluation committed her to the hearing inpatient unit. (There was no specialized deaf unit in this state.) An interpreter was requested for her admission and would arrive within 3 hours.

Before I left the hospital that night, I did three things. I spoke to the psychiatrist about the significance for deaf people of being able to use their hands and asked that his staff ask Peggy as soon as possible if she felt she could be safe if they released or loosened her arm restraints. I let him know that she could read well (when not psychotic) and that she and staff could write back and forth until the interpreter arrived.

Second, I wrote a note to Peggy myself telling her what would happen next, in the simplest language I could. Although she is skilled in English, I wanted her overloaded brain to take in as little stress as possible. The note was factual and neutral: It did not discuss feelings, nor did it blame Peggy for her behavior or apologize for my part in this awful situation. When I went into the room to give it to her, she was asleep and relaxed at last. I left it nearby and asked staff to show it to her when she awoke.

Third, I walked down to the psychiatric unit, introduced myself to the charge nurse, and let her know I would be available for consultation on working with a deaf patient. I gave her a quick "Deafness 101" chat on how to use the interpreter when she came, on the inaccuracy and stress of lipreading, and on getting Peggy's attention visually and in good light before beginning to talk.

I told the charge nurse briefly what I knew from my record about Peggy's clinical issues and her ability to read and write when not psychotic. (Because this was a crisis involving the patient's safety, I shared clinical and communication information in the absence of a release from Peggy.) I stressed how small the Deaf community is and how complete confidentiality is even more vital than with hearing patients, because a deaf patient could be identified so easily from a story without a name.

I left a note for the social work coordinator with my work number and some good times to reach me, and I went home. It was late, and I decided to preserve my own energy by not waiting until the interpreter arrived. The additional 45 minutes I stayed to complete these three tasks seemed well worth reducing potential trouble and misunderstanding, which could take much longer to help unravel.

Ongoing Treatment Plan.   When Peggy's urine screen came back the next day, the precipitant to her decompensation was clear: her system had contained large amounts of cocaine, and her drug-induced psychosis cleared within the next 3 days. She stayed in the hospital for 3 weeks, gradually eating and sleeping better. I saw her weekly for an hour and sat in on a half-hour treatment team. Her paranoia improved somewhat. She agreed to go to AA meetings with an interpreter (but not the Deaf AA meeting) and to see me for outpatient therapy.

When Peggy returned home and our outpatient therapy began, we needed a common language with which to form our treatment goals: a viewpoint that included her idea about what was wrong as well as my concerns about improving her substance abuse, paranoia, and other PTSD symptoms. Because of her cognitive set that everyone was out to get her and wanted her to suffer, the approach I took was: "You deserve better than this." We looked at her history, and I became outraged along with her at her father's physical abuse, the teasing at NTID, the rape.

A dilemma in treating people with histories of abuse who also have personality disorders or major mental illness is the risk of exploring such history due to their fragile emotional makeup. Unless clear flashbacks or memories are occurring, focusing on "here and now" coping skills tends to be more useful to supporting daily functioning.

I listed with Peggy all the negative results of her various abuses, including her trouble with drugs and alcohol along with her nightmares and overdeveloped startle response. I insisted that she deserved to have a better life and mentioned that living well is the best revenge. Peggy was able to accept my framing of her problems and could tolerate a model of brief, solution-focused psychotherapy. We agreed to look at our progress after 10 sessions and decide whether to recontract or not. In fact, Peggy worked with me for over 3 years.

As we discussed her family history, I acted puzzled by her parents' attitude about sign language, asking her to explain it to me. I told her I could not understand how sign language or interpreters could have hurt her. She was clearly so intelligent; she should not have had to work so hard to do well in school. Whenever she implied she should have been able to do without interpreters, I insisted it was her right to have a choice and then decide herself. This was language she could understand and accept, and slowly her image of herself as deaf began to change.

Communication Strategies That Shape Treatment.   Peggy's view of herself as a helpless, angry victim and her negative opinion of the Deaf community were intertwined, as shown by the way she communicated. Throughout the treatment process, I used communication as a medium to test her receptivity to change her self-image.

Our communication began as Sim. Comm. using MCE. I had trouble with some endings and took a one-down position with her, asking her to correct me if I forgot an ending or was not clear. Initially, she was not responsive to any ASL classifiers or idioms and asked me to repeat or clarify if I used one. As our bond strengthened, I occasionally (and without planning it!) would use a sign that had no good English equivalent, without mouthing a word along with it. She would say, "Huh?" I would grope for words, using a few English sentences to explain. After a while, I could use such signs in a course of conversation and she would understand them and not challenge me. Over the few months that this process was happening, Peggy met a hearing woman in AA who signed and began to hang out with her. She also decided to request an interpreter at her weekly department meetings at work "because it's less boring, and it's my right."

As we worked together over the first year, I gradually dropped endings as I signed, sliding slowly toward more PSE. Most of the time, Peggy accepted these changes and even began dropping endings at times herself, causing her sign to be more fluid and easier for me to read. Her signing, her view of deafness, and her opinion of herself all seemed to improve together.

Outcome of Peggy's Treatment.   Peggy and I had our ups and downs, typical of treatment with a person with personality disorder. Whenever she would get enraged at me or refuse to come for a month, I would always interpret it the same way: She had suffered enough; she did not deserve to feel all this pain or to keep pushing people away with her behavior; she had a right to heal from this abuse and learn to control her behavior better so she could feel better inside. This attitude, while holding her responsible for her behavior and imposing natural consequences (such as charging her for "no-shows"), translated her treatment goals into her language, her own worldview, so she could feel understood and supported as a person no matter what.

As I persistently held Peggy responsible for the consequences of her actions, she began to channel her anger more appropriately. Her sobriety strengthened, and her slips appeared only at particularly difficult times. She was hospitalized again after another drug-induced psychosis but was able to go willingly and with less trauma. She could actually accept some responsibility for her actions that led up to the hospitalization. When she came home, she began to attend the Deaf AA meeting.

Shortly after this, I informed Peggy about a Deaf community campaign to fund a Deaf substance abuse program. I told her about the next meeting because I thought she was ready to take another step in her increasingly positive Deaf self-image. She passionately joined this cause. She went to meetings at the state Deaf association (the first time she had gone there) and wrote a letter to her state senator as a consumer who had needed this type of treatment in the past. She told me in therapy: "This Deaf substance abuse program is my right!" Although her attitude was often still strident and provocative, Peggy was learning to value herself as a person, and in so doing, was able to open up to the support of the Deaf community—and to contribute to it as well.

For clients with personality disorders, who can often direct anger and struggle into the therapeutic relationship, it can be healing to direct their anger and struggle toward the state system that should be providing more services—and sometimes see results.

Expansion of Therapist Role.   How and why did I choose to expand my role with Peggy? In the midst of the initial crisis, I empowered her to be in control of my presence and of my communication approach, while insuring her safety and gently encouraging her to accept communication that could be easier for us both. I chose *not* to act as interpreter with an unknown client in crisis. I also chose to stay an extra 45 minutes to leave a note for Peggy, educate the inpatient unit, and make contact with the social worker. I felt this investment of time was minimal in order to smooth the way for Peggy and the staff—and I expected my supervisor to find a way to give me comp. time for it! I decided not to stay until the interpreter arrived. We all must find our own personal boundaries, and this was mine.

While Peggy was in the hospital, I decided to spend 1-1/2 unpaid hours per week forming a bond with her and consulting to the treatment team. (When a client is inpatient, usually the outpatient therapist cannot bill for services.) Fortunately, this inpatient unit allowed collaboration with outpatient therapists and welcomed my input.[8] Had I chosen not to be involved during these 3 weeks, my job would have been infinitely harder after Peggy's discharge. She would have had a harder time engaging and might never have come to therapy; after all, the last time she would have seen me would have been recommending her inpatient stay. The inpatient unit would have probably missed many of her needs, not gotten interpreters, and done treatment that was unhelpful or made things worse. Because I did not have other patients in the hospital at the same time, because the hospital was on my way to work, and because I had a supportive supervisor who allowed me to miss some meetings during this period, I was able to become involved in an optimal way.

---

[8]Even on an inpatient service that usually does not allow outpatient therapy involvement, I have often found my involvement welcomed because staff do not know how to deal with a deaf patient.

During our 3 years of therapy, my role was somewhat more complex than that of a therapist treating a hearing personality-disordered client with a trauma history. Our communication match symbolized the emotional work we were doing together: I first unconditionally supported her style and then gradually raised my expectations of her, both emotionally and linguistically. She was able to respond by becoming less rigid in both areas. Her changing feelings about herself were reflected in her growing acceptance of Deaf culture. I used her cognitive set ("It's not fair!") to help her draw connections between the ways her needs around deafness were not considered growing up and the daily issues she struggled with now. I was able to offer her resources as she was ready to learn about them and to help her advocate appropriately for herself. Without these expansions of role, Peggy's therapy would have been less successful and had a far more limited impact.

Summary

This section has used three composite stories to demonstrate the complexity of evaluation and treatment of deaf people. A multidimensional model has been used to show how assessment of communication, clinical, cultural, and resource issue weave together to guide intervention. The therapist's decision-making process about how and when to expand her role has been highlighted.

Ethical, Culturally Appropriate Therapy With Deaf People . . . and the Real World: Can They Peacefully Coexist?

As we learn to do therapy, we are taught and continue to develop ethical standards of professional conduct with our clients. As we get to know the Deaf community and culture better (or as we grow up, if we were born into it), we absorb community norms, values, and expectations. At times, such sets of clinical and cultural values seemingly conflict with each other or with the expectations of agencies and insurance companies. We can easily feel torn between what we know is needed to serve this deaf client properly and what we can realistically get approved.

The rest of the chapter focuses on such real life professional and institutional dilemmas. In the first section, issues around the ethics of dual roles, therapeutic touch, and home visits are explored. The second section focuses on writing effective treatment plans that are living, functioning guides that clients and agencies can accept. Finally, the third section offers suggestions about juggling conflicting agency demands of paperwork and productivity with client needs of case management and nontraditional therapeutic approaches.

ETHICAL AND ROLE CONSIDERATIONS

The codes of ethics we learn in hearing professional programs do not take into account norms of the Deaf community. As we integrate our knowledge of Deaf culture with our therapeutic skills, each of us must form a construct that holds the safety of the therapeutic process while respecting and supporting the comfort and safety many deaf clients find in the Deaf community. We must confront the almost inevitable overlapping of roles in a small community. We must find a way within ourselves to balance the clinical and cultural viewpoints as we sit with each client and each set of individual needs.

Some of the ethical dilemmas around overlapping roles, or contexts other than therapy where therapists may see clients, are explored in this section. Guidelines are presented to help with decision making about expansion of the therapeutic role, including "emergency interpreting" and home visits.

Dual Relationships or Roles: Boundaries Versus Parameters

> I am at a rally at the statehouse urging the governor to sign a relay service into law. One of my MR clients, carrying a diligently hand-lettered sign, runs up to me and begins complaining about how his housemate was teasing him on the bus on the way here.

> I am invited to sit on the advisory board of a new psychiatric day program, which has a goal of becoming accessible to deaf clients. I accept. The following week, my schizophrenic deaf client tells me enthusiastically that she has been asked to attend the same advisory board.

> A case conference is called for one of my multiagency clients. Her ILS specialist has moved, and she has just been assigned a new ILS specialist, who will be attending the case conference. That new staff is also one of my clients.

In the Deaf community, some overlapping of roles is unavoidable. But when is two roles too many? When should a therapist attend an advocacy board, meeting, or rally where clients may be present? Are there situations where a therapist can or should accept the role of interpreter for a client? This section explores the crucial difference between therapeutic *parameters* and *boundaries* and offers guidelines to differentiate them when faced with a potential dual role with a client.

In the field of psychotherapy, we constantly make decisions about how we can and should relate to clients, from the simple matter of how often a client can call between appointments to the inappropriateness of dating each other. Traditionally, every conceivable therapeutic limit or stance has been termed a boundary. My colleague Fran Demiany, one of the first signing psychologists in Massachusetts, helped me clarify a useful distinction between boundaries and parameters:

Boundaries are fixed, enduring stances that must be kept and are set up for the benefit of client safety and for the sanctity of the therapy. Examples of boundaries shared by most reputable therapists include: Therapy is a professional relationship, different from a social one; the focus of therapy is on the needs of the client and not the therapist; the therapist is paid for services; there are no sexual relations between therapist and client; what is said in therapy is confidential. Clients can depend on boundaries being immutable and unchanging, which helps to create a nurturing, expectable structure within which therapy can occur.

Parameters are more flexible and can be expanded or adapted based on a client's history, emotional challenges, developmental stage, and current needs, as well as the stage of the therapy and the time availability and financial constraints of the therapist. Examples of parameters would be fees, appointment times, whether phone calls are allowed between sessions and how a client may access the therapist, what to do if there is a crisis, and what to do if therapist and client bump into each other outside of therapy. Parameters may and should be dealt with in the context of therapy in order to process the client's feelings and to maintain safety in the therapy as parameters shift.

According to this definition, there are some areas that one therapist considers a boundary (clients may never call my home) and another therapist treats as a parameter (clients in crisis may call my home; if it happens too often, we will work through it as a therapeutic issue). This section demonstrates how I make such distinctions. Each therapist may do this a bit differently, as long as decisions flow from an ethical and clear framework that is consistent enough to keep clients safe and flexible enough to respond to changing needs and circumstances.

Traditional psychotherapy teaches extremely clear and formal roles between client and therapist. There are many fixed boundaries and few parameters. The therapist and client meet only in an office setting, never have dual roles (such as teacher or colleague or fellow advocate), and never discuss anything about the private life of the therapist. If they happen to run into each other outside of the office, they do not interact. They never hug or have other physical contact.

Although many modern practitioners criticize such a stance for being overly rigid and distant, these policies were originally set up as a protection for the client. Clients should never have to worry about their therapist's needs or preferences. If a therapist and client go out to dinner together as friends, or if a client cleans a therapist's house in exchange for therapy sessions, such safeguards are no longer automatically there: The nature of the situation causes the client to consider the therapist's wishes and can harm the therapeutic relationship. It is all too easy, in a relationship with such a power imbalance, for a therapist to exploit a client sexually, financially, or emotionally. Boundaries must be clear and explicit to guard against this risk.

Boundaries are also a protection, at times, for the therapist. A therapist's role is to be totally available for the client's needs, within the clinical 50-minute hour. If they become friends, a therapist is no longer protected by the limits and safeguards of the office. If a client wants to visit the therapist's home, for example, at a time the therapist wants time alone, two sets of wishes are conflicting. Outside of the office, the therapist cannot and should not comply with every wish of her client. But once the relationship is other than purely therapeutic, exactly where and how does the line get drawn without hurting either the client, the therapist, or the therapeutic relationship?

Transference and the Myth of the Value-Neutral Therapist

Transference (a client projecting feelings and wishes about parents or important others onto the therapist), when positive, often makes a client view a therapist as infinitely wise and powerful; Negative transference can make the therapist the object of rage and disappointment. Exploring these feelings and helping the client see where they come from in his life can be one of the most valuable aspects of treatment, helping increase insight and change lifelong self-defeating patterns (yes, even in short-term work at times).

Transference happens not only with clients bright enough and linguistically skilled enough that therapists can explain it to them: It also occurs with clients with no formal language system, with mentally retarded clients, and with paranoid clients, to name just a few. With such clients, we carry the particular challenge to be aware of potential transference, minimize its negative impact, and discern which clients would be helped by discussing it.

In particular, hearing therapists who see deaf clients must bear in mind how we (transferentially) may represent the whole hearing world and what it has done to them. In this society, we as hearing people truly have more power than our deaf clients. Our social responsibility is to acknowledge that and work professionally and politically to equalize that power. Our responsibility with each deaf client in our office is to use the power of transference and of "hearingness" judiciously and with the greatest respect.

Proponents of pure therapy point out, with good cause, that any dual role (what they would call "blurring" of boundaries) has the potential of affecting transference and diminishing the therapy. The learning potential of transference is that it helps us understand childhood reactions and modify them when unhelpful in the present. Any interchange outside the therapy office between client and therapist may evoke feelings, which could then confuse the process of sorting out past and present.

For example, if a client sees a therapist speak at a board meeting and another advocate criticizes the therapist's position, the client may feel upset and protective of the therapist, or angry at the therapist for saying something that was attacked, or have any number of reactions that make him feel less safe in the therapy.

However, even in our offices, therapists are not computers. We are human beings to whom clients react on a number of dimensions, including our appearance, age, ethnicity, signing ability, therapeutic stance, and so on. Furthermore, we are not value neutral, and I believe that any attempt to portray ourselves as such is dishonest. We have strong ethics, ideals, beliefs, and values that influence our therapeutic styles. We have unconscious cultural assumptions that affect our work.

Knowing our own cultural biases and values is as essential to being good therapists as is understanding our emotional triggers. This awareness enables us to consciously choose when our ethics and values should appropriately influence the therapy and when they must be put aside. For example, if I believe stealing is wrong, and a client tells me she is stealing, I need to know how much of my value I ethically should include in the therapy. Should I let a client know I think stealing is wrong? Is it my job to make the client stop stealing? Or is it my job to help the client think through, as much as possible, the potential legal and other consequences of stealing and develop her own judgment and decisions about what to do?

In a similar vein, if a deaf client hates being deaf, is it my job to help him like his own deafness or other deaf people? Well, the part of me that supports Deaf culture says, "Of course! No deaf person can have healthy self-esteem without being proud of the Deaf culture and community." But is that really true? The truth is, my job in therapy is to help a deaf person feel good about all of who she is, including her deafness. Then, if she has been exposed to Deaf culture but at an age or in a situation that makes her feel uncomfortable about it, or if she chooses to stay with her hearing familiar community, that must be her choice. (I believe that most deaf people, given the option early in life to be involved in the Deaf community, will develop a comfortable bicultural identity and feel at home in the Deaf community. Some will not, and each must make his own decision.)

Handling Dual Role Situations

Now we return to the examples of dilemmas around dual roles. My view, which is a controversial one, is that there is no fixed set of correct parameters for every therapeutic situation. In the small Deaf community, some types of dual roles and social interactions are at times unavoidable. Mutual advocacy by client and therapist toward common goals, for example, is a necessary and vital way to advance deaf services and improve/empower clients' lives. So we must struggle with the impact of different parameters and mesh the clinical and cultural components as best we can.

> I am at a rally at the statehouse urging the governor to sign a relay service into law. One of my MR clients, carrying a diligently hand-lettered sign, runs up to me and begins complaining about how his housemate was teasing him on the bus on the way here.

Most of us have probably experienced this type of dual role: a client who, due to developmental disability or naiveté, expects us to do therapy when he meets us in a public place. The only context in which he knows how to interact with us is therapist–client, and he does not have the sophistication or social skills to manage a context shift in a different situation.

What are the issues we need to be concerned with in handling this situation?

1. *Confidentiality*: The client has not announced specifically that I am his therapist, and my response needs to preserve his confidentiality.

2. *Respect for him as a person*: Although I need to set limits around what is appropriate for us to discuss now, in this public context, I want to be sure he does not end up feeling ashamed, put down, or as if he has done something terribly wrong.

3. *Power and hierarchy dynamics*: In this inherently unequal relationship, I hold more power. My actions and emotional response to this client carry more weight and impact than those of another person. My ability to welcome the client as a person, to make him feel I am glad to see him, even as I redirect his actions, will help make this dual role a therapeutic encounter, although it is not therapy.

4. *My own wishes and needs, as this is not a therapeutic hour for my client*. I am not obligated to spend the rest of the rally with him (nor would it be therapeutically desirable), even if he may wish this. I have my own agenda for this rally, perhaps people I want to talk with or tasks I have agreed to do, and it is necessary for my client to see me role modeling a real person in the community with my own life. I would explore whatever feelings my client may have about this next time we meet together in my office.

I am invited to sit on the advisory board of a new psychiatric day program, which has a goal of becoming accessible to deaf clients. I accept. The following week, my schizophrenic deaf client tells me enthusiastically that she has been asked to attend the same advisory board.

Awareness of this possible dual role before it occurs adds some responsibility for me. I need to decide whether to prevent the dual role from happening or to discuss it with my client and decide together.

Should I tell my client that I have been asked to join the same board? That depends. I would have to consider this person's clinical picture and whether it would be to her benefit for us to work together. In some cases, it would be clear to me immediately that such a dual role would be harmful to her. In other cases, it might be unclear or might even seem helpful to the treatment—empowering and providing a role model.

I cannot think of a situation where the ethical decision would be to ask the client to withdraw from the board, although there could conceivably be one: for example, if I were the only deafness professional in the state, and as such I have irreplaceable expertise that a program needs. Even in this situation, I could consult to the chair of the board without actually attending meetings, although my name could be raised as an expert and my client would need to deal with her feelings about this.

If it would be harmful for this client to sit with me on a board—for clinical reasons such as paranoia or because competitiveness or mushy boundaries in her family are a big issue in treatment—then my choices would be to withdraw without telling the client (in order to avoid her feeling guilty, too powerful, or whatever else she might feel) or to tell her I have also been asked, to explain to her why I will withdraw, and to assure her that I will do so in such a way that her confidentiality will be preserved. I might make the second choice if a client could experience my decision as supportive, as having faith in her abilities, or that she could learn something about her own style and about appropriate boundaries by my action.

If it seems a dual role would not be harmful—or might even be desirable—I would discuss the opportunity with her and arrive at a joint decision. Why might it be helpful for some deaf clients to have their therapist on the same board? A client might feel very supported and more able to take risks, to know someone in the room is interested in her opinion. She might benefit from having a role model, someone she respects who is unafraid to push for deaf rights. She may appreciate having the chance to talk in a meeting and then ask her therapist for feedback about how she came across.

It would be important to bring up the subject in a way that empowers the client to make the decision, as well as to explore (within her capabilities) how she would feel in different situations with or without me on the board. If we decide to try it, we would, in advance as well as ongoing, discuss confidentiality and other issues to help her feel safe.

A case conference is called for one of my multiagency clients. Her ILS specialist has moved, and she has just been assigned a new ILS specialist, who will be attending the case conference. This specialist is one of my clients.

Deaf professionals who come to us for therapy are aware of these potential dual roles. It is likely that the ILS specialist and I have already discussed such possibilities and have decided together how we would handle them. If not, it would be a good idea to discuss the issue in our next therapy session if time allows, or for me to call him to decide what to do. It would be fine for us both to attend if he feels comfortable with this and I can process it with him before and after the case conference. It would also be fine for one of us to be "unable to attend," if this is needed to preserve our therapeutic relationship, and to send input to the chair of the meeting. If it is important to our therapy relationship that we do not both go to the meeting, then we would step into our professional roles with the client we share and decide, from the standpoint of her needs, which of our roles is most vital to the case conference.

Guidelines for Setting Clinically and Culturally Appropriate Boundaries and Parameters

Here are some guidelines I follow in distinguishing parameters and boundaries with clients:

1. *The client's needs are always primary within the therapy hour and are to be considered extremely strongly outside therapy as well.* No action should be taken that will harm or invalidate the therapy. No interaction should be primarily for the therapist's benefit rather than the client's. Sexual contact with a client or family member of a client, or even socializing in each other's homes, is clearly inappropriate because the therapist's needs are involved, and the client's safety can be compromised. A hearing therapist going to a Deaf club for social reasons is for the therapist's benefit and could be felt by some deaf clients as an intrusion on their space. (For a Deaf therapist, this issue is more complex, as he probably has no other Deaf club from which to choose. He must decide for himself what he will do to fulfill his social needs in his community and deal with his clients about it as well as possible.)

2. *No action should be taken that uses the therapist's greater power or authority to advantage.* For example, asking a client if she wants to buy something from me is unfair. The client may see me as a parent figure to whom she cannot say no or may be worried I would be angry if she declined. (This obviously applies even more strongly to romantic or sexual contact—another reason why such relationships are unacceptable with current clients, and I believe with former clients as well.)

Anytime a client and therapist encounter each other outside of the office, the client should have the power to decide if or how they will interact (within the bounds of the therapist's comfort zone): Does the client wish to say hello? Hug? Ignore me? Discussing this possibility in therapy and putting the client in charge of what happens decreases unintended abuse of authority.

3. *When parameters change or dual roles are a possibility, one always must have clear roles and role expectations for different situations.* I was recently on an organizing committee to lobby the legislature for funds for more Deaf and hard-of-hearing services. My home number was on the organizing flyer as a contact person. One of my clients, a young man struggling with a personality disorder, joined the organizing committee and was part of a smaller delegation formed to visit key legislators in

person. We discussed our dual roles at length, including the fact that if he had to call me on committee business, it would be appropriate to call my home number, but that for anything therapy related, he must call my office—even in an emergency. He was able to respect these limits well.

4. *Process feelings before (if possible) and after a dual role occurrence.* In a predictable situation, clients' feelings and wishes can be discussed in a predictive and retrospective way. For example, prior to Gay Pride each year, I talk to my gay, lesbian, and bisexual clients who know I belong to this community about dual role possibilities. We discuss how they might feel if they saw me and how they might want me to respond. We can use the opportunity to work on internalized homophobia, role modeling, and empowerment—including clients' right to control the interaction with me. Clients who have never been to a Gay Pride parade might discuss their fears of attending, and clients "in the closet" can get full support for this position while being exposed to other options. There is a therapeutic opportunity following the event to discuss clients' feelings about seeing or not seeing me there.

If an unpredicted dual role situation occurs, I follow up with the client during the next session to ask how it felt and to work with the transference, if appropriate. With more V–G clients, much of this work must be done through role plays, sometimes with different parts of the room representing what happened already and "what-ifs," or reality and fantasy. With clients where even limited abstraction is beyond our best communication together, I might simply draw or role play when and where we saw each other and pointing, ask "Feel happy? Mad? Upset? What?"

In an ongoing dual relationship such as sitting on the same advisory board, therapist and client can and should process the client's experience from time to time and renegotiate parameters if appropriate. For example, a client who wanted me to sit next to her at the first meeting may prefer a few months later to sit across the room from me with a new friend.

5. *If a therapist decides to interpret or facilitate communication, immediate physical and emotional safety must be weighed against ongoing therapeutic safety and legal liability.* There may be informal situations or even emergency situations where a therapist who is not a certified interpreter helps facilitate communication between deaf and hearing. Even if the therapist is a certified interpreter, such a major role shift entails some risk. The following are emergency interpreting guidelines I follow. During a crisis, if as a therapist, I must facilitate communication at any point because there is no interpreter available, two of my choices are:

(a) to talk to the client and report to the emergency worker or police officer, and vice versa—but to be clear I cannot interpret; or (b) to interpret with the client's permission and with the caveat that I am not in a legal capacity as interpreter. When considering the second option, *caution is advised.* If an interpretation results in a client being committed against her will to a hospital or jail, a noncertified interpreter could be held accountable if a suit was ever initiated.

Personally, I would agreed to interpret only for immediate safety or a client's short-term comfort until an interpreter arrives but not as part of a psychiatric decision about placement or a decision about medical treatment. My only exception would be to interpret for a first aid situation: I could still be held liable if miscommunication occurs, but I would take the risk to save a life. Another person might make a more or less conservative decision.

If I do decide to interpret, I remind all parties frequently (especially hearing ones unused to interpreter ethics) that I am not an interpreter and am only helping them communicate about what to do until an interpreter arrives—even if I must leave soon and the client must stay in the emergency room for 16 hours awaiting an interpreter.

A therapist's precise role in each interpreting situation must be clear: am I bound by interpreter confidentiality, or might I need to include in my chart what is said? Am I an interpreter/participant in the discussion who will need to derole and add information or my opinions? If the latter, a move to a different chair or another concrete visual cue may be needed to clarify a role change for V–G clients or many others in crisis.

6. *Hugs and other forms of therapeutic touch carry both benefits and risks; these choices must be made consciously.* The issue of using touch in therapy deserves much careful discussion and is clearly beyond the scope of a few paragraphs.[9] Yet touch is both a clinical and a cultural issue when working with Deaf people.

In the Deaf community, hugging is a common expression of social connection, and rejecting a client's hug could seem culturally "odd" or standoffish. However, transference and certain clinical syndromes can make hugging confusing or overstimulating for some clients.

Therapists who choose to hug or use other forms of touch in therapy would do well to explore what touch symbolizes to them and to get training and supervision in this important area. Any therapist uncomfortable with touch for any reason should not feel pressured to use it, cross-cultural sensitivity notwithstanding.

7. *Home visits may deepen trust and allow access to crucial information.* If a home visit is indicated and possible, it should be made clear ahead of time and when a therapist arrives, that this is a professional visit, not social. However, to feel comfortable having a therapist in their space, clients may need to offer coffee or tea, give the therapist the comfortable chair, or serve food. It is sometimes quite a tricky balance to be clear that clients do not have to meet a therapist's needs and also not to transgress some ethnic/cultural values and offend them.

> I remember visiting the mother of a Latino gentleman, with whom I had worked in the hospital for several months. He was finally well enough for his first visit home, and I accompanied him along with a Spanish/ASL interpreter. When I had met with his mother in the hospital previously, she had been quite reticent about her son's childhood. She had been appreciative of my efforts to communicate in my halting "Spanglish", before the interpreter arrived and made communication smooth, and seemed to trust my treatment of her son. But she seemed either not to remember or not to want to disclose huge pieces of family history.
>
> When we arrived at her home in mid-afternoon, we three were welcomed like royalty, given three of the four chairs around the kitchen table (the eldest brother took the fourth) and immediately served a small feast. When I protested that my client's other brothers and mother should sit at the table with him, I was shushed soundly and waved back to my place. I had sense enough to understand how important this ritual was to this mother's sense of welcome. Even though I am a vegetarian, I ate pork for the first time in 15 years!
>
> After the meal, we all moved into the living room, whereupon she proceeded to tell me every detail of her son's growing up years for the next 2 hours. She had fed me in

---

[9]Some in-depth reading on the use of touch in psychotherapy can be found in the following references: Barnard and Brazelton (1990) and Heller and Schiff (1991).

her home, and I had become family in a sense; what was once privileged information was now able to be shared with me.

Home visits, although often impractical from a productivity standpoint, can provide invaluable information and connections difficult or impossible to obtain in the office setting. The more a therapist knows about the culture of each family (including but certainly not limited to Deaf culture), the more he can understand what is appropriate for this family and fully enter their world. Developing a clear role of visiting professional, who expects no special favors from clients and is here to listen and support fully—but who is flexible and sensitive enough to graciously accept the hospitality that is offered—is crucial for ethical, responsible, culturally sensitive home visiting.

Conclusions About Ethics and Expanding the Traditional Therapeutic Role

Dual roles are frequently inevitable in a small community and can be used therapeutically in a clear framework where client safety, confidentiality, and empowerment are essential priorities. Each therapist must develop a personal model of unchanging boundaries and flexible parameters for the therapeutic relationship to be protected. The realities of transference and countertransference issues should be integrated into decision making. Home visits, therapeutic touch, and informal interpreting can be helpful when used in a clinically boundaried and culturally sensitive manner. Ongoing discussions with clients about dual roles before (when possible) and after each event facilitate growth, promote anticipatory functioning, and clarify expectations.

Doing cross-culturally sensitive therapy with deaf clients poses challenges regarding maintenance and expansion of the traditional therapeutic role. Understanding the risks and benefits of differing roles in changing contexts helps therapists operate from a consistent, ethical, and growthful model that protects clients and ourselves in the best ways possible.

SETTING TREATMENT GOALS WITH CLIENTS THAT AGENCIES/PAYORS UNDERSTAND

Therapy works a lot better when therapist and client have shared goals. Therapy gets reimbursed a lot more when agencies and clients' insurance companies support these goals. So how do we develop such treatment plans, when insurance companies do not know deafness and many deaf people do not understand the concept of setting treatment goals? This section focuses on how to set therapeutic goals that both clients and agencies can accept: goals that are concrete, achievable, and clinically and culturally appropriate.

Most agencies and insurance companies require a treatment plan model that addresses problems, interventions (plans to help problems diminish), and treatment goals. So as we talk with clients, we need to fit their concerns into these categories. We want to arrive at a shared understanding of the problem, a shared vision of where we are going (goals), and at least some overlap in our approaches to get there.

First, we must start where clients' pain or discomfort (and therefore motivation to change) is—or where they perceive it to be. If a client is convinced that if his former girlfriend would only come back to him, he would be happy, we must start there. But "getting girlfriend back" is not a clinically sound nor a reimbursable treatment plan!

I might ask such a client what his problems and feelings are, now that his girlfriend has left him. I may be able to elicit a list of symptoms with which he can agree, such as depression (including trouble sleeping, eating more or less than usual, decreased interest and motivation, feelings of loneliness and despair), anxiety (vague irritability, inability to settle down and relax, restlessness, even actual fear or panic at being alone or in certain situations), or losing his temper more easily. If he has any type of thought disorder or personality disorder, this added stress may be causing increased paranoia, delusions or hallucinations, stealing, helplessness, or whatever symptoms are related to his particular diagnosis. If he feels his heart has been broken, I would empathize with this image and also help him translate his chief complaints into concrete descriptions the agency will understand. We would then have a list of symptoms, or treatment problems, to address.

With court-ordered clients, this process is tricky. A client may show up in my office because she thinks someone has "forced" her to come. I always introduce the idea of choice:

"If you chose not to come, what would happen?"

"My probation officer would bring me back to court."

"Oh, I see. So you decided to come here because you prefer therapy to court again?"

This is a process of empowerment: even when one has two options that appear lousy, she still gets to make a choice; she is not helpless.

The reasons the court sends a person to therapy may be vastly different from what this person wishes to change. Suppose the court wants a client to stop hitting people when he is angry. The client believes he hits people because they insult him, do not treat him right, or discriminate against him due to his deafness. What is the problem from his perception? Perhaps one problem is the stress or anxiety of having a probation officer looking over his shoulder all the time, running his life. Another problem could be that people do not treat him fairly. I might write a problem list that includes:

1. Joe, very anxious, pressured by Mr. Jones (his probation officer);
2. When people around him act unfair, Joe has a hard time sticking up for himself without hitting.

As Joe and I develop the interventions to help him meet his goal of getting off probation, we might create a strategy of assertiveness training to help Joe stick up for himself proudly as a Deaf person, know his legal rights and how to use them, channel his anger into filing complaints, and learn to avoid hitting in order to get off probation and not give "them" the satisfaction of seeing him get into trouble. (Adults with sociopathic problems sometimes can identify with the same logic I offer 5-year-olds: If she teases you and you hit her and get in trouble, who won? She did. But if she tries to tease you and you ignore her, who won? You!)

We also need to give each client (or one client of a family or couple) one or more diagnoses from the current *DSM*. The symptom list I develop with each client, plus some family and personal history, is vital in helping me make my diagnosis. Most insurance companies do not want to treat chronic or longstanding problems such as personality disorders or mental retardation, so it is important to focus on the acute or current problems that are different from the norm and therefore more responsive to treatment.

Whenever clinically and linguistically possible, sharing diagnoses with clients and explaining which symptoms led to which diagnosis is part of empowerment, demystifying the therapeutic process and increasing teamwork. (With some clients, such as those with paranoia, such a sharing may increase the symptoms and prevent therapeutic bonding, especially at first.) I often use a holistic approach by introducing the ancient concept of "dis-ease," meaning an absence of ease or a discomfort, a not-rightness within the self that the client and I will fix together. As a team, we can monitor the list of symptoms and work to mitigate this diagnosis or make it no longer applicable, if possible. With higher functioning clients, I explain the political functions of diagnosis as well as the clinical ones: None of us fits neatly into such categories, but we need to approximate the closest one or ones for insurance purposes—and sometimes for our own clarity as well.

Returning to the treatment plan, I would next ask this client what his life would look like and feel like if his girlfriend did return to him. As he describes this, we develop a shared vision of treatment goals. It is important for the goals to be observable (to an outsider), concrete, measurable, and realistic. If a client says, "If my girlfriend came back, I would feel wonderful all the time," I might ask, "How would you act differently if you felt that wonderful? If a person saw you at work or at the Deaf Club, how could they tell you were happy by watching you?" He might respond, "I'd be smiling." I would continue, "What else?" giving him suggestions if necessary, based on his problem list. "Would you be sleeping better? Eating better? Calling in sick less often? Arguing with your boss or mother less?"

Most agencies want goals to be measurable, so everyone can agree when they are met. I try to help clients get a sense of what is reasonable to expect in a given amount of time. For example, I might say:

> We need to set up a treatment plan for our first 3 months of work together. I don't know if your girlfriend will come back, but I can help you sleep better and get to work more so you don't lose your job. How about if we set up a goal that in 3 months, you will be sleeping at least 6 hours every night and missing work less than once a month?

(I might explain that he can freely express his feelings to me about missing his girlfriend, that this may help him sleep and work better, but that his situation with his girlfriend is private and the agency reviewers or insurance company do not need to know that.)

When I have specific treatment problems and measurable, concrete, doable goals, I need to assess the best interventions. Is the modality of family, individual, group, or couples therapy indicated? Would a treatment approach of cognitive–behavioral, psychodynamic, reality therapy, or brief solution-focused therapy be helpful? (Of course, often we combine such approaches, but with this particular client, would one predominate?) Would therapeutic tools such as expressive therapy (drawing, mime, role plays, movement) be helpful?

Suppose group therapy seems the treatment of choice, but no appropriate therapy group of Deaf members exists, what are the options? I could try to start a group: a great idea, but time consuming and difficult at best. I could try to identify other clients on my caseload who would benefit from such a group. I could check with other signing therapists in my area to see if together we would have enough clients for a group of this kind. Should I run the group if I am seeing one or more of the clients individually, or should someone else? Can I manage all the differing communication styles in the group effectively, or should there be an interpreter? Does the clinical mix require a co-leader to work well? Are there Deaf people who do not want to be in a therapy group with other Deaf people because they are worried about gossip and do not believe that other group members can be taught to be confidential? Each of these questions should be considered.

I could try to mainstream my client in a hearing group with an interpreter. Some sophisticated clients actually prefer this, even culturally Deaf people, because of the anonimity it affords. For most, as we have witnessed, it is sadly inappropriate. Even if we conscientiously train the group leader in deaf cultural and clinical issues and use of interpreters, typical issues that emerge are:

1. The deaf person does not have an equal chance to participate, due to interpreter lag time and inexperience of the group leader in mixed deaf–hearing meetings. A communication ball can be used (we use a brightly colored Koosh ball because they are light and easy to throw and catch) to show visually where the speaker is and to slow down turn-taking somewhat, but inexperienced people often throw the ball as they finish their last word and forget to wait for the interpreter to catch up. (A strong, deafness-experienced facilitator seems almost always necessary in order to have truly equal access to communication.) A significant number of Deaf group members (more than 30%) helps balance the communication access, as does a Deaf leader or paraprofessional co-leader.

2. The hearing members are nervous about how to interact with a deaf person, have a hard time learning to use the interpreter well or to speak directly to the deaf person, and unwittingly exclude the deaf person from the developing group norm.

In both cases, the deaf member risks feeling doubly isolated and worse than before she started.

Suppose family therapy seems the treatment of choice: Should an interpreter be used? Should I observe routine communication in the family without an interpreter? (Entire articles have been written on this subject, such as those by Mike Harvey, 1982, 1984.) How might family therapy be different with a suicidal young adult who has lived in the dorms at the state school for the deaf since age 5, only going home on school vacations? If he becomes suicidal on graduation, is the emotional "family" really his hearing parents and siblings or the Deaf dorm counselor and teachers with whom he feels strong ties? Culturally Deaf people, like gay and lesbian people, did not grow up in a family with a shared culture. For such folks, their "chosen family," people from the same culture with whom they spend a lot of time and from whom they get emotional support, may be the significant family with whom to work.

As you read this description of treatment planning, which involves fairly high level concepts, you may be thinking: But many of my clients have no formal language! They have no idea what therapy is, why they are here, or what agency requirements or insurance companies are! How do we help such clients have some basic involvement and investment in a treatment plan?

With such clients, we can both show by example what happens in therapy and explain what we do not do by referencing their experience of other helpers. For example, by respectful listening and empathy, we can help clients experience what a therapy relationship feels like. By asking how they feel inside today: happy? sad? frustrated? worried? mad? what?, we can begin to define our role. (Much of this questioning takes place via mime, drawing, and role plays.) By making charts or role playing what we do not do and what other professionals do, clients can begin to understand the limits of our role. For example: "A vocational rehabilitation counselor helps you get job, hearing aid, and so on. A case manager goes with you to help you apply for welfare, Supplemental Security Income, and so on. A doctor checks your body, how it feels, sometimes gives you medicine to feel better. In therapy, you express, I ask questions, you express, we think, think, find way to improve life, feel better, feel relieved."

I used to simply write my usual complex English treatment plans and attempt to translate them into mime, ASL, or a combination before asking such clients to sign them. My colleague Daria Medwid from the Deaf program at South Shore Mental Health in Quincy showed me a beautiful way to simplify plans in ASL gloss (writing English words in capital letters to roughly represent ASL concepts) to help clients see what they were endorsing. She showed me a sample plan, written with a woman who lived with her hearing mother and hearing children. The children looked to their grandmother as the authority and often ignored their mother's attempts at parenting. No family members signed. This concept (see Fig. 8.8) helped me revamp my treatment plans to give clients limited in written English more ownership over the written part of the plan.

After initial development of the treatment plan, my client and I review it periodically as a tool to discuss progress, frustrations, and modifications that might improve the therapy process. I use such opportunities to notice and bring up interventions that my client may not have been ready for or rejected in the past, or that have not been available until now. These could include Deaf community activities, job training, an ASL class for a late-deafened person, or AA for a person who initially denied problems with alcohol (but with whom I now have enough history or enough of a relationship to help him see the

PROBLEM:	INTERVENTION:	GOAL:
Conflicts between Ginny and children: lack of respect for her status leads to children acting out.	Weekly 1 hour individual therapy with Ginny to teach concrete parenting skills.	Ginny will demonstrate understanding of praise, consequences, importance of consistency. Will report increased respect from children.
GINNY, KIDS FIGHT. KIDS IGNORE, GINNY UPSET, MAD.	GINNY TALK DARIA MONDAYS 2 P.M. MOTHER SKILLS LEARN, IMPROVE	GINNY SKILLS LEARN, PRACTICE. KIDS IMPROVE. KIDS IGNORE LESS.

FIG. 8.8. Example of treatment plan "translated" into ASL gloss.

connection between alcohol use and increased problems in his life). My supervisor at the South Shore Mental Health Deaf program, Kim Kelly, taught me an approach with alcoholism that I have found useful in many other areas as well:

> You seem convinced you can limit your drinking to two beers and aren't alcoholic. Let's try it your way and see what happens. Do you agree now that if it doesn't work your way, you will then try it my way?

The process of treatment planning does not have to be a choice between clinically and culturally appropriate goals. In fact, a clinical goal that is culturally inappropriate will probably not succeed; and a cultural approach that is clinically ineffective will be unhelpful. Of course, in specific instances, the clinical or cultural needs may need to predominate for a while. For example, if a client is suicidal, she may need to be hospitalized even if there is no unit where staff sign. A threatened funding cut of his state Deaf school may cause a client and therapist to focus on cultural and advocacy issues, while putting on hold relaxation techniques to control anxiety. But in the long run, clinical and cultural goals interweave and complement each other in sound treatment planning.

Treatment plans are not just pieces of paper. They are living, organic, changing, and changeable concepts that guide our clients and ourselves together toward making clients' lives more satisfying, and obtaining insurance reimbursement for that change whenever appropriate. We are the interpreters between the client and the agency. We must be bilingual in "agency language" (the psychological terms that bring in reimbursement) and in "client language" (the framing of problems and goals in ways that help clients feel understood, supported, and cared about). As with all interpreter training, this one takes some practice, and we get better at it as we go along.

JUGGLING AGENCY NEEDS AND CLIENT NEEDS

In my mailbox at work are three managed care forms, two Medicaid travel forms, a letter asking me to call my representatives to prevent slashing of welfare benefits, a phone message that a client was hospitalized last night in a hearing psychiatric unit, and a list of the seven treatment plans due next week. It is 3:00 p.m. on Friday afternoon. My one free hour today was taken up by several phone consults to distraught workshop staff trying to de-escalate one of my assault-prone clients.

More and more, it seems, the gap is widening between client needs and agency requirements. The list of nonreimbursable tasks that need doing—crisis phone consultations, advocacy, education of hearing institutions, coordination with other providers—seems to grow exponentially even as productivity demands increase.

It is easy to feel that the only way to both help clients and maintain productivity is to work 70 hours a week. I disagree. This section offers some concrete ideas to help meet productivity and paperwork requirements, while still providing the nonbillable services and coordination that are an integral part of treatment for many of our clients. It also discusses the importance of time off and ways to nurture oneself and minimize burnout.

Do Necessary Advocacy as Part of the Therapy Hour

Much needed advocacy can and should be part of the treatment plan. Part of our goal is to empower clients to take charge of their own lives as much as possible, to be assertive rather than aggressive, to take responsibility for their own actions, and to change the circumstances of their lives. The more they can do this, the less they will need therapy in the future, so this approach saves money for insurance companies as well.

The treatment process should move clients (within their cognitive and emotional limits) from being done *for*, to doing *with*, to doing *independently*. This is a basic tenet of the ILS movement but has not filtered sufficiently into therapeutic circles. Social workers, who historically paired personal growth and social change as inseparable, whitewashed our profession of its progressive political overtones in order to become more acceptable and licensable to the professions with greater social status and political power: psychiatrists and psychologists. As a result, many social workers now refer to themselves only as "therapists," attempt to focus on pure psychotherapy, and have lost their connection with the advocacy process. As deafness therapists, if we do not advocate with and for clients as part of the therapy process, our treatment can be sadly ineffective.

If clients do not have advocacy skills, they often feel helpless, enraged, passive, or explosive. These symptoms can be included in a treatment plan with the intervention of assertiveness training. An important part of that training is doing some advocacy together within the treatment hour: making calls through relay or with a staff interpreter, writing letters together to agencies or representatives about needed services, calling an ILS center together to make a referral and to turn over the advocacy training to the ILS-client team as much as possible.

Suppose a client is working with an ILS specialist toward getting into subsidized housing—but in my office the lack of it is the highest stress and the most upsetting element in her life. Of course, I can empathize with feelings and talk about ways to hang on until something changes—but helping a client to take concrete action with me, to make a call to her state senator together, to be able to feel my tangible support may make the biggest difference in her well-being right now.

For clients who are not skilled in using an interpreter by phone or the TTY relay, they have an opportunity to role play what they want to say before the phone call, to be coached by me during the call, and to do some self-assessment and reflection on their accomplishment afterward. Therapeutically, this process helps increase healthy risk-taking behavior, build confidence and self-esteem, and promote planning and problem-solving abilities. As clients learn these skills, "homework" can be assigned. Clients can be asked to make calls from their TTY at home after they have successfully done so in my office with coaching and report back about the experience. Newfound assertiveness skills can be transferred to other problems in their lives as well.

Hold Reimbursable Case Conferences
With the Multiagency Treatment Team

Incorporate requests for regular case consultations into treatment plans so insurance companies pay for them. Many companies will pay for one conference per quarter, with clinical justification, especially if the client is in the meeting (which they should be whenever possible).

Case conferences can help delegate tasks, clarify roles with the client and other providers, increase communication and decrease potential splitting (by clients or even providers!), and help clients feel a sense of teamwork and containment. (Again, preparing for the case conference with the client and discussing it afterwards provides important therapeutic continuity.)

Bill for Crisis Sessions When Appropriate,
Including the Adjunct Work Involved

If we are called to squeeze in a crisis session for a client, we usually bill for an emergency. But if a client comes to see us at his regular time and reports suicidal or assaultive feelings or intent, we often do not have the time to resolve this situation safely within our scheduled time. Perhaps we see this client for a half hour every 2 weeks, and clear communication about the distinction between feeling like hitting and planning to hit takes 45 minutes to accomplish that day. Perhaps a client brings up the risky material 5 minutes before the end of the session.

Some of us work under a system where most at-risk situations are immediately referred over to a crisis team. Even if a crisis team is available, there would not be interpreters there for hours, and we deafness clinicians are often asked to perform assessments ourselves (with consultation from the crisis team). Where there is no crisis team, we can feel very alone and isolated handling such a high-stakes situation.

Crisis evaluation is difficult work. It takes a lot of time and involves more liability, so it must be done with unusual care. This is why most insurances reimburse at a higher hourly rate for emergencies. Deafness clinicians deserve to get this higher rate, or if on salary, higher productivity, for this type of work. In fact, because of the idiosyncratic communication styles of many of our clients, our work is *more* complex and *more* tricky.

Emergency services workers bill for the hours they spend on the crisis: including the interview of the client, phone calls with collatorals, placement calls to respite programs or hospitals if necessary. When we are needed to do this work, these should all be part of our crisis charges as well.

If I see a V–G client at 10:00 a.m. for a half hour appointment, and by 10:20 she is showing assaultive potential, I change over to crisis mode (and crisis charge) at that point. Whatever time it takes to clinically assess whether or not she is dangerous, whether she can return safely to the workshop or needs respite or hospitalization, is billable time for emergency services. This includes role plays and drawings; phone calls to family, residence, workshop, and/or case manager to gather information about recent behavior; phone calls to the crisis team if possible for a consult; and calls if needed for placement (including brief phone training/consultation to orient hospital or respite staff unaware of deafness and interpreter issues).

If there is a limit to what can be billed as an emergency (for example, Massachusetts Medicaid will pay a maximum of 90 minutes), I might discuss with my supervisor beforehand what to do if a crisis is still unresolved by that time: Would the agency like to give me extra money or productivity credits in order for me to finish up? If not, who will take over and finish the process? If I will be handing over an unfinished situation to someone else, I would do the most specialized part of the process first and warn my boss, the crisis team, or the person in the system designated to take over for me about what time I will be passing on the client with my recommendations for further action.

Consider Home Visits

Even when a home visit is clinically indicated, it may or may not be practical. However, if the client's home (or daily environment at a workshop) is 10 or 15 minutes away, I can legitimately drive there, have a shorter session, and return within 60 minutes. If such a session will provide me with crucial information I do not have access to in my office and that will make treatment more effective, I can ethically justify it in my records. If such a visit would be helpful for a client who lives on my way home, I might take my last hour of the day to stop along my way home.

When home visits to a client are not possible, I could use creative techniques (such as both of us inviting staff into our sessions at times, calling her residence or workshop staff together during a session, or asking her family into a session to role play a dinner hour) in order to access some of this information.

Actively Use the Appeals Processes Available

Many utilization review committees in agencies and most insurance companies have appeals processes when claims or requests for treatment are denied. Keeping a record of my appeals shortens the time needed to write the next one, as I can reuse material I have already written about general deafness needs. One can describe in detail the greater needs of language-deprived clients, the longer time required to make accurate diagnoses and effect change in behavior, and the necessity of case conferences with several collatorals in order to do effective treatment. Referencing the rich book on assessment by Elliott, Glass, and Evans (1987),[10] the present volume, or other deaf mental health research may strengthen one's case by making it appear more "official."

Show the Agency the Logic of Lowering Productivity When Working With Deaf Clients

When I began setting up the Deaf inpatient psychiatric unit in Massachusetts, the normal caseload for a social worker at the state hospital was 10 patients. Because our unit was to have only 10 patients, the administration reasoned that we would only need one full-time social worker. We were lucky to have the precedent established by the Massachusetts Rehabilitation Commission that the Rehabilitation Counselors for the Deaf had a caseload significantly lower than their hearing counterparts, due to the complexity of the cases and the slower evaluation and rehabilitation process. That information, and the fact that we were a statewide unit, convinced our higher-ups that we could set a caseload of 5 clients per full-time social worker. Even this caseload proved sometimes to be difficult for a deaf social worker who had to spend a large part of her day on TTY relay, networking and advocating for nonexistent aftercare services for severely disturbed deaf psychiatric patients.

Due to years of advocacy and education of the Massachusetts mental health system, most of our outpatient deaf mental health programs have a lower productivity requirement than do hearing programs in the same agencies.

Constantly Reprioritize

When Neil Glickman, one of the editors of this volume, and I began running the deaf inpatient unit in 1987, he noticed I seemed overwhelmed one day and suggested I write a daily "to-do" list, as he did. "I'll try that!" I sighed, "but what do you do with all the things you don't get to every day?" Neil looked taken aback. "I don't put more on the list than I can get done in one day," he explained.

---

[10]This book has been out of print since September 1990. However, it can be ordered from Pro Am Publications at 512-451-3246 if there are copies left.

Most of us are simply not as organized as Neil. But I have learned a lot from this attitude. I try to begin my day with a list of priorities, with the most important at the top of the list and so on. Then, if I only manage to get the first three items accomplished, I know that at least I have done what most needed to be done first.

Of course, crises come up, my boss stops by with a form that must be done today, someone I have been trying to reach for weeks finally returns my call. But in each situation, I can look at my priority list and ask myself, "Which is more important—my top priority on the list or this new interruption?" If it is a clinical crisis, that always "wins"—unless I'm leaving for the day (and truly do not have 10 minutes extra to stay) and must delegate it to a coworker or the crisis team. (Yes, there are times I do stay late for a crisis, and I make sure I am compensated for it; there are other times I cannot stay and have learned to say "no.") If my boss requests information, I can ask her, "If I can't do both, would you rather I gather that data today or finish my late treatment plans?" In this way, I am asking her to help me reprioritize.

We each have our own "pah" or approach to a crisis: some panic, others withdraw or become passive, yet others become controlling and try to "do it all." Being in the last group, I have learned over the years to take several deep breaths and delegate, delegate, delegate! For example, if a case is exploding and necessary tasks seem overwhelming, I may call the case manager and say, "This client needs X, Y, and Z done right away. I'll do X, the part her therapist must do clinically. Can you do Y and call her residence to do Z?" Know your own unhelpful tendencies and create your own personal crisis plan that helps you guard against them.

I often must rewrite my top five items a few times during the day. But when I have reached the end of my scheduled work day, there are far fewer items that "simply can't wait until tomorrow" than there used to be!

Videotape Trainings to Professionals

If you train hearing clinicians about deafness, deaf culture, and interpreter use, videotape the training to save yourself time. Then, as new staff join the crisis team or mainstreamed program, they can watch the video and have a short discussion with you afterward. If you offer mental health trainings to deaf staff, or if hearing clinicians offer trainings where interpreters are present, videotape the trainers and interpreters in order to show new deaf staff as they arrive.

Set Good Limits With Work Hours to Avoid Burnout

Human service jobs have endless work, all of it important. We could work 24 hours a day and not get it all done. We can all be far more effective if we can end work every day at a predictable time, and have time to relax, do nonwork activities, or simply do nothing. If we take a lunch break—even 10 or 15 minutes to relax or take a walk—our work the rest of the day will probably be more efficient and of higher quality than if we work through lunch.

For some of us, setting these limits is not hard at all. For the majority of us caretakers, trying to unlearn family patterns set during our early years, it is a constant struggle. Some of the elements that help are: (a) a clear vision of what our number of work hours should be, (b) how many hours we are willing to work over these on a regular basis, and (c) what we can do to compensate ourselves if we need to stay longer due to an emergency.

A supervisor who understands the field of deafness, the complex nature of our clients, the communication barriers, and the scarcity of resources is invaluable in supporting good limits. If you do not have a supervisor knowledgeable in deafness, create one! You may need to teach her, but a good supervisor is willing to learn. Even in agencies that have official policies of "no compensatory time," a sympathetic supervisor may find ways to compensate you with additional productivity or flexibility to come in late after you have had to stay late for a crisis.

Actively Replenish and Nurture Yourself
Outside of Work and Regularly During the Work Day

Many of us enjoy advocacy, Deaf community events, and other activities containing elements similar to our jobs. This is fine, but it is equally vital to do things outside of work that are totally different—hobbies, sports, whatever makes you feel joyful, alive, and whole and makes you forget about work completely.

Many people, especially in the high-stress human services, have found that soothing activities such as meditation or yoga or expressive activities such as dance are particularly good at helping their stress meters drop to zero on off-hours.

Besides good physical boundaries around work, we need to set good mental limits as well. It is a learning process not to ponder work issues outside of work. Many people new to a field or even to a position find themselves thinking about work constantly, trying to figure out places they are stuck, even dreaming about it. As we mature in our jobs and get more skillful at relaxation techniques, we can practice more and more what we are teaching our clients: visualizations of sending thoughts about work back to work in a hot air balloon, for example, or spending a prescribed amount of time writing down thoughts or questions and putting the paper away until the next day. We can go to therapy ourselves at times to take in nurturance, learn how to let go better, understand our own issues at a deeper level, and become increasingly more effective clinicians. We can form interdisciplinary support groups with other deafness professionals to create mutual validation and information sharing.

If you find thoughts about work problems plaguing you, remind yourself frequently that you are doing the best you can, that none of us finishes everything, and that your clients are better off with all your work than if you were not doing it. Of course, in a profession where lives can be at stake, it can be difficult not to worry. But ultimately, worrying will do nothing except decrease effectiveness.

During the work day, take a few minibreaks to help your stress level drop and renew your efficiency. Teaching relaxation tools to clients can help you learn them better yourself. While you are breathing deeply or doing progressive muscle relaxation with a client, you are also helping your own body relax. A 2-minute break can be enough time to relax fully, and return to your next client or paperwork with a clearer mind and higher motivation.

This section has listed strategies for juggling competing agency and client demands, including teaching and delegating advocacy to clients and collaterols; getting paid for crisis work; working home visits into a work day; and educating agencies and payors about the need for more services and lower productivity than is needed in work with hearing clients. Also discussed were ways of reducing burnout, such as reprioritizing, setting physical and mental limits, and actively replenishing oneself emotionally.

Key ingredients to implementing any of these approaches effectively and consistently are self-confidence, a grasp of deafness and resources to back up one's knowledge, a good personal support system, and the firm belief that one person cannot and should not save the world single-handedly.

Summary and Conclusions

Therapists who work with the full range of deaf people often are case managers, advocates, emergency clinicians, and educators of clients and systems. Balancing this variety of roles with grace, clinical skill, cultural sensitivity, and compassion is far from easy. Such a task demands openness, flexibility, willingness to expand the traditional therapeutic parameters when needed, and determination not to do for clients anything they can do for themselves—or that appropriate, accessible professionals could do with and for them. In order to decide when to expand our role and when not to, we need to understand deeply the clinical, cultural, and ethical implications of doing so and of not doing so: what is lost and what is gained from each option.

Using the multidimensional model of evaluation presented in this chapter highlights areas of strength and need, guides clinically and culturally appropriate intervention, facilitates development of treatment plans that make sense, and clarifies priorities so we can do first things first and model good limit setting and self-care.

Clear, unchanging boundaries and flexible parameters responsive to differing client needs and changing situations are crucial in dealing ethically with the dual roles or overlapping relationships that often occur in the small Deaf community.

Interpreting with clients should generally be done only with their permission, in a crisis, and not in a legally or psychiatrically sensitive situation. It should never be done beyond the limits of one's abilities and without clear, repeated explanations to hearing and deaf consumers about one's role, limitations, and boundaries.

Most of our clients need far more than traditional therapy, and accessible resources besides ourselves are often nonexistent. We must decide which types of advocacy are essential in order for the therapy to move ahead.

Teaching clients to self-advocate is an integral part of therapy. We intervene on a continuum: At one end, advocating for clients in areas where they cannot do it themselves; in the middle, helping develop the supports they need to help themselves advocate; and at the other end, teaching them the assertiveness and practical skills to do all their own advocacy. Even in cases where clients are severely limited, the process should always be to involve them more and more in the advocacy process over time, as they learn how to do parts of it and to feel good about themselves as a result.

I believe part of our mandate as therapists is not only to improve the lives of individual clients but also to improve society in general so it is a better and mentally healthier place for all to live. Part of our work is to advocate within the larger system for permanent systems change, not only for this individual client. Doing so benefits this client and all others in the same situation. It also benefits therapists, to prevent us from having to do it over again next week or next year. The fact that deaf people are both a cultural–linguistic minority and are considered a "disability" under the federal Americans with Disabilities Act (ADA) means there are two sets of advocacy groups with whom we can ally for greater political impact and more service delivery. During these times of budget cutting, advocacy work may feel more discouraging. Today is actually an even more vital time to be a visible advocate, to teach clients to advocate, and to hold a vision and hold the line against more service cuts.

Our job is a juggling act! Most of our clients need far more than the traditional therapy with which payors, and some supervisors, are familiar. Each geographic and work setting has different political and financial constraints: Each of us must decide when to work to change a policy inappropriate for deaf clients, how to pick our battles carefully and fight them respectfully and professionally, when to organize with other agencies and when to go home and take a hot bath. Competing and pressing demands are the very fabric of our work lives; we need to make sure they do not rule our daily work but that we can juggle them as we need to, letting our visions guide our priorities and directions, and remembering that we cannot and should not do it all.

As you become increasingly familiar with the four dimensions of assessment described in this chapter, you will integrate them into your style and create new ones for your own use. You will develop your own set of guidelines for when to expand your clinical role and when to stand fast, how to negotiate dual roles in ways that protect your clients and yourself, which types of ongoing limits and self-care prevent burnout for you. Perhaps you will share your vision by writing or teaching about it, thus further enriching our community of deafness providers.

As we continue to learn from each other and refine our professional roles, we will appear more and more like jugglers on the circus tightrope: balancing with apparent ease, skillfully tossing balls to and from each other so that nobody has too many balls to handle at one time, sometimes missing a catch and simply going on. We are building this skill within each of us, individually, and among us it grows exponentially. In this way, we keep enthusiasm alive for improving our therapeutic skills with the varied and challenging populations of deaf people.

Appendix A:
Questions to Guide Assessment
on the Four Dimensions

COMMUNICATION ASSESSMENT QUESTIONS

1. At which age was this person exposed to meaningful communication (if at all)?

2. How is this person used to communicating? What is her natural communication style? Is it primarily linguistic or alternate methods (such as tantrums when angry, working when lonely, withdrawing when depressed)?

3. Is either receptive or expressive language considerably stronger than the other mode?

4. Can the client communicate (and if so, how well) over phone line with TTY, relay, or amplified handset? Would she be able to get across a message or ask for help this way in a crisis?

CLINICAL ASSESSMENT QUESTIONS

1. Is the client at risk to hurt himself or others?

2. Does the client show evidence of a personality disorder or a thought disorder?

3. If the person feels disempowered, where do the feelings of disempowerment stem from? (Understanding where a person experiences lack of empowerment in the past or present helps a therapist know how to help the empowerment process take place. Most acting out behavior is at least partially rooted in feeling trapped, disempowered, helpless, or ignored.)

4. Which cues in the present seem to trigger inappropriate behavior? Where could the particular form of behavior (self-mutilation, throwing things, running away, sexual behaviors, etc.) have been learned?

5. Is there a trauma history (or symptoms of a possible trauma history), particularly physical or sexual abuse? (Disclosure of trauma often takes months, if not years, of building therapeutic alliances. Some clients do not even remember traumatic events until a great deal of trust and safety has been established in therapy. Deaf children, often unable to communicate clearly to adults, are particularly vulnerable targets for abuse. The astoundingly high percentages of female and male victims of childhood abuse is probably even higher in the deaf population. Therefore, our adult deaf clients are likely to have a high rate of childhood abuse histories.)

6. How does this person's communication style change—if it does—during a crisis or a temporary psychosis?

7. Which interventions seem to "fit" with this person? Can she reality test? Understand cause and effect? Show insight?

CULTURAL ASSESSMENT QUESTIONS

1. In which stage of Glickman's cultural identity model (see Glickman, chapter 5, this volume) would this person be?

2. When did this person first meet another deaf/Deaf person? What was the context? What messages about deafness did he get and from whom?

3. If the person is in Glickman's marginal stage, what exactly does she feel and think about the Deaf community and Deaf culture? Has she experienced ridicule or rejection from deaf people—in school, Deaf clubs, or other situations—and generalized this experience to all deaf people? If the client's feelings toward deafness are negative, are the feelings rigid or do they seem open to change with education and exposure?

RESOURCE ASSESSMENT QUESTIONS

1. What is this person's level of intelligence and maturity? What are her ego strengths, both at this moment and in general?

2. How well does he understand the process of problem solving and of therapy? How much confidence does he have in himself? If his confidence is low, can the therapist find in his history examples of successes, of skills, and can he take in these examples to modify his self-perception?

3. What supports does the person currently have in her life (family members, friends, neighbors, priest, doctor) even if they are not deaf or do not sign?

People who care and have an ongoing relationship with a client may be able to encourage her to take risks and try new things, or may be the ones who sabotage any new growth, unless they are brought into the therapy process.

4. What are the stressors (Axis IV) in this person's life currently? Is he unemployed? Has she recently lost a loved one through death or divorce? Has he recently been diagnosed with a new illness or disability, or is he dealing with a progressive one?

5. Which community resources (both Deaf and nondeaf supports) are available in the local area? Do they cost money? Are they mandated to be accessible through federal ADA legislation? What is the referral process? Is there a waiting list? Can a therapist advocate (or help a client advocate herself, or both) for a hearing agency to pay a deafness provider to give services if this fits the client's needs better? (I have been pleasantly surprised at how quickly managed care plans that rarely refer out have been willing to pay me privately to see a Deaf client.)

6. What is the client's general level of functioning (Axis V)? What is her level of behavioral control, social skills, education, vocational functioning? How much is he able to advocate with the therapist's support and guidance, and how much

does the therapist have to do this for him? Does she understand what advocacy is, what her rights are as a deaf person and as a U.S. citizen in general? What can he learn about his legal rights and how to access them?

7. Which disabilities or differences (Cerebral palsy, AIDs, Jewishness, lesbianism, etc.) does the client have, besides deafness, that might cause oppression or discrimination? How aware is she of how these differences affect her life and how to constructively manage these pressures?

REFERENCES

Barnard, K. E., & Brazelton, T. B. (Eds.). (1990). *Touch: The foundation of experience.* Madison, CT: International University Press.

Elliott, H., Glass, L., & Evans, J. W. (Eds.). (1987) *Mental health assessment of deaf clients: A practical manual.* Boston: Little, Brown.

Harvey, M. A. (1982). The influence and utilization of an interpreter for deaf persons in family therapy. *American Annuals of the Deaf, 127*(7), 821–827.

Harvey, M. A. (1984). Family therapy with deaf persons: The systemic utilization of an interpreter. *Family Process, 23,* 205–213.

Heller, M. A., & Schiff, W. (Eds.). (1991). *The psychotherapy of touch.* Hillsdale, NJ: Lawrence Erlbaum Associates.

Maslow, A. H. (1968). *Toward a psychology of being.* New York: Van Nostrand.

Chapter 9

Mental Health Service
And The Deaf Community:
Deaf Leaders As Culture Brokers

Tovah M. Wax
National Technical Institute for the Deaf
Rochester Institute of Technology

As is well known to those who tried, successfully or otherwise, providing mental health services to deaf people is a formidable task. Until recently, mental health service providers have joined the medical and rehabilitation professions in subscribing to what Lane (1990) called the infirmity model of deafness, a view that deafness is a medically defined deficit typically accompanied by mental health complications caused by communication difficulties and related sequelae. Today, practitioners increasingly recognize the sociocultural implications of deafness as a different way of living as well as communicating (cultural model; Lane, 1990).

Given the current cultural view of deafness, mental health practitioners need to develop an in-depth understanding of experiential and cultural characteristics among people in the Deaf community. Within other (ethnic) minority populations, one effort to compensate for the scarcity of trained mental health professionals who are themselves from specific minority groups has been the selection of individuals from those minority groups to serve as bridges, or "culture brokers," between pertinent mental health providers and clientele from their communities (Lefley & Bestman, 1991; Schwab, Drake, & Burghardt, 1988). For example, Lefley and Bestman (1991) developed teams of social scientists, clinicians, and paraprofessionals who were themselves members of targeted minority groups. Service, teaching, and research activities were conducted by these team members through a network comprised of university, medical center, and surrounding community. The culture broker (or equivalent) model has also been applied to rural clients (Heyman & VandenBos, 1989), Vietnamese refugees (Brown, 1987), Latino clients (Rosado & Elias, 1993), and even to chronically mentally ill clients with a "culture" of their own (Schwab et al., 1988).

According to Eng and Young (1992), who summarized case studies using lay advisors to facilitate health education and awareness, important functions of culture brokers include reducing disparities between professionals' intentions and clients' expectations and increasing accessbility and sustainability of health services for individuals in the community. By serving as a mediator between professional agencies and clientele, the broker can be in a position to negotiate for more and better services; to accomplish these outcomes, culture brokers require relatively specific kinds of skills.

Apart from anecdotal evidence of attempts to do so—including the one proposed in this chapter—hardly any research exists about the application of the culture broker concept to the relationship between mental health providers and the Deaf community specifically. One study reviewed attempts by the Parks and Recreation Department to provide leisure programs and services to deaf residents of Winnipeg, Canada; according to Munch and Mulligan (1991), training was provided to selected deaf adults to help increase access to park and recreation services. Among the outcomes of interest were the need to modify training for deaf adults by using fewer materials in written English and the need to modify "standard" marketing approaches from the use of printed materials (brochures, posters) to more direct face-to-face contact. One dilemma faced by the Parks and Recreation Department was that as increasing numbers of deaf people used their services, the need for accessibility services (e.g., interpreters, assistive devices) also increased, creating questions about division of responsibility and cost.

Assisted by a number of undergraduate and graduate students[1] over time, the writer conducted an informal survey of mental health providers serving deaf clientele, to ascertain whether or not any extant programs or services have developed and/or applied the culture broker concept within their Deaf community cachement areas, since publication about a similar model was proposed by Wax (1990). Several respondents indicated that such a model was under development or attempted; in fact, one respondent indicated that the model was tried and dropped due to the low participation rate of the Deaf community clientele. In the few cases when the culture broker model was approximated, each respondent indicated that advisory boards and outreach networks were the primary sources of significant members from the surrounding Deaf community. In two cases where specific deaf persons could be identified in the culture broker (or "bridge") role, neither was given any specific training for the role but voluntarily assumed responsibility for serving as a link between mental health and Deaf communities. Among the roles assumed by these persons were those of educator, problem solver, advisor, and listener/counselor. In a number of instances, the broker also served as facilitator of communication between the two cultures as well as translator of culture differences. Of note also was the

[1]The assistance of Rebecca Hurth, Tanya Duarte, and Suzanne Burley is gratefully acknowledged.

observation that the problems confronted by these "bridges" were not limited to mental health issues. As is typical of many deaf clientele, there were multiple problems ranging from housing, employment, and educational and communication accessibility needs to conflicts with families or friends, substance abuse, and emotional distress.

Respondents also indicated that people from the Deaf community, including family members and friends of clientele, leaders of organizations, and deaf professionals in other fields (e.g., teaching, ministry), comprise an untapped resource with respect to enhancing mental health service delivery to this population. Although some respondents felt thrust into the role of mental health provider without the necessary training or expertise, they nevertheless attempted to assist individuals seeking their help. In one community, for example, an elderly couple who often provided shelter to deaf runaway teenagers or aggrieved spouses indicated their sense of inadequacy in trying to address the mental health issues involved. In still other communities, teachers or other staff in schools for deaf children or clergy with significant deaf congregations are approached with appeals for help in situations involving mental health issues. Because helper and helpee alike often perceived local mental health providers as inaccessible or inadequately trained to work with deaf clients, or they wanted to avoid community gossip or opprobrium, they usually ended up backing down from attempts to make appropriate referrals and trying to solve the problems more discreetly among themselves.

This chapter briefly describes the evolution of attempts, in the 3-year period from 1984–1987, to provide more adequate mental health services to the Deaf community residing in the state of Washington, with a proposed model for a more effective program to serve this population. Because of the continuing shortage of qualified deaf or hearing mental health professionals with expertise in deafness, one alternative may be to train recognized leaders or other credible members of the Deaf community to serve as culture brokers between deaf clients and mental health service provider systems. Properly selected/elected and trained, these brokers can contribute in-depth understanding of the differences between mental health and Deaf community systems, "translate" these differences, and negotiate for better mutual accommodation in order to achieve more accessible/effective mental health services for deaf clientele. Even as increasing numbers of qualified mental health professionals with expertise in deafness enter the field (especially since the establishment of Gallaudet University's MSW and PhD programs, and the passage of the Americans with Disabilities Act in 1990), the proposed model can be adapted to incorporate those professionals and deaf community culture brokers (DCCBs) as collaborators.

THE WASHINGTON STATE EXPERIENCE

A Coordinator of Statewide Mental Health Services for Deaf and Hard-of-Hearing Persons was hired in 1984, in response to the identification of deaf people among the populations most underserved by the Washington State Division of Mental Health (DMH). A deaf mental health (MH) professional was hired as part of a contract between a speech/hearing agency in King County and the DMH. King County was selected as the central location of the MH Coordinator's office because of its size and concentration of deaf people; the MH Coordinator was responsible, however, for working with county-designated mental health programs across the state to develop accessible and cost-effective mental health services for this population.

Questionnaire surveys of the county-designated community (outpatient) and institutional (residential, inpatient) mental health service providers revealed a significant lack of familiarity with the needs of deaf clientele as well as a desire for more education and training about Deaf culture, the Deaf community, sign language communication, and mental health issues specifically pertinent to deaf people (Wax, 1985). Logically enough, these results led to the development of a training program combining curricula about mental health and deafness as well as guidelines for the use of sign language interpreters in mental health treatment.[2] Additionally, the MH Coordinator was able to develop contracts with each of the county-designated mental health service providers, stipulating that such training would take place at regularly scheduled intervals to accommodate personnel and program changes. Consultation was also available to these providers as needed for particular deaf client situations.

During the same period, focused discussion group surveys of Deaf community members across several ($N = 6$) of the most densely populated counties revealed both lack of knowledge about and low utilization of existing mental health resources. When deaf participants were asked why professional mental health services were not used, responses ranged from perceived or actual lack of accessibility or availability of mental health specialists in deafness, embarrassment or discomfort about acknowledging the need for professional services, and a desire to avoid exposure of mental health problems within the Deaf community. Again, the logical outcome of these survey findings was to design a series of workshops to educate deaf consumers about mental health and mental health services. Built into these workshops was a needs assessment process to ascertain what deaf people perceive as most pressing mental health service needs.

It should be mentioned that although convened by a deaf mental health professional, these workshops were poorly attended. Participants tended to be professionals themselves, parents of deaf children, or deaf leaders already fairly knowledgeable about mental health services or, more precisely, the lack thereof. The intended audience of the "regular" deaf consumer never fully materialized at these workshops. Several conjectures are offered to explain the difficulty of engaging deaf consumers in discussion of mental health issues. First, the mental health coordinator position was filled by someone from out of state and therefore relatively unknown to that Deaf community. As an "outsider" (Higgins, 1980), the new mental health coordinator did not yet have the reputation or credibility of a trusted member of the community—a critical issue in dealing with sensitive mental health issues. It took about 3 years for the MH Coordinator to establish a sufficient base of trust and rapport with the Deaf communities across the state, as reflected, for example, in the increasing number of referrals to the MH Coordinator's office and increasing attendance at sub-

---

[2]This part of the curriculum was taught by Lisa Holmberg, Mental Health Interpreter Consultant.

sequently scheduled workshops.

Second, it is the tradition within the Deaf community for younger newcomers to be introduced to the community by older more established leaders (Higgins & Nash, 1987; Padden & Humphries, 1988). When scheduling the initial mental health education workshops for selected local Deaf communities, the MH Coordinator did not consult with local deaf leaders; consequently, their lack of support, advocacy, or presence undoubtedly contributed to poor attendance. In at least one case, the meeting was unknowingly scheduled in conflict with a Deaf community wedding—something that could have been avoided if the leader(s) had been invited to assist or participate in the planning and implementation of the workshop in the first place.

Third, the subject of mental health itself continues to be a source of discomfort and stigma among the Deaf community. Given the central importance of both positive and negative gossip in the Deaf community (Higgins, 1987), the desire of deaf people to build and enhance a nonpathological "image" of Deaf culture (Dolnick, 1993), negative experiences related to misguided or inappropriate mental health services (Lane, 1992; Paul & Jackson, 1993) and lack of understanding of preventive and palliative mental health services, resistance to mental health intervention at any level remains high.

During this time, the DMH also had an office of specialists coordinating services to refugees, another underserved population. Because of its relative proximity to the Pacific Islands and the Asian mainland, Washington state has had a signifiant Asian population, many of whom were refugees from the war in Vietnam and subsequent political danger zones. While sharing concerns with these specialists about lack of attendance of deaf consumers at the mental health education workshops, the MH Coordinator discovered that they were experiencing similar problems providing outreach to their minority populations and had discovered that working closely with their leaders—in this case, Buddhist monks—was a particularly effective way of communicating about mental health services to the Asian refugee population (see also Brown, 1987). Because Asian people and deaf people share similar characteristics of not wishing to be identified with mental illness and of tending to approach the "elders" or leaders of their communities with what would be described as mental health problems, the MH Coordinator developed the proposed model for improving rapprochement between mental health service providers and deaf consumers/clients.

DEAF COMMUNITY CULTURE BROKER MODEL
FOR MENTAL HEALTH SERVICE DELIVERY

Given the assumption that the mental health program and service culture is significantly different from the Deaf community culture (and specifically the Deaf culture, comprised of about 2 million people; Higgins, 1980; Schroedel, 1984; Padden & Humphries, 1988), it follows that some cross-cultural process is needed to facilitate access of existing services to this population. It would appear that a cost-effective method for providing such access would be to identify key people in the Deaf community who are also educated about the hearing community and its resources; these people can then be trained in specific skills (e.g., listening/screening, problem solving, advocacy) that they could translate into increased interaction between cultural systems. Ideally, deaf people who have attended college and/or obtained graduate degrees in mental health fields appear to make prime deaf culture broker candidates, because of their presumably positive reputation and credibility as respected members of the Deaf community and because of their knowledge of the mental health system and access to resources in the hearing community. Other members of the Deaf community who, because of their ability to use both sign language and the spoken English language, their pursuit of careers in mainstream work settings, or their otherwise fortuitious contacts in the larger hearing community, and/or who have ended up in leadership capacities within the Deaf community, would also make excellent candidates for this role.

It is important to point out that "obvious" leaders, such as presidents of Deaf clubs or mental health professionals assigned the task of providing services to deaf people are not always the best candidates. Frequently these leaders are selected/elected for "utilitarian" reasons such as ease of communication be-tween deaf and hearing worlds and not necessarily because they are accepted representatives of the local Deaf community or Deaf culture (Higgins, 1980). Leaders sought as candidates for the culture broker role can be identified by a "key informant" approach (Warheit, Bell, & Schwab, 1970)—those who are named by most members of the Deaf community as the person(s) most likely to be approached for help with mental health problems, because of their perceived empathy and wisdom. These people can range from being the volunteer bartender at the local Deaf club, to the aforementioned elderly couple who provide temporary shelter to runaway teenagers and upset or abused spouses, to the well-liked and respected deaf alcoholism counselor (Cowen, 1982; Froland, Pancoast, Chapman, & Kimboko, 1981). It is also important that the person be deaf, both to provide a model for interaction and communi-cation to the prospective mental health service provider and to demonstrate the abilities of deaf people to act as informed consumers on their own behalf.

Functions served by deaf community culture brokers could include, but not be limited to, the following:

- help identify or screen potential mental health problem situations needing professional help,
- serve as consultant or advisor to the local mental health program and service providers,
- guide and facilitate access of potential deaf clients to mental health system resources when needed,
- serve as "translator" between deaf client(s) and mental health professional(s) in terms of understanding cultural differences in perspectives or experiences (not to be confused with sign language interpreter services), and
- act as advocate on behalf of deaf clients experiencing difficulty obtaining access to needed services or treatment.

These functions can be identified from the following suggested flow chart (see Fig. 9.1). For example, identifying/screening functions most likely would occur during the "intake" and "assessment" phase of a DCCB's contact with individuals from the Deaf community; the guiding/facilitating functions would most likely occur at the "referral" phase; the translating and advocacy activities would most likely occur as mental health resources are being utilized, and the consultation/problem solving functions would most likely occur during this phase as well at other times, when providers may have specific questions or issues. After the DCCBs have been oriented and trained, ongoing contacts between the MH Coordinator's office and the DCCBs would probably most frequently occur when they have made referrals to the agencies where service is requested on behalf of deaf client(s). At that point, the MH Coordinator can reinforce the training and consultation activities with the agencies involved. Also noteworthy about the flow chart in Fig. 9.1 is that inherent within each question/decision point is the potential for evaluation research to determine effectiveness of the role and function of DCCBs as well as of the process itself.

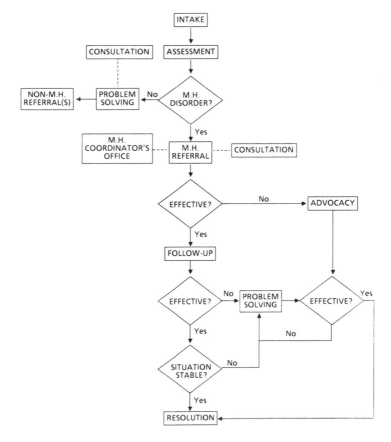

FIG. 9.1. Flow chart depicting key activities of deaf community culture brokers.

PROPOSED CURRICULUM MODULES FOR DCCB TRAINING

Intake and Assessment Skills

Deaf community leaders approached by friends or relatives with what can be identified as mental health problems sometimes feel that these problems are beyond their scope. As a result they may feel helpless and frustrated. One way of increasing effectivness of those leaders in dealing with these situations is to teach active listening skills as well as some tools for initial "screening" of the problem to ascertain the need for more professional assistance. Table 9.1 suggests some subtopic areas that could be reviewed with DCCBs, such as active listening skills for empathy (Hackney & Cormier, 1987) and the importance of

Table 9.1

Outline of Intake, Assessment, Referral, and Follow-up Skills Training
for Deaf Community Culture Brokers.

INTAKE

    A. Active Listening Skills

        1. Attention

        2. Reflection

            a. Cognitive Reflection

            b. Affective Reflection

            c. Cognitive–Affective Reflection

        3. Confirmation: Accurate Empathy

    B. Assuring and Protecting Confidentiality

        1. Scope and Limits

ASSESSMENT

        a. Warning Signs of mental Illness

        b. Problem-Solving Strategies

        c. Use of Consultation

REFERRAL

    A. Understanding the Mental Health System

        1. Public vs. Private

        2. Profit vs. Nonprofit

        3. Mental Health Assessment

        4. Mental Health Professionals

        5. Mental Health Intervention, etc.

    B. Relationship and Rapport Building

        1. Negotiation

        2. Mediation

        3. Conciliation

        4. Arbitration

FOLLOW-UP

    A. Evaluation

        1. Effectiveness: Is intervention appropriate/working/satisfactory?

        2. Adequacy: Is intervention enough?

        3. Efficiency: Is intervention timely/too costly?

    B. Advocacy Revisited

confidentiality. The latter is an especially significant consideration because of
the cohesiveness of the Deaf community (e.g., Baker & Cokely, 1980) . The
DCCB will be in a position to credibly explain the distinction between getting
help from friends and confidential mental health therapy. By acting as role
model for this distinction, the DCCB can facilitate a translation of the issue of
confidentiality between mental health service providers and the Deaf community. Examples of outcomes of this kind of facilitation resulted in a mental health
agency providing visually separate entry and exit doors so deaf clients would
not see each other in passing; in another agency, appointments were scheduled
so as to minimize the chance of deaf clients passing each other during entry and
exit. With respect to assessment of presenting problem(s), DCCBs can be taught
to recognize the typical indicators of mental illness (see Table 9.2).

It will also be helpful to teach problem-solving strategies (Christie & Maraviglia, 1978) and effective ways to use consultation (with the MH Coordinator
and/or mental health service providers in local agencies), in order to prepare
the way for possible referral(s) (Long, High, & Shaw, 1989).

Referral

To make appropriate referrals—that is, to steer deaf individuals to appropriate
possible resources—DCCBs need some information about different facets of
the mental health system, such as type of agency, varieties of staff, and typical
assessment/treatment procedures. With this information, DCCBs can then
develop relationships with key providers in the local agencies and help explain
or translate the system to the prospective client, who may otherwise be reluctant
to find out for oneself. Conversely, the DCCB can help prospective client(s)
translate mental health problems in the context of the Deaf community culture,
so that the provider can conduct more accurate assessments and formulate
more effective or appropriate interventions. An illustration of a framework that
can be used by DCCBs to provide this kind of translation can be found in the
work of Harvey (1985), who distinguished between the paradigms, or "lenses,"
of family therapy and deafness.

Often mental health service delivery to deaf people is hampered by discrep-
ant financial and political priorities; consequently, DCCBs need to be prepared
to advocate on behalf of prospective clients and community mental health
needs. Advocacy skills include the ability to negotiate, mediate, conciliate, and
arbitrate (see Fig. 9.2), depending on the situation (Nierenberg, 1973; Zartman
& Berman, 1982). To illustrate, if a DCCB wants to establish a working
relationship with a particular mental health provider/agency because of perceived benefits for Deaf community clientele, he or she may try to negotiate a
reciprocity of favors. Perhaps the DCCB will offer a free workshop about deaf
awareness (e.g., Sheetz, 1993) for agency personnel in exchange for agency
personnel attending a Deaf club meeting and explaining about agency services
(see Fig. 9.2, Situation A, Direct Participant in Negotiation). DCCBs often find
themselves in the role of mediator, as when trying to help patch up things
between fighting spouses (see Fig. 9.2, Situation B, Mediator); in such cases,

Table 9.2
Ten Warning Signs of Mental Illness*

 1. Gradual, marked personality change
 2. Confused thinking, strange or grandiose ideas
 3. Prolonged severe depression, flat emotions, or extreme highs and lows
 4. Excessive anxieties, fears, or suspiciousness
 5. Withdrawal from others, friendliness
 6. Abnormal self-centeredness
 7. Thinking or talking about suicide
 8. Numerous, unexplained physical ailments, sleeplessness, or loss of appetite
 9. Anger, hostility—range or violent behavior
10. Growing inability to cope with problems and daily activities such as school, job, or personal needs

*Philadelphia Psychiatric Center (now the Belmont Comprehensive Treatment Center), Philadelphia, PA. From a brochure distributed to incoming clients.

having active listening and clarification skills as well as ready suggestions for marriage counseling resources will be helpful for the DCCB. In still other cases, a DCCB may try to persuade a deaf person to seek alcoholism treatment services and will be working both with prospective treatment provider and prospective client and/or client's family. In these situations, the DCCB acts in the role of conciliator, who can—in contrast to the mediator who acts strictly as facilitator—exercise persuasion or influence on the parties involved (see Fig. 9.2, Situation C, Conciliator). Finally, there may be cases in which a DCCB may be asked to serve temporarily as a legal guardian or guardian ad litem to a runaway deaf teenager, for instance, in order to ease family tension or until mental health resources take effect (see Fig 9.2, Situation D, Arbitrator). In these cases, authority and decision-making powers are vested in the DCCB to protect the welfare of the client during that time.

POTENTIAL ISSUES AND CLINICIAN INVOLVEMENT

Mental health therapists who work with deaf clientele invariably find themselves in a variety of roles, including not only clinician but also case manager, advocate, community planner, and politician. On the one hand, if DCCBs could be trained to take over more of these nonclinical functions, then mental health providers could maintain a clearer and less complicated role therapeutically with deaf clients. By educating and training DCCBs in some aspects of screening and intake (including active listening and rudimentary counseling skills), clinicians would be able to focus more directly on therapeutic issues rather than having to take the extra time involved in didactic aspects of counseling (e.g., teaching deaf people how to be "clients"). On the other hand, DCCBs—particularly those who are especially adept at empathic and problem-solving functions—could be perceived as a threat to the viability of psychotherapy with deaf clients, who may not bother to come in for more extended "talking therapy" once their more immediate problems have been resolved.

Mental health service agencies may have difficulty incorporating and collaborating with DCCBs for a number of reasons. As is the case with many cross-cultural endeavors in mental health service provision, there is a period of time in which DCCBs need to help break down initial resistance to working with the deaf population through significant advocacy, education, and training efforts. And as providers become more aware of the specific needs of the Deaf community clientele, they also become aware of the demands for additional resources (e.g., sign language interpreters, specialized equipment, inservice training, hiring of deaf professionals); in turn, administrators will need to incorporate these resource needs into budget planning and administration. At a time of major cutbacks in mental health care spending (e.g., the current health care reform debates), programs and agencies may be reluctant to engage in partnerships with DCCBs because of these relatively labor-intensive implications. In these cases, clinicians can be allied with DCCBs in advocacy efforts and through the DCCBs have access to experts in deafness issues, in order to be more informed in their own advocacy efforts within the agency.

Conversely, DCCBs themselves may be caught in a number of cross-cultural dilemmas. As members of the Deaf community, with its predominantly negative attitudes toward mental health systems, DCCBs risk alienation from their own communities by attempting to advocate mental health education and the use of mental health services. If DCCBs become involved in mental health situations of Deaf community members and help them connect with mental health services, they become bound by the expectations of the mental health service providers for maintaining confidentiality and subscribing to professional mental health codes of ethics. To illustrate, when a deaf person receives a phone call in a Deaf club, he or she is generally expected to explain who called and what the call was about to those in the same room. If a DCCB happens to receive a call from a mental health provider requesting help with a deaf client in that

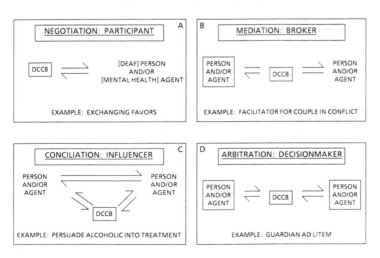

FIG. 9.2. Types of bargaining for advocacy work by
deaf community culture brokers (DCCBs).

same situation, he or she is bound not to discuss that conversation; therefore, the DCCB is caught between the mental health culture of confidentiality and the Deaf culture of sharing information about an intruding phone call. In these instances, DCCBs would benefit from the expertise of clinicians in teaching about the mental health culture, and both would benefit from the process of negotiating ethical guidelines that would be acceptable to both cultures.

CONCLUDING REMARKS

The proposed DCCB model was intended as a cost-effective means of using community people and resources to improve existing mental health service resources by making them more accessible and effective for deaf mental health clientele. Notwithstanding the need to demonstrate the cost effectiveness of this concept, however, the DCCB role can still serve a number of important purposes. Though conceptualized as an opportunity for key members of the Deaf community to volunteer for community service in specifically utile ways, the skills required can increase the employment potential of such volunteers for paid positions with similar functions, such as case manager for deaf clients within the involved local mental health agency. Furthermore, when more deaf people graduate with mental health degrees and expertise in deafness, then these DCCBs can work closely, perhaps in a paraprofessional capacity, with these professional experts in mental health. Hopefully, of course, some DCCBs may be inspired to pursue further formal mental health education and training themselves and be hired by those agencies to provide a broader spectrum of fully accessible mental health services to deaf clients.

REFERENCES

Baker, C., & Cokely, D. (1980). *ASL: A teacher's resource text on grammar and culture*. Silver Spring, MD: T. J. Publishers.

Brown, F. (1987). Counseling Vietnamese refugees: The new challenge. *International Journal for the Advancement of Counseling, 10*, 259–268.

Christie, C., & Maraviglia, F. (1978). *Creative problem-solving: Think book*. Buffalo, NY: D. O. K. Publishers.

Cowen, E. (1982). Help is where you find it. *American Psychologist, 37*(4), 385–395.

Dolnick, E. (1993, September). Deafness as a culture. *Atlantic Monthly*, pp. 37–53.

Eng, E., & Young, R. (1992). Lay health advisors as community change agents. *Family Community Health, 15*(1), 24–40.

Froland, C., Pancoast, D., Chapman, N., & Kimboko, P. (1981). *Helping networks and human services*. Beverly Hills, CA: Sage.

Glickman, N. (1986). Cultural identity and deafness and mental health. *Journal of Rehabilitaiton of the Deaf, 20*, 1–10.

Hackney, H., & Cormier, L. (1987). *Counseling strategies and objectives (2nd. ed.)*. Englewood, NJ: Prentice-Hall.

Harvey, M. (1985, October). Toward a dialogue between the paradigms of family therapy and deafness. *American Annals of the Deaf*, 305–314.

Heyman, S., & VandenBos, G. (1989). Developing local resources to enrich the practice of rural community psychology. *Hospital and Community Psychiatry, 40*(1), 21–23.

Higgins, P. (1980). *Outsiders in a hearing world*. Beverly Hills, CA: Sage.

Higgins, P. (1987). The deaf community. In P. Higgins & J. Nash (Eds.), *Understanding deafness socially* (pp. 151–170). Springfield, IL: Thomas.

Higgins, P., & Nash, J. (1987). *Understanding deafness socially*. Springfield, IL: Thomas.

Lane, H. (1990). Cultural and infirmity models of deaf Americans. *Journal of the American Rehabilitation Association, 23*, 11–26.

Lane, H. (1992). *The mask of benevolence*. New York: Knopf.

Lefley, H., & Bestman, E. (1991). Public-academic linkages for culturally-sensitive community mental health. *Community Mental Health Journal, 27*(6), 473–488.

Long, G., High, C., & Shaw, J. (1989). *Directory of mental health services for deaf persons*. Little Rock, AR: American Deafness and Rehabilitation Association.

Munch, A., & Mulligan, R. (1991). Responding to the deaf community. *Journal of Leisurability, 18*(1), 19–24.

Nierenberg, G. (1973). *Fundamentals of negotiating*. New York: Hawthorn.

Padden, C., & Humphries, T. (1988). *Deaf in America*. Cambridge, MA: Harvard University Press.

Paul, P., & Jackson, D. (1993). *Toward a psychology of deafness*. Cambridge, MA: Allyn & Bacon.

Philadelphia Psychiatric Center. *Ten warning signs of mental illness*. Philadelphia: Author.

Rosado, J., & Elias, M. (1993). Ecological and psychocultural mediators in the delivery of services for urban, culturally diverse Hispanic clients. *Professional Psychology: Research and Practice, 24*(4), 450–459.

Scheetz, N. (1993). *Orientation to deafness*. Cambridge, MA: Allyn & Bacon.

Schroedel, J. (1984). Analyzing surveys on deaf adults: Implications for survey research on persons with disabilities. *Social Science Medicine, 19*, 619–627.

Schwab, B., Drake, R., & Burghardt, E. (1988). Health care of the chronically mentally ill: The culture broker model. *Community Mental Health Journal, 24*(3), 174–184.

Warheit, G., Bell, R., Schwab, J. (1970). *Planning for change: Needs assessment approaches*. Bethesda, MD: National Institute of Mental Health.

Wax, T. (1985). *MHCO progress report*. Olympia, WA: DMH/Seattle Hearing, Speech and Deafness Center.

Wax, T. (1990). Deaf community leaders as liaisons between mental health and deaf cultures. *Journal of American Deafness and Rehabilitation Association, 24*, 33–40.

Zartman, I., & Berman, M. (1982). *Practical negotiator*. New Haven, CT: Yale University Press.

Chapter 10

Deaf Therapists, Deaf Clients, and The Therapeutic Relationship

Linda Risser Lytle
Washington, DC

Jeffrey W. Lewis
Gallaudet University

In this chapter, the authors focus your attention to the therapeutic alliance and how it is played out between the therapist and the deaf client. The relationship between therapist and client has been defined and examined by various theorists and researchers and there is now an extensive body of knowledge on the topic. There is very little written, however, about the therapeutic relationship when one or both members are deaf. In this chapter, we will take a brief look at the general body of knowledge about the therapeutic relationship and examine implications pertinent when the client or the therapist is deaf. We will also consider communication issues, the hearing status of the therapist, cultural responsiveness to the deaf community, and the impact of parental hearing status as these pertain to psychotherapy with deaf persons.

The therapeutic alliance is seen as an important and essential part of the therapy process by theorists and practitioners from various backgrounds. Some therapists believe that the relationship between client and therapist is the essence of effective treatment, whereas others give this relationship considerably less prominence. However, regardless of orientation, therapists agree that it is an important variable in treatment (Gelso & Carter, 1994).

The alliance is defined as the patient's collaboration in the tasks of psycho-therapy (Frieswyk, Colson, & Allen, 1984). Freud (1913) dealt with this topic early in his career, when he addressed the benefits of a positive transference process in aiding the therapeutic work. Later in his writings he appeared to acknowledge the existence of a real relationship between therapist and client, quite apart from the transference, that also allowed the work of therapy to occur (Freud, 1958). One way we conceive of the therapeutic relationship is to imagine a small glass ball, the kind where snow falls if the ball is held upside down for a few seconds. Depending on which side of the ball we are looking through, we see different things; our perceptions of this universe change. For there are towns and people and even dreams in our glass ball, where sometimes the universe snows and sometimes it is calmly still. So it is with the therapeutic relationship, which is seen differently by client and therapist and which some-times bears a very close resemblance to a blinding blizzard, other times proceeds at an orderly pace, and sometimes seems to move not at all.

Rogers (1951, 1957) addressed issues of the therapeutic relationship from a client-centered orientation and a great deal of research was generated as a result of his work. A review of this research (Orlinsky & Howard, 1986) suggests that it is the client's perception of the therapist as an empathetic individual which makes the difference in therapy outcome. Social influence theory carries this one step further and hypothesizes that the therapeutic alliance is enhanced when the client perceives the therapist as expert, trustworthy, and attractive (Cartwright, 1965; Hovland, Janis, & Kelley, 1953). Later in this writing, we will examine how researchers in deafness and mental health interpret the relevance of these findings to psychotherapy with deaf persons.

Luborsky (1976) and LaCrosse (1980) postulated that the initial alliance between therapist and clients depends on whether the therapist is perceived as helpful, caring, sensitive and sympathetic and that the client's past experiences in similar relationships plays a part in the perception. This raises the question of how deaf clients perceive empathy and, if this perception is colored by their past experiences with deaf and hearing people, how is this played out in the therapy process? It also raises the question of how we as therapists can enhance this process for our deaf clients so that appropriate issues within the relationship are addressed, and the relationship is ultimately strengthened. Growing up deaf and becoming deaf later in life are both experiences that lead to different perceptions of deaf and hearing people. Other variables specific to deaf people that may impact on psychotherapy include whether parents are deaf or hearing, the type(s) of school attended, communication mode used and when it was learned, and one's attitude towards one's deafness. All of these variables may also influence how deaf clients see their therapist.

THE THERAPEUTIC ALLIANCE

Clients walk into the therapist's office in various ways. Some stride in confi-dently, take a seat, and proceed to talk about their most pressing issues. Others seem to slink in, quietly, primly sit down and seem to be waiting for an invitation to begin. Of course, there are lots of variations in between as well. Although perhaps less noticeable, there are an equally great number of ways in which therapists begin sessions and how both client and therapist react to the others' appearance and behavior (both verbal and nonverbal). Thus begins the therapeutic alliance.

Deaf clients most often enter therapy with only a sketchy idea of what the therapist will be like and of what the client's own role will be in the treatment process (Lewis, 1987). When encountering a therapist for the first time, one's life experiences, including one's stage of cultural identity development, influence initial impressions of the therapist (Harvey, 1993). Feelings and expectations based on past experiences and now superimposed upon the therapist are called transference. For a deaf client, a considerable portion of the transference will be related to his/her particular worldview of being deaf.

Just as deaf clients bring their past perceptions of the world and the people in it, so do therapists bring their past experiences and perceptions, including their own deafness or hearingness and their experiences with deaf and hearing people. We believe that therapists can maximize the base of similarities and differences between themselves and their clients in the therapy work. Therapists who have similar experiences as their clients (for example, when both are deaf, or have divorced parents, or lost parents when they were young) share similar frames of reference, social symbolism, and may have a common basis for understanding, responding to, and caring about issues raised by their clients (Winter & Aponte, 1987). This increases therapists' ability to empathize and join with clients. It can create an immediate attraction and bond. Therapists need to be aware that conversely, sameness can lead to an overidentification that induces blindness and reinforces mutually shared, perhaps unhelpful, patterns that can lead to stagnation and even acting out. As with many countertransference issues, therapist overidentification with patients or patient issues may occur, specific or not specific to hearing loss.

Differences between therapists and clients, on the other hand, can create distance that allows for a dialectic of differences that can be most useful (Winter & Aponte, 1987). Therapists may be able to find ways to connect with clients' differences in a manner that results in clients feeling understood and accepted as well as providing opportunities for new insights and motivation to change. One deaf person we know was told by her therapist (a hearing, nonsigner) that it was not until she saw a group of deaf people casually talking at the airport that she realized on a profound level that she was missing a tremendously vital and important part of her client. The deaf person on hearing that felt immediately engaged and connected with her therapist on a level she had not experienced before. Much significant work was accomplished through this simple, but profound, shared experience. The differences between client and therapist and their joint struggle to communicate and to understand these differences forged a bond for them. Of course, differences do not always support such growth. Therapist–client differences can also result in a lack of understanding and basis for connecting between them. Therapists who do not challenge themselves to explore unknown territories are particularly vulnerable.

We are two deaf psychologists with vastly different backgrounds. As we wrote this chapter together, we discussed similarities and differences in our viewpoints. We realized how differently clients perceived us and how differently we reacted to our deaf clients. Our own counter-transference issues (that is, our personal biases aside from our professional objectivity) had much in common and also much which was uniquely ours. We would like to share this with you in the hope that our experiences as deaf psychologists and our circumspection as human beings may illuminate aspects of your work with deaf individuals.

Our orientation as therapists is principally psychodynamic, although we have also been influenced by humanistic and existential views of humankind. Our experience is primarily with deaf and hard-of-hearing adolescents and adults. Views and issues appearing here are particularly salient and of interest to us, as two deaf therapists, reflecting who we are and where we are at this point in our professional development.

BASIC ISSUES RELATING
TO THE THERAPEUTIC RELATIONSHIP

Four basic issues relevant to deafness and the therapeutic relationship are discussed: (a) communication, (b) hearing status of the therapist, (c) client and therapist cultural responsiveness to the Deaf community and, (d) impact of parental hearing status. Case material is presented in discussion of each issue, and transference and countertransference issues are elaborated on.

Communication Issues

We take the general position that therapists regardless of hearing status can do effective therapeutic work with deaf people if effective communication is present and the therapists are informed and sensitive to variations in the deaf experience. We feel it is important to give the utmost consideration to clients' feelings about communication between themselves and their therapists. This is true regardless of the hearing status of the therapists; however, these communication issues become most apparent when the therapists are hearing, as we see later. We consider the utilization of a sign language interpreter in the therapy session when the therapists do not know how to sign a completely different scenario which in no way can be considered equivalent to therapists communicating for themselves. While this issue deserves much more attention, our present focus is on direct communication between clients and therapists.

Discussion of communication issues seems best conveyed through case vignettes. The first one addresses deaf clients who use communication issues as a defense against the therapeutic alliance. A hearing therapist we know was trying to work through an impasse with her deaf client and was accused of not signing well enough. The client said that the therapist's signing skills discouraged her from wanting to express herself in the session and she felt that the therapist was not qualified to work with deaf people. This therapist met with two deaf therapists following the session to discuss their perceptions of her communication skills. She was told that she signed quite well and that it was felt that her communication skills might not be a valid reason to accept the client's resistance. Buoyed by this feedback, the therapist told her client that she had discussed her signing skills with the two deaf professionals and that their feedback fit with her own perception of herself, and that perhaps the two of them needed to explore further why the client did not feel comfortable with her therapist.

In this situation, the client devalued her therapist through criticism of her sign language skills. The therapist was able to deal with this criticism by checking its reality base with her deaf colleagues, who both supported and validated her. She was then able to help her client to realize what was occurring and to point out that this kind of resistance is a very easy way to keep someone at a distance. Therapy was able to continue productively.

Another situation where resistance toward a hearing professional surfaced included a deaf family working with a hearing, nonsigning family therapist and a sign language interpreter. After four sessions, the family expressed their desire to work with a deaf psychologist employed at the school and threatened to refuse to attend further sessions with their present therapist. It was decided that the deaf psychologist would join the next session to evaluate the communication process and to consult with the hearing therapist. During the session, the deaf therapist was able to see that the family's resistance was more related to uncovering sensitive material than to the hearing therapist, who was herself a very sensitive, perceptive, and caring individual. Both therapists worked in unison to confront the family on this issue and agreed that the family needed to work through their transference issues.

What is important to note here is that in both situations, deaf and hearing professionals worked together on therapeutic issues with deaf clients that involved the primary therapist's *hearingness*. This term hearingness is the counterpart of *deafness* and reflects not only hearing ability but also one's attitudes, beliefs, and values about Deaf culture. Deep mutual respect and support between deaf and hearing therapists is a model that we strongly support. As therapists we should probably strive for personal biculturality between Deaf and hearing worlds. Collaboration with Deaf professionals by their hearing peers when dealing with questions about the impact of their hearingness on the therapeutic relationship with deaf clients is surely one way in which we can stretch our knowledge of our clients' world and become more bicultural.

The interpersonal byplay between therapist and client is like an external map of what is going on inside the patient. This can be viewed as a microcosm of deaf–hearing encounters in that client's life. Clients' dealings with their therapists have meaning on many levels. This is illustrated in the next vignette when a deaf therapist was asked by a nonsigning hearing mother to meet with her to discuss her deaf son. With the son's permission, the therapist met alone with the mother for three sessions. The mother, although she could not sign, asked to see the therapist without a sign language interpreter and it was agreed that they would try it. In the first session, the mother spoke very fast and it was extremely difficult for the therapist to follow her. No matter how often the therapist asked her to slow down, she would pick up the pace and speak too quickly for him. It was as if she did not want him to understand her. When the mother was confronted with the fact that she was hard to understand, she tried to deny that and credited the therapist with fantastic lipreading abilities. She proved to be very resistant to exploring what was going on in the session. The therapist considered using an interpreter, however, he felt it would be more meaningful to struggle without one, to re-enact the microcosm of the deaf son's struggle with the mother. In the second session, the therapist shared his frustrations once again with the mother and finally she broke down and while sobbing, said that she hated the idea of her son being deaf. She wanted to believe that the therapist refused to play along, rather than that he, like her son, could not hear her. This work was a step toward helping her to accept her son and paved the way for both son and mother to work on other issues. The remainder of the time in that session and the following one were more meaningful and focused on the exploration of her grief about her son's deafness and acceptance of it. It was by utilization of this byplay between the therapist and the mother that allowed the therapist to arrive at the core issue.

In the previous vignettes, we dealt with the most apparent communication problems, that is a discrepancy between the hearing status of client and therapist. It is important to note that these communication issues do not disappear when both client and therapist are deaf. The deaf therapist needs to be particularly astute in order to pick up some of the more subtle issues that surface.

A college student peer advisor, on finding out her trainer was deaf, was elated, "Oh, great! We're all deaf. There will be no communication problems." She totally ignored the fact that all of the group members did not have equal sign language skills. Although delighted to be so easily accepted and included, the therapist/trainer and other group members were also under considerable pressure. Any asking for clarification or not understanding something would be judged as lacking, as not "deaf" enough for this peer advisor. During her training, she was helped to look beyond the obvious and to see individuals with all their strengths and weaknesses.

Another example is the typical response from an American Sign Language (ASL) user when recommended for group therapy, which is, "I don't think that the other group members will sign as well as I do, so I am not interested." We as therapists need to accept such comments as normal resistance and anxiety about beginning something new and scary. Communication is a real issue, but we also need to take the client past the obvious: yes, other group members might not sign as well as you. What else are you scared/worried about? These are very basic issues of acceptance, fear of rejection, and being judged by others. Communication is sometimes only the tip of the iceberg, and we will be missing a lot if we do not examine beyond it. We as therapists need to be secure enough in our knowledge of our skills in communicating, so that we can explore deeper issues.

Hearing Status of the Therapist

Although overlapping considerably with communication issues there are also some special points to be considered in the hearing status of the therapist. Social influence theory postulates that clients tend to be attracted to therapists of the same gender, culture, and ethnic origin (Corrigan, Dell, Lewis, & Schmidt,

1980). Thus, we would assume that deaf clients would be naturally attracted to deaf therapists. This is borne out in the results of Lewis' research (1987) on deaf female college students' preferences for and perceptions of counselor–client relationships that showed an overwhelming, statistically significant number of students preferred to work with therapists of the same gender and same hearing status (in this case, a deaf female therapist). However, this should not be construed as a statement to the effect that male or hearing therapists are not appropriate for this population. These students, when viewing a simulated counseling session, rated the same counselor significantly higher when told that the counselor was deaf than when they were told the counselor was hearing. However, the ratings of the "hearing" counselor were also favorable because the counselor could communicate effectively with her client (in this case, in sign language). Thus, we postulate that deaf and hearing therapists are in good position to do effective therapy with deaf clients, assuming that effective two-way communication is occurring and the client feels understood by a competent and caring therapist.

A therapist's hearing status impacts on the relationship in many ways and is rarely, if ever, of no significance to what happens over the course of treatment. A deaf client with a hearing therapist constitutes cross-cultural counseling (Glickman, 1986) and a deaf client with a deaf therapist also raises issues stemming from either assumptions or actual cultural differences. Deaf clients often enter therapy dealing (either consciously or unconsciously) with issues of identity. They need to know in which world they fit—deaf or hearing—and how much of both worlds they want to own. Likewise, deaf clients need to know where their therapist fits culturally, and if this is not made obvious by direct communication and behavior, it will certainly be one of the first strokes brushed in on the therapist's tabula rasa. Assumptions will most certainly be made about cultural belongingness of both client and therapist, and in learning about these assumptions, much rich therapeutic work occurs.

Some clients are able to directly voice their preferences for a deaf or a hearing therapist. Unlike the clear preference for a deaf client that our research suggests, our own experiences teach us that expectations and preferences are complex.

Client Issues When Therapist is Deaf

Positive reactions to having a deaf therapist are generally straightforward. There is happiness and relief that communication will presumably not become a problem and that, again presumably, their deafness will be seen as a cultural and linguistic variable instead of as a loss. It is important to remember that these initial feelings are based on assumptions. The therapist is a recipient of a positive transference. It remains to be seen as the therapy unfolds which other issues are beneath the transference and if the therapist will be able to meet those initial positive assumptions.

Negative reactions to discovering one's therapist is deaf are more varied. A deaf college student came to his first therapy session and learned that the therapist was deaf. The initial reaction of the client was astonishment and doubt that another deaf person could help him. Subsequent analysis of this perception showed that the client felt that deaf people were inferior to hearing people, and that because of this inferiority, only hearing therapists were qualified to work with deaf clients. The client agreed to continue with the deaf therapist on a trial basis and immediately plunged into valuable and insightful work. In this therapist's own supervision session, countertransference issues related to anger brought on by the client's perception of the inferiority of deaf professionals was addressed.

Sometimes clinical issues reflect and influence feelings about one's therapist's hearing status. Clients with histories of familial abuse are in great pain, and their experiences of abuse are colored by such issues as: Was the abuser deaf or hearing? Have they told others of this abuse, and if so, what were their reactions? Were their confidants deaf or hearing? The answers to all these questions help to build the transference in the therapy relationship. One young man from a deaf family was both an incest victim and had experienced sexual molestation by a family friend. There was, as is typical in families where physical and sexual abuse occur, a very closed and secretive family structure. Confidentiality became a big issue. As he began talking about his family, his sense of betrayal became quite intense. He began to be increasingly angry at his therapist, becoming intensely critical of her sign language and accusing her of not understanding his ASL. It gradually became apparent that this young man had put his therapist into a hearing category so that he could talk more freely to her. As a deaf person, she was too big a part of his community. As a hearing person, she was more distant, and his feelings of betrayal and disloyalty no longer interfered with his ability to open himself up in therapy. Once this interpretation was made to him, issues more central to the actual sexual molestation were expressed. The therapist's knowledge of Deaf culture, particularly the tendency to see all Deaf people as a kind of extended family, helped her to realize the issues of conflict and family betrayal and to make a helpful interpretation.

Individuals who begin therapy shortly after learning sign language are frequently seen as most confused with their identity and are still culturally marginal (Glickman, 1986). This confusion surfaces in interesting ways when the therapist is deaf. A young woman requested a hearing therapist during the intake process, but was assigned to a deaf therapist. During intake, the client explained that her request for a hearing therapist was based on her not yet feeling comfortable with signs. She explained she liked to drop her signs while talking. Early in the course of therapy, the client discovered that her therapist was deaf but appeared unconcerned about this revelation. The therapist inquired as to how she felt about being assigned to a deaf therapist. The client replied that because the therapist could talk, she met her definition of a hearing person, and thus this was no problem for her. This initial work paved the way for discussions of the client's feeling about her own deafness.

A positive therapeutic relationship with a deaf therapist makes it much more likely that an individual new to sign language will continue on that course towards a culturally Deaf identity. However, our experience is that a negative or weak therapeutic alliance with a deaf therapist results in not only a premature termination of therapy, but also an increased likelihood of the individual not continuing identity explorations and retreating to their old position of identification with the hearing culture. The cognitive dissonance created by the circumstance of having a deaf therapist while they themselves are not comfortable with a Deaf identity is so great that flight and premature termination become a viable course toward easing that inner conflict. Perhaps there are deaf therapists who can successfully navigate those waters, however, our experience tells us that we may not be the best therapists for such individuals unless the therapeutic alliance feels positive from the very beginning, as it was in the recent example.

Late-deafened individuals present a similar dilemma. Late-deafened individuals themselves are frequently outspoken in their opposition to seeing deaf therapists. Almost equally strong is the message from many friends that a deaf therapist would be "good for you." After repeatedly falling into that well-meant trap ourselves, we are inclined to trust and believe the clients' initial feelings, that they are truly not ready to be so strongly confronted with their own or their therapists' deafness. A recently deafened client was referred to a deaf therapist. In the initial session, the client expressed great reluctance to working with this therapist because of the therapist's deafness and requested an immediate transfer to another therapist. The client was not willing to explore the underlying issues and proved to be very resistant throughout the session. It was decided that it was in the client's best interest to transfer him to a hearing therapist, and his therapy continued for 1-1/2 years. The new therapist reported that the encounter with the deaf therapist provided much material for exploration, including discussion of his feelings about his deafness.

What we believe happened here was that the client needed space to feel free enough to explore his dark side, that is, all his negative, angry, hostile feelings about his becoming deaf and that he simply could not, at that stage of his life, do that with a deaf therapist. However, there is no question that the brief encounter with the deaf therapist was enormously therapeutic. To insist that the client continue with the deaf therapist would not only most likely have resulted in his dropping out of treatment but may also have been therapeutically harmful.

Client Issues When Therapist is Hearing

When the therapist is hearing, different issues play themselves out. Generally, when the client is culturally Deaf, there is resistance to working with a hearing therapist. Because of past negative experiences at the hands of hearing people, many deaf people have felt both angry at and hurt by hearing people. The initial transference feelings for such individuals to a hearing therapist is often negative. However, as we see from some of the previous vignettes, there are some deaf clients who prefer hearing therapists.

Two different deaf clients were initially assigned to two different hearing therapists. Both clients immediately expressed resistance to the idea of working with a nondeaf professional and asked to transfer to deaf therapists. One hearing therapist immediately confronted the issue at hand, that the deaf client was transferring onto the therapist past experiences, anger, and frustrations with hearing people. This therapist was able to engage the client in an exploration of these issues and to help the client to see that her reaction was based on previous experiences and not on what had actually happened between them in the session. The client agreed to continue to work with the therapist.

This is in contrast to the second situation, in which the client accused the therapist of not being competent to work with deaf people because the therapist was hearing. The therapist at the time was dealing with her own issues of competency in sign language and being accepted by deaf people and responded to the client by apologizing for her hearingness and acknowledged that maybe the client did have a point. The client responded by becoming almost belligerent in his approach to her, criticizing her for her perceived inadequacies, and reinforcing in her, her own sense of maybe not being good enough for deaf people. Although the client did not pursue his own request for a transfer, he did seem to gain satisfaction from his constant attacks on the therapist. Only when the therapist received feedback on her own acquiescence and encouragement from her supervisor and colleagues to confront this client with his behavior did therapy begin to occur for the client.

There are clients who idealize their therapists. Two issues need to be considered when thinking specifically about deaf clients. One is the common idealization of the therapist, which occurs among clients regardless of hearing status. This is usually resolved by encouraging such clients to talk about their feelings toward their therapists, to look for the client's withholdings, and to help them to openly express their feelings (including anger and worship) to their therapists. The second issue is of the idealization of hearing people by some deaf people and how this can be manifested in working with hearing therapists. This can be dealt with by encouraging the deaf clients to talk openly about their idealization, in reinforcing the deaf clients' self-esteem and sense of competency and in allowing deaf clients to experience therapists as human beings, also fallible. Because of commonplace feelings of inferiority shared by many deaf people, there is often much work to be done to repair their negative and harmful self-images. Because hearing people may be idealized, they can be in an ideal position to challenge both this idealization of hearing people and this negative view of deaf people.

The examples given show how much material can come up during the initial session between a deaf client and the therapist related to the therapist's hearing status. This is because hearing status and cultural identity are important themes in Deaf culture. Deaf people often interpret the meaning of interpersonal interaction on the basis of "how deaf or hearing" the participants are.

However, definitions of deaf and hearing are not always so clear cut. Hearing people who sign well are frequently accepted as deaf, whereas some deaf people have difficulty being accepted as such. For example, although both of the authors are deaf, there are important differences in how they are perceived. Lewis, who has deaf parents and has been signing since birth, is typically perceived immediately as deaf by both hearing and deaf clients. Lytle, who learned sign language when she entered college, is perceived as deaf by her hearing clients because of her speech but presents more of a dilemma for her deaf clients. Clients typically judge her to be deaf or hearing based more on how they view their own deafness and on what deafness means to them. Accordingly, she tends to use this issue of her deafness as a therapy issue, for example: "Suppose I am deaf, or suppose I am hearing, how do you feel about both?"

This leads to an often-asked question about how much exploration should be given to the issue of the client's hearing loss. The way we handle this issue with our clients is to allow them to talk about what is on their minds and to seek out the themes that arise in the sessions. We react to their presence and respond to it. Very often our clients bring up their own feelings about being deaf or hard-of-hearing, and we then encourage exploration of the issues. If we sense that their deafness contributes to their life problems or relationship problems, then we ask questions that lead clients into that area. When we encounter resistance from our clients, it becomes material for discussion and analysis. It may be a different experience for deaf therapists and hearing therapists to probe into this area. Deaf therapists, by virtue of their perceived similarity to clients in the area of hearing loss, may be in an initially better and more comfortable position to delve into their clients' experiences of being deaf, whereas hearing therapists may have some initial reluctance to be seen as intruding into this area. However, clients' feelings about their own deafness provide rich materials for therapy and transference analysis.

Cultural Responsiveness To The Deaf Community

Therapists working with this special population should learn as much as they can about deafness and the Deaf community, so they do not rely on their deaf clients to teach them about deafness. Such reliance on deaf clients takes away opportunities to use possible transference materials because therapists remain too dependent on clients' accounts of experiences, filtered through the clients' biases and vision, when it comes to the experience of being deaf or the Deaf community. What therapists see and sense in the sessions is at the heart of the matter, and it is enhanced by therapists' understanding of what is relevant and not relevant about deafness. Therapists need to help clients become aware of their own perceptions at some time in the course of therapy.

We have noticed that many of our deaf and hard-of-hearing clients talk about themselves in regards to their feelings about the Deaf community. The Deaf community plays a big role in many of their lives. If we think of the Deaf community as a map, individuals both deaf and hearing, have positions on various areas of the map, depending on their knowledge and experience with deafness, ability to communicate with other deaf people, and their own allegiances to various segments of the deaf world (i.e., sign language, oral). Deaf culture is a part of the Deaf community accessible to deaf people and perhaps a few hearing people: those whom possess skills in American Sign Language, a pro-Deaf attitude, the right social connections, and several other criteria. Clients' feelings about Deaf culture and the Deaf community and their own positions in it, as well as their therapists' positions in it, are a rich source of therapeutic material. Helping clients make the connection between their feelings about the Deaf community and about themselves can be a valuable source of insight. For example, some clients devalue the Deaf community but do not realize that they may be talking about themselves.

An example of this is a young deaf man from an oral background who was seen in a group by a deaf, female therapist and a hearing, male therapist. This client was from a very disturbed family that was able to give him little but that made enormous demands on him. For example, when he tried to tell his mother of his homosexuality, she replied that his being such would literally kill her. This young man had enormous contempt for African Americans, women, and, of course, deaf people. He transferred all of his negative feelings of self-worth onto the deaf, female therapist, while endowing the hearing, male therapist with great wisdom and knowledge. However, these negative feelings were attributed not to the therapist herself, but to the whole Deaf community, and of course, the other deaf members of the therapy group. In spite of his insults to the therapist of how deaf people have no manners, are rude, and nothing much can be expected from them, he was astounded and extremely hurt to find this deaf, female therapist did not like him. His extreme superiority and snobbery was seen as a defense, and in the group, he was gradually helped to see himself as he really was and to make some limited progress in relating with the other deaf group members.

The smallness of the Deaf community is often manifested in the therapeutic encounter, where it is not unusual for clients to devalue the therapist with information obtained from the Deaf community. With deaf therapists, the devaluing can emerge in the form of questioning the competencies of deaf professionals by using real or imaginary information gained via the Deaf community. For example, a deaf client confronted his therapist with the information that she (the therapist) was a lesbian. When asked about this, the client said that a friend in the deaf gay community had told him that his therapist was "not straight," and the client became upset. It was only by helping the client appreciate his own perception of what he was doing to the therapeutic relationship and how undermining the relationship was serving as a vehicle for his anger to the therapist that the client was able to explore the sexuality issue and not permit it to interfere with his therapy.

Through our work, we have come to respect our clients' concerns for confidentiality and trust because of the smallness of the Deaf community. We feel that their concerns are very real and do not deserve to be viewed as overly defensive but as manifestations of our clients' wise caring of themselves. Early exploration of these issues make later work much more possible. Perhaps therapists working with deaf patients need to be more thorough in discussion of confidentiality.

This brings up the question of how therapists can demonstrate cultural responsiveness. Our work and interaction with professional colleagues and our experiences in training graduate level clinicians indicates that cultural respon-siveness can be acquired from immersion in the Deaf community for a period of time that allows for ASL fluency to develop along with cultural sensitivity and acquisition of cultural rules. Cultural responsiveness is a demonstrated level of easy familiarity and comfort with themes that are salient and relevant to culturally Deaf people. It may be communicated by reflecting an understanding and acceptance of the central value of communication for deaf people both as a means of communication and as a central organizing theme of Deaf culture (Higgins, 1980; Padden & Humphries, 1988). Cultural responsiveness includes appreciating the view of deafness as a cultural difference rather than as a disability and the view of the Deaf community as "home" and hearing people as "other." It also includes an in-depth understanding of the mixed feelings that deaf people may have about other deaf people and about hearing people; feelings which may reflect a healthy state of development. It also includes appreciation of potential minefields such as issues of entitlement, which are a way of life for some deaf people. This entitled view includes the sense that society in general and schools, parents, and employers in particular owe them a living and should take care of them. Being culturally responsive certainly would permit therapists to more easily discuss this sensitive topic. This area of cultural responsiveness is of paramount importance and reader is referred to the chapter by Humphries (chapter 4, this volume) for further edification.

Cultural responsiveness by therapists, while crucial, also raises important issues related to boundaries. It is often a fine line that clinicians, particularly deaf clinicians, walk when it comes to respecting client boundaries while participating in Deaf community, professional and social events. It is not at all uncommon to meet clients at such functions. Therefore, this must be discussed in therapy, both prior to and after such events. In a sense, it is a Catch-22 situation because the Deaf community would view participation in Deaf community events as a sign of cultural responsiveness, whereas the psychotherapy community would view therapist participation in events where clients are frequently present as countertherapeutic. This aspect is recognized by professional members of the Deaf community as part of the uniqueness of our deaf world.

Impact of Parental Hearing Status

It is the authors' experiences that our clients' backgrounds as to having either hearing or deaf parents makes a considerable impact on therapeutic progress. Here we are on shaky ground, and we wish to acknowledge this instability at the start. This field of research is so new! However, we are going to venture into making some broad generalizations about deaf people with hearing parents and deaf people with deaf parents, in the hope that these generalizations may generate some research in this area.

How do deaf individuals perceive their parents' parenting styles, and how does this perception impact on their expectations of the therapeutic relationship? Our experience is that clients with deaf parents and those with hearing parents perceive their parents differently and that these differing perceptions are reflected in their work with us.

Research by Lytle (1987) supports this assertion of differences in perception between college women with deaf parents and those with hearing parents. Women with deaf parents more frequently saw their parents as functioning within a democratic style of parenting, where discussion and open disagreements were encouraged. These deaf parents were able to provide their children with proper guidance during the formative years but with a definite expectation that during adolescence they were to begin making their own decisions.

Those women who did not perceive their deaf parents in such a way frequently came from homes where they, for various reasons, were seen as much more competent and/or intelligent than their parents. In these families, the women frequently perceived themselves in the caretaking role and perceived their parents as giving them considerable freedom, but little else.

Women with hearing parents, on the other hand, experienced their parents as being more frequently overcontrolling and/or inconsistent. If inconsistent, they alternated between offering little or no guidance to being intrusively over involved in their children's lives. Hearing children, raised in an inconsistent environment, are generally either pampered or neglected, resulting in low self-esteem and lack of confidence (Dreikurs, 1968; Dreikurs & Stoltz, 1964). We can assume the same would be true for families of deaf children. These are extremely destructive parenting styles as they convey both lack of interest in the children and low expectations for their future success. In hearing families where there is more communication with their deaf children at a young age, a more democratic, healthy style of parenting is expected.

In the therapist's office, these deaf clients who have deaf parents are often easily identified. They have more outward confidence, they relate on a more equal level with their therapist at a quicker pace, and they are more expressive. This seems to be true of those clients with deaf parents regardless of their degree of inner disturbance or turmoil. These individuals have the skills to outwardly present themselves as self-confident and empowered. This presentation is sometimes intimidating to therapists new to deafness; to others, it is just one more facade behind which our clients hide.

A vignette of a deaf male with deaf parents illustrates the previous discussion. This client, a high achiever, sought out a deaf male therapist. In the course of his therapy, it became clear that his parents, who were not well-educated, viewed him, their oldest son, as a very capable and bright person and entrusted him with the care of his younger siblings. He assumed this role quite well and carried out his responsibilities with distinction; however, he had unknowingly sacrificed much of his childhood play because of the additional expectations placed on him by his parents. He was experiencing anxiety attacks, periods of restlessness when he could not concentrate on anything, and was finding himself overcommitted to his activities in school. Through therapy, he was able to explore his feelings of anger at his parents for depriving him of a childhood of play and learned how to let the child within him come out more often to play. His anxiety attacks disappeared.

Deaf clients with hearing parents are a considerably larger percentage of our caseload. Clients who have been either pampered and overprotected as children and/or neglected as children represent two large groups with whom we have come into contact. Those clients who have experienced parents who pampered them are frequently demanding of the therapist to do a great deal for them and respond angrily and hurtfully when this expectation is not met. In addition, they frequently present themselves as helpless and easily overwhelmed by life. "Life is not fair!" they rant. "Life is too hard!" In some cases, they are very protective of parents whom they perceived as giving them so much, and they cannot understand or tolerate their intense anger at these same parents. It seems likely that many of the entitlement issues presented by some deaf clients stem from these early parenting styles.

An example of such a pampered, overprotected child is John. He initially came to therapy because of his difficulties getting along with peers. From a well-to-do hearing family, he had been adopted as an infant, prior to his diagnosis as deaf. The parents were unable to enforce any rules or expectations for their child, for example, allowing him to sleep with them up until the age of 9, to eat whatever and whenever he desired, and purchasing each and every electronic gadget he asked for. This extreme acting out by the parents effectively diminished John's self-hood while at the same time reassured him he was "special." John had been scapegoated all of his school years, teased unmercifully by his peers for being a spoiled mama's boy. When he arrived in the therapist's office his narcissistic personality was in full bloom. He was described as a "pest" and "obnoxious" by the secretarial staff who encountered him, put off by his ingratiating and intrusive ways. In therapy, he was overly grateful for whatever he received—sincerely so, sometimes with tears. However, he was completely unable to take in and retain what he received. During his last months in treatment, he started dating a young woman about whom he had serious doubts—she "embarrassed" him as she was not attractive enough, not cool enough, did not sign well enough, and so on. It was clear in everything he did that he felt he deserved more and better than what life was dishing out to him. Through therapy, he was able to see just how badly this old expectation hurt him, although he could not let it go.

Frequently pampered lifestyles are mingled with neglect. In families where there is money, a familiar scenario is the parents giving money and material things while withholding love and attention. For a child, it is very difficult to reconcile this neglect with all the materialistic possessions they receive under the name of love. For a deaf child this neglect is often expressed by sending the child to residential schools or to live with another family closer to a school. Under the guise of "good for the child" or "be grateful that you went to a good school," it is a very difficult task to recognize and feel permitted to express anger at not getting enough from one's parents. The client is unable to reconcile the good parent who gives expensive gadgets and clothes and the bad parent who does not bother to call or visit. There are so many issues here that provide grist for the therapeutic mill.

We believe that growing up in a deaf or hearing family provides very different life experiences and that we as therapists can learn much about the experience of deafness by learning more about each of these unique family backgrounds.

In closing, we feel we have touched on just a few of the possible variables associated with having deaf or hearing parents, and we hope that we have stimulated your curiosity in exploring this largely untapped and uncharted area.

CONCLUSION

We hope that this chapter has increased your awareness of how the hearing status and cultural identity and sensitivity of therapist and client impacts upon the therapeutic relationship. Both client and therapist influence each other. Many therapeutic issues that are contained within the client's life have meaning and relevance for the therapist. Other client issues are most likely different from those the therapist has faced (Winter & Aponte, 1987). We hope that through reading this chapter, you have become more aware of how this sameness and difference between client and therapist impact on the therapeutic fit, both on conscious and unconscious levels.

Therapists who work with deaf clients, be they deaf or hearing, may profitably explore with clients the issues we discussed here: what it means to be deaf or hearing, the impact of the type of schooling they received, whether or not their parents are deaf, and how they were treated as deaf members of the family. Therapists may explore how clients perceive them to be similiar or different and what this perceived similarity and difference means for the clients' own emerging identity.

REFERENCES

Cartwright, D. S. (1965). Influence, leadership and control. In J.G. March (Ed.), *Handbook of organizations* (pp. 1–47). Chicago: Rand McNally.

Corrigan, J., Dell, D., Lewis, K., & Schmidt, L. (1980). Counseling as a social influence process: A review. *Journal of Counseling Psychology, 27*, 395–441.

Dreikurs, R. (1968). *Psychology in the classroom.* New York: Harper and Row.

Dreikurs, R. & Stoltz, V. (1964). *Children: The challenge.* New York: Duell, Sloan and Pearch.

Freud, S. (1913). On the beginning of treatment: Further recommendations on the technique of psychoanalysis. In J. Starchey (Ed.), *The standard edition of the complete psychological works of Sigmond Freud.* (pp. 122–144). London: Hogarth.

Freud, S. (1958). The dynamics of transference. In J. Starchey (Ed.), *The standard edition of the complete psychological works of Sigmond Freud* (pp. 99–108). London: Hogarth.

Frieswyk, S., Colson, D., & Allen, J. (1984). Conceptualizing the alliance from a psychoanalytic perspective. *Psychotherapy, 21*(4), 460–464.

Gelso, C. J., & Carter, J. A. (1994). Components of the psychotherapy relationship: Their interaction and unfolding during treatment. *Journal of Counseling Psychology, 41*, 296–306.

Glickman, N. (1986). Cultural identity, deafness, and mental health. *Journal of Rehabilitation of the Deaf, 20*(2), 1–10.

Harvey, M. (1993). Cross cultural psychotherapy with deaf persons: A hearing, white, middle class, middle aged, non-gay, Jewish, male, therapist's perspective. *Journal of Rehabilitation of the Deaf. 26*(4), 43–55.

Higgins, P. C. (1980). *Outsiders in a hearing world.* Beverly Hills, CA: Sage.

Hovland, C.I., Janis, I. L., & Kelley H. H. (1953). *Communication and persuasion: Psychological studies of opinion change.* New Haven, CT: Yale University Press.

LaCrosse, M. B. (1980). Perceived counselor social influence and counseling outcomes: Validity of the counselor rating form. *Journal of Counseling Psychology, 27*, 320–327.

Lewis, J. W. (1987). *Counselor attitude influences on the counselor preferences and perceptions of counselor characteristics held by female deaf college students.* Unpublished doctoral dissertation, New York University.

Luborsky, L. (1976). Helping alliances in psychotherapy. In J. L. Cleghhorn (Ed.), *Successful psychotherapy* (pp. 92–116). New York: Brunner/Mazel.

Lytle, L. R. (1987). *Identity formation and developmental antecedents in deaf college women.* Unpublished doctoral dissertation, The Catholic University of America. Washington, DC.

Orlinsky, D. E., & Howard, K. I. (1986). The psychological interior of psychotherapy: Explorations with the therapy session report questionnaires. In L. S. Greenberg & W. M. Pinsof (Eds.), *The psychotherapeutic process: A research handbook* (pp. 477–503). New York: Guilford.

Padden, C., & Humphries, T. (1988). *Deaf in America: Voices from a culture.* Cambridge, MA: Harvard University Press.

Rogers, C. R. (1951). *Client centered therapy.* Cambridge, MA: Riverside.

Rogers, C. R. (1957). The necessary and sufficient conditions of therapeutic personality change. *Journal of Consulting Psychology, 21*, 95–103.

Winter, J. E., & Aponte, H. J. (1987). The family life of psychotherapists: Treatment and training implications. In F. W. Kaslow (Ed.), *The family life of psychotherapists: Clinical implications.* (pp. 97–133). New York: Haworth.

Chapter 11

Concluding Thoughts

Neil S. Glickman
Mental Health Unit for Deaf People
Westborough State Hospital
Westborough, MA

Michael A. Harvey
Boston University
Gallaudet University

Our intent with this volume was to apply a culturally affirmative model to the theory and practice of providing psychotherapy with deaf persons. The previously dominant medical–pathological model of deafness—a framework that purports to help deaf people cope with their disability and adjust to the dominant society—in fact, from our perspective, has contributed to the oppression of the Deaf community. Culturally affirmative psychotherapy corrects that oppression. It is a paradigm shift—a way of thinking—that includes therapist self-awareness, knowledge of Deaf culture, and culturally-syntonic intervention skills. Culturally affirmative psychotherapy contributes to the growing movement for equality and reciprocity between Deaf and hearing people. As such, it is a stance of profound respect.

We have emphasized how clients as well as psychotherapists are bound by sociohistorical and cultural factors. Our task as clinicians is to bridge the sociohistorical differences in life experiences between us and our clients; to use language, narrative, and method that contribute to client empowerment. We ask many questions: What will move our clients forward? How is "help" conceptualized? Is what we are offering culturally appropriate? We humbly acknowledge that our professional training—which is itself bound by a sociohistorical context—has often not provided the answers; it has given us both the tools of liberation and of oppression.

Effective treatment begins with therapist self-awareness. We hope that this volume has opened up the "psychology" of hearing people for discussion and research: Which conscious and unconscious motivations guide hearing professionals to enter and remain in the field? Which kinds of experiences do hearing people need to truly assist deaf people? These questions go beyond the realm of emphasizing the need for adequate therapist communication skills, a dictum that—as in other major texts on deafness—is emphasized throughout this volume.

Increased knowledge of Deaf culture and the Deaf community make it possible to develop culturally syntonic ways of understanding and treating a Deaf individual in psychotherapy. We delineated a framework for analyzing the development of a culturally Deaf identity, the Deaf self in relation to "the other," marginality, and other knowledge-based requirements for conducting culturally affirmative treatment. Our knowledge in these areas guides our therapeutic inquiry and, in turn, guides our interventions. In this volume, we have discussed the utilization of traumatic transference in treatment, culturally syntonic metaphors and narrative, the inclusion of Deaf community leaders in treatment, and the use of one's own deafness as an essential therapeutic tool.

Today's socioeconomic context includes managed health care. We continue to struggle with the question of whether culturally appropriate psychotherapy can coexist with that system. As therapists of all persuasions are increasingly forced by insurance carriers to be brief, structured, and symptom focused, we lose the opportunity to provide so-called pretherapy: the necessary time to develop a therapeutic relationship with nontreatment-ready clients, frequently those who are disadvantaged and/or culturally different. In the era of managed care, clients are expected to immediately be able to contract for specific treatment goals. This threatens to eliminate from mental health facilities those clients who are not psychologically minded, that is, who do not have the educational and cultural experiences that sanction and legitimize psychotherapy as a form of healing.

We need to formulate and implement ways of advocating for the complex needs of such deaf clients with insurance carriers and state facilities whose bottom line is short-term service delivery. This volume included practical suggestions for serving a broad range of deaf clients within a public sector agency.

Which limitations do we see in our endeavor? To begin with, although we have included several articulate deaf contributors and owe our understanding to the guidance of many of our deaf teachers and colleagues, we as editors—albeit somewhat defensively—admit that we are *hearing* clinicians. Inevitably, there are ways in which our "hearingness" limits our understanding of deafness.

We have not specifically addressed the multiple linguistic and cultural challenges of providing diagnostic assessments of truly language-impaired deaf people: those without a full linguistic (signed or spoken) system. Nor have we addressed the issue of cultural diversity within the Deaf community. What is the cultural experience, for instance, of African American Deaf persons? Of gay and lesbian Deaf persons? Which different issues do they face? We look forward to future discussions about therapy with Deaf people of such widely differing backgrounds and perspectives.

The culturally affirmative psychotherapy framework opens up many new questions for research and clinical work:

What is the relationship between cultural identity and mental health in Deaf persons?

Which factors promote healthy cultural identity development in Deaf persons?

What is the impact of various educational and social policy matters (kind of educational environments, medical interventions with deaf children) on cultural identity and mental health in Deaf persons?

How does cultural identity develop in Deaf persons who share multiple cultural orientations (African American, gay, female, etc.)?

Which cultural dilemmas are faced by hard-of-hearing people?

Which interventions facilitate resolution of cultural marginality?

What constitutes culturally appropriate diagnostic assessment of Deaf persons?

How can we create psychological assessment procedures that are culturally appropriate?

What constitutes helping and healing in the Deaf community?

How can therapists draw on the resources for healing that the Deaf community possesses?

Perhaps the greatest asset of the culturally affirmative treatment model is that it guides Deaf and hearing people to show mutual respect and understanding. Through dialogue comes increased knowledge and clarity, along with more questions and increased complexity. In our case, as hearing clinicians, we remind ourselves that we are not experts in the treatment of "the deaf"; we are collaborators with our clients. We hope this volume, following the lead of the Deaf community, nudges our profession in this direction.

Author Index

Subject Index